FIGHTER ACES

Colonel Raymond F. Toliver
and Trevor J. Constable

FIGHTER ACES

The Macmillan Company

NEW YORK

First Printing

The Macmillan Company, New York
Collier-Macmillan Canada, Ltd., Toronto, Ontario

Library of Congress catalog card number: 65-21463

DESIGNED BY RONALD FARBER

Printed in the United States of America

DEDICATED TO THE WINGMEN
WITHOUT WHOSE EYES, GUNS AND
DEVOTED VIGILANCE THERE WOULD
BE MANY FEWER LIVING ACES.

Acknowledgements

THE AUTHORS GRATEFULLY acknowledge the assistance they have received from the many persons who contributed information and effort towards the publication of this book. It is quite impossible to give credit to everyone by name since the research and writing took 15 years of work, 1950 through 1965. Special thanks, however, are due the late Patrick J. Cassidy, the late Hans Otto Boehm (German Fighter Pilot Association Historian), General Adolf Galland, General Johannes Steinhoff, Lt. Colonel Erich Hartmann, Bill Hess, Hans Ring, Ernst Obermair, Martin Caidin, Robert S. Johnson, Falk Harmel, Dr. Maurer Maurer, The Research Studies Institute personnel of the Air University of the USAF, The American Fighter Aces Association, Cletus J. Cattoor (special accolades), Margaret A. Story, Joan Hall Wheatley, F. Claire Amabile, Del Hannasch, Mrs. R. F. Toliver, Suzanne Toliver Kemp, Nancy Toliver Belknap and Janet Toliver Moskal. The authors appreciate the efforts of everyone concerned, and above all, wish to thank the relatives and friends of those fighter pilots who lost their lives in combat for their invaluable assistance.

Contents

FIGHTER ACES

1

★ ★ ★ ★ ★

The Making of a Fighter Ace

THE CLASHING DYNAMISM of the medieval joust was reborn in this century in the form of aerial combat. While anonymous millions in the 1914–1918 war were mowed down in the mud of Flanders, high above these scenes of unprecedented mass slaughter individual combat was having its renaissance. There was nothing glorious in the dull butcheries of trench warfare. But in the clean and open combat in the air, where it was man against man and plane against plane, the issue was easy to comprehend and therefore easy to glorify. The result was the emergence of the fighter ace as this century's most glamorous warrior.

Amid the sputtering of primitive engines and the whine of the wind in struts and wires, all the lineaments of the knightly joust reappeared in the infant art of aerial combat. While whole divisions were decimated a few thousand feet below, chivalry and sportsmanship ruled the fighting in the skies. While every bond between man and man was being sundered by the sheer impersonality of mighty artillery barrages, gas attacks and storms of machine-gun fire, the men in the crazy flying crates could still salute and wave to an opponent.

The kind of war the airmen fought bore little relationship to the mass effects of modern armies and navies. Their individualistic type of fighting was an echo from the past, before the juggernaut of technology intruded upon the settlement of disputes. Many of the elements and much of the spirit of a *game* were present in aerial combat in World War I and continued down to the present day. As a consequence, the men who flew fighter planes, regardless of the uniform they wore, are joined by a common bond. Among the thousands so joined there is an inner and elite brotherhood—the fighter aces.

Just as the fighter pilots literally rose above the impersonal nature of modern warfare, so did the fighter aces rise above their fellow fighter pilots. The factors that make a fighter ace are so variable, so elusive of analysis and so far beyond the grasp of the ordinary fighter pilot that the United States has been able to produce only 1,300 fighter aces in this century. In the nine years of warfare involving America since 1917, over 45,000 fighter pilots have taken the air for Uncle Sam. Less than three percent of these men became aces.

Motion pictures, novels and wartime publicity have etched an archetypal fighter ace in the public mind. He is often depicted as a devil-may-care girl-chaser, a hard-drinking, glamorous hedonist who flies, fights or loves on a prodigious scale. Orgies into the wee small hours are supposed to be his stock in trade. Despite these exertions, he is always first into the air as the Dawn Patrol goes bucketing up to challenge the hated Black Baron.

If this fighter ace of fiction ever existed in the world of reality, few real aces ever knew him. There have always been aces who were drinking men, and plenty of playboys and ladies' men, but these frivolous aspects of personality invariably concealed sterner qualities, without which few could survive in aerial combat, let alone become aces.

The real fighter ace is likely to be a man of better than average intelligence and education, but even this is not typical. There are many men woefully short on academic training whose character, will power and natural ability enabled them to win through to the coveted title of "ace."

The fighter ace is likely to be a direct and plain-spoken man, and often forceful of manner. The overwhelming majority of aces are individualists. This might be expected, for no other individual fighting man in any era, dependent in the end entirely on his own abilities, has wielded the deadly powers conferred on a pilot by a fighter plane.

America's aces include many professional aviators, men who made aerial combat and the preparation for it their life's work. The majority of them, however, have come from other occupations or direct from school in wartime. All shared a common attraction to the magnificent adventure of flying. War brought this adventure within the reach of many who otherwise would never have known its magic.

Combat flying developed in many men personal capacities and skills that would otherwise have lain dormant. The awakening and sharpening of these qualities have always been central to the making of a fighter ace. Skill, dash, courage and judgment have all been required in an exceptional degree—all qualities drawn from the individual's inner resources. They are not things that can be taught. Such qualities have had to be blended, balanced and brought under control both by training and experience.

These inner resources have met and mingled with such uncontrollable external factors as luck and opportunity. Interwoven with these in turn, and exerting a decisive influence on the success of the individual pilot, has been that special plexus of powers and skills that makes a *good shot*.

Contrary to popular ideas, shooting ability and not flying ability has always been the fighter pilot's most important asset, and the asset most likely to make him an ace. Air-to-air shooting ability is an esoteric skill, and few indeed are the fighter pilots ever to master it thoroughly. Those blessed with the native ability to shoot at a moving target from a moving platform, the movement of both being in three dimensions, were almost certain to become aces, even if they were not exceptional pilots.

This volume contains a number of interesting observations on air-to-air shooting from the aces themselves. Strangely enough, it was the smooth-as-silk pilot who often went to his doom under the enemy's guns, while cruder pilots of lesser experience escaped repeatedly. This was because the slick pilot's reactions in the air were predictable to an enemy pilot of similar skills. When the smooth pilot took evasive action, his enemy could sometimes predict it in advance, and the evading pilot would make a lethal rendezvous in the sky with a well-aimed stream of bullets or cannon shells.

The ham-fisted rough pilot, on the other hand, often reacted unpredictably when bounced. His salvation lay in his sheer crudity as an airman. He might wrench his aircraft into turns an experienced pilot would never have attempted. But smooth or rough, the fighter pilot who could shoot was likely to become an ace if given adequate opportunity.

Good eyesight was important to the pilots of World War I, but not as crucial as it became in World War II and Korea. At 150 mph in the 1914–1918 conflict it was difficult to close a target that could be easily seen miles away. In World War II, with its straight and level fighter speeds of around 400 mph, a target could be attacked if it could be seen at any distance under most conditions. The same was true in Korean jet combat.

The pilot with good eyes, able to pick out the tiny speck in the heavens that an aircraft becomes at five miles, had another of the attributes of an ace. Spotting the enemy at great distances permitted the pilot to place himself in an attacking position and get the enemy machine on the defensive. This kind of advantage, combined with shooting skill, resulted in many an aerial victory and many an ace.

Physical toughness has always been an essential in the making of an ace. With the evolution of aerial combat and aircraft, the physical requirements have undergone a metamorphosis, World War I, World War II and Korea each requiring a different kind of toughness. But all three conflicts demanded the highest qualities of endurance, both physical and mental.

The aces of World War I had to be able to take outright physical punishment. In their own cockpits, they received a merciless buffeting from the elements. The roar of the wind, of their guns and their crude engines frequently left them deaf for days. They would descend from flights half-frozen, and many World War I pilots carried circulatory ailments throughout the rest of their lives.

The pioneers shared with their World War II and Korean War counterparts the savage demands made on the human structure when a man fights literally for his life. Psychologically, the World War I pilot in addition was haunted by the possibility that his machine might shed its wings, especially after a few hits. The inflammable nature of these early machines made a fiery death in the heavens an ever-present likelihood, from which the only deliverance was a horrifying death leap—without a parachute.

In World War II, improved aircraft design brought a measure of pilot comfort, but with it came a new set of physical demands. In the

300–400 mph bracket, where most World War II aerial combat occurred, the controls of the fighters became extremely heavy. Fifteen minutes of combat would test the physical strength of an Atlas, and pilots often fought soaked in sweat from these exertions.

A fighter pilot could not hope to become an ace in World War II without strong arms and shoulders, and a powerful back. The leading aces on both sides could invariably sense any physical weakening of an opponent in the air. If a pilot's strength began to fail, his enemy would probably notice it as soon as he did. In gladiatorial fashion, such a pilot was actually physically overpowered—but by an enemy who had never laid a hand on him. All this while they had pirouetted thousands of feet above the earth.

The same physical rigors were not required of the jet aces. In the waning days of World War II, hydraulically operated controls were just being designed into aircraft. America's jet-aces, mounted on the F-80 Shooting Star and F-86 Sabre in Korea, had hydraulically operated flight controls. The machines could be maneuvered at speeds approaching that of sound with no more physical strength required than that of the proverbial "97-pound weakling."

The jet aces nevertheless landed after combat in an exhausted condition. To the fierce strain of fighting for their lives had been added the exacting mental demands of feather-touch flying and teamwork at speeds approaching mach one. A weakling could not meet these requirements, and only the strongest of those who could became America's jet aces.

The ace of World War I had a 1,500-pound aircraft of wood and fabric to fly, with an engine of perhaps 350 hp in the later days of the conflict. Top speeds of 200 mph in a dive represented the zenith of performance. The aces gained their glories in fighters that flew in combat at considerably less than the stalling speed of the jets flown by the aces of the Korean War. Such is the spectrum of aircraft performance in which America's aces won their laurels.

In the making of an ace, knowledge of the enemy's strengths and weaknesses played a substantial role. While it is generally true that the machine imposes limits on the man, the great aces have always been able to stretch those limits. In each of the three wars, the aircraft flown had technical flaws. If he was ever to become an ace, a pilot had to know those things about his machine that might kill him, rather than the enemy. He had also to know where the weaknesses were in the enemy aircraft and, if possible, exploit these in combat by appropriate tactics.

No fighter plane of World War I, World War II or Korea was without drawbacks, either innately or by combat comparison with enemy aircraft. The P-47 was a case in point. Affectionately known as the "Jug" by all who flew it, the P-47 Thunderbolt could dive as fast as anything in the air prior to the German Me-262 jet. Nevertheless, the "Jug" had one serious fault that claimed the lives of a number of its pilots.

The P-47's control stick would freeze in a dive from high altitude at high speed. No amount of human strength could budge the stick. What did the pilots do? By instinct and training they rolled back on the trim tab in an effort to raise the nose. No luck. The heavy machine kept going headlong for the deck. The desperate pilot rolled in more trim tab and pulled with all his strength on the stick.

At about eighteen thousand feet the aircraft reached heavier air. Here the pilot's strength and the trim began to take effect. In a few seconds the effect became violent. Hitting between 500 and 600 mph in its dive, the P-47 was hurtling downward at better than 800 feet a second. The tail of the aircraft was simply torn off in the resulting fifteen- to thirty-G pullout, and seldom was the pilot able to recover his senses in time to bail out.

Even the beautiful "pilot's aircraft," the German Focke-Wulfe 190, was cursed with a mach limitation that caused it literally to fall out of control. This flaw was quickly spotted by the Allied pilots and exploited to the full. The ingenious manipulation of technical strengths and weaknesses brought many an American pilot into the fraternity of aces.

Knowing the enemy's capabilities, and respecting them, was a firm step toward becoming a living ace. In World War I, the German aircraft were generally superior in performance, with the exception of range. Their superiority in climb, speed, maneuverability and firepower governed the tactics used by the Allied pilots, with most of the aerial combat taking place over German-held territory.

In World War II, the German fighters were again a tough proposition. The American pilots who fought them did so at the end of a long flight from British bases, or from makeshift strips behind the advancing Allied armies in the late months of the war. Technical superiority over the famed Me-109 in its own airspace came only with the advent of the equally famed P-51 Mustang.

The Japanese Zero was the dogfighting master of the Pacific skies in the early months of the conflict. The leading American aces of the Pacific Theater were men who intelligently exploited the superior aspects of aircraft like the P-38 Lightning and avoided the close dogfighting so favorable to the Japanese. The vulnerability of the Zero to gunfire was not only a technical flaw, but also gave the hard-pressed Americans a psychological advantage. The American machines proved far more robust than the Japanese. Japanese pilots needed many hits to down an American machine unless they happened to kill or wound its pilot.

The aggressive competitive spirit essential to the making of an ace had to be constantly tempered by technical awareness. In this respect, the blundering rush of the medieval knight, with its all-or-nothing outcome, had disappeared from the aerial joust. Here the thrusts were coldly calculated as well as deadly.

Tactics in aerial combat developed erratically, and were modified mainly by technical innovations and the see-saw changes of fortune they offered to each of the combatants in turn. In the pioneer days before the First World War, there was no accepted concept of *aerial combat* accompanying the military advent of the aircraft. The Army had a limited view of aircraft, seeing them primarily as mobile observation platforms. To the demonstrable tactical value of the balloon, they added the vital and novel factor of mobility. Aircraft were not looked on as new weapons in their own right. This was true on both the German and the Allied sides.

The brilliant Italian, Giuilio Douhet, who accurately foresaw the rise of airpower as the primary tactical and strategic factor in future warfare, was rewarded with jail for his views. He became the Clausewitz of airpower later, but was a joke in his own time. His devotees in America, who included "Billy" Mitchell, did not have sufficient influence to get the air weapon the attention it deserved. The same situation applied in France, Britain and Germany.

The early military aircraft in World War I were slow machines, intended to fly over the battlefield and its environs and report on the progress of the ground war. Generals ensconced in chateaux miles behind the front found them a handy innovation.

These reconnaissance pilots, German on the one side, British and French on the other, frequently spotted each other while making their aerial rounds of the battlefield. They often waved to each other as they flew close. It was as though the very fact that they had managed to get off the ground and stay airborne united them in a grateful and chivalrous brotherhood. Aggressive acts soon followed, however, and aerial combat was on its way out of the womb of ideas and into the world of reality.

One daring English pilot, a Lieutenant Norman Spratt, made such hostile moves toward a German two-seater that the German pilot did the World War I version of "hitting the panic button." He landed, jumped out and set his plane afire with a signal pistol. He then scurried back to the German lines on foot. This is believed to be the first aerial combat victory on record, although neither aircraft was armed. But weapons were not long in coming.

Observation planes began carrying bags of bricks, hand grenades and other lethal objects. The original intention was to drop this material on enemy troops in the trenches. Soon the possibilities of a new mode of warfare began to dawn on the airmen. They began dumping their loads on each other's aircraft. Rifles, pistols and eventually machine guns were added to the aerial arsenal. Pot-shots at the enemy became standard operating procedure.

More than one of these early crates was sent plummeting to earth by an avalanche of bricks released from a machine flying above. Another cunning tactic was to drop lead pellets by the bagful into an enemy's propeller arc. Tiny though these pellets were, they were sufficient to shatter the wooden props of the day and destroy an aircraft.

The pellet tactic, which seems like a relic from the past, has recently undergone a resurgence in the space age. Research has shown that millions of tiny BB-sized pellets might bring down a satellite or an ICBM. Where the World War I pioneers had to drop their pellets down on the enemy flying below them, their space age descendants must find a way to boost the pellets up into the path of the missile or other object they wish to bring down.

In the early aerial combats, long before the term "ace" had ever been applied to airmen, the ideal tactic was to fly formation with the German and knock him down with pot-shots to the engine, propeller —or pilot. Before long, pilots on both sides began to seek some form of advantage, and this gave birth to the first tactical maneuvering of aerial combat.

To gain advantage on a German pilot, the Allied flyer with a rear observer-gunner would try to get in front of the German machine. This made the German vulnerable to the observer's machine-gun fire. The German was prevented from returning the fire, lest he blow off his own propeller in the process.

The same maneuver gave protection to a pilot who had run out of ammunition while his opponent had not. By staying in front of the other machine, a fleeing pilot could avoid being sprayed with lead, unless his pursuer happened to be a "pusher" type of aircraft such as the British FE-2B, which had the gunner in a front nacelle with an enormous field of fire forward.

All the tactics involved in these early encounters underwent a decisive change due to the brainchild of a determined Frenchman named Roland Garros.

A famed and experienced stunt and speed pilot, Garros set aerial combat firmly on the path it was to follow right down to the days of the heat-seeking missile. He could see what the consequences would be if pilots could fire machine guns through the propeller arc. His approach to the problem was terrifyingly direct.

Garros attached heavy steel deflectors to the propeller blades of his plane. Then he mounted a machine gun on the aircraft so that it fired forward through the propeller arc. A percentage of the bullets hit the deflector plates and ricocheted. The bulk of the bullets sped on through the propeller arc.

The Frenchman could now aim his gun by aiming his whole aircraft, something that was impossible previously. The days of formation flying with a foe were now numbered. Instead of avoiding a tail-chase of a German aircraft, Garros did everything possible to promote this maneuver, and in the beginning it was easy. The German two-seater pilots felt they were gaining the advantage on Garros when he finished up behind them.

Certainly the Frenchman's early victims must have been among history's most surprised pilots. Serene in their assurance that they had outmaneuvered the French *schweinhund*, they suddenly found themselves in a storm of machine-gun fire. In a few seconds they had become statistics in a deadly scoring game.

In two weeks, Garros scored five kills with his forward-firing gun. Then the ingenious Frenchman, who diced with death every time he pulled his triggers, fell victim to the law of averages. With a German machine in his sights, he opened fire and blew off his own propeller despite the deflector plates. The resulting vibration caused a joint in his fuel system to separate and Garros was forced to land behind the German lines.

The Germans reacted with typical energy to their good luck in capturing Garros and his deadly scout plane. Anthony Fokker, Dutch builder of Germany's greatest warplanes, took Garros' idea and made it a practical addition to German aircraft. Fokker designed the interrupter cam, which prevented the machine gun from firing when a propeller blade was in front of the gun muzzle. The fully synchronized machine guns in pairs followed shortly afterward, and the way was now open for a new kind of aerial jousting.

Appropriate tactics soon developed. With the new device, the ideal attack was to steal up silently behind an enemy and get as close as possible before opening fire. Accuracy diminished with distance, and the pioneers established the practice of closing in before striking. Even as late as the Korean War there was one American ace who said: "The hell with gunsights. Stick some chewing gum on the windshield, shove the gum up the other guy's tailpipe and let drive!"

As the World War I pilot closed in, if his opponent spotted him and turned quickly, then the attacker would try to turn even more sharply and get behind the enemy plane. This action best resembled two dogs trying to nip each other's hindquarters, and was soon known to all the Allied pilots as a "dogfight." The Germans called this kind of battle a "rhubarb."

The forward-firing machine guns also permitted the emergence of the First World War's most popular fighter tactic—the dive out of the

sun. With the sun at his back and as much altitude advantage as possible, the attacking pilot bounced his foe. His foe in turn was blinded by
the sun when he searched the sky and could be taken unawares from
this quarter.

In all the wars in which America's fighter aces were made, the
bounce out of the sun was a fundamental. Pounded into three generations of fighter pilots in their training, it served all of them well in
combat. Failure to remember the importance of altitude and the sun
usually resulted in dead pilots. To attack with altitude and sun advantage has remained the first principle of aerial warfare down to this day.
The living aces continue to emphasize the value of these fundamentals.
How much they have been altered or modified by electronics and the
various types of air-to-air missiles, only the dynamics of another war
will reveal for certain.

Another enduring maneuver developed in World War I after the
advent of the forward-firing machine gun was the "inverted vertical-
reversement." This maneuver was intended to remove an enemy aircraft from a position of advantage astern. Two aircraft in aerial
combat eventually wound up in a vertical bank, each trying to close the
circle, get on the enemy's tail and "give him a couple of squirts."

The winner in such an encounter was usually the pilot who could
slowly close the gap between the planes, thereby putting himself in
position to shoot. It was at this moment, when the pursued pilot was
about to feel the full force of the enemy's guns, that he would execute
the dramatic "inverted vertical-reversement."

The pursued pilot would suddenly increase his bank so that his
machine would roll 180 degrees under. At the same time, the pilot
would slap the stick back into the full rear position, including the full
bank, and the aircraft would snap-roll through the inverted position.
The pilot would then stop the roll in a vertical bank going in the
opposite direction.

Since the other pilot in the firing position had to have his quarry
under his nose in order to gain the necessary firing lead angle, he was
usually unable to see his target make the reversement until it was too
late. In a split second the maneuver was completed. The hunted suddenly became the hunter, lining up his adversary for a lethal burst.

The inverted vertical-reversement was a tricky maneuver to perform, but a deadly one when pulled off by a good pilot. The maneuver was used in different ways in World War I, World War II and Korea. In all three conflicts it brought many aerial victories to America's aces.

In World War II, aircraft like the Me-109, P-51, P-47 and Spitfire were too fast and heavy to execute the snap portion of the inverted vertical-reversement if the speeds exceeded 300 mph. The maneuver was also a speed-killer, and tactics usually demanded that all combat be fought at full throttle. Under these conditions, the classic maneuver was modified simply to a high-speed reversement, with no attempt to make it a snap maneuver.

The Royal Air Force called this modification a "three-quarter underneath roll" and used it to advantage with the Spitfire and Hurricane when attacked by Me-109's and F-190's. The Germans used it also, and several of the Luftwaffe's leading fighter aces were masters of this tactic.

In the Korean War, the inverted high-speed reversement was used to perfection by F-86 pilots battling the MIG-15's. As the Soviet-built jets had a higher ceiling than the American Sabres, the MIG's would dive from their superior altitudes to open combat. The Sabre pilots would wait until the MIG's opened fire, and then break violently into the attacking jets.

Hurtling down in their dives with superior speed, the MIG's would overshoot and pass behind the Sabres. The American pilots would then execute an inverted, or perhaps an overhead high-speed reversement on to the tail of the fast-departing MIG's, opening fire immediately. If a pilot got a hit that holed the MIG's canopy or damaged its engine, it was then a relatively simple matter to close on the damaged machine and shoot it down. In this way, the basic tactic of the reversement has served America's aces in all three conflicts.

The speed-killing properties of the snap maneuver were also applied to definite purpose. A snap roll at 275 mph in a P-51 would kill 75 mph of speed in less than two seconds. Two snap rolls would kill nearly 180 mph. Some pilots used the snap roll against a fast-closing enemy. Others learned to use it to prevent overshooting a target. The maneuver could kill so much speed so quickly that a skilled pilot could often place himself suddenly and squarely behind his enemy. The well-timed use of this aerial brake could put an able pilot in perfect shooting position against a foe who only seconds earlier was in the role of aerial executioner.

In the view of most of America's top surviving aces, overtaking and passing (overshooting) was one of the cardinal sins of aerial combat. Why? Because if the pilot on his firing run missed or only damaged his enemy and then overshot the hostile aircraft, all the enemy pilot had to do was put his gunsight on his erstwhile attacker and press the triggers. Pilots who overshot were actually shooting themselves down. Nevertheless, untold dozens of pilots on both sides met their doom through this example of a fatal mistake.

There are some American aces very much alive today, however, who often overshot and lived to tell of it. These aces are men who believed that speed should *never* be slackened in aerial combat, since it is the only thing that can be traded for altitude. They planned their attacks on full speed and with absolute confidence in their marksmanship. They always had a plan for the breakoff, which usually consisted of a break underneath the enemy pilot in his blind spot before he could discover where his attacker had gone. During this brief period, the Americans would put all possible distance between themselves and the enemy plane. Without such a planned overshoot, which depended on a high rate of closure, overshooting was likely to be fatal no matter how brilliant the pilot at the controls.

In the light of these explanations, it seems incredible that any combat pilot would have been stupid enough, in breaking off from his overshoot, to pull up in a zoom directly in front of and above the enemy he had just attacked. Nevertheless, it happened all too often. Almost every experienced fighter pilot has at least one recollection from his combat days of someone doing this. Even a mortally wounded enemy pilot could not fail to riddle such a sitting duck. The hot-shots who tried this maneuver never lived to join the circle of aces.

As aerial combat began to take definite shape in World War I, team work and tactics with large formations of planes all combined to oust the aerial lone wolf. The highly individualistic plane against plane, pilot against pilot way of fighting began to disappear. Occasionally, a lone wolf like America's Frank Luke would blast his way to glory, but such pilots were exceptions. The lone wolf pilot simply could not prevail against well-led formations.

Pilots who were commanders, in the highest sense of the word, with a flair and instinct for aerial tactics, found the road to immortality open. The last year of World War I belonged to such men. The Royal Air Force's Major James T. McCudden and Major Edward Mannock were probably the outstanding Allied tacticians, and their counterparts were Oswald Boelcke and the famed "Red Knight of Germany," Baron Manfred von Richthofen.

Richthofen's formations and the tactics he developed gave America's first fighter aces a hard row to hoe and influenced the air war long after the Baron had gone to Valhallah. Almost uncannily, Richthofen grasped the mechanics of teamwork, which he introduced on the German side. He saw that a two-, three- or four-plane formation could quickly box in a lone plane, making maneuver impossible for the Allied pilot. Often by its very presence, the larger German formation terrified the lone Allied pilots into making fatal errors.

As formation flying developed on both sides, Richthofen's strategy was to dive out of the sun into the Allied formations, hoping to break them up and scatter them into individual elements which could be downed easily.

Richthofen has often been criticized in retrospect for his tendency to pick on inexperienced pilots, which he shot down while his formation protected him. Such views cannot be accorded much value when aerial combat is considered realistically. The name of the game is "shoot the other man down." All great aces have had the instinct for spotting a lack of aggressiveness in the air. Richthofen had it in high measure, combined with outstanding flying, gunnery and leadership talents. It is significant that at the moment of his death, Richthofen was hotly pursuing the aircraft of Lt. Wilfred May of the RAF, who that morning was on his very first combat operation.

Although he may have had personality traits that made him an unpleasant man to serve with, Richthofen's reputation was awesome among Allied fliers. His leadership, tactical skill and the technical superiority of the German aircraft made him a legend in his own lifetime. He dominated the air war until his death, and his eighty aerial victories were to become a landmark and the cherished goal of another generation of German pilots twenty years later.

Fortunately for the Americans, Baron Richthofen was killed before the U.S. Air Service became active on the Western Front. But the Baron's demise has long been a matter of controversy, with the popular records of World War I crediting the downing of Richthofen to Canadian Captain Roy Brown. Contemporary claims that the Baron had been machine-gunned from the ground were lost in the numerous glamorized versions of the affair that found print between the wars.

However, gunner Donald Buie of Australia claimed in 1959 to have shot down Richthofen with a machine gun, using a homemade sight that he had designed to give him the proper firing lead angle. The violent controversy that followed led to an exhaustive investigation of the whole matter by the eminent British aviation historian, Mr. D. A. Russell.

Mr. Russell's conclusion was that it was impossible in view of the facts he uncovered to credit the victory to Captain Brown. But nor would he hand the coveted honor to Donald Buie, whose claim he considered virtually as implausible as that of Captain Brown.

Mr. Russell attributed the Baron's death to ground fire, and held no doubt of this fact. The investigation proved that several machine-gunners fired on Richthofen from the ground, and Buie was ruled out because of his position relative to the Baron at the fatal moment. The incident has been termed "the dogfight that will never end," and that is the truth of the matter.

The best lesson to be gained from Richthofen's demise is the mortal danger to which even the most formidable aerial fighter exposes himself when he flies close to the ground. In his final months, Richthofen had become contemptuous of this danger, and it led to his undoing.

The air-to-ground role for the fighter pilot always reeked with danger. It called for the highest qualities of mind, heart and skill. There was no combat with other aircraft, but only low-level strafing, tactical support of infantry and armor, and the beating-up of enemy concentration and supply dumps. Though the role has never produced a fighter ace, it would be unfair in a work dealing with fighter aces not to say a word about the fighter pilots who were almost entirely confined to the air-to-ground role. With little or no chance to try their wings in aerial combat, they succeeded in earning the admiration of the aces.

Fighter pilots in all wars, with the possible exception of Richthofen, have disliked flying low over ground targets. The possibility of becoming a statistic in strafing operations mounted alarmingly as flak weapons multiplied in numbers and efficiency. A man might be unconquerable in the sky, but if he flew close to the ground in the combat zone long enough, his chances of survival diminished to zero.

Aces like Duane Beeson and the seemingly invincible Francis Gabreski, tops in aerial combat, were shot down and taken prisoner as the result of ground-strafing operations. To fly in the ground-support role month in and month out, as so many unknown American pilots did in World War II and Korea, took plenty of guts and nerves of steel.

In the making of a fighter ace, statistics play almost as large a role as all the various qualities and attributes outlined previously. Through the years, long after the wars had ceased, there has been almost as much fighting over victory credits and official scores as there was in the air during wartime. Most of this controversy is due to the completely *nonofficial* nature of the "ace" title.

In the early days of the U.S. Air Service, officialdom blew hot and cold on the question of aces, the qualifications for an ace, and how these qualifications were to be assessed. The French were the first to recognize that the *chasse* (pursuit) pilot of outstanding achievement should have some suitable and distinguishing title. They coined the term "ace."

The British and the Germans followed suit, although the British, like the Americans, have never officially accepted the title in their military establishment. Frederick Libby of Sterling, Colorado, an American who served with the Royal Flying Corps in 1916 and 1917 and became an ace, recalls that it was mid-1917 before he ever heard the term used. At that time, a resplendent French pilot who made a forced landing at the field where Libby was stationed quickly informed all the British pilots that he, the Frenchman, was an ace.

Libby recalls the Frenchman's chagrin at finding that most of the British pilots had more kills than he and had never heard the word "ace" used before.

The British, French and Germans set ten confirmed aerial victories as the standard qualification for an ace. Since the warring powers between 1914 and 1917 did not include the United States, there were already dozens of Allied and German aces at the time of America's entry into the war. The only American aces were expatriates flying in the service of Britain and France.

American development of the air weapon had been extremely slow. The possibility of there not being a single American ace in an American unit became very real. When American air units had still not gone into action at the beginning of 1918, the likelihood of any American pilot scoring ten kills before Germany's collapse seemed remote.

Accordingly, it was decided to reduce the American qualification for an ace to five aerial victories rather than the ten recognized by the other Allied powers and Germany. The value of the ace for morale purposes was not underrated, especially in the isolationist areas of the United States where a certain antipathy for the conflict existed. The ace was to become an easily comprehended symbol for the American public, one that would enable it to say, "We're really in it."

As it happened, a number of American fighter pilots in World War I exceeded ten aerial victories, despite America's late entry into the air war. The original departure of the U.S. ace standard from ten to five aerial victories has nevertheless applied from World War I to the present day. The "five down" standard applies in this book and in all the lists in the Appendix. The same standard of five now applies generally throughout the world, and is even given in dictionaries.

The war of statistics has been going on ever since World War I, and only the Korean War aces seem immune from continual reviews of their scores by official and quasi-official historians. The changing standards of victory confirmation, the various means of recognizing and documenting aerial victories once scored, the matted tangle of different procedures in different commands have created a historian's nightmare.

Typical of the problems presented to any researcher in this field seeking to follow official guidelines is the explanation given in this extract from a letter written by the Director of Air Service, U.S. Army, and dated January 5, 1920:

The U.S. Air Service does not use the title "ace" in referring to those who are credited officially with five or more aerial victories over enemy aircraft. It is not the policy of the Air Service to glorify one particular branch of aeronautics, aviation or aerostation at the expense of another. . . .

. . . the work of observation and bombardment is considered equally as hazardous as that of pursuit, but due to the fact that observation and bombardment pilots are not called upon merely to destroy enemy aircraft, it should not be allowed to aid in establishing a popular comparison of results merely by relative victories.

In this letter may be detected the germinal sentiments from which the "bombardment *vs.* pursuit" controversy came to dominate American military aviation until World War II. The order accompanying the letter, in addition to being a masterpiece of jabberwocky, drops the following statistical bombshell:

An addition of the victories listed herein does not furnish the number of enemy aircraft destroyed, due to the fact that the Air Service method of crediting gave each person who participated in the combat one victory. Thus, if three were concerned in one fight to the destruction of one enemy airplane, each U.S. combatant would be credited with one victory, if properly confirmed, but the enemy loss would still be but one airplane.

The list published by the Director of Air Service in 1920 actually contains, therefore, the names of flyers who really did not shoot down an enemy aircraft. Historically and statistically they received one full victory credit, a practice which has since been erroneously attributed to the World War II Luftwaffe.

A few of the World War I pilots whose names are published in the Ace List of this book are not actually entitled to membership in the elite fraternity. Under the rules of World War II and Korea they would have received fractional credits, and this would have reduced their victory totals below five.

To try and go back into these matters, to make everything from the beginning completely accurate, is not only an impossible research task but a trespass beyond rational limits. It would serve only to strip American combat pilots of an ace standing they have had for forty years—surely a picayune approach to accuracy!

Such historical probings of the ace issue as have been made by official American sources are unable, by the nature of things, to give any proper credit to American aces who flew in the service of foreign nations. The authors believe that if an American citizen became a fighter ace, then he is entitled to be considered an *American* fighter ace regardless of the uniform he wore while winning his spurs in the air.

This is the approach that is being taken in this book to the statistical mess and to the assorted political factors involved in the recognition of aces. Since the Americans who fought with the French and British in World War I and with the RAF and RCAF in World War II fought in the same cause as the United States, they rightly belong in the American fraternity of aces.

While the achievements of many of these expatriate aces have been remarkable, information on their careers is exceedingly difficult to obtain. Their omission from past books dealing with the history of American combat flying and flyers has been unfortunate, and repair of this omission is long overdue.

The same 1920 Air Service List, in which pilots who actually did not shoot down five enemy aircraft are included, specifically excludes "victories by members of the U.S. Air Service prior to their becoming such while in the service of the Allied countries." If this standpoint aided nationalist sentiment, it was at the expense of injustice to a number of courageous Americans who helped make history in the air.

These included such luminaries of early American combat flying as Major Raoul Lufbery, 17 victories; Second Lieutenant Frank L. Baylies, 12 victories; First Lieutenant Paul F. Baer, 9 victories; Captain G. De Freest Larner, 8 victories; Lieutenant James A. Connelly, 6 victories; Captain David McKelvy Peterson, 5 victories; Lieutenant Colonel William Thaw, 5 victories. These men all fought with the famed Lafayette Escadrille. They go to their rightful places as American fighter aces in this book.

For the purposes of this book an ace is considered to be the *pilot* of a fighter-type aircraft credited with five or more confirmed aerial victories. Aerial victories are considered to be against piloted enemy aircraft, with observation balloons included for the period of World War I.

While there have been gunners on aircraft who have been credited with five aerial victories or more, they have not been considered as fighter aces for the purposes of this book. Some pilots of bomber-type aircraft made the Ace Lists where they were at the controls and did the firing, but gunners are not included.

Worthy of mention here is the fact that prior to the advent of the forward-firing synchronized machine gun, a number of aircraft types were devised on both sides that put the observer-gunner in a forward nacelle. In those days, the observer was often an officer, the pilot an NCO.

Survivors of this era emphasize that victory in aerial combat depended then upon the observer-gunner rather than the pilot. In the brief training given to Royal Flying Corps observers it was pounded into these men that they had their pilot's life in their hands, and it was the RFC practice to credit aerial victories in this period to the observer who actually did the shooting.

The only American to be concerned with this transitional period is Frederick Libby of Sterling, Colorado. In his special case it is not necessary to make an exception to the "pilots only" rule for acedom. Observer Libby later became a pilot and made his ace rating anyway. His career is exhaustively covered in Chapter Two.

Confining the ace title to pilots is not intended to take anything away from the aerial gunners for their feats. However, to be considered a fighter ace a flyer must have been in control of the aircraft he flew in and have directed its firepower against manned enemy aircraft. This is the broad, general interpretation of a fighter ace preferred by the American Fighter Aces Association, one of its aims being to exclude credits toward ace standing for aircraft destroyed on the ground.

Wherever possible, the lists compiled by the authors are based on the records. During the period of World War II each air force and theater of operations had its own methods of formally acknowledging aerial victories. For this reason, the facts concerning all aerial victories will never be finally determined. Even today, the Air Force Historical Division is revising World War II victory statistics.

Where the authors have come into possession of authoritative data concerning aces, this statistical material has been incorporated in the lists. The lists in this book may not necessarily agree in every case with studies or surveys published either by official or quasi-official sources.

In World War II, divergent views existed in every theater of operations, as well as in each branch of the service, regarding aircraft destroyed on the ground. Most fighter pilots considered that an air-craft destroyed on the ground included those destroyed while rolling their wheels during takeoff or landing, as well as taxiing, hangared or parked aircraft.

"On the ground" kills were dubious for many reasons. The attack-ing pilot could not always tell whether the aircraft was actually de-stroyed, unless it blew up. If it blew up, it was impossible to know whether it was a real aircraft or a dummy loaded with inflammables. The Japanese talent with dummies in the Pacific Theater of Operations became legendary. When an enemy aircraft exploded *in the air* there was no doubt of the authenticity, either of the victory or the enemy machine.

Another reason for excluding ground kills from credit toward an ace standing is an anomalous scoring situation created in Europe in 1945 by the 8th Fighter Command. The Germans began to refuse aerial combat. The Luftwaffe would not take off to challenge Allied aircraft, sometimes because they lacked fuel and parts and sometimes because the Luftwaffe's waning strength was being conserved for the ground support role. The USAAF's 8th Fighter Command took emer-gency countermeasures.

They announced that full victory credits would be given for air-craft destroyed on the ground. This was an inducement to the fighter pilots to abandon the relative safety of air-to-air combat and enter the low-level hell of the air-to-ground fighter pilot. To descend into the undiminished hails of flak that still protected the surviving Luftwaffe airfields certainly required some incentive. Giving full victory credits for on-the-ground kills was the 8th Fighter Command's way of getting its pilots to face this most dangerous of all fighter operations.

Pilots avoided low-level strafing work mainly because they lost most of the advantages of being airborne. Their piloting skill and aerial combat experience meant little. If their aircraft were badly hit, or they were hit themselves, the deck came up to meet them in a hurry. There was opportunity neither to limp back to base nor to bail out. A forced landing was the best they could hope for, and a fiery crash was much more likely.

All fighter units everywhere faced these facts, but the 8th Fighter Command was the *only* unit of the U.S. forces in World War

II that ever gave full victory credit for ground kills. The Navy, Marine Corps and the rest of the Army Air Force kept track of ground kills only haphazardly, for the very nature of the operations forbade any exact tallying.

Some of the outstanding pilots of the 9th Air Force in Europe destroyed dozens of enemy aircraft on the ground, but never received credit toward an ace title for any of them. The anomalous nature of the ground-kill credits given to the 8th Fighter Command pilots is dramatically illustrated by the twenty ground kills credited or attributed to the Navy's top ace, Captain David McCampbell. Added to his thirty-four aerial victories, these would bring his official total to fifty-four, had McCampbell been functioning with the 8th Air Force in the 1945 emergency.

Many American fighter pilots will look in vain for their names in this book and its appended ace lists. These lists, as has been pointed out, are based on the records but do not necessarily duplicate them. Where the records say four aerial victories and two on-the-ground victories, then that individual is not an ace under the definitions applying in this book.

In compiling lists involving over 1,300 men and a period of almost four decades, there may well be unintentional omissions. For these the authors offer their apologies, while standing firmly by the "five aerial victories" criterion. This criterion is strictly observed, despite any 8th Air Force orders that may have been published, naming a particular pilot an ace after one or more ground kills built his victory total to five or more.

Kills shared in the air count as fractions. The method of assessment has been straightforward. If two pilots attacked an enemy machine and successfully shot it down, with neither pilot able to claim individual credit for the kill, the victory was split. Each pilot was given half a victory credit. All fractional credits have been similarly determined.

These then are the human and statistical factors that go into the making of an ace. There can be no doubt that statistical requirements have prevented many outstanding pilots from entering the elite fraternity, just as statistical anomalies have admitted some pilots who do not rightly belong to the fraternity.

The arcane blend of shooting and flying ability, intuition and eyesight, luck and opportunity, instinct and technology will never be truly fathomed or accurately analyzed, any more than will the statistics. But it is certain that the medieval knight never needed to bring such formidable powers to the joust, nor required such a host of seconds and supporters to make the joust possible and record its outcome for posterity.

2

☆　☆　☆　☆　☆

Aces of World War I

WHEN WORLD WAR I began in 1914, there were no eager hordes of dashing young pilots waiting to fly themselves to glory as aces. On the contrary, there was only the dimmest apprehension by military thinkers of the potential and significance of aircraft. In the eleven years between the first powered flight by the Wright brothers and the outbreak of World War I, aviation technology had developed at a snail's pace.

Between 1914 and 1918, under pressure of war, the aircraft was transformed from an invention of dubious military value into a revolutionary new fundamental of war. While aircraft were not decisive in World War I, the speed with which they added a dynamic new dimension to military thinking clearly showed that they would dominate future wars. Symbolic of this new military dynamism was the new warrior to whom it gave both birth and scope—the fighter ace.

In retrospect, the foundations of American military aviation on the outbreak of World War I were pathetically inadequate. Almost five years passed following the Wright brothers' first flight before trials were conducted on the first U.S. Army aircraft. These trials killed Lieutenant T. E. Selfridge and injured Orville Wright. There was pressure in the Army to abandon the airplane. Fortunately, the idea was bigger than its opponents.

On August 2, 1909, the U.S. Army took delivery of its first airplane. By June the following year, the service boasted one officer, nine enlisted men, one Wright airplane, one Baldwin airship and three captive balloons. From this beginning, a more rapid development might have been expected. The outbreak of World War I five years later and the subsequent development of the air weapon prior to America's involvement in the war provided a major incentive for the accelerated development of U.S. military aviation. But surprisingly little was actually done.

By April 6, 1917, when America entered the war, the Aviation Section of the U.S. Army had increased to only 65 officers, of whom only 35 were flying officers. Fifty-five aircraft and 1,087 enlisted men completed the inventory of American aerial strength. History now fairly characterizes this as a deplorable record for the land of the airplane's birth. America's tardiness was to have far-reaching consequences.

Although flying schools were in operation at Memphis, Tennessee, Mineola, New York, Essington, Pennsylvania, and San Diego, California, the foundation for the production of fighter pilots was limited. Many additional flying schools were subsequently opened, but the lack of facilities *in being* on America's entry into the conflict, meant that it was well into 1918 before U.S. fighter pilots got seriously into action. This largely accounts for the relatively small number of American aces in World War I and for their limited victory totals compared with both Allied and German aces.

One of the bright spots in this period was the appointment of Lieutenant Colonel William "Billy" Mitchell as Army Aviation Officer. Destined to become one of the world's dominant aviation prophets and America's most controversial aviation advocate, Mitchell's exertions played a leading part in getting American airpower off the ground. Special impetus was given to the expansion of the U.S. Air Service by General Pershing's call for a minimum of sixty-nine Balloon Companies in France by the autumn of 1918.

In July, 1917, the 29th Provisional Squadron left the United States for Europe. This unit went first to England, and on September 1, 1917, redesignated the 1st Aero Squadron, landed in France to enter the fray. The first official U.S. Aviation unit to go overseas, the men of the 1st Aero Squadron had some illustrious unofficial predecessors.

The adventure of flying, the challenge of the new form of combat in the air, and a hatred for the Kaiser's imperialism brought a number of Americans into the fight well ahead of their countrymen. Impatient for action, these Americans volunteered to serve with the French and British forces, and many of them made history. Not a great deal has been published about the Americans who flew with the British, but most of the Americans who volunteered for the French Army finished up in Nieuport 124, a unit specially formed for them by the French Air Department. Activated on March 21, 1916, this unit was initially known as Escadrille Américaine.

Escadrille Américaine subsequently became the immortal Lafayette Escadrille. This unique force probably received more publicity during and following World War I than any other combat unit involving Americans. Stories about the Lafayette Escadrille, both fact and fiction, are being written to this day, and the names of its leading lights are household words to America's aviation buffs.

Strong emotional factors swirled around the Lafayette Escadrille, a unit that epitomized the tradition of kinship and help in time of trouble that has existed between France and the United States since the American Revolution. Those factors served to almost obliterate historically the large contribution made to Allied victory by the Americans who volunteered to serve with the British forces.

These expatriate Americans were not integrated into special units of their own, but served with great distinction with the Royal Flying Corps, Royal Air Force and Royal Navy. As a consequence, very little is known about them today, historical data concerning their war careers is sketchy, and they still dwell in the shadow of the glorious Lafayette Escadrille. To the extent that historical research allows, this book gives all due credit to these men by listing their victory totals in the Appendix.

Typical of this long lost and elite corps of American aces is Captain Frederick Libby of Sterling, Colorado. Because it has been possible to locate Libby in Los Angeles, California, and finally obtain the details of his incredible career, it is proposed to deal with him at some length. The following section of the book will then be representative of the numerous American aces who served with the British in World War I without receiving any historical credit or recognition. The correction of this lamentable omission is long overdue.

Raised as a Colorado cowboy, Frederick Libby had just turned twenty-two when World War I broke out. In Canada at the time, he immediately joined the Canadian Army. Shipped to France the following year, Libby found life in the trenches in the rainy spring of 1916 to be more than he could stand. When the Royal Flying Corps sent out a call for observers by circulating bulletins in the trenches, Libby jumped at the chance to get away from the rain, mud and muck. The possibility was held out that successful applicants would be made second lieutenants in the RFC after a probationary period. To Private Libby, this was a substantial inducement. He did not know that, at the time he volunteered, the life expectancy of an observer was a scant ten operational hours. He now tells his own story of his first day in the RFC:

On arrival at HQ, 23rd Squadron, Royal Flying Corps I was questioned by the CO, Major Ross Hume, concerning my military experience. I had to tell him point-blank that I had never touched either a machine gun or an aeroplane in my life. He sent me immediately for half an hour's instruction on the gun range, after which I was to go up on a training flight with Lieutenant Price.

Coaching with the Lewis gun came easy. At that time the standard armament on most British aircraft, the Lewis used a drum of forty-seven rounds. This doesn't seem like much by today's standards, but in 1916 and to a cowboy who'd been used to making every shot count, forty-seven rounds seemed like a hell of a lot of firepower.

When I came back from the range, Lieutenant Price's plane was being wheeled out. It was an FE-2B, a pusher type of machine in which the observer sat in front of the pilot in an open nacelle. When you stood up to shoot, all of you from the knees up was exposed to the elements. There was no belt to hold you. Only your grip on the gun and the side of the nacelle stood between you and eternity.

Toward the front of the nacelle was a hollow steel rod with a swivel mount to which the gun was anchored. This gun covered a huge field of fire forward. Between the observer and pilot a second gun was mounted, for firing over the FE-2B's upper wing to protect the aircraft from rear attack. This second gun was at least as dangerous to the observer as it was to the enemy.

Adjusting and shooting this gun required that you stand right up out of the nacelle with your feet on the nacelle coaming. You had nothing to worry about except being blown out of the aircraft by the blast of air or tossed out bodily if the pilot made a wrong move. There were no parachutes and no belts. *No wonder they needed observers.*

I was to fire at a petrol tin on the ground as Price whizzed over the field at low altitude. I was instructed to fire bursts. The three firing passes proved my amateurism. On the first pass, after being hurled to the floor of the nacelle on takeoff, my unprotected eyes filled with tears and I couldn't even see the tin, let alone shoot at it. On the two subsequent passes, I hit the tin, but on each occasion let the whole drum of bullets go in one burst. I figured that I needed a lot of training, even if the torn up petrol tin was proof that I could still shoot like a good cowboy was supposed to.*

I was just settling down for a nap after lunch when an orderly arrived with an armload of flying gear. I was flying again at three PM, and was to be on the field at two-thirty. I figured it was more training, but it turned out to be an operational flight deep into enemy territory. I was flabbergasted. I'd only been in the RFC half a day.

On the field I got a thumbnail course on aerial tactics from my pilot, Lieutenant Hicks, to supplement my gunnery and flying training of that morning. "If another plane doesn't show his colors, Libby," said Hicks, "*let him have it.*" And we were off in formation, six aircraft in all, with our FE-2B flying upper back escort. This put us behind and above the other machines, and was considered to be the roughest and most vulnerable spot of all.

As we droned above the trenches, I could hardly believe that yesterday I was down there wallowing in the mud. Ringing in my ears were my instructor's words, driving home to me my life and my pilot's life depended on my vigilance and shooting.

I had just scanned the rest of the formation below us when out of the blue and to our right came an enemy ship. He was slightly higher than us. The tell-tale bluish puffs of tracer ammunition were coming from the German plane, and I grabbed immediately for the Lewis gun, which was resting in a clip on the left side of the nacelle.

I meant to throw the gun over to the clip on the front of the nacelle so I could get into action. I was overeager and all thumbs. I completely missed the clip and fell back in the nacelle with the heavy gun on top of me. Furious with myself, I kicked the gun off my chest and struggled it into shooting position.

The German machine passed in front of us and went into a vertical bank. The iron crosses on his wings looked huge and menac-

---

* Captain Price describes Libby today as "a deadly and economical gunman, whose length of vision was fantastic."

ing. Still off balance, I squeezed the trigger of the Lewis, and again committed the same error as in the morning's training flight. The whole forty-seven rounds went spurting off into the sky, leaving me there with an empty gun and the German still as large as life.

To my immense relief, the German slipped from view below us, going about his business. I put another drum on the Lewis in case he came back, and, crouched in the nacelle on my knees, I prayed he wouldn't. Looking up, I could see that the German's bullets had riddled our upper wing. Little tatters of fabric fluttered from the holes, and I got comfort from concluding that the German was probably as green as me.

The rest of the flight passed without incident, and when we touched down at Le Hameau, I noticed that there was a big bunch of officers milling about by the hangars. I caught a glimpse of the red tabs that usually went with high rank, but it meant nothing else to me.

As I swung down out of the plane, I was confronted by a very agitated sergeant major. He said that Colonel Shephard, CO of our wing, was on the field and wanted to see me immediately. The colonel was beaming when I walked over to him. As I went to salute, he grabbed my hand and pumped it furiously.

"First flight, first fight . . . wonderful, wonderful. When they go down in flames, Libby, by God, they don't come back up again."

I must have looked as though a mine had gone off under me. I didn't even know I had even hit the German machine, let alone sent it down in flames. My brief aerial battle and the blazing demise of the German had been observed and reported back to our squadron by artillery observers as soon as it had occurred. This was why the elated colonel was on the field waiting for me.

On my first day in the RFC I had my first contact with both aircraft and machine guns. I had my first day's training, my first operational flight and scored my first aerial victory. All this took place between ten in the morning and four in the afternoon. There were to be many more aerial battles before I left the RFC, and many other victories, but if ever an aviator had luck for his angel, it was me on that unforgettable day.

Frederick Libby holds a unique place among American airmen. He was the first American to shoot down five enemy aircraft in aerial combat. Only the fact that he performed this feat as an observer instead of a pilot prevents his occupying the historic spot of first American ace. He shot down his fifth confirmed German plane on August 27, 1916.

Under the definition of "ace" preferred by the American Fighter Aces' Association, the distinction is confined to those scoring aerial victories as a *pilot*. After scoring ten aerial kills as an oberver, under the difficult conditions prevailing before the introduction of the synchronized gun on the Allied side, Libby took pilot training. As a pilot, he downed a further fourteen German aircraft, bringing his World War I victory total twenty-four.

He was awarded the Military Cross in September of 1916 for "conspicuous gallantry and devotion to duty in the field." His British contemporaries included Captain Albert Ball, to whose guns and daring Libby attributes the fact that he is alive today, and Sholto Douglas, famed British fighter pilot who rose to the highest commands in the RAF in World War II.

Libby's place in history is rendered a special quality by one particular act of his, which was at once sublimely patriotic and historically significant. For the reasons outlined previously, when America entered World War I there were no American fighter pilots in U.S. units to carry Old Glory into action in the air. Frederick Libby filled the gap.

Shortly after America's entry into the war, Libby was presented with an American flag by a British squadron mate. His CO suggested that the former Colorado cowboy cut the flag into strips and use it as streamers on his aircraft. The idea was that the flag would be carried over the German lines every day by an American pilot, thus signifying to the enemy that the United States was in the war.

Libby carried the historic flag on his aircraft on every operational flight from May to September, 1917. It was the first American flag to fly over enemy territory in World War I. When Libby left the RFC in September of 1917, after transfer to the U.S. Air Service at the request of "Billy" Mitchell, he took the precious flag with him.

When he returned to the United States, the Aero Club of America auctioned off the flag at a Liberty Loan drive at Carnegie Hall on October 18, 1918. The historic bunting brought $3,250,000 into the Liberty Loan coffers, but Libby contrived to retain possession of the relic. He has it today at his Los Angeles apartment, still with the castor oil stains of World War I on it. One day it will find its proper resting place in the Smithsonian Institution.

The only incident in his military career that Libby looks back on with regret was the cool reception he got in Washington, D.C., on his return to the United States. Air Service nabobs who had never flown a plane in combat or fired a gun in anger found the presence of a real, live American ace in their midst to be more than a little disquieting. Numerous mean-spirited humiliations were heaped on Libby, such as the kind of pilot wings he was allowed to wear, questions concerning his citizenship and so on. The fact that he was one of Billy Mitchell's protégés did not help him, either.

Libby's story and career exemplify much of the color, mystery and interesting early history that surround these expatriate pilots who flew with the British and French. Those who flew with the British suffered at least a temporary loss of citizenship, and indignity that was not visited upon the members of the Lafayette Escadrille.

On August 31, 1916, just four days after Libby shot down his fifth German plane as an observer-gunner, an American flying as a pilot in the Royal Flying Corps downed his fifth German plane and became the first American fighter ace. He was Captain Alan M. Wilkinson, twenty-five years old and already a veteran of a year's aerial combat. He was commissioned on June 14, 1915.

By war's end, Wilkinson was a major with nineteen aerial victories to his credit. He was certainly among the first Americans actually to fly in combat in World War I, but he never transferred to the AEF from the RFC and is almost unknown to most aerial combat buffs.

Wilkinson was flying with 24th Squadron RFC from January 16, 1916, until October 13, 1916. He scored his first five kills between May 16, 1916, and August 31, 1916. Wilkinson was credited with four probables in the same period, which involved daily forays far into Germany territory and made confirmation of many victories impossible. There is no more adequate testimony to the bravery and courage of Alan Wilkinson than his being awarded the British Distinguished Service Order *twice* in 1916. This is the highest decoration that an officer of the British services can win other than the coveted and rarely awarded Victoria Cross.

Serving with the Lafayette Escadrille from the days of its foundation was the man more generally accepted as America's first fighter ace—Raoul Lufbery. He was flying during the same period as Wilkinson, and under the same difficult conditions. Lufbery was a fitting figure to enrich the Franco-American traditions. French-born, he was taken to the United States by his immigrant parents and was naturalized in 1910. In his personality, citizen status and deeds, Lufbery united the two great nations of which he was a part.

In 1914, aged twenty-nine Raoul Lufbery returned to France and enlisted as an airplane mechanic in the French Army. His background for this was excellent. For several years before the war he had barnstormed around the world with the famed French pioneer aviator, Marc Pourpé. Both men returned to France to fight on the outbreak of World War I.

When Pourpé was killed shortly after the Battle of the Marne, Lufbery set out to avenge his death and applied for pilot training. He flew in action for the first time on October 7, 1915, as the pilot of a Voisin bomber.

Despite some earlier difficulties with his training, Lufbery proved to be an exceptional combat pilot with a talent for improvising tactics suited to the machines and armament of the day. Transferring to fighters in 1916, he scored his first aerial victory on July 30, 1916, and by Christmas Day the same year had confirmed his sixth kill. Although not yet an ace by the French yardstick of ten aerial victories, the United States had its first ace when Lufbery was reluctantly released to the U.S. Army by the Lafayette Escadrille.

He was transferred to the U.S. Air Service on January 21, 1918. He was assigned to the 94th Aero Squadron, First Pursuit Group. Because of his foreign birth and Lafayette Escadrille service, Lufbery's final status was not formally decided until many years after the war. His score has been the subject of many disputes, and it is generally acknowledged to have been far higher than the seventeen kills with which he is officially credited.

Since the overwhelming majority of fighter combat took place in 1916 and early 1917 behind the German lines, most Allied fighter pilots who were active during this period probably shot down at least twice the number of aircraft with which they are officially credited. Confirmation of these kills, often far from friendly observation, was frequently impossible. In addition, until the "ace" concept became associ-

ated with aerial victories, there was no special urgency or significance
attached to the confirmation of kills.

Hence, when Lufbery confided to some of his contemporaries that
he had downed as many as fifty German planes, with the bulk of these
kills unconfirmed due to their being far behind enemy lines, he was
probably talking fact and not fiction. His demonstrated abilities in
front of his fellow pilots were sufficient proof that he could have done
it.

Lufbery's place among the immortals of the air is assured by his
development of the "Lufbery Circle"—a useful and enduring aerial
tactic that saved the lives of many Allied pilots in two world wars.
When Richthofen's Circus was at the height of its power, the Baron's
uncanny grasp of the essentials of aerial fighting enabled him to inflict
terrible losses on his foes. The "Lufbery Circle" was intended to partially offset the technical disparity between the German and Allied
aircraft, which added to the Red Knight's assets.

Lufbery and his pilots would fight until the Germans, mounted on
superior aircraft, began to gain the advantage. Then Lufbery would
enter a tight turn or circle with the other members of his squadron
following close behind him. Friend was behind friend, so that if any
German machine entered the circle and tried to get into firing position
behind any of Lufbery's planes, the German would be immediately
under the guns of the following American pilot.

The German might shoot down his intended victim, but he would
certainly be shot down himself. The odds against successfully penetrating a Lufbery Circle were high, and discouraged most German pilots
from tackling the Americans when they went into this formation.
Lufbery would continue the circle, all the while working the formation gradually back to the Allied side of the lines. Once the circle
reached Allied territory, the Germans usually gave up and flew
away.

Raoul Lufbery was killed on May 19, 1918, with the 14th Pursuit
Squadron. He tackled a massive German photo-reconnaissance aircraft
near Toul airfield. The German machine was armored, and on Lufbery's first pass his hits had no effect. As the ace made a second
firing pass, the German rear gunner threw a burst into Lufbery's engine, and the little Nieuport was soon a flying ball of fire. Lufbery

jumped in midair from this inferno, his flying suit smoldering as his body cartwheeled down. There were no parachutes for the pilots of those days, and he plummeted into a small stream, there to be crushed to death by the impact.

Lufbery was the third-ranking AEF ace of World War I and is credited with seventeen victories. If Alan Wilkinson is excluded because of his British service, Lufbery was the first American ace.

Lufbery once said to a group of pilot companions, "There will be no 'after the war' for fighter pilots." His death in combat verified this prophecy in his own case, but the Lufbery Circle kept his name before America's fighter pilots for almost forty years after his death. "Luf's" historical niche is secure, and he lives on as a dominant pioneer figure.

Among Lufbery's fellow Americans in the Lafayette Escadrille was Major Charles J. Biddle, who came to the elite formation from Escadrille 73. Like Lufbery, Biddle was later transferred to the U.S. Air Service, and he spent the remainder of his flying career with the 13th Aero Squadron, 4th Pursuit Group. He is credited with seven serial victories.

Charles Biddle's 1919 book *Way of the Eagle* contains a number of letters written by the American ace during war. These missives provide interesting insight into the thinking of a World War I pilot. They have a powerful sense of immediacy usually missing from retrospective writing. Like Lufbery, Biddle came out second best in an encounter with an armored German plane, less than a week after Lufbery was killed.

It is not inconceivable that Biddle battled the identical machine that downed Lufbery, for the German gunner was evidently a very bright boy. Biddle tells the story of this fight, and its sequel, in a letter he wrote on May 25, 1918, from the Ocean Hospital, La Panne, Belgium:

> . . . Ten minutes after the first fight we were flying along inside our own lines, when I noticed a peculiar two-seater circling very low down between the trenches, he could not have been more than six hundred meters up. I took him for an English infantry liaison machine, which he very much resembled, but then noticed that he seemed to circle into the Boche lines with remarkable impunity considering his very low altitude, so decided to investigate. Sure

enough, there were the old black crosses on him showing plainly as he swung almost under me in making a turn over our lines. . . .

It was the first Boche machine of the kind that I had ever seen, and, indeed, I have never heard of any one that I know running into one like it. He had a rounded body like some French machines, the tail was square and the lower wing much shorter than the upper, like many of the English two-seater observation planes. All the Hun two-seaters that I have ever seen or heard of before have both the upper and lower wings approximately the same length. In addition, it was the slowest bus you ever saw, and I think I could go two miles to his one.

All this leads me to believe that it was a new type of German armored plane which they call "Junkers" and which I have read about in the aviation reports. They are built especially for this low infantry liaison work, and are heavily armored about the fuselage to protect them from fire from the ground. In consequence of their great weight, they cannot go very high and are extremely slow.

This fellow must have been a squadron leader or something, for he had four big streamers attached to his wings, one on the top and another on the lower plane on each side. . . . it is very common for patrol leaders to carry such streamers so that their pilots may easily distinguish them from the other machines in the patrol.

Whether or not this fellow was what I think he was, I hope that when I am flying again, I may see him and have another go at him. He certainly got the best of me, and I don't feel at all vindictive about it, as it was a fair fight. But just the same, it would give me more satisfaction to bring that boy down than any five others. It would also be interesting to see whether his hide is thick enough to stand a good dose of armor-piercing bullets at short range. An incendiary bullet in his gas tank might also make his old boiler factory a warm place to fly in.

As soon as I was sure that the machine was really a Hun, I dove down after him and made up my mind this time to get at good close range. I did, and ended up fifty yards directly behind his tail and just below, but I had one bad mistake, a real beginner's trick which was the cause of all my troubles.

I was not far enough below him, and I had not fired more than one or two shots when I got caught in the back draught from his propeller, which joggled my machine about so accurate shooting became an impossibility. I saw one bullet go to one side of him, and another several feet on the other side, so stopped shooting for a second to get in better position. Anyone with a little experience should know better than to get himself caught like this, especially

myself, for I had the same thing happen with the first Hun I ever
brought down.

That time I dove down a little before shooting at all, and then
fired from a good position a little lower down. I tried to remedy the
situation in the same way this time, but in doing so I entirely failed,
for the instant, to appreciate the very slow speed of the Hun. I was
already close to him, and when I dove down and then pulled up to
shoot, I found that I had overshot and was almost directly under
him—so much so that it was impossible to get my gun on him.

He started swerving from side to side to get me out from under
him, so that the machine-gunner could shoot, and I tried to stay
under him, swerving as he did and at the same time slowing down
my motor to the limit so as to let him get ahead of me enough to
allow me to start shooting again. The Boche and I were at this time
about twenty yards apart, and if he had only had a trap door in his
bottom he might have brought me down by dropping a brick on my
head. However, he did not need it.

The Hun gave a twist which took me for an instant beyond the
protection of his fuselage. It was only for a second or two, but it
was sufficient for the observer, who proceeded to do the quickest
and most accurate bit of shooting that I have yet run up against. As
a rule in such a situation, you see the observer look over the side of
his machine at you, and then swing his gun around on its pivot and
point it in your direction. While he is doing this, you have time to
duck.

In this case, I saw a black-helmeted head appear over the edge of
the Hun machine and almost at the same instant he fired, as quickly
as you could snap-shoot with a pistol. In trying to slow down as
much as possible, I had gotten into almost a loss of speed, so that my
machine did not perhaps answer to the controls as quickly as it
otherwise would have.

This, however, made no difference, for . . . he was as accurate as
he was quick, and his very first shot came smashing through the
front of my machine above the motor, and caught me just on top of
the left knee. How many bullets hit the machine I don't know, and
never had a chance to find out, but my motor went dead at once, so
that knocked out all chance of any further shots at the Boche.

I dove under him out of his line of fire, and then twisting sharply
around, planed back for our own lines, trying to make the most of
what little height I had. . . . I kept working away till the last minute,
trying to get the motor going, for anyone who knows this country
knows that it is utterly impossible to land any machine in it without
crashing, let alone a Spad, which requires at least as great speed for
landing as any other type.

All my efforts were useless, however, and I saw that there was nothing for it but to smash up as gracefully as possible. The thing that bothered me most was not the smash, for that would probably result only in a little shaking up, but I thought I was further in the Hun lines than I was, and had most unpleasant visions of spending the rest of the war in Germany. . . .

Just at the last moment I veered the plane a little to avoid landing in the middle of a barbed-wire entanglement, and then the instant my wheels touched ground, over my machine went in the middle of its back with a loud crash. . . . Scrambling out, I lost no time in rolling into a nearby shell hole.

Biddle dived from shell hole to shell hole, avoiding by turns the strafing runs made on him by his late adversary, German artillery fire and the combined small-arms efforts of several hundred German infantrymen. Wallowing through mud and stagnant water, with his sodden flying suit adding an almost intolerable burden of extra weight to his wounded leg, Biddle eventually stumbled to safety in a position occupied by the Royal Irish Rifles. He survived World War I.

The Americans of the Lafayette Escadrille had learned the essentials of air fighting as they had developed. This know-how was passed on to the inexperienced American pilots coming from the United States after America's entry into the war. Since aerial combat was a dynamic art, only a participant could learn its lessons and provide authentic guidance for green pilots. In this respect, the American fighter pilots of the Lafayette Escadrille made an invaluable contribution to the success of the U.S. Air Service.

The Aviation Section's own first aerial combat did not take place until April 12, 1918, a year after America's declaration of war. Reconnaissance planes of the First Squadron were attacked by German fighters and a brisk battle ensued. Eager for a victory over the new foe, the Germans tried desperately to score a kill, but were unsuccessful. The dogfight was a draw.

Two days later, the Americans drew first blood. Lieutenants Douglas Campbell and Alan F. Winslow each gained credit for one victory, and the official American scoring account was opened. Despite this encouraging beginning, the Germans exacted a heavy toll of men and machines from the AEF by virtue of their superiority in both experi-

ence and equipment. In due course, the Americans developed the skills
and acumen that only actual war can provide, and redressed to a great
degree the technical disadvantages under which they flew.

As the final year of the war progressed, tactics became more and
more important. Daylight fighter operations built up from two- and
three-machine formations to mass flights and battles involving thirty to
forty aircraft on both sides. The American squadrons played a leading
role in these events as American strength flowed into the conflict.

The first ace with the AEF was Captain Douglas Campbell of Mt.
Hamilton, California. Introduced to combat flying by Raoul Lufbery,
Campbell shot down his first enemy plane on April 14, 1918, as previously related. Six weeks later, after a rousing dogfight over the German front lines, Campbell became an ace by scoring his fifth kill.
Wounded in combat shortly afterward, he was returned to the United
States. He joined W. R. Grace in 1919 and served twenty-four years
with Pan American Grace Airways. Campbell retired in 1963 and lives
in Cos Cob, Connecticut.

The second AEF pilot to win acedom in an American uniform was
Captain Edward V. Rickenbacker. He became in due course the American "Ace of Aces" in World War I. By every measure, Rickenbacker
is the most famous American pilot of his time.

A man of energy, daring and imagination, Rickenbacker was already a nationally famous auto-racing driver at the time of American
entry into World War I. His later achievements as an ace pilot and as a
businessman have overshadowed this earlier phase of his career, but his
racing experience was responsible in a great degree for the development of Rickenbacker's fantastic mechanical sense and coordination.

He enlisted in the Signal Enlisted Reserve Corps in New York City
in May, 1917, and was assigned to the Aviation Section. Three days
later, Rickenbacker was on his way to France. He served as a chauffeur
with Aviation Headquarters of the AEF in Paris. In this capacity, he
came into contact with Billy Mitchell and impressed the pioneer leader
with his determination to fly combat.

Since Rickenbacker was considered "too old" at twenty-eight for a
fighter pilot, it took the intervention of someone like Mitchell to pave
the way for Rickenbacker's flying training. He trained at Tours, and
found his way eventually to the 94th Aero Squadron as a pilot. This

was the famed "Hat in the Ring" squadron, which found immortality due to the deeds of Rickenbacker and others who served with the 94th.

In command of the 94th when Rickenbacker joined was the sagacious air fighter Raoul Lufbery. Under "Luf's" experienced eye, Rickenbacker broke in and began his spectacular climb to the top scoring spot. He scored his first kill April 29, 1918, and the following month he was an ace.

Rickenbacker went on to score twenty-five aerial victories, consisting of twenty-one aircraft and four balloons, in the remaining five months of the war. Thirty years later, he was given confirmation for a fifth balloon he had knocked down, bringing his final official score to twenty-six aerial victories.

History does not confine such caresses solely to the famous, as another American pilot of World War I can testify.

Captain Charles R. D'Olive was credited with a World War I score of four victories, and spent forty-five years outside the elite fraternity of aces. Then, on June 18, 1963, one of his two additional victory claims was finally confirmed by the USAF, and Captain Charles D' Olive, late of the 93rd Aero Squadron, became an ace. This incident is mentioned to illustrate that even the best historical records can be incomplete, and that unknown fighter pilots are just as likely to benefit from fresh historical facts as the more famous men of the air war.

From August to September, 1918, Rickenbacker was hospitalized. He made his brilliant fighting record in a scant three months of combat, and no other American pilot surpassed his twenty-six victories until well into World War II. Billy Mitchell is reputed to have said, "If the war had lasted a few more weeks, Eddie Rickenbacker would have been a general."

Rickenbacker was an exponent of the classic bounce from out of the sun. He believed in the fundamental value of altitude to the attacking pilot, and this, combined with his natural aggressiveness, outstanding piloting skill and superlative shooting, placed him among the greatest combat pilots produced by the United States.

A legend in his own lifetime, Rickenbacker's philosophy has been born of the incredible physical disasters he has survived. He once turned end over end in a race car at Indianapolis. A fearful airline crackup in February, 1941, near Atlanta, Georgia, broke his hip, elbow and nose and scooped his left eye out of its socket. The following year, he almost died of exposure after a crash in the South Pacific. His spirit and indomitable courage kept both him and his younger companions alive until rescue.

What does the "Ace of Aces" himself say about these numerous flirtations with death? "The thought I had held since boyhood never deserted me. I was a dynamic part of progress and life. Some Power was taking care of me, keeping me alive for some purpose, some fulfilment."

Recently "Captain Eddie" laid down his business burdens. He has played a substantial role in building American civil aviation, and has been the dominant figure in Eastern Air Lines for decades. He has announced that he will write his memoirs, and aviation buffs the world over look forward to the appearance of what should be a significant work of history, written by one who has made history.

Behind Rickenbacker among the aces of the AEF is Frank Luke of Arizona. He holds a special niche among American aces because fourteen of his eighteen victories were balloons. The fury and the success with which he hurled himself on the gasbags earned him the immortal nickname of the "Arizona Balloon Buster."

Luke's career was as brilliant as it was brief. To term his career "meteoric" is finally to do justice to an overworked word. Lieutenant Luke shot down his first aircraft and confirmed this aerial victory, September 12, 1918. Seventeen days later, Luke's score had risen to fourteen German observation balloons and four aircraft, and Lieutenant Luke was dead. He was killed in the wreckage of his crashed fighter by German infantry in an episode that epitomized his phenomenal courage.

The best-known biographical study of Frank Luke comes from the files of the U.S. Air Force.

Frank Luke (World War Ace). Born Phoenix, Ariz. May 19, 1897, son of Mr. and Mrs. Frank Luke, Sr.

Frank Luke, the most spectacular air fighter of the World War, enlisted in the Signal Corps, U.S. Army, on September 25, 1917, as a private.

He was then sent for flying training to Rockwell Field, San Diego, California, on January 23, 1918, and was subsequently com-

missioned a Second Lieutenant in the Aviation Section, Signal Officers Reserve Corps.

Arriving overseas for advanced flying training, he was stationed
at the 3rd Aviation Instruction Center, Issoudon, France, where he
remained until May 30, 1918, leaving for Caziaux. On July 26, 1918,
he was ordered to active duty at the front with the 27th Aero
Squadron, 1st Pursuit Group, in the Aisne-Marne salient. Three
weeks later he engaged in his first aerial combat and shot down an
enemy airplane, the beginning of a long list of victories. During his
active flying at the front he was officially credited with the destruction of eighteen enemy craft—four airplanes and fourteen balloons.

Luke stood out among his contemporaries because at a time when
formation flying and team tactics were coming to dominate aerial warfare, he was the epitome of the lone wolf. He was a throwback to the
spirit that held sway in the air war's earlier years. To his lone-wolf
nature, Luke had coupled an iron will and a fierce determination. He
made his attacks in this way even against the repeated orders of his
commanding officer. Like a talented artist, Luke did not take kindly to
controls on his work, and he was courageous almost to a fault.

Balloons were not easy targets. They were protected by bristling
batteries of antiaircraft and machine guns. Frequently fighter squadrons were assigned to protect the balloons, often known as the "eyes of
the artillery." For a lone fighter plane to tackle a balloon was by 1918
little more than heroic madness.

Luke ignored the risks. He made observation balloons his specialty.
Balloon attacks were elevated to the stature of an art by the youthful
American ace. In one week of September, 1918, two days of which
he did not fly, Lieutenant Frank Luke sent down no fewer than thirteen of the gasbags in flaming tatters.

His only departure from his lone-wolf ventures was his brief aerial
partnership with a kindred spirit in 27th Squadron, Lieutenant Joseph
F. Wehner, who was killed in action September 18, 1918. Wehner was
also a balloon buster, and his five aerial victories were all balloons.
During the St. Mihiel offensive, the two aces shot down five observation balloons between them. Returning from one of these encounters,
Luke and Wehner were separated, and while returning alone to his
airfield, Luke downed three German aircraft.

Lieutenant Luke absented himself from his squadron on September

28, 1918, without permission. For this his CO severely reprimanded the young Arizonan. He was also grounded. This did not sit well with the mercurial Luke. Telling a born combat pilot that he could not fly while the war thundered all around him was like ordering the tide to stay out.

Without permission Luke took off in his plane and landed at a neighboring field. Orders for his arrest were issued, and then countermanded from higher up before they could be carried out. Luke took off again, his target three German balloons in the Meuse region.

Luke destroyed two of the balloons. In the second strike, the law of averages caught up with the balloon buster. He received severe wounds from the protective fire. Ignoring his wounds, he pressed home his attack on the third balloon, sent it down in flames and turned for home.

Grinding along at 150 feet, fighting to retain consciousness, Luke spotted German troops on the road near Murvaux. He made several strafing runs on the road, killing six Germans and wounding many more. This effort led to more hits on his aircraft, and he was forced to land. He rolled to a stop in the middle of the German positions.

Surrounding the American pilot, the German infantry called on him to surrender. There would have been no dishonor for the Arizona Balloon Buster in surrender under such conditions, but the idea of surrender never entered the ace's mind. Standing in the wreckage of his riddled ship, he drew his pistol and opened fire on the German infantry. A crash of rifle fire closed the incredible career of America's most spectacular World War I ace.

Captain Alfred A. Grant, Luke's CO, who had opposed the ace's unruly conduct as a matter of discipline, was the first to urge the award of the Congressional Medal of Honor. This decoration was added to the Distinguished Service Cross and Oak Leaf Cluster awarded Luke for earlier bravery. The decorations were presented later to his father, Frank Luke, Sr.

At the time of his death, Frank Luke was only twenty-one. In spite of his youth, he had blazed a glorious chapter in the history of American aviation and set a standard of courage and boldness that no pilot would ever surpass. More than any other American pilot, Luke epitomized the classically heroic aspects of the fighter ace. A statue of him was erected in the Capitol grounds at Phoenix, and the USAF has a permanent commemorative link with the Balloon Buster through Arizona's Luke AFB.

Ranked for scoring laurels between Rickenbacker and Luke are a number of Americans who served exclusively with the British, never transferring to the U.S. forces. These Americans were:

CAPTAIN STANLEY ROSEVEAR, RFC, 23
WILLIAM C. LAMBERT, RFC, 22
CAPTAIN F. W. GILLETTE, RAF, 20
SUB-LIEUTENANT JOHN J. MALONE, RNAS, 20
MAJOR ALAN M. WILKINSON, RFC, 19

There is also the anomalous and colorful figure of Captain Frederick Libby to bear in mind, with ten kills as an observer and fourteen as a pilot, all of them airplanes—more airplanes downed in aerial combat in World War I than any other American aviator.

Lieutenants Frank Hale and Paul T. Iaccaci, both of the RAF and both with eighteen kills, rank in the overall American scoring in World War I with Lieutenant Frank Luke of the AEF.

Many of the expatriate American aces in the service of the British received high awards for bravery. Wilkinson's double award of the DSO was probably the greatest distinction won by any of these men, but Sub-Lieutenant John J. Malone of the Royal Navy also won the DSO. He was killed in action in May, 1917.

Captain Clive Warman of Philadelphia served with 22nd Squadron RFC and won both the DSO and the Military Cross. He is credited with fifteen aerial victories, which ranks him high among America's World War I aces. Captain Stanley Rosevear won the British Distinguished Service Cross. These decorations are adequate testimony to the quality of the service rendered to the Allied cause by these Americans.

Ranked behind Rickenbacker, Luke and Lufbery among the AEF aces is Lieutenant George A. Vaughn of Brooklyn, New York, who flew with the 17th Pursuit Squadron. A superlative shot with an instinct for combat tactics, Vaughn shot down twelve German planes and one observation balloon for a total of thirteen victories in World War I.

Enlisting directly from Princeton University in 1917, Vaughn trained in England and Scotland, and was then assigned to 84th Squadron, RAF. While with this British outfit, Vaughn shot down seven planes and a balloon. Transferred to the AEF in August, 1918, he was assigned to 17th Pursuit Squadron as a flight commander.

While with the 17th, he downed another four German aircraft, and this put him fourth among America's AEF aces. An extract from the citation to his Distinguished Service Cross gives insight into his qualities as a pilot:

> For extraordinary heroism in action near Cambrai, France, September 22, 1918. Lieutenant Vaughn, while leading an offensive flight patrol, sighted eighteen enemy Fokkers about to attack a group of five Allied planes flying at low level. Although outnumbered nearly five to one, he attacked the enemy group, personally shot down two enemy planes, the remaining three planes of his group shooting down two more. His courage and daring enabled the group of Allied planes to escape. Again on September 28, 1918, he alone attacked an enemy advance plane, which was supported by seven Fokkers, and shot the advance plane down in flames.

Vaughn maintains an undiminished enthusiasm for aviation. He lives on Staten Island in New York, and is a partner in the Casey Jones Academy of Aeronautics at La Guardia Field in New York City.

With twelve aerial victories, one less than Vaughn, Captain Elliott White Springs is usually ranked fifth among the AEF aces, a distinction he shares with Captain Field E. Kindley of the 148th Aero Squadron. In terms of fame, however, Springs ranks second only to Rickenbacker among the aces of World War I. His is an unusual case.

Elliott White Springs' books on aerial combat made him a far more famous flyer in the postwar period than he had been as a war ace. A whole new generation of American boys were introduced to aerial warfare through his books. He glamorized the fighter pilot more than any other American writer. In fact, his books could easily lead the reader to believe that the fighter pilot had the most glamorous of all jobs.

Another notable American ace credited with twelve victories is Frank L. Baylies, who flew in the Lafayette Escadrille with Raoul Lufbery. One of the best combat pilots in the famed French unit, Baylies' victory tally suffered in the same way as Lufbery's from inability to confirm. Both pilots had numerous kills far behind the German lines, and like Lufbery, Baylies probably had twice the kills that the records show. He was killed in aerial combat in 1918.

Also unable to confirm a number of victories was Arthur Raymond Brooks, an MIT graduate of 1917 who joined the Aviation Section right after winning his degree. Trained in Canada at Toronto, Brooks went overseas early in 1918 and shot down ten German aircraft. Unfortunately, only six were confirmed, with the others classed as "probables."

Brooks contributed a vivid account of World War I aerial combat, set down in December, 1918, while the events were fresh in his mind and not embellished by time and memory.

On the 14th of September, 1918, with a section composed of six Spads, we attempted to clear the area for a reconnaissance plane. Three Fokker groups composed of five, six and twelve planes were observed, and our leader and squadron commander, whom I call "big fellow" for more than reason of his stature, headed for the center group of six. Intent as we were upon the center group, the last formation of twelve Fokkers got around on our right rear and jumped us. I saw them as they neared us, but had no time to warn the leader of our flight, other than by just nosing down, gaining speed, and then turning to the right over his head into the Fokkers.

Before a second or two I had penetrated the Boche formation and from that time on I never saw another of my mates. But I was treated to fine display of daytime pyrotechnics. We were at 5,000 meters (about 15,000 feet), the "we" in this case referring to myself and at least eight red-nosed Richthofen Circus Fokkers bent on an eight-to-one shot. We were about ten miles on the German side of the front line. My chances of escape were so slight that I figured I had come to my end.

I was scared, but in spite of much high tension and yelling at the top of my voice, I calculated, by the nature of my training, I suppose, that I would get as many Fokkers as possible before the inevitable. For ten minutes from our three-mile height down to a few hundred feet, and through that distance behind the lines to our own side, I passed through rather a mystery.

I side-slipped continuously, and whenever a Fokker would get on my tail, I would go through the most absurd gyrations as quickly as possible. Twice I tried to ram Fokkers. One red-nosed nightmare came in from right, endeavoring to draw me under. . . . I had just time to dip enough to see his features before I fired incendiaries, and he was aflame.

I turned immediately on another, feeling that a vigorous offense was the best defense. After a short burst from very close quarters I was satisfied that the second Fokker was out of the fight, although he did not catch fire. It was being surrounded that had saved me thus far. The Germans could not shoot at me without being in their own way most of the time, or bringing one of their own aircraft into the line of fire.

White tracer ribbons would cut through between my wings often, so close that if I reached out my hand the stream of bullets would have cut it off. My engine worried me because the pressure in my gas tank failed in certain positions of the airplane. My gravity feed was so low that I had to conserve it.

Then my prop stopped dead before I could switch over to the gravity tank. I stared at the stationary blade, and instinctively nosed down just as an enemy burst swept in front of my forehead, shattering my windshield and clattering into my right gun, rendering it useless except for single shots. Two more Boche planes, in their tactical work, happened to get in the way of my now single gun line of fire, and down they went. My spirits soared as the odds diminished.

I now had the better feeling that came with finding myself over Lake Lachausee, with a good two thousand meters of altitude and only four German planes still paying me attention. This was still too much attention to suit me. I figured the danger was greater for me now than with the whole swarm, because there was less chance of the Germans getting in their own way.

A 220 hp Spad can outdive a Fokker D-7, and for 1,500 meters with full motor I spun, nose-dived and then slithered toward the ground, flattening out just over rolling country with a fair chance over the four Germans. Two of these, and then one finally, kept up the chase for a short distance. They retreated to my glad astonishment before crossing the lines.

I don't know how I got back. One incendiary bullet had burned itself out in the main spar of my upper wing. Five bullets went through the fuselage within four inches of my back. Holes were scattered all over my poor Spad. The aircraft had to be salvaged.

Had gun cameras been installed in Brooks' aircraft, he may well have been the first American ace ever to score a quadruple kill. His last three kills in this encounter were never confirmed under the victory rules of the day. By such vivid interplays of luck, skill, courage and aggressive determination were fighter aces made in World War I.

Captain Brooks not only survived the war, he remained in the Air Service until December, 1922. He returned to the service of the USAAF at the beginning of World War II, determined that he would again take a fighter plane into combat. Fate decreed otherwise. A series of spinal operations denied Brooks the fulfilment of his courageous dream. Still a dashing figure, he is Publications Manager of the Bell Telephone Laboratories at Whippany, New Jersey.

Lieutenant David Sinton Ingalls was the U.S. Navy's first and only fighter ace in World War I—a historic distinction. He joined the First Yale Unit and went to France for training with the French forces at Claremont Forand. This was followed by further training with the British at Gosport, Turnbury and Ayr. Ingalls flew fighters while assigned to the U.S. Naval Air Station at Dunkirk. During this period he downed a Rumpler observation plane, and he tells the story of this incident here in his own words:

On September 24, 1918, Hobson and I went out about 5:30 PM in our Camels. We flew along the lines at fifteen thousand feet for some time, got disgusted and started home as it was getting dark. Saw some Archie off La Paune, and also a German Rumpler. I caught up with him between Newport and Ostend, but he was so slow I overshot. So I dove again. He would turn one way to give his observer a good shot at me, and I would try to keep under him, making a bigger circle so his observer could not shoot.

I came up underneath him, again overshooting, but succeeded in firing a few rounds. Nothing happened, so I dropped and worked for a good position. On a turn he almost got me, for before I could make the outside circle, his observer fired about ten shots, the tracers going between the struts on my left side. We were only ten yards off at the time, and I could see the two Huns in their black helmets.

All the time we were getting further behind their lines . . . and I was getting madder. Finally, I gave up the careful, cautious tactics, got straight behind him and kept firing for probably one hundred rounds. At last a big puff of smoke came up like an explosion. I felt fine. It was a long way over, so I had to contour-chase (hedgehop) and was shot up by a ground machine gun. My Camel had to be scrapped and I was given a new one.

After the war, Ingalls left the Navy and entered the publishing business. His career between the wars included service as Undersecretary for Air on the staff of the Secretary of the Navy. In World War II, Ingalls went into the Navy again, this time on the staff of Pacific Air Command. He later became Executive Officer of the Air Central Coordination Group, Forward Area, and also served on the staff of ComAir South Pacific.

A successful businessman, David Ingalls is President and Publisher of the Cincinnati *Times-Star*. In terms of long service to his country, he has few rivals among America's aces. His five aerial victories include an observation balloon shot down in combat. He was awarded numerous decorations including the Distinguished Service Medal from his own country, the Legion of Honor from the French and the British Distinguished Flying Cross.

By November 11, 1918, there were 111 Americans who had earned the "ace" distinction. Possibly another fifty actually downed the required number of German aircraft without confirming the victories. America's late entry into the war held down the number of aces, and considering the extremely short time that AEF pilots were actually in combat with the enemy, the American record is a good one. Approximately forty Americans earned their acedom in the service of either Britain or France.

U.S. military aviation had undergone a phenomenal expansion by the end of the war. Few military leaders in 1914 could possibly have foreseen the rise of America's airpower between 1917 and 1918. From its April, 1917, skeleton status, the U.S. Air Service expanded to 45 squadrons and 767 pilots in the AEF. There were 491 observers, 23 gunners and 740 aircraft assigned to the various armies.

American aviators had flown more than 35,000 hours over the enemy lines in 13,000 pursuit flights. In 1,100 bombing flights, American pilots had dropped more than 275,000 pounds of bombs. America's airmen had shot down 781 enemy aircraft confirmed, while losing 289 machines to the enemy in combat. Impressive as these statistics might be, they veiled the immeasurably greater power that had not yet had time to uncoil.

The sleeping giant of American productive power had been stirred into reluctant wakefulness. Had World War I continued another six months, there may well have been a fulfilment of the politicians' assertions that the skies of Europe would be darkened by American aircraft. A wise man studying the aerial power that would have been in

America's grasp by early 1919 would probably have decided that under no circumstances should the sleeping giant be stirred again. But wise men were not to prevail in the postwar affairs of Europe.

By the middle nineteen-thirties, war clouds were gathering in Europe once again, and in Spain, the Civil War provided a trial ground for new weapons and techniques. The significance of this conflict, and what it revealed about the future role of airpower in warfare, was largely lost on the onlooking United States.

As they took part in the Second World War's "curtain raiser" in Spain, two more Americans joined the elite fraternity of fighter aces. Lieutenant Frank Tinker of the U.S. Army and Lieutenant Albert J. "Ajax" Baumler fought for the Loyalist Air Forces as soldiers of fortune. They were the first Americans to shoot down the new generation of Fiats, Messerschmitts, Heinkels and Junkers in aerial combat. Directing the German Condor Legion flyers were such famous German fighter leaders as Adolf Galland and Werner Moelders.

Baumler, who later served as a major with the 10th Air Force in the Far East during World War II, gained eight aerial victories in Spain. When he gained a further five kills during World War II, he made history as the first American to become an ace in both of two separate wars. Lieutenant Frank Tinker, from Little Rock, Arkansas, flew in Spain from January First to August First, 1937, and shot down eight Italian and German aircraft in aerial combat. Tinker also served again in World War II with the American Volunteer Group in China, but did not add to his score.

The participation of Baumler and Tinker in the Spanish Civil War was an adventurers' attempt to stay in tune with the times. These two aces did more to meet, in a practical fashion, the dominant menace of the nineteen-thirties than most Americans of their time. Between their individual effort as aces and the stagnation of official American airpower at the same period, there is a stark comparison.

The best military minds had failed to grasp the future significance of airpower. Like the tank, it was regarded more as a novelty—an embellishment—than as a new dimension to warfare. Only sacrificial efforts like those of Billy Mitchell and the devotion of a hard core of less famous airpower advocates stood between the United States and disaster.

What the best-trained experts could not understand or grasp certainly went far beyond the public's ken. But the lay public, right down to the schoolboy on whom all would depend in the near future, could certainly understand the fighter ace. While it is true that in the period between the wars the fighter ace was over-glorified, this process kept aircraft and the men who flew them firmly in the public's mind. That American boys were inspired to do as well as or perhaps better than America's aces of World War I can hardly be doubted. The overwhelming majority of living American aces from World War II confess to being inspired through books about fighter aces and their deeds.

The ace was a bold, new and valiant figure in modern combat. He had won his spurs in World War I. He was also the bearer of a message for the future, for behind him loomed the unknown terrors held for posterity by the new air weapons—the flail that the aces of World War I had wielded in its most primitive form.

The statistics tell the dry facts of American aviation's baptism of fire, but the facts were made by men, 111 of them, who represented a typical cross-section of American manhood. Raoul Lufbery, the immigrant boy; Frederick Libby, the cowboy and expatriate soldier of fortune; David Ingalls, the gentleman patriot; Eddie Rickenbacker, the mechanical genius; Frank Luke, heroism incarnate; and the dozens of less colorful but equally courageous Americans who found their way into World War I's fraternity of aces.

They symbolized for over twenty years a new and vital kind of military prowess. What they won so arduously in blood and struggle was almost lost in the years that followed the winning of their glory. Then came the new generation of fighter pilots—the young men they had inspired—to snatch back the fortunes of their country from the years between the wars.

3

★ ☆ ☆ ★ ☆

USAAF Aces of World War II–
Pacific Theater

THE EUROPEAN WAR was little more than a series of daily news-paper reports to the residents of Hawaii in December, 1941. There were no American combat units involved or located anywhere near the conflict. The few adventurous Americans who had donned foreign uniforms to enter the struggle fought in anonymity. All this changed at 7:56 A.M., Sunday, December 7, 1941, as Japanese naval aircraft at-tacked Pearl Harbor.

By 0830 the same morning, an American fighter pilot flying in an American unit and wearing the uniform of the United States had shot down the first Japanese aircraft of the war. History has given no final verdict on who scored this first aerial kill. Lieutenants George S. Welch, Harry M. Brown, John J. Webster, John L. Dairns, Kenneth A. Taylor and Robert J. Rogers of the Army Air Corps all got air-borne and made contact with the raiders.

Several Japanese planes were shot down. Welch* claimed four kills. Since each of the pilots mentioned claimed at least one Japanese air-craft, the only certainty is that one of these six men drew first blood. In the heat of battle, and under the shocking circumstances of the attack, every pilot forgot to note the time of his first kill, an omission for which they could hardly be blamed.

* George S. Welch gained sixteen confirmed victories in World War II.

Short, sudden and devastating, the Pearl Harbor attack was over in a few hours. Hawaii went on its way, shaken up and injured, but destined to stay out of Japanese reach for the rest of the war. Six hours after Pearl Harbor, the Japanese began raining blows on the Philippines. They attacked and subsequently took Clark Field on Luzon, sixty miles north of Manila.

In the Philippines, the Army Air Corps and the Philippine Air Force were pathetically unprepared for war. In spite of the fact that Japanese "Nell" reconnaissance aircraft had been regularly overflying Manila and other American bases in the Pacific, the preparations for the conflict by the Americans were meager. The world situation had impelled no special vigilance or precautions.

A few new P-40E fighters had arrived for the Army Air Corps, but many of these were not actually in commission. The machines had not been processed through the Manila Air Depot. On the day the war began in the Philippines, the 24th American Pursuit Group gave a status report showing ninety aircraft in commission. This group's task was to defend the Philippine Islands from air attack.

The 24th had fifty-four P-40E's, eighteen P-40B's and eighteen P-35's on the base. Of these, only the P-40E's could be considered first-line aircraft by the standards then prevailing. More than one pilot considered even the P-40E to be obsolescent and a stopgap at best.

The Americans in the Phillippines, no less than at Pearl Harbor, were "caught with their pants down." When the first Japanese bombs fell on Iba Field, four American fighters of the 3rd Pursuit Squadron were caught landing on the field. Five minutes after the blow at Iba, the Japanese poured the punishment on Clark Field. An American staff meeting was in progress, and the field was loaded with ninety B-17 Fortresses and some twenty P-40 fighters.

As the attack went in, four of the 24th Pursuit Group fighters were taking off. These four machines were the only ones to survive this devastating early stroke by Japanese airpower. All the other aircraft were pulverized on the ground as the Japanese bomb pattern made a shambles of Clark Field. The big base was immobilized, but the four fighters that were airborne made their presence felt against the Japanese enemy.

Lieutenant Joseph H. Moore, commander of the 20th Squadron and

FLIGHTLINE: A squadron of Nieuport 28 Pursuits are being prepared for takeoff by crew chiefs and pilots somewhere in France. The date: 1918.

LT. EDDIE AND FRIENDS: Here Rick poses with his SPAD III-CI. Left, Rick stands between other members of the 94th Aero Squadron: (left to right) Lt. Joseph Eastman, Capt. James Meissner, Rick, Lt. Reed Chambers, Lt. Thorne Taylor.

All photographs courtesy of
Colonel Raymond F. Toliver

FAMOUS FIRST: Lt. Alan Winslow (above, left), first AEF pilot to score a "kill" over the Germans. BALLOON BUSTER: Lt. Frank Luke, Jr. (above, right), the "Arizona Balloon Buster," and a German plane he destroyed. HIGHEST AWARD: Capt. Fred Libby, after winning Britain's Military Cross, with (right) his pilot, Capt. Price, and a Scotland Yard man.

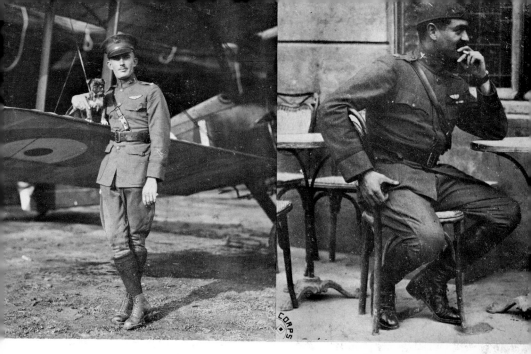

EVEN DOZEN: Capt. Field Kindley (above, left), credited with 12 victories. TACTICIAN: Maj. William Thaw (above, right), the fourth American to join French Aviation Service, was an important tactician for the Allies. NIGHT FIGHTER: Capt. Jerry Vacsoncells, Flight Commander of 27th U.S. Aero Squadron, which was later the only U.S. night pursuit squadron.

RECORD SETTERS: Above, left, America's first ace, 1st Lt. Douglas Campbell (center), Capt. Rick, America's top World War I ace (left), with Capt. Kenneth Marr. Below, right, Capt. Fred Libby, estimated to have flown over 1,000 operational sorties against the Germans, more than any other American airman.

CAROLINA ACE: Capt. Elliott Springs (below, left) of Lancaster, S. C., who scored 12 "kills."

FRENCH PURSUIT PLANE: Above, the 220-h.p., French-built SPAD XIII-CI Pursuit, introduced in 1918, could outdive the German Fokker D-7. CURTISS "JENNY": Below, the Curtiss
JN-4D "Jenny," the plane in which most U.S. aces of World War I won their wings as pilots.

GERMAN FIGHTER PLANE: Above, the German "Fokker" D-7.
ALL-PUPOSE BOMBER: Below, the De Havilland-4 bomber, with a Liberty engine, the American-made aircraft sent to France for all purposes.

WORLD WAR I OBSERVATION PLANE: Above, the Salmson 2A2 observation plane, used in World War I. SCOUT PLANE: Below, The Thomas Morse scout plane.

SOPWITH CAMEL (above). NIEUPORT 28 PURSUIT: Below, the Nieuport 28 Pursuit, used by the 94th Aero Squadron, 1st Pursuit Group. The hat in the ring on the plane was the trademark of the squadron.

of the surviving flight, took his small but angry force thundering up toward the Japanese, driving for the bombers. The covering Japanese fighters quickly spotted the Americans, dove on them, and the first aerial battle over the Philippines began.

Second Lieutenant Randall Keaton whipped his P-40 into a stern chase on an enemy fighter. Winding the P-40 into as tight a turn as he dared, Keaton gained a firing lead angle on the enemy machine. He let drive with his guns and the Japanese fighter exploded and plunged earthward. Looking around for more targets, Keaton saw his flight commander, Lieutenant Moore, flame two more Zeros in quick succession.

The four Americans were so heavily outnumbered that they could do little more than maneuver defensively once the Zeros swarmed in on them. They learned quickly that the P-40 and P-35 were no match for the Zero in close dogfighting. Since all fighter pilots up to that time had been trained to dogfight in the tradition of World War I, the Zero forced some hurried reeducation.

The maneuverability of the Zero and the lethal punch of its twin 20mm cannon made meeting with the Japanese on their own terms something akin to suicide for the American pilots. The Japanese pilots at this time were already masters of their craft, with extensive combat experience over China. As Japan's "first team," they knew how to exploit the Zero's qualities. They also knew the weaknesses of the American fighters, and were therefore among the most formidable opponents faced in the air by American pilots at any time in history.

These early days in the Philippines served to verify with special force the warnings concerning the Zero issued to the USAAF from China by General Chennault. In one desperate encounter after another, the American fighter pilots learned the limitations of the P-40 in combat with the Zero and how best to use their machines against the elusive, fast-turning Japanese aircraft.

Tactics meant hitting the Nip at top speed, and then making a run for it. The pilots who learned this lesson often went through the agony of watching other Americans die who would not learn. The slick Japanese pilots took pride in shooting their enemies out of the top of a loop. They would pick their moment to strike with the cool professional aplomb of a surgeon making an incision.

Lieutenant Boyd D. "Buzz" Wagner became the first American ace of World War II in the Pacific area. The same Lieutenant Joseph Moore who led the four lucky fighters in their escape from embattled Clark Field remembers Wagner's efforts in those dark days. Writes Moore:

> Buzz shot down three Jap I-97's (single-place, fixed-gear aircraft) over Appari on one flight. He also burned ten-plus on the ground while strafing a field near San Fernando on the coast of Lingayen Gulf. Later, out of New Guinea, he led a flight of P-40's to Lae and Salamaua and was bounced by a larger number of Zeros. Buzz got two on that flight.
>
> He was subsequently ordered to cease participation in aerial combat and concentrate on directing air operations out of New Guinea. Shortly afterwards, he returned to the United States and was killed in the crash of a P-40 after departure from Eglin AFB in the early months of 1943.

Moore is today a Major General in the USAF. He was erroneously listed in the records at one time as an ace with five kills. Moore himself has always denied most emphatically his right to belong to the exclusive club. He wrote to the authors:

> I have three confirmed Nips, all in the air, but the balance of the action in the Philippines was one-sided and obscure. I am sorry that I am not eligible to be among the aces.

A review of the official records agrees with General Moore, although many quasi-official lists include him as an ace. He earned himself a niche in history nonetheless as a fighter pilot who survived American airpower's grimmest days.

The second of the Pacific aces was Lieutenant Ed Dyess. He fought to the end in the Philippines, was captured and took part in the infamous Bataan Death March. Dyess later escaped from his pesthole prison in April, 1943. He got back to the United States, only to be killed in a P-38 crash near Burbank, California. He is usually credited with five aerial victories, although the records of this period are understandably indefinite.

The Pacific Theater produced the two top American aces of

World War II, Richard Bong and Thomas B. McGuire. Both were majors and both flew the P-38, an aircraft generally considered by pilots to be third best of the P-51, P-47 and P-38. Bong's forty victories make him the greatest American ace of all the wars, and McGuire's thirty-eight kills make him second only to Bong.

Major Dick Bong has become one of the immortal American heroes. His legendary career as a fighter ace has been extensively recorded, and there is little that can be said about him that has not been said a hundred times before.

He was an expert at teamwork. A firm believer in having a strong, aggressive protector of his flanks, he usually flew with the most capable and battle-tested wingman available. Bong was a master tactician and an outstanding shot. His special experience with his marksmanship serves to endorse what has been said earlier in this book concerning shooting skill in the making of an ace.

Already an ace at the end of his first tour of combat duty, Bong was returned to the United States for rest and recuperation. After this, he went to the Air Force Gunnery School. Major Bong said many times, after his return to the Pacific:

> If I had only known as much about aerial gunnery on my first tour as I did when I came out of that gunnery school, I might easily have scored eighty kills.

Since Bong was not a boastful man, why did he make such a statement? He was rough on himself with his answer.

> The Jap fighters I failed to down escaped mainly because I just did not know enough about the mechanics and art of air-to-air shooting.

Coming from a pilot who was already considered a top-notch deflection shot in combat, this surely indicates that, like all arts, air-to-air shooting can be improved by diligent study of the mechanics involved. Bong's statement serves to confirm and support the postwar statement of Saburo Saki, the greatest living Japanese fighter pilot. He said that many times American fighters had him cold, and yet their shooting was so poor that he escaped from what he considered to be certain death at their hands.

Bong always told the story of one of his missions a little ruefully, since he was no neophyte at the time it occurred. With twenty kills to his credit, Bong intercepted a Japanese formation escorted by fighters and made ready to hack some of them down. Bong suddenly realized that the aircraft on his wing was not that of his usual wingman. He glanced at the machine. The vivid red meatballs of Japan glared back at him. His wingman was a Zero!

Bong slapped his left throttle closed and flipped the P-38 into a split-ess and a vertical dive. Unable to locate the Zero in his mirror, he leveled off at fifteen thousand feet to see if he had actually lost the Jap. Once in level flight, the Zero popped into his mirror again. The Jap was still behind him, just a little too far away for accurate shooting.

Bong flipped quickly to the right, split-essed once again and drove the P-38 wide open to the deck. Leveling off just a few feet above the waters of Oro Bay in New Guinea, he had gained a few hundred yards on the Zero. The Japanese machine could not dive with the P-38. As Bong now pulled away to about a mile lead over his pursuer, both engines wide open, he whipped the P-38 into a tight left-hand turn.

This maneuver zoomed him into the middle of an unobserved formation of nine Zeros—all of them suddenly intent on the demise of Richard Ira Bong.

Like Captain Arthur Brooks of World War I fame, who landed in a similar mess with a covey of Fokkers, Bong decided there was only one course of action—aggression. Like the ace he was, Bong tore at the Zeros, gaining an immediate psychological advantage as he flew head-on at the lead Zero and exploded it with a short burst.

The other eight Zeros, higher and diving to the attack, seemed unnerved by the sudden, dramatic loss of their leader. They wavered, and their fire went wild. Bong exploited their confusion. He picked out another Zero, exploded it, and twisting upwards at full throttle, threw a snap shot from his vertical climb squarely into a third Zero. This machine did not explode, but it slowed, smoldered and went waffling out of the fight.

Pulling every ounce out of the P-38's screaming engines, Bong went streaking away from the scene. He outdistanced the disorganized and shaken remnants of the Japanese formation, and returned successfully to base.

The great ace frequently told this story on himself to fledgling pilots under his command and to others he later trained. The melee which almost cost him his life illustrated in classic fashion why a fighter pilot must know everything going on around him in combat. Many pilots have flown similarly into enemy formations never to emerge. And as Bong put it, "There is nothing more frightening in this world than to look off your wingtip and see a long line of enemy propeller spinners lining up *for a pass at you.*"

Fifth Air Force pilots who flew with Dick Bong have often said that they believe the Dick Bong-Thomas J. Lynch team to have been the hottest fighter combination in the Pacific. Certainly it was the hottest Army team in the theater. Lynch was an exceptional leader in his own right and, with a final score of twenty kills in World War II, proved himself to be among America's best fighter pilots. When he teamed with Bong, it was a formidable alliance, as numerous Japanese pilots discovered.

Bong and Lynch would trade the leadership position during a rhubarb with such perfection and precision, it was as though each of them was intuitively flying the other's aircraft as well as his own. They were like two men constantly able to read each other's thoughts. In battle, one was always in firing position on the enemy, while the other kept the shooting aircraft's tail clear.

Flying as Major Bong's wingman near the end of the ace's final combat tour was another aggressive fighter pilot, Captain James W. McCrary of Commerce, Texas. "Tex" McCrary has provided the details of Bong's thirty-eighth and thirty-ninth aerial victories, and one of them could fairly be claimed as the most novel victory scored by any American pilot.

With McCrary flying wing, Bong was vectored by radar toward a bogey. Searching for the enemy, McCrary spotted two Jap machines several thousand feet below the two fighters and called into the radio, "Two rats directly below."

"Jettison your bomb," ordered Bong, intending that thus lightened, he and McCrary would quickly wipe out the Jap bombers.

The two 500-pound bombs plummeted down from the American

fighters as Bong led into a split-ess dive. As they pulled into the nearly vertical dive position, both Bong and McCrary gasped to see Bong's 500-pounder, set to "safe," smash through the tail of one of the Japanese machines and send it spinning down to destruction. Still incredulous, Bong lined up the second Jap aircraft and shot it down with a short burst.

Like so many of the top aces who survived innumerable deliberate attempts on their lives by the enemy in the air, Bong lost his life in an aircraft accident. A glorious figure, immortalized by his deeds and already a part of American folklore, Bong was killed in the crash of an F-80 jet at Burbank, California, on August 6, 1945. He was decorated profusely. His awards included the Congressional Medal of Honor, the DSC, two Silver Stars, seven DFC's and fifteen Air Medals.

In a little over twenty months of combat, Major Thomas B. McGuire scored thirty-eight aerial victories. Hailing from Ridgewood, New Jersey, McGuire was not only a brilliant combat pilot, but a splendid comrade-in-arms to inexperienced pilots. Blessed with a knack for guiding fledgling pilots, he saw to it that flyers fresh from the States got the fruits of his experience. He gave freely of the lessons he had learned the hard way.

This deep concern for his fellow pilots, which in no way prevented McGuire's own prolific scoring, was probably responsible for his untimely death in combat. On January 7, 1945, McGuire and another experienced fighter pilot were taking two newly arrived Air Corps captains on a sweep over Los Negros Island when they were bounced by a single but audacious Japanese Hamp.

The Hamp made a perfect run on the American formation and sent the leader of the second flight down in flames before being spotted. McGuire saw the Hamp almost in firing position on one of the inexperienced pilots, and made an extremely sharp turn in order to rescue this man. McGuire was famous for the tight turns he was able to wring out of the P-38, but on this occasion he turned a little too tightly.

The twin-boomed fighter entered a high-speed stall, followed by a spin. At fifteen hundred feet altitude, McGuire had no chance to recover control. His fighter plunged into the ocean while the Hamp escaped unharmed. As an air fighter, McGuire was superb, and an accident rather than the enemy prevented his going on to even greater glories.

Postwar research has indicated strongly that McGuire and his formation were shot down by Shoichi Sugita, Naval Air Pilot First Class, of the Imperial Japanese Navy. Sugita was a brilliant pilot too, with eighty kills to his credit when he met his end three months after the battle involving Major McGuire. Sugita's career is dealt with in Chapter Nine, devoted to the enemy aces.

Captain John R. Alison is one of the many modest World War II aces whose victory claims are less than the official records. Alison claims six victories in the China-Burma-India Theater, but his official tally is eight. He is unlikely to forget one combat experience that he almost did not survive, and which he relates here:

Flying a P-40 over Henyang, China, twelve thousand feet at night, I picked up the exhaust of three Jap bombers at fifteen thousand feet. I had closed to within two hundred feet when a Jap gunner in a turret position on the bomber hit my P-40 broadside. He stitched a line of holes from the prop to the tail.

I started firing at very close range. The first bomber I hit pulled up into a steep climb, badly hit but not burning. I moved from one to the other of the remaining two bombers, and they exploded one after the other. The concussions shook my aircraft.

I tried to get down to a friendly field just below, but as I started a landing approach, my aircraft caught fire. I had to ditch quickly—and into the river I went. I emerged wet and wounded, but had two confirmed victories plus one probable.

Alison lives in Los Angeles, California, today, where he is an executive in the aviation industry. He is also a lively figure in the affairs of the American Fighter Aces' Association.

Blind flying is one thing, but blind shooting is quite another, as Captain Ernie J. Ambort of Little Rock, Arkansas, can testify. Sometimes fighter pilots have taken long odds when the chips were down. Ernie Ambort is one of them.

We had just relieved the first flight, and started to orbit at 8,000 feet to cover a destroyer evacuating wounded from the Philippines. Out of a 3,500-foot lower broken-cloud layer came two Jap fighters in a dive-bombing attack or Kamikaze on the destroyer. . . .

In the ensuing near-vertical dive at full throttle to intercept these Japs, I knew that in order to properly lead the Jap for a full deflection shot I would not be able to see him. My wingman, Lieutenant H. A. Hammett of Boston, Massachusetts, would get a better sighting on the number two Jap.

I hastily calculated that my P-38 was probably worth more than any destroyer, but due to the number of people involved, and all those sick and wounded boys, I decided I'd ram this Jap if necessary. On the open channel I called the destroyer's fire control officer and asked him to hold their fire and watch for me if I bailed.

Trusting in luck rather than ability, I put in lead, held my triggers full down and waited. When I flew through billows of black smoke and saw pieces of the Jap aircraft lodge in mine, I knew he had blown up just before our flight paths crossed. I pulled up in time to see Hammett's hits blow up the second Jap, who crashed into the ocean one hundred feet astern of the destroyer.

Sometime later, when things had quieted down, Hammett and I buzzed the destroyer before returning to base. The gratifying waves of crutches, bandages and plaster casts told me that this had truly been my most thrilling aerial victory.

Ernie Ambort survived the war. He served with the 49th Fighter Group and is credited with five aerial victories.

Getting personal stories from some of the aces was very much like asking these men to pull out a good front tooth. Colonel William M. Banks of Raleigh, West Virginia, proved to be one of these. Bill Banks would much rather talk about other pilots at length, praising and admiring their skills. Banks' own nine aerial victories in the Pacific give him plenty to talk about. His wingman probably saved his life in this incident:

During combat with some Japanese fighters, I found myself in the embarrassing position of having lost my airspeed at very low altitude. At this time, I spotted a Jap fighter closing in on my tail for the kill.

But the Japanese pilot had forgotten Banks' able wingman, Lieutenant Malcolm Rand, of Mexico, Maine. Rand's own combat report provides the rest of Colonel Banks' story:

I was in range astern and closed on the Zeke to about fifty yards before firing. The first few shots burst on the right elevator. I corrected a little and there were shots bursting all over his wings and fuselage. I fired until flames shot out from all parts of his plane. I pulled up and saw him crash in the water. The action took place from one thousand feet on down. Captain Banks saw the plane crash. The enemy pilot appeared skilled and eager for combat, but I don't believe he saw me protecting Captain Banks' tail.

Lieutenant Rand was later killed in action in a fighter strike against Bobo Airfield, Dutch New Guinea. His memory is safe with Colonel Banks who says of Rand today: "He was one of our most outstanding pilots. At least three other pilots in our squadron owed their lives to his skill, courage and devotion to duty. His death was a great loss to his country." Many aces feel similarly towards gallant wingmen who failed to survive the conflict or make ace themselves.

Still flying with the Air National Guard at Savannah, Georgia, is Captain Philip E. Colman, a fighter pilot officially credited with nine kills gained in two wars. Colman fought first with the 5th Fighter Group of the 14th Air Force in the Pacific from 1942 to 1944. He fought again in Korea with the 4th Fighter Interceptor Group in 1952, where he came within one frame of 16mm gun-camera film of confirming his fifth MIG-15 kill. This victory would have put him into the ultraexclusive inner circle of aces who scored five kills in two wars.

Phil Colman recalled his most memorable combat experience with frank words: "Every damned one of them was exciting."

Captain Robert Marshall De Haven is an ace who maintained his connection with aircraft following World War II. He knocked down fourteen Japanese aircraft while flying with the 14th Air Force in the Pacific. De Haven is currently with Hughes Aircraft Corporation in California, and is married to singer Connie Haines.

De Haven's first ten victories were gained in the P-40, an aircraft that could excel its mediocre qualities in the hands of a pilot who knew his stuff. A number of skilled American pilots learned how best to use the obsolescent machine against Japanese aircraft, and did well with the P-40. De Haven flew also in flights with Dick Bong, Thomas McGuire and Gerald R. Johnson during the Philippine campaign. This incident sticks in his mind:

On November 2, 1944, I was leading a squadron flight of fourteen P-38's out of Tacloban airstrip on a dive-bombing strike against
Jap shipping in Ormac Bay, on the west side of Leyte. Intelligence
reported a concentration of troop transports, with destroyer and
cruiser escorts, landing troops in the area.

Our strategy was to take the first six aircraft across the bay at
low level, drawing naval ack-ack. This would permit the remaining
eight aircraft, carrying 500-pound bombs, to make their attacks
with minimum opposition. Although reports of enemy aircraft in
sizable numbers came in, we went unmolested during the first portion of the attack, and one of our pilots got a direct hit with a 500-
pounder on a troopship.

About the time decoy flights were pulling up at the far end of
the bay and the dive-bombing runs were almost over, enemy aircraft were spotted in several directions by our pilots. One was
sighted at six o'clock to me.

I went into a tight climbing turn to meet the enemy head-on.
Since my wingman stayed glued to me during the turn, the enemy
pilot lost his enthusiasm and broke off into a climbing turn. My
position was better now, and the chase was continued.

Gradually I gained on the Jap, climbing in the process to 16,000
feet. He was identifiable now as one of the new Jack fighters. For
some reason, he elected now to enter a shallow dive, which against
the P-38 was decidedly unwise. I needed full power for quite a
while to catch him, but at 10,000 feet and indicating 400 mph he was
in front of me at point-blank range.

Two short bursts produced no apparent effect. But on the third
burst the Jap disintegrated with a violent blast. Flying debris thundered against my P-38. My windshield was smothered in Japanese
engine oil, and I had to use side vision and the careful directions of
my wingman to get back to base.

During the disassembly of my P-38, in one of the oil cooler
scoops, a large portion of one of the Japanese pilot's maps was
found. This memento is today a prized possession. Another memento of this combat is a copy of the orders sending me Stateside
from the Philippines after twenty-two months overseas. They are
dated November 1, 1944. My most memorable mission had been
unknowingly "on my own time."

Warren D. Curton of Spring City, Tennessee, was a young Second
Lieutenant flying with the 49th Fighter Group in the Pacific when
plain old fighter pilot's savvy brought him a spectacular aerial victory.
Curton is a major in jets now, but he was mounted on a P-38 on

December 5, 1944. With three other P-38's, he was flying cover for a Navy convoy off the Leyte coast:

> Suddenly my number four pilot reported that an Oscar had come out of the clouds and was closing on our tail. We immediately turned into the enemy plane, whereupon he broke off his attack and raced westward, climbing into the sun.
>
> I closed in, but I couldn't see the Oscar because I was looking directly into the sun. By using my tinted goggles, I could see everything except within the diameter of the sun itself. Knowing I was in range, I fired directly into the disc of the sun. My wingman, over to one side, reported that I was getting hits on this Jap I couldn't even see.
>
> The Oscar now turned right. As he did so, I fired a 30–45-degree deflection shot, getting hits in the wing root and cockpit area. He started flaming and tried a crash dive into a nearby landing craft. He missed and plunged into the ocean.

Warren Curton ended World War II with five aerial kills credited during his service with the 5th Air Force.

Colonel William D. Dunham of Nez Perce, Idaho, scored sixteen aerial victories over the Japanese. He flew with the 5th Air Force. Bill Dunham also sank two Japanese troopships estimated at ten thousand tons apiece. Now in the regular USAF, he recollects best a melee in which aggressive American action demoralized a superior Japanese force.

> While flying cover for skip-bombing attacks on Jap shipping, my eleven-plane squadron attacked thirteen Jap fighters. I shot down two on the first pass, and in the next ten minutes shot down two more. We completely routed the attacking Japs.

The four quick kills Bill Dunham passes off so modestly conceal a talent that ranks him high on the aces' own list. He is recognized as one of the most formidable deflection-shooting artists among the aces. Dunham demonstrated this skill in an aerial battle that cost the life of one of America's outstanding pilots, Colonel Neel E. Kearby, who is credited with twenty-two aerial victories.

Kearby, intent on a Nip kill, did not know that his wingman had been taken out of position in the fight. An alert Japanese pilot promptly latched on to Kearby's tail. Seeing this disastrous turn of luck, Bill Dunham swung quickly in an attempt to scare the Jap off, and began firing at one thousand yards from ninety degrees deflection.

The Japanese plane disintegrated in a gout of orange flame, but its pilot had already held his triggers down on Major Kearby. The famed pilot, ace and Medal of Honor winner, crashed to his death. Pilots who flew with Bill Dunham speak in awe of his shooting skill, which is belied by his relatively modest sixteen kills. In Dunham's case, opportunity to use his skills did not come as often as it might have done, something that is true of a number of other superb American marksmen.

There is no more vigorous advocate of the art of aerial gunnery than Major Nelson DeCoursey Flack Jr., whose views on the subject were gleaned from the hard school of experience. An erstwhile member of the 49th Fighter Group in the Pacific, Flack tells this story on himself:

Arriving in combat with fifty hours of P-40 experience and negligible fixed-gunnery training, like all the others I concentrated on back-breaking acrobatics as the *sine qua non* of successful combat flying. For a year I scattered ammunition profusely at several dozen Japs, primarily from large deflection angles and maximum to minimum range, but without success.

Then I decided on serious application of gunnery principles, and I really studied the 100-mil sight. Shortly afterward, I ran into a Jap fighter at 10,000 feet. With deflection 120 degrees, and range about 2,000 feet, I estimated his speed at about 300 mph.

Just as though I was operating a slide rule, I slowly eased in exactly three radii with the P-38, and then began firing at about 1,000 feet and 90-degree deflection. Instantly the center wing section exploded violently. The shattered Jap fighter tumbled down in fragments. I was convinced. A combat pilot is a gunner, not an aerial acrobat.

Major Flack successfully applied these same principles on four other occasions against the Japanese, and thereby gained admission to the fraternity of fighter aces. He is also credited with five probables.

Three versus twenty-four are long odds in aerial combat, but time and again the power of aggressive pilots to reduce such odds has been demonstrated. Psychological factors, and especially an aggressive spirit, bulk large in aerial combat. Captain Richard H. Fleischer of Quincy, Mass. took part in an aerial battle in which a bold assault paid big dividends.

With two other pilots, I engaged approximately ten enemy dive-bombers and fourteen fighters which we had caught bombing and strafing U.S. PT-boats. In just a few minutes we had destroyed seven. When the rest of our squadron arrived, we knocked down another seven. The U.S. Navy confirmed sixteen kills, although we only claimed fourteen, without loss to ourselves. The action took place in December, 1943, south of New Britain. I received credit for one fighter and one dive-bomber.

Captain Fleischer flew with the 248th Fighter Group in the Pacific Theater and is credited with six aerial victories.

Known in the Air Force as the "Kankakee Kid" after his home town in Illinois, William Kenneth Giroux shot down ten Japanese aircraft in the Pacific Theater. One of his combat reports gives insight into the aerial pyrotechnics of this colorful ace.

A. Mission number 6-385, 2 November 1944, 12 P-38's.
B. Cover for B-24 to Mindanao Sea Area.
C. Time and altitude of attack: 1215/L at 8,000 feet.
D. We were escorting B-24's to look for a task force in the Mindanao Sea. We found quite a few ships in Ormac Bay. I could not say just what type they were or how many because we were climbing, and I saw an enemy fighter right after we got to the target. The ack-ack was very heavy from the ships as our bombers neared the target on their bombing runs. I saw the first fighter going in on the bombers just as they were over the target. He did not seem to mind his own ack-ack, so I followed him in.
   I shot at ninety degrees deflection just as he started to fire on the bombers, and he broke away. He was smoking a little, and I figured he might go down. But he kept going, and as I pulled up into the sun, I waited for him to start for the bombers again. He did, and I dove, coming up under him. I closed in to twenty-five yards, gave him a short burst, and he blew up. This was a Hamp-type fighter.

Up until this action I had been alone, but as the Hamp was going down, Lieutenant Loh joined me. By this time the bombers had made their run and were on course for home. They were about twenty-five miles west of the Camotes Islands. Lieutenant Loh and I started back for the bombers, and I saw one enemy fighter drop a phosphorous bomb. I overtook this fighter and got three shots at it, all ninety- to forty-degree deflection. On the third shot we were about a hundred feet above the water. I got a short burst in the wing root and he also blew up, splashing into the water. He too, was a Hamp.

Another enemy fighter had joined the flight by then, and I noticed him about five hundred feet above me and to my left. I started a fast climb and turned into him, but he only got a very short burst. He then did a wing-over, and Lieutenant Loh got on his tail. Lieutenant Loh fired a few shots and the enemy fighter turned left. As Lieutenant Loh pulled up I got in a forty-degree deflection shot. This third Hamp burst into flames and crashed on Pacijan Island just south of a small lake.

For this action the Kankakee Kid got the Silver Star. He shot down four other Japanese planes with similar applications of the deflection shooter's art, but these machines were not seen to crash by others and are credited to Giroux only as probables. He also sank a 10,000-ton tanker by pressing home a determined attack, and for this action he was awarded the DFC.

An air show at San Diego on Independence Day, 1947, saw the tragic end of Colonel John C. Herbst, one of the outstanding Air Corps aces of the Pacific Theater. He crashed while piloting a Lockheed F-80 Shooting Star. His death was a deep loss to the Air Force and to his country.

Although not among America's top-scoring aces, Herbst is revered and remembered today not only as a brilliant pilot and top marksman, but also as a man of outstanding leadership talent. Few doubt that Herbst could have easily joined America's top scoring aces had he been given adequate rein by his superiors.

General Claire Chennault grounded Herbst after his seventh kill, ordering him to "plan operations instead of taking part in them." Herbst complied, like the good soldier he was, but he managed nevertheless to shoot down another seven Japanese planes during "training and indoctrination flights"—no mean feat.

Colonel John C. Herbst also numbered a German Me-109 among his fifteen officially confirmed victories. He had six additional kill claims, which were never confirmed, at the time of his death. The bulk of his war service was with the 14th Air Force.

Lieutenant General Bruce K. Holloway USAF was among the professional aviators who became aces in World War II. He graduated from West Point in June, 1937, and from the West Point of the Air at Kelly and Randolph Fields in Texas in October, 1938. His most memorable combat experience came in May of 1943:

I was on a lone visual reconnaissance over Formosa, in a P-40 out of Henyang, China, with staging-out of five-gallon cans at Kienow. I saw many large Japanese training formations, and avoided detection by ducking in and out of a thousand-foot overcast. I encountered a single bomber offshore, and closed to ten yards range. I shot the bomber down using about fifteen rounds of ammunition.

Lieutenant General Holloway's distinguished service in China won him the coveted Chinese Order of the Sacred Tripod from Generalissimo Chiang Kai-shek.

The P-40 built by Curtiss, and used by General Holloway in the mission he describes, was the aircraft type that bore the brunt of the early Pacific aerial fighting. There were a few older and earlier types of aircraft battling the Japanese in the first days, including a handful of Boeing P-26's, but the P-40 was all America had to begin the war in the Far East in numbers sufficient to hurt the enemy.

The pilots of the American Volunteer Group used the P-40 for fighting, bombing, reconnaissance and for hauling cargo. As one ebullient Flying Tiger said, "If we only had a periscope for it, we could use it for a submarine, too." Considering that the P-40 was well below the standard required for fighter combat in the European Theater, its record in the Pacific must rank it historically as among the great fighter aircraft of World War II.

In three years of combat in China, where it was the mainstay of the 23rd Fighter Group, 941 Japanese aircraft went down under its guns. This was a ratio of fifteen Japanese losses for every loss by the 23rd, and it is doubtful if any other Pacific unit could claim such a record.

The American Volunteer Group under Chennault made their

P-40's count in the struggle. They gained official confirmation for 297 Japanese aircraft destroyed during the AVG's relatively short life. Every fighter pilot who flew the P-40 in combat recalls with affection and gratitude the machine's incredible ability to absorb the punishment of cannon fire from the Zero and still keep flying.

The P-38 Lockheed Lightning was introduced into the Pacific fighting primarily to extend combat range and to give American pilots twin-engined safety while flying over long stretches of open ocean. The P-38 was greeted with soaring enthusiasm. This became somewhat dampened when the Japanese pilots began shooting the Lightnings down with alarming ease and in large numbers.

No small element in these early failures was a certain tactical ineptitude on the part of the Americans. As they learned how to exploit the Lightning's strong points, and as improved versions of the P-38 came forward from the United States, the aircraft did well. As American teamwork evolved the Lightning did even better.

In a turning dogfight, the Zero could usually take the measure of the P-38, and unfortunately there was a tendency on the part of many American pilots to get into this kind of battle. Most of them had spent their early years reading about World War I dogfights, and prewar training tended to follow in the World War I groove. Reeducation was quickly forced when the turning ability of the Zero proved to be so formidable.

Aces like Bong, Lynch and McGuire soon turned the tables on the best of the Japanese pilots. The high altitude, speed and dive superiority of the P-38, intelligently translated into tactics, permitted many Pacific aces to run up strings of kills in the sleek, twin-boomed fighter. For one thing, the superior altitude capability of the Lightning permitted the American pilots to choose combat as they wished. The inferior ceiling of the Zero, like the inferior Japanese teamwork, proved to be something that Japanese skill, courage or fanaticism could not overcome.

The P-51 Mustang, which appeared somewhat later in the Pacific war, became the top-notch all-around fighter there even as it proved to be the best all-purpose fighter in Europe. Old P-47 and P-38 pilots often rise to dispute this, but the statistical record, as well as the postwar testimony of the Japanese pilots, leaves little doubt that the P-51 was the superior aircraft of the three.

Major John Alden Tilly USAF, of Mill Valley, California, flew with Major Thomas McGuire in the 431st Fighter Squadron. He recalls an incident in flying the P-38 that reveals how much depended on the man rather than the machine:

My second victory provided particular satisfaction, because it was a classic example of the P-38's little-known but nevertheless excellent maneuverability. At first glance, the aircraft seemed large and ungainly. But in this combat, I was able to stay behind *and* *inside* the enemy's turn at approximately 1,000 feet above the water and 100 mph. That P-38 shook and shuddered, but never snapped a spin. The hits from my guns finally turned the Jap plane into a ball of flames. I was close to this Jap while firing—so close that oil from his stricken engine completely covered my windshield. When I got back home, I had to slow down just above stalling speed, roll down the side window and wipe a clear spot on the windshield with my handkerchief before I could land.

Tilly flew 159 missions in the P-38 and is credited with five aerial victories. He is extremely proud to have flown with McGuire, whom he considers to have been the complete master of the P-38. "He knew of the P-38's surprising maneuverability," recalls Tilly, "and more than a few of his thirty-eight kills were due to his willingness to turn with the Jap fighters—something most of our boys thought impossible."

Despite the performance disparity between the P-38 and the P-51, the Lightning had its devoted advocates. There can be no doubt that the faith and ability of a P-38 pilot, wherever he plied his trade, could wring from the Lightning superior and often surprising performance. For the run-of-the-mill fighter pilot, such attainments were impossible. For the exceptional pilot, who loved, studied and flew the P-38 with everything that was in him, the enemy held no terrors.

Such a P-38 devotee was, and is, Colonel John H. Lowell of Denver, Colorado. Lowell served in the ETO, and on one occasion, with his whole group watching and a beer bust riding on the outcome, he took on an RAF Spitfire Mark XI in mock combat.

The encounter took place over Lowell's home base of Honington, in East Anglia, and Lowell administered a sound thrashing to the fabled British fighter. Lowell believed that the P-38L was able to fight anything that flew, and in this instance, with him at the controls, the P-38L proved superior even to Britain's great thoroughbred.

Lowell is credited with 7.5 aerial kills in Europe, but few other pilots in the USAAF could make the P-38 perform as he did. For the most part, the journeymen pilots who forsook the Lightning for the Mustang as the newer machine flowed out to the squadrons were rarely sorry to say goodbye to the P-38.

Colonel John S. Stewart was in command of the 76th Squadron of the 23rd Fighter Group, 14th Air Force, when the fabulous and long-awaited P-51 arrived in the China-Burma-India Theater. The impact of this superb machine on pilot morale forms Colonel Stewart's outstanding memory of aerial combat:

In early 1944 the 176th Squadron received its first P-51B's, and 'for the first time in nearly two years, we had an aircraft that could perform with or exceed the capabilities of the best Japanese fighter planes. Their Tojo had been able to out-dive, out-turn, out-run and generally out-perform our P-38's and P-40's.

These wily Japs had developed their deadly "high-low" tactics, and were giving us fits. Then in came the P-51B's. One of our squadrons took off in P-38's, and we followed with two flights of Mustangs. At 21,000 feet, a flight of twelve Tojos bounced the P-38's, but for the first time, we had aircraft above them. Our Mustangs were at 30,000 and 32,000 feet.

I led my element down on a Tojo which had shot one engine out of a P-38 and was circling to finish him off. The Jap saw us coming, and started a sharp turn. He was visibly shaken when we out-turned him, so he dove for the deck. We found then that we could out-run him too, for when he leveled off at a hundred feet above the deck, we steadily closed in on him.

He tried evasive action, but it was to no avail. I got to close range, gave him about seventy rounds, and he exploded violently. One Tojo was eliminated, but best of all, we all knew that we were flying a better fighter than the Japanese.

Colonel Stewart is credited with eight aerial victories, all of them gained in the Pacific Theater.

Lieutenant Colonel Gerald Richard Johnson of the USAAF in World War II has frequently been confused with two namesakes among America's aces—Gerald W. Johnson of Owenton, Kentucky, and Robert S. Johnson of Garden City, New York, both of whom won fame in the ETO as fighter aces.

Gerald R. Johnson called Eugene, Oregon, his home town, although he was born in Kenmore, Ohio. He enlisted in the Air Corps in 1941, and in May of 1942 was sent to Alaska. Over the Aleutians he had his first aerial combat, downing two Japanese planes, but without confirmation of the victories. Later assigned to the 49th Fighter Group in the Pacific, in fighter pilot's parlance Johnson "got hot." He ran up a string of eleven confirmed kills and eleven probables before being sent to the United States for rest and recuperation. On his return to the Pacific in late 1944, Johnson got hot again and ran up another eleven kills and eight more probables by war's end.

With twenty-two aerial victories, the DSC, Silver Star and Legion of Merit among other awards, Johnson was commander of the Atsugi Air Base near Tokyo right after the end of the Second World War. On October 7, 1945, he was acting as pilot of a B-17 Fortress which got hopelessly lost in a typhoon. The aircraft's radio was knocked out, and under these grim conditions, Johnson gave his parachute to a passenger who had come aboard without one. All on board the B-17 who jumped were picked up, but Johnson and his copilot were killed in the crash of the aircraft.

Because he did not survive this postwar incident, Gerald R. Johnson's career has been confused with those of the other Johnsons. Pilots who knew Gerald R. are warm in their praise of his gallantry, and his admirers include General George Kenney, wartime commander of the Far East Air Force. General Kenney told Johnson's father: "You are the father of the bravest man I ever knew, and the bravest thing he ever did was the last thing, and when he did not need to be brave."

When the Japanese attacked Pearl Harbor, Verl E. Jett of Belle Missouri, was based at Wheeler Field in Hawaii. He managed to get an *unarmed* fighter into the air during the attack. This probably made him the most frustrated fighter pilot in history. All he could do was save the aircraft from certain destruction while he witnessed the fury of the attack from a fighter plane's cockpit, powerless to intervene.

Subsequently, Jett was sent to Australia, where he qualified on P-39's. He joined combat with the Japanese in the New Guinea area, this time with his guns loaded and ready. One incident made a special impression on him:

While leading a flight of P-39's, I spotted a Norma-type bomber at ten thousand feet. I made a 180-degree turn and got on his tail for an attack. The sky was full of cumulus clouds, and breaking in and out of this stuff as I tried to stay on this Jap's tail, I nearly collided with him four or five times. Each time I managed to recover position and give him a full burst of all guns. Then both of the Jap's engines burst into flames. By this time, I had pulled excessive manifold pressure, causing the rocker-arm bolts to break. Two cylinders would not fire. With the engine missing, I turned back to Milne Bay, a 150-mile flight over an ocean teeming with sharks. I wondered if I was going to become a victory myself.

My wingman saw the Norma crash into the sea and sink fifteen miles north of Watutu Point on Goodenough Island. When I landed, I was assigned another aircraft and ordered to return to the scene of the Norma's crash and search for survivors. The bomber was supposed to have been carrying Jap VIP's, but at the spot where the Norma went in there was only an oil slick.

Lieutenant Colonel Jett ended the war with seven aerial victories confirmed, and with the unforgettable experience of having watched the Pearl Harbor attack from the air.

The top living ace of the USAAF in the Pacific is Colonel Charles Henry MacDonald, credited with twenty-seven aerial victories over the Japanese. Pennsylvania-born MacDonald was commissioned into the regular USAAF in 1939 and was a fighter pilot stationed at Hawaii's Wheeler Field when the blow fell on Pearl Harbor.

The din of the Japanese attack woke him up, and it was a somewhat bewildered young Lieutenant MacDonald who made his way to Wheeler through the rubble and smoke. He set up an alert system with the remaining serviceable P-36's and P-40's, and flew patrol along the west coast of Oahu until it was determined that the Japanese were not going to send in a second attack.

After an apprehensive hour and a half aloft, MacDonald and his fellow pilots flew back to Honolulu, and there ran into a veritable hornet's nest. The trouble came not from the long-gone Japanese flyers, but from the jittery American gunners on the ground. A fierce hail of flak rose to meet the friendly fighters. With gas low, MacDonald had no option but to run the gauntlet, landing back safely at Wheeler Field in spite of stiff American opposition.

A thorough professional, MacDonald's later career included command of the famed "Satan's Angels," the 475th Fighter Group whose alumni included Thomas B. McGuire. Only Bong, McGuire, the Navy's McCampbell (thirty-four kills) and the Marines' "Pappy" Boyington (twenty-eight kills) topped MacDonald's score in the Pacific. He recently retired from the USAF after a distinguished postwar career.

The American fighter pilots in the Pacific had many "characters" in their ranks, and numerous funny stories have found their way into legend concerning these men. A typical character is Captain Richard L. West of Chillicothe, Missouri, a comrade-in-arms of the "Kankakee Kid" mentioned earlier.

West became the "Samson of the South Pacific" when he swore he would not cut his hair until he had downed his first Japanese plane. His hair had reached an oppressive length under the tropical conditions of the South Pacific when he finally splashed a Zero.

West was then seized by the dread that if he now cut his hair, he would never get another Jap. He fought over Australia, New Guinea, the Celebes, Borneo and the Phillippines, racking up twelve aerial kills and needing a haircut so badly he was afraid it would shatter the shears. West survived both the war and his first haircut, and lives today in his native Chillicothe. His first aerial action is the one he remembers best. Why? Because, in West's own words, "I was near immobility with fear."

In the middle nineteen-fifties, the Air Research and Development Command made a study of the personality traits of fighter pilots, and concluded that practically all aces are "characters" in some degree or another. The ARDC Study indicated that aces generally are those who set their hearts and minds on becoming aces. Those who made the grade strongly desired further aerial combat, which is generally the opposite of the nonaces.

Studies of this kind can only deal in broad generalities, for there are surviving aces who take a dim view of personal glory and of special recognition for aerial victories gained in battle for their country. This substantial but nevertheless minority faction has an eloquent spokesman in a U.S. Navy ace, Lieutenant Commander Edward Overton, Jr., of Washington, D.C. Overton puts his views this way:

Most men fight because they have to. A few, perhaps, find glory beyond their wildest dreams. Most develop an understanding of teamwork, cameraderie and give-and-take, which will always be helpful to them. But one's perspective concerning awards and aces becomes significantly altered when one considers the "unknown" ones. Victories and awards, I suppose, are part of the game, but each individual knows in his heart whether his "well done" was deserved or not. . . . the records really belong to those who are not listed.

Among the personality traits of aces, a disregard for or obliviousness to danger is frequently found. It is this kind of character who can recall, almost conversationally, the petrifying experience of flying head-on into the hail of fire put up by a formation of bombers. Colonel Franklin Nichols, of Wewoka, Oklahoma, is a typical instance. With three accompanying P-40's, Nichols tackled a flight of eighteen Jap Betty bombers near Buna, New Guinea, on the first anniversary of Pearl Harbor.

We bounced them and broke up the bomb run before a single bomb was dropped. We knocked two of the Bettys down and I got got credit for one of them.

This laconic description conceals the special kind of courage it takes to fly into a storm of bullets pumped out by upwards of eighty guns, turned on four lonely fighter planes. Colonel Nichols ended World War II with five aerial victories confirmed.*

Major Sammy A. Pierce of Ayden, North Carolina, scored seven aerial kills with the 49th Group of the 5th Air Force. He remembers a melee that took place while he was flying out of Dobodura, New Guinea, in March of 1943:

We were scrambled for an intercept mission. I was flying the number two position on the third flight leader. Right after takeoff, the number four man in the flight had to return with propeller trouble, making it a three-ship flight. Due to sketchy radar facilities, the controller could give us only approximate locations, so the four flights split into patrol formations to sweep the whole area. My

* Colonel Nichols was another member of "Satan's Angels," the 475th Fighter Group.

flight sighted the Japs at 25,000 feet—headed for the harbor under construction at Oro Bay. The enemy formation was still about fifty miles out at sea.

Our flight climbed to the right-hand side above the bomber formation, which consisted of twenty-seven Bettys with a top cover of sixty Zekes. The flight leader rolled into an overhead 180-degree pass, picking out the lead ship in the first element of the bomber formation. I followed him in, picking up the lead ship in the second element of the Jap formation. I was firing from a position relatively straight down, and my windshield began to fog. I tried to clear it off, and as a consequence, my pull-out was a little late. I damned near rammed the Jap wingman in the outside element of the formation.

I cleaned my windshield of fog and moisture. While rejoining, I spotted a Jap fighter making a pass on the number three man in our flight. The Jap was slightly above and forty-five degrees to my right. I pulled the nose far enough in front of his line of flight to at least shoot in front of him. It was all I could do to take him off the number three man. When I fired, I saw hits on the Zeke around the wing root and just forward of the wing in the fuselage. He fell off to the left in a steep diving attitude. I followed him, and fired one more burst into him until he hit the water.

Climbing back up, I found I'd been separated from the flight leader and number three man. I climbed above the bombers, which by this time had jettisoned their bombs and were hightailing it for New Britain. I made my next pass on the third element of the bombers, and knocked one engine out of a bomber which lost altitude. As he dropped, I made three more passes at him until I ran out of ammo.

Now the Zekes were on me. A three-ship element came down after me. It was my turn to run. Heading for home and nosing down, I managed to outrun my three pursuers. I was just congratulating myself when I ran into a single additional Zeke—head-on!

He had about three thousand feet of altitude on me. He rolled over and started a diving pass. I held my heading until I thought he was just about in range, then I pulled up into a direct line with him. He broke off and pulled up to my right. I made a diving turn to the left and held her wide open all the way to Dobodura. Although I only got two credits out of this, our three-ship flight got seven Japanese aircraft and caused the bombers to jettison bombs and bolt before reaching the target.

Sammy Pierce himself later became a victim of Japanese aerial gunnery in October, 1943. After being shot down, he landed near the

Japanese lines. He managed to evade capture, and by a turn of good luck stumbled across some Australian infantrymen. The Aussies got Pierce back to his unit, and he survived World War II to become a career USAF officer.

Another victim of the Japanese fighter pilots was Captain John E. Purdy of Wyandotte, Michigan. He had seven aerial victories to his credit when he was shot down over Luzon in the Philippines. After more than two weeks with the guerillas, Purdy was finally picked up by an Air Corps PBY. On the flight back to his unit, he had time to reflect on the naïve newspaper stories published in the United States, which told of Japanese pilots with two-dimensional eyesight who could neither shoot nor fly well.

Purdy remembers another incident in the same area:

I was leading a flight of four P-38's on patrol over the West coast of Leyte, when I spotted six Jap Vals heading toward Cebu Island. I closed on a Val from dead astern at 500 feet altitude, and found we were directly over the Jap airbase at Cebu City. I fired a short burst and hit the Val's port engine. It smoked, exploded and crashed north of Cebu City. I tackled another Val at the same altitude, but as I approached it from behind, the Jap plane banked to the right. I closed to 250 yards, fired a short burst at forty-degree deflection. Hits and explosions peppered the Val, and he rolled over and plunged straight into the ground.

Everything had been going my way up to now, but suddenly all hell broke loose. My wingman, Lieutenant John A. Nelson, called and said he'd been hit by flak. The shell had exploded in his parachute, injuring his legs. At the same time, Lieutenant Ettien, the other wingman in my flight, called that a group of Jap fighters was directly over our heads.

It was impossible to try and race out from under these Japs, and each time they would close in on us, we would have to go into a Lufbery Circle for mutual protection. We couldn't get back home that way. Strangely enough, the Jap fighters broke away after a while, and we made it home. Whatever caused that breakaway—fuel shortage, fear of other P-38's or what, saved our skins, because our fuel was very low.

The payoff came at home base. Captain William Grady, my tentmate, who had a flight of Lightnings in the area at the time, accused me of trying to shoot down all the Jap planes myself. It seems he could hear our flight conversations on the radio, but we could not hear his urgent pleas to let him know where the fun was. I doubt if he'll ever believe I couldn't hear him.

Credited with twenty-two aerial victories, Colonel Jay Thorpe Robbins of Coolidge, Texas, emerged from World War II as the tenth-ranking ace of the PTO. Most of these victories were gained in the P-38, although Robbins also flew the P-40 and P-39. He once lived a lifetime in a few seconds, in a combat experience he is unlikely ever to forget:

I was leading the 80th Squadron in low level escort for B-25's attacking Rabaul, New Britain, in November, 1943. While the B-25's went in for the attack, we fought a dogfight with Zeros, lasting about twenty-five minutes. I shot down three of them for sure, and another one I wasn't sure about. The Zeros withdrew, and with almost all my ammo gone I climbed to 24,000 and started home. Then I spotted one lone Jap fighter, who had already seen me and was making a suicidal head-on attack. There was no doubt he intended to ram.

He opened fire at 800 yards, and though our rate of closure was very rapid, he gave no indication of intent to break. I held my fire until range was 250 yards, then aimed at his wing root and pulled the trigger. Only two of my guns responded. They fired about twenty rounds and then quit. I was out of ammunition, but the Jap's left wing flashed and sheared at that same instant. I broke hard right, barely missing the Zero and flying through a shower of debris which damaged my Lightning. The firing of that twenty rounds seemed like an eternity.

Throughout the Pacific air war, the American urge for competition, so much a part of the national heritage, had to be disciplined in dealing with the tricky and highly maneuverable Zeros. Although the abler American pilots often won victories by dogfighting with the light Japanese aircraft, the surest way for the average pilot to survive was to avoid close dogfighting.

In spite of the fact that these tactical truths were impressed on tyro pilots during their training, there still came to the squadrons in the Pacific a steady stream of hotheads who had to be shown, often at the cost of their own lives, that the Zero was a superior aircraft for this kind of close action.

Teamwork and the right tactics eventually demoralized the Japanese fighter pilots, but to the very end it was a sort of aerial picnic for a skilled Japanese pilot if he could inveigle an American into a dogfight with him. One audacious and able Japanese pilot, whose feats are dealt with in the chapter on the enemy aces, made a specialty of taking on and defeating even the greatly superior Mustang in this kind of combat.

The Japanese were never short of tricks, lures and decoy gimmicks, even though their teamwork never approached that of the Americans they flew against. Japanese tactics of this kind form the outstanding combat memory of Major Leonard Randall Reeves of Texas. Since the incident almost cost "Randy" Reeves his life, it is well etched in his mind and he recalls it thus:

In March, 1945, our squadron was supposed to hit Nanking in order to keep the Japs busy there and prevent their concentration on the Okinawa landings. Eight hit the airfields to strafe parked bombers, and the other eight were to engage the Jap airborne patrols.

The Jap radar was working, and better than thirty Jap fighters were waiting for us as we bored in. They were the new Jacks, not as maneuverable as the Zekes, but faster and much more rugged. They were above us, and some were level with us as we came in at 27,000 feet.

The Japs would send out their usual decoy, a guy simulating a novice pilot flubbing around and not knowing what to do. When you concentrated on this decoy, the rest of the Japs would bounce you. In this case, the "professional novice" got too far from his flock. I shot him down before his pals could get to us.

Right after this contact, the air was jumping with enemy planes. My wingman, Lieutenant Beck, and I spotted a "squirrel cage" of Japs. It wasn't a vertical one, but one halfway between a Lufbery and a loop, with eight Jap planes in it. One Jap had closed up too tightly on the man ahead of him, so we snuck in, shot him down and snuck out again before the Jap astern of us could close the distance and save his overeager comrade.

Soon all my ammo had gone, and I called to Beck to join up and we would go home. He came in, but instead of joining up, he seemed to be taking lead on me. I immediately thought he must be mistaking me for a Jap. I was so concerned I yelled "Don't shoot, Beck, this is ole Randy!" But the next instant *blam*—I was hit by gunfire.

I realized instantly that a Jap had closed on me while I was watching Beck. Out of control, my ship rolled over, buffeting like hell and throwing the stick back in my guts. I chopped the power and rolled in full tail down trim. The nose started to come up—slowly. Finally on an even keel, I found myself completely alone, with no Beck or anyone else in sight and the weather closing in.

An hour and a half from home, I managed to join up with two of my flight. They checked my plane and reported part of my tail planes shot away. I landed without flaps, and when I got out and saw the damage, I wondered how in hell she flew at all.

Randy Reeves came through World War II with six aerial victories officially credited. These kills were gained in ten months of service with the 10th Air Force in India, and a further nine months with the 14th Air Force in China. He was a member of the famed 530th Squadron, known to the Japanese as the "Yellow Scorpions" because of the yellow noses and tails on their aircraft.

A single wild aerial battle elevated William A. Shomo to the fraternity of aces, won him immortality among combat pilots and gained him the Congressional Medal of Honor. Shomo was flying with the 82nd Tactical Reconnaissance Squadron in the Pacific at the time of his epic encounter. Time: January 11, 1945. Place: Over Luzon, P.I. Shomo modestly makes light of it:

As flight leader of two P-51 Mustangs on an armed reconnaissance mission over Northern Luzon, I sighted twelve Tony fighters escorting a Jap Betty bomber near Tuetubaro in the Cagayen Valley. My wingman, Lieutenant Paul Lipscomb, and I attacked the formation. Lipscomb shot down three fighters, while I shot down six and the bomber as well. The remaining three fighters fled. A ranking Japanese air marshal was later confirmed as killed in the bomber, hence the heavy fighter escort.

Bill Shomo's seven kills in this encounter have earned him a special place among American fighter pilots. He finished the Second World War with eight victories, and is a career Air Force officer.

An outstanding fighter pilot may not necessarily be a high-scoring pilot. Leading, guiding and planning fighter operations has called for exceptional talent and has not always led to large tallies of aerial kills. The capacity to function in the sphere of leadership rather than in individual brilliance has been given to very few men. Fighter leaders of this kind who also made ace are extremely rare.

Epitomizing this breed was Brigadier General Clinton D. Vincent, affectionately known in the USAAF and USAF as "Casey" Vincent. He downed six Japanese aircraft himself, but his leadership paved the way to many kills by others. As long as the enemy's planes went down, and plenty of them, "Casey" felt that his job was well done.

A vigorous and dedicated missionary for fighter aviation, which always seems to fall on hard times when America is not at war, "Casey" Vincent's death in 1955 was a heavy blow to all who knew and followed him. He believed the fighter arm should continue to develop to that ultimate point where missiles would completely replace manned fighters for aerial defense. The fighter arm and fighter aviation were first in Vincent's heart. He devoted his life's energies to this goal, and rightly belongs among America's most dedicated airmen.

Born in Gale, Texas, in 1914, General Vincent called Natchez, Mississippi, and San Antonio, Texas, his home towns. He saw his first aerial combat with the 35th Pursuit Group in the China-Burma-India Theater. He was Chief of Staff of the China Air Task Force and of the 14th Air Force. He later commanded the 68th Composite Wing in the CBI.

He became a brigadier general in 1944, aged twenty-nine. His most exciting combat experience was recorded for the authors shortly before his death:

> We were escorting B-24's over Hongkong, and ran into a new type of Jap fighter, later called the Hamp, which gave us a start. I shot down one just as he slid into position fifteen yards from a B-24. It was a great feeling of elation to see him explode and know that the bomber boys had been saved. Low on gas, I almost landed in the river on the way home, and barely made it to an abandoned air strip near our base.

The overwhelming majority of fighter operations in the Pacific were conducted by the U.S. Navy and Marine Corps, working hand in glove in their island-hopping progress towards Japan. The Army Air Force produced only 165 fighter aces in the Pacific Theater of Operations, against more than twice that number of Navy and Marine aces.

The USAAF was in action in the Pacific from the opening explosion to the final victory, and the few stories and combat sketches here are a sampling of the kind of fighter activity USAAF pilots undertook in this theater. The Army and the PTO produced the two top American aces of all time, Richard Bong and Thomas McGuire. From being ground down almost to nothing in early 1942, the AAF fighters made a dramatic comeback in the next three years to help the Navy and Marines drive the Japanese from the skies.

In the European Theater of Operations, the USAAF had the lion's share of the fighter combat, against an equally rugged foe mounted on much better aircraft than the Japanese. The aces of the ETO fought a war different from the Pacific struggle, and also had much the better of the wartime publicity. Nevertheless, the contribution of the USAAF aces to Pacific victory was considerable, and their glory second to none.

4

☆ ☆ ☆ ☆ ☆

USAAF Aces of the European Theater of Operations (I)

THE AMERICANS who made their way to England to fight with the RAF and RCAF between 1939 and 1941 were Uncle Sam's only representatives in the European air war at the time of Pearl Harbor. Their presence was unofficial, but nevertheless welcome. There were no USAAF combat units deployed anywhere in the European area, in contrast with the Pacific, where the USAAF was widely deployed and presumably ready for war.

As a consequence of these dispositions, the first American bomber raid on the Continent did not take place until June 12, 1942, with the now famous attack by B-24 aircraft on the Ploesti oil refineries in Rumania. The next American raids came on July 4, 1942, when four airfields in the Netherlands were attacked by twelve RAF Bostons (American-built A-20's), six of these machines being manned by American pilots and crews as a familiarization operation.

Not until August 14, 1942, did a fighter plane manned by an American pilot in a USAAF unit make its first kill against the Germans. Flying a P-39 fighter, Lieutenant Shafter shot down a Focke-Wulfe "Kurier" over Iceland when the lumbering German reconnaissance plane came under his guns. On August 19, 1942, the first German machine to be shot down over Europe by a USAAF unit was claimed following an aerial battle over Dieppe.

During the first six months following Pearl Harbor, U.S. airpower was fighting with its back to the wall in the Pacific. This immediate and urgent involvement prevented any rapid build-up of U.S. air strength in the European Theater of Operations. There were other consequences that upset many of the best-laid schemes of American war planners.

The planners had concluded that by producing large numbers of bombers with high speed, good defensive firepower and high-altitude capability, it would be feasible to make deep penetrations into Germany by daylight. The tragic experience of the RAF in the 1941 experimental use of the B-17 in this type of operation compelled a modification of the plan. It was decided that the first bomber missions would be heavily escorted by fighters until they proved the theory that they could defend themselves against enemy fighters.

General Henry "Hap" Arnold wanted to hold off all commitments of the B-17's and B-24's against the Luftwaffe until he could send them in great numbers. In this way, the awesome firepower of the formations could take the starch out of the German fighter opposition. General Arnold was not to realize this goal.

Due to circumstances beyond Arnold's control, it became necessary to commit the B-17's and B-24's virtually piecemeal. As a result, an urgent demand developed for swarms of American fighters. Heretofore played down in the officially adopted American aerial policies, fighters now came into their own as the hard realities of war swept away the superficialities of war theory. Until American fighters were provided, the burden of defending the bombers fell to the RAF.

Fighter aircraft were ferried from the United States to units in England. Initially, the 31st Fighter Group (P-39's) had to leave its aircraft in America because the B-17's assigned to lead them across the Atlantic were diverted to the Pacific. The pressure was on and the Fortresses were needed at Midway Island.

The 31st therefore went to England by sea, minus aircraft, and was equipped with RAF Spitfires. The 52nd Fighter Group followed the same procedure. Hence these American units saw their first fighter combat in the ETO in British aircraft bearing U.S. insignia.

American fighter pilots entered the ETO with well-founded misgivings about the experienced German pilots they were to face. American bomber losses were already high. Fighter losses rose sharply when they began escorting the bombers. German pilot quality in 1942 was very good, although it went into decline in the period 1943–45. The top Germans were always formidable.

The German aircraft were rugged and could take punishment. Unlike the Japanese planes, of which reports had already flashed through USAAF units, the Luftwaffe's sturdy Me-109's did not burst into flame from a few hits and explode like the Japanese Zero. The top German pilots, some with experience dating back to the Spanish Civil War, often turned the tables on green American pilots. The neophyte Americans were sometimes shot down by these habile Germans even when the latter were themselves flying seriously damaged machines. This kind of German pilot talent caused considerable tremor in USAAF units in England. More will be said concerning the Germans in the chapter devoted to the enemy aces.

American fighter pilots lost many a battle in these early days because they failed to learn the value and the theories of the high-angle deflection shot. The enemy was hard to surprise. He was wily. Consequently, it was difficult to get into a stern chase position on him.

A good high-deflection artist could often damage the Me-109's oil coolers, disable the hydraulic system that allowed the landing gear to drop in midair, set a gas tank alight or create an engine malfunction. Any such damaging blow could dramatically swing the odds in the deflection shooter's favor, often forcing the German to make a wrong move or straighten out—just long enough for the classic final kill from dead astern.

New gunsights, designed in 1942 and produced in 1944 and 1945, were intended to solve the problem of trajectory for American pilots, but the war ended before more than minor results could be attained. Even at the time of the Korean War, American fighter pilots were still not sold on new-fangled sights. Many of them opposed radar sights. "Kentucky windage" was employed, or in the classic expression of one of America's leading aces—"Stick some gum on the windshield, then ram the gum up their tailpipe and let go."

As the bomber sorties into Germany mounted, it was soon evident that the major threat to this offensive was the German fighter force. Bomber raids with fighter escort were much less costly in casualties and aircraft than were unescorted raids. The long-range escort fighter became the *sine qua non* of successful daylight bomber operations. The clamor for its rapid development found a response in the production of the Republic P-47 Thunderbolt.

The P-47 was the first USAAF fighter to provide the badly needed long-range protection to the bomber streams. The 4th Fighter Group, based at Debden RAF Station near Saffron Walden, Essex, was the first unit to receive the new aircraft. A better unit to blood the P-47 could not be found.

The 4th Fighter Group had been formed in September, 1942, from the 71st, 121st and 133rd Eagle Squadrons of the RAF. These tough, combat-tested pilots were a valuable cadre around which to form a new unit. Under the command of Colonel Edward W. Anderson, they said goodbye to their slender, greatly esteemed Spitfires in March of 1943 and mounted the massive Thunderbolt with considerable misgivings.

At 14,000 pounds, the Thunderbolt weighed almost three times as much as the Spitfire. Many of the American pilots, accustomed to the heavyweight punch of the Spitfire's four 20mm cannons, did not like resigning themselves to the Thunderbolt's eight .50-caliber machine guns. Despite the experience of the pilots flying with the 4th Fighter Group, enemy kills came slowly. The P-47 scored its first kill south of Dieppe on April 15, 1943.

Other squadrons, new ones, were being equipped with the P-51 Mustang, destined to prove itself the outstanding single-engined fighter of World War II. Colonel Hubert "Hub" Zemke's 56th Fighter Group, dubbed the "Wolf Pack," had clawed down 300 German aircraft by the time the 4th had racked up its 150th kill with the P-47. When the 4th Fighter Group was reequipped with Mustangs on February 26th, 1944, the American race for high scoring Group honors started in earnest.

By war's end, the initially laggard 4th Fighter Group claimed to be the best, with 550 enemy aircraft destroyed in the air and 466 destroyed on the ground for a total of 1,016. However, two other groups reported more air-to-air kills. Zemke's Wolfpack claimed 671.5 aerial victories and the 557th Group claimed 586.5 aerial kills. For the purposes of this book, which is devoted to aces and counts aerial victories only, Zemke's Wolfpack is the top USAAF Group of the ETO.

By comparison, the most successful German fighter unit on the

Western front was JG-26 "Schlageter," known to the Allied pilots as the "Abbeville Boys." In more than five years of aerial combat, the "Abbeville Boys" claimed over 2,700* Allied aircraft shot down. It should be noted that the German unit had almost three full years of combat before the first USAAF Fighter Group in Europe was formed. Nevertheless, the German record is impressive.

The ETO is deemed to include all aerial activity over Europe proper, as well as such areas as Italy and North Africa. The top American ace of the ETO was Colonel Francis S. Gabreski, with a total of thirty-one confirmed kills. Blonde, blue-eyed and sharp-featured Gabreski hails from Oil City, Pennsylvania. Of Polish descent, he is possessed of all the traditional charm of his ancestors. Greying now, but still a compact dynamo of a man, "Gabby," as he is known in the fraternity of American aces, is America's top living ace.

Gabreski was going great guns at the time of his World War II downing. Like many another seemingly invincible combat pilot, he was either nailed by flak or bent his propeller against a rise in the terrain during ground-attack operations. He was taken prisoner. He is one of the six American pilots to win acedom in both World War II and Korea.

Gabreski took to jets easily. Six and one-half communist jet fighters fell to his guns in Korea, bringing his all time victory total to 37.5 kills. Only Bong and McGuire, with 40 and 38 victories respectively, surpass Gabreski, and both died in crashes.

Robert S. Johnson of Lawton, Oklahoma, flew himself into second place among America's ETO aces as a member of Hub Zemke's Wolfpack—the 56th Fighter Group. Johnson shot down his first German aircraft in June, 1943, and went on to become the leading ace of the ETO. He held this distinction until Gabreski passed him in April, 1944. He is credited with twenty-eight aerial victories.

Johnson is another of the many aces who is of shortish stature. Five feet seven inches tall, he has to a marked degree the cold blue eyes atributed to aces so often in fiction. Notwithstanding this striking physical feature, he is a friendly man with a fine sense of humor and extremely modest. Even in bull sessions he never exaggerates. Johnson

* JG-52s, on the Russian front shot down over 6,500 aircraft.

always gives the impression of poise, confidence and a razor-sharp intelligence. He was undoubtedly one of the deadliest American aces of World War II.

Bob Johnson flew his last combat mission on May 8, 1944, and returned to the United States to finish his career in the service. Johnson's removal from combat flying while at the zenith of his career typifies a practice that was prevalent in the Allied air forces. When a man had run up a good score of kills, higher commanders showed a readiness to remove such a pilot from combat flying.

The reason was not only the likelihood of losing the man eventually if he went on flying combat, but the very real need to exploit the experience and prestige of such fliers in training new recruits. This Allied practice was not followed on the German side, where, in the words of General Adolf Galland, "our aces flew until they were killed."

Bob Johnson was released from active duty on January 1, 1946, a well-decorated and distinguished airman. He holds the DSC, Silver Star, ten DFC's, the British DFC and four Air Medals. He required only thirteen months to amass his score of twenty-eight aerial victories. Johnson was the first member of the Wolfpack to break Captain Eddie Rickenbacker's World War I record. Very much alive today, Johnson is a sales engineer for Republic Aviation in Farmingdale, New York.

Johnson advice to fellow pilots and fledglings alike was a telegraphic distillate of common sense: "It's better to come home tired with a sore neck from looking constantly in every direction than it is to leave the thing you sit on back in enemy territory."

He was a firm believer in teamwork, and made this generous salute to the wingman and his vital but unspectacular job:

"Any time you lose your wingman, you've lost 75 percent of your eyes and fighting strength. Jerries will shoot at anyone. Never think you're a favorite to them. Anyone can get it, some of the best have gotten it, so keep your eyes open."

When asked to recount for this book his most memorable combat experience, Bob Johnson said: "The victories were not nearly as impressive or as memorable to me as was keeping from being a victory."

The third-ranking American ace in the ETO was Major George

Earl Preddy Jr., of Greensboro, North Carolina. He was killed in
action on Christmas Day, 1944, aged 25, after flying in combat in both
the Pacific and European Theaters. He is credited with 25.83* victories
against the Germans. He won his other victory in 1942 while flying
fighters out of Australia against the Japanese.

Preddy's death was one of Fate's more ironic twists. On December
25, 1944, Preddy bounced a formation of four German aircraft, shooting down one of them on the first surprise pass. In the ensuing dogfight, Preddy exploded a second Me-109. The two remaining Germans
split up and fled, one racing eastward, the other diving for the deck
with Preddy in hot pursuit.

Allied ground troops, watching the aerial battle after the fashion of
soldiers in the trenches in the First World War, sent up a stream of
flak and small-arms fire in an effort to hit the Me-109. The ground
gunners failed to lead the diving Me-109 far enough. The hail of fire
struck the pursuing Preddy's Mustang instead, and he crashed almost
on top of the friendly troops who had killed him.

Although Preddy is at present only credited with two kills in this
engagement, German records indicate that the third Me-109 was also
his victim. Preddy may be credited eventually with the extra victory,
as was the case with Eddie Rickenbacker and his long-delayed victory
credit in World War I.

The less famous fighter aces of the ETO came from all walks of
civilian life, and the talents of some of them were by no means confined to flying. Gerald Lynn Rounds, an ace with the 97th Fighter
Squadron of the 82nd Fighter Group, is a man with several strings to
his bow.

Today Rounds is a research chemist with the Kaiser Steel Corporation at Fontana, California. His experiences while flying with the
famed "Forked Tailed Devils" Squadron at the controls of a P-38
provided him with the raw material to exhibit an unusual talent for
narrative writing. Rounds' description of operations with the P-38 is a
lively classic of the feelings, apprehensions and emotions of a World
War II fighter pilot:

---

* Preddy's score may be 26.83, but positive confirmation is lacking on kills
scored on his final mission. The fraction (.83) came from a kill shared with a
wingman (.5) and a kill shared with two other pilots .33⅓.

The "Forked Tailed Devils" stood cold and gaunt at the 9 A.M. briefing on February 8, 1943. The target is to be Gabes, two hundred miles south of Tunis in North Africa, being used as an evacuation port for Rommel's army as Montgomery presses in from the south. We're escorting B-25 Mitchells. We're told to expect a little fighter opposition, 109's and 190's.

Escorting the B-25 has been expensive, one pilot and one plane per mission on the average. Some of our best men have got the hammer. We are green and are up against an experienced enemy in good aircraft. Our boys are scared, but they're learning.

We are all thinking about this as we walk out to our P-38's. The sky is overcast, and the air is cold and wet. Spam and powdered eggs for breakfast sit in a stagnant ball in the stomach. The crew chief meets us and the tension eases a little as we slide into the familiar cockpit of the P-38. She's a dream, an honest aircraft, she always warns you of impending trouble.

The engines are warm, thanks to the crew chief, and catch easily with a heavy blurp through the turbosuperchargers, then run smoothly and solidly. You check each engine instrument, as you watch the first flight taxi out from its dispersal point. Then the other flights are moving.

You release the toe-pedal brakes and glide ahead off the smooth dispersal pad on to the rough, waterlogged taxiway. You are one of two spares for this mission. The flights are getting off in good shape, and your engines check clean at forty-five inches of mercury as you sit on the end of the runway.

Number four flight is off and you clear the two Allisons and give her loose reins. The counter-rotating props cause no torque, and the takeoff is easy except for the drag caused by the soft spots in the wet dirt runway. The belly tank necessitates a little trim after the wheels are up into their wells.

A quick count of the four flights looks discouraging. All sixteen planes are forming up. After sweating out the mission the night before, then thorough briefing, and takeoff, you expect at least one of the boys to have some trouble . . . so it won't all have been in vain.

Radios are being checked at low altitude, so the enemy won't pick them up. You listen anxiously as all the boys check in with their code and number "Meatball 2-2" . . . "Meatball 2-3" . . . "Meatball 2-4" . . . then Major Whittliff flattens out on course and the flights assume escort position at his side and to the rear.

In five minutes, our rendezvous course will bring us to the circling bombers. Already in the distance you can see the small swarm of bee-like objects milling in slow motion against the mountain backdrop. Then you get a break. A man in number three flight peels off sharply from formation and chandelles over you and the other waiting spare P-38. Oil streaks from the left oil cooler to the empennage tell you why.

As you look over your shoulder you see his left engine slowly feather up and the prop blades stand motionless as he cuts it off. You hope he makes the tricky one-engined landing okay. The other spare closes in to the vacated position just as the number two man in the second flight glides slowly out of formation. There's no visible reason, but you know that an instrument is telling the pilot that his plane is not fit for combat.

You increase your manifold pressure to forty inches, and close up rapidly into the 2-2 position. As you slide into tight formation to get the attention of the leader, letting him know that he has a new wingman, you remember that Captain Petersen is in this 2-1 position. He recognizes you. There's a friendly hand gesture, and you slip out into the loose, flexible combat formation.

You drank green French beer with your element leader after the mission the night before last. You've flown a lot with him, and are confidant of his judgment. You're proud to be his wingman and feel an added sense of responsibility because of it.

On course for Gabes, you begin the slow tactical weave back and forth over the B-25's. This weave will increase in tempo as the target and danger of attack approach, until it is violent but coordinated shifting of each four-ship flight from one side of the bombers to the other, all the while covering their most vulnerable area—to the rear and above.

The thought runs through your mind that this is an odd place to be sitting—you're 5,000 feet up, in a comfortably warm cockpit, moving at 225 mph toward someone who wants to kill you. This prompts a look over your gondola nose at the top two gun barrels jutting into the slipstream. You know there are two more below those, and nestled in the center of the four fifties is a cannon. One explosive shell from that cannon will down an aircraft.

You jump. No gunsight! A quick twist of the rheostat shows it to have been turned too dim to show up in the daylight. Now it stands out well, a solid orange circle with a pipper in the center. Good! A water pistol would be as good in aerial combat as a plane without a gunsight.

You are reminded to flick on the small switch on the panel marked "guns." The two black buttons under your right thumb and forefinger are now "hot." Better watch how you hold the column with your right hand.

You burn every landmark below into your memory. You might

get caught alone and have to come back "on the deck" where navigation is much more difficult. You might even have to walk back—or maybe die of thirst in that waste down there.

Your mind goes back to the dirty Arab woman who does your laundry. Will she have it by tomorrow? Wait! Where's the fourth plane in number three flight? Didn't see him leave. Watch yourself and be careful, he could have been a Kraut coming in instead of a friend leaving.

At noon the Tebessa Mountains are falling behind, and with them the dismal cloud that cloaks their environs. The warm sun sparkles through the plexiglass canopy, and for a moment you forget that this marvelous thing in which you sit enjoying the beauties of the world below can also be a greased runway to hell.

You check your map. There's the Gulf of Gabes ahead. The map goes back into your knee pocket and you pull the zipper shut. Everything must be secure for combat.

The tempo of the weave is increasing. You're twisting your neck as far as it will go. The sun is at nine o'clock high, and you squint at it through your spread fingers. No "bogies." Captain Pete is wrapping in tighter on the outside of the weaves now and you have to be on the ball to stick with him.

The coast is under your nose. You look down and see streaks of dust below the formation, and another batch of these streaks over to the north. *Airfields*. Those are fighters taking off in abreast formation.

The bombers are turning on the bomb run. You're losing Captain Pete—manifold pressure forty-five inches—you increase the rpm from 2,200 to 2,600—now you close up nicely on your leader. Perspiration pours down your ribs from under your arms, the shirt, dress shirt, flying suit and leather jacket are soaking wet in the middle of your back and armpits. Both your thin pigskin gloves are sodden, but your experience has shown that this hide hangs to the wheel well when wet.

You're cranking your head 'round for a glimpse of the fighters who'll soon be up to try and nail you. You glimpse bombs drifting down from a trio of B-25's. Good! Now the formation can pick up some speed. The oil temperature's too high now. You flick the oil cooler flap switch to wide open and jam the coolant valves forward.

You're headed homeward, but why don't the damned bombers put their noses down? Let's have a little more speed. Let's get the hell out of here before we're jumped.

"*Eight o'clock high!*" blasts in your ears from the phones. Your head yanks around to left and right. Damn it, there they are . . . little sharpened sucker sticks with an afterthought wing. 109's, eight of them. They're climbing hard, will be going like hell when they come through.

You reach down and snap the two fuel selector valves to "reserve." Up goes the tank release switch. You push the button, and there's a surge upward as you lose 500 pounds of tank and gasoline. The sleek, teardrop tanks tumble awkwardly earthward in a shower underneath the whole P-38 formation.

"*Here they come*" hits you from both sides of the head. You see them, you're on the other side of the formation from the attack. The 109's have their pencil noses pointed down in a steep dive. Our left flight breaks into them.

"*Timber—four o'clock high!*" Hell. That's my side of the formation. Pete slams in full right rudder and aileron. His plane snaps over into a vertical bank. He hauls the column into his stomach and the 38's tail sinks into a blackout turn. Then you're right behind him, and as you sneak a glance through the top of your canopy you glimpse three 109's with the leading edges of their wings winking flame from their guns. Two of them are winking at *you*. The 109's whip through and under like comets, and you complete your turn just short of a high-speed stall.

Your turn puts you and Pete behind the formation. You're now tail-end Charlies and you both hasten to catch up. Rpm levers are jammed to the stops. Throttles are shoved *through* the stops. Manifold pressure climbs to an engine-torturing sixty-five inches. The engines are way beyond their limits, but you have to have the power.

Garbled warnings pour through your radio. Three 109's come drilling down from four o'clock high. You press your mike button to warn Pete. He doesn't answer. You yell to him to break right as the 109's come in. You feed in right rudder and aileron fast and suck the stick back. You know that Pete hasn't heard you and this is the only reason for abandoning your element leader. One 109 is ahead of you, firing at Pete and about to cross your bow. You clinch both buttons. The first belch of the four fifties and the 20mm cannon seems to stop your thirty-eight dead in the air. Then the guns settle down to a steady hammering.

The 109 slips through your lethal stream and disappears below your nose. You continue turning tightly until the Germans behind you slide over the top. You reverse your turn rapidly on the top to prevent being left too far behind. You're on your back and hauling your nose down hard. Through your canopy top, looking down at the ground now, you don't see Pete. Maybe he broke with you and completed the turn. No, no, you argue with yourself, he wouldn't do that, he'd know better.

You keep her nose down to pick up speed as you flash above the desert. You're all alone. "What in hell do I do if I'm jumped now?" you think. You roll your head and eyes, checking the whole sky. There's another 38 below you. Must be Pete! Both his engines are smoking.

You dump your column forward and the nose plunges down. You slam up into your belt and your head thumps against a rib in the canopy. A clump of dried mud from the floor floats oddly up in front of your face. As you dive, you get a good view of the ground 8,000 feet below and of the whole battle. Two pillars of black smoke billow up from the desert brush. You wonder if they are 38's.

The main part of the squadron is a mile ahead, and still beating off 109 attacks. You see one 38 half a mile ahead and well below the rest. He's going down, with white smoke from the prestone system streaming behind him. The wings are turning slowly one over the other and the tail is washing around sloppily. You think of the boy slumped over the column.

As you pull up behind Pete he snaps into a left bank. You see that a 109 has tried a long-range cannon shot on the rear of the formation far ahead. Pete closes in and the German pilot doesn't see him until it is too late. Pete comes in behind him and the German makes a mistake. He tries a tight climbing turn to shake you and Pete. The German hasn't learned that a 38 will turn inside him at any speed.

Pete's guns start pumping and his withering fire takes its toll. The 109 pilot tries to squeeze a little more out of the turn and snaps uncontrollably. One and a quarter turns later the German recovers on his back, dives out in a split arse and Pete ceases fire.

You watch the 109 as he begins his pullout. There's a livid yellow flash, and all that's left of him is a black ball of smoke, like a flak burst.

Pete slams tight right and loses you. Just as you get tipped into the turn, a 109 shoots over the top of Pete and one streaks past your tail in a steep dive. Pete reverses his turn and banks back toward course. This is your chance to catch up on him by "cutting across the pie," but as your tired right arm forces the wheel up, you catch a glimpse of something disappearing under your right wing. You reverse the bank, and there's a 109 closing behind Pete and leaving a trail of black powder smoke behind. Perfect! He's lined up for an eighty-degree deflection shot for you.

You've got to hurry, or the Kraut will have Pete bored in. The radio's clogged, so you can't warn Pete. You go into a left bank and find the 109 in your gunsight ring. Back on the stick and the pipper pulls ahead of the German. He's following the pipper nicely. But

whoa! The pipper is sitting right on Pete's canopy. You'll be shooting directly at Pete.

You won't hit Pete because there's no "lead" on him. You hesi-
tate a moment to quickly query the laws of motion and relativity in
your head. You hope they're still in force as you clamp both black
buttons. Again the initial burst jars the 38's whole airframe.

You follow the 109 round the bend as the guns hammer. He sits
in position as though you have him chained to the pipper. Flashes
pepper along the upper surface of the 109's wings. The flashes
sparkle and crackle all over the German's canopy as the incendiaries
appear to explode on contact. Shrouded in white smoke, the 109
falls off your pipper, and you release the buttons and fall in behind
Pete.

The 109 goes into a steep spin, belching thick black smoke. You
can't follow him down, or even watch him, you've been too long
already without sweeping the sky with your eyes. Unless Pete hap-
pens to see the German crash, it will go into the books as a "probable."

Magically, the 109's have gone and the sky is clearing up. Everyone is weaving over the bombers protectively. The radio is silent
and you wonder if it is out of commission. You count the 38's.
There are five missing.

You settle down to escort the bombers, your mouth feeling like
one of those dry wooden paddles that the doctors use. You snap the
right side of the mask off the helmet and fish out your pipe from the
knee pocket. Tobacco? Damn it, it's in your shirt pocket under
the chute buckle, under the flight suit. Five minutes later, when you
are half undressed and finally have fished out the tobacco, it's sodden
with sweat.

You stuff it in the bowl and light up anyway. It doesn't burn
worth a damn, but it tastes good. You're tired and time drones easily
away. When the bombers split off for their field, you begin looking
for the half-green slush hole that your aircraft calls home. The
peeloffs look tired as you moan over the strip at 300 mph.

On the pad, the crew chief is waiting. He spots you in, the
engines are cleared and the props suddenly transform themselves
from shimmering discs into sharp knife blades. You heave yourself
out, and while you walk to the interrogation center a lone 38 roars
over the field, a jagged hole gaping in his horizontal stabilizer.
"Lucky boy", you think to yourself as you realize what that 20mm
cannon might have done to him and his machine.

Then Captain Pete grabs you and all but kisses you with excitement because you knocked the 109 off his tail. "But I thought sure
as hell you were going to shoot *me* down," he says. The formal

scoring sobers you a little. Four bombers and a 38 are gone, maybe more.

Then the tension slowly ebbs. By evening the adrenal pit in your stomach is gone and your hand is steady again. Steady enough at least to hold another glass of green beer with Captain Pete.

Gerald Rounds was born in Imlay City, Michigan, on April 26, 1921, and shot down five German aircraft while flying while flying eighty-two combat missions in P-38 aircraft. He saw action from December, 1942, until September, 1943, engaging in combat over Africa, Sicily and Italy, with the 12th Air Force.

If young fighter pilots in World War II had a common dream, it was to be an ace overnight. Eighth Air Force Captain William H. Allen USAF, of Los Angeles and Long Beach, California, made this dream a staggering reality in one of the most unusual feats in the history of fighter aviation. He became an ace in *one mission*, with five victories in just a few minutes.

Modest in the manner of many of the aces, Captain Allan provides a terse explanation for his success.

"I got into the middle of a large group of German aircraft, and was able to chase them at will. I believe the pilots were relatively inexperienced, because their evasive action was ineffective." With those few words, Captain Allen dismisses his rare distinction among America's fighter aces.

Lieutenant Colonel Clarence E. Anderson Jr. of Oakland, California shot down 16.25 enemy aircraft while flying with the 363rd Squadron, 357th Fighter Group of the Eighth Air Force. His story is a graphic example of the demands placed on a fighter pilot during combat.

"G" is the term used to indicate the force of gravity. A 4-G turn forces a pilot into his seat in such a way as to make his body weigh four times its actual static weight. Thus, a 200-pound pilot for the duration of his 4-G turn weighs 800 pounds. Physical strain like that combined with the manipulation of a gunsight, throttle controls and careful listening on the radio require almost phenomenal concentration. Keeping the aircraft at the proper speed and in the proper attitude are added to this burden. On top of it all, during battle, is the never-ending watch for the enemy. Some pilots cannot do all these things simultaneously, and as a consequence fail to survive.

These tasks are graphically described in Clarence Anderson's story:

We were escorting bombers to the Ludwigshaven-Mannheim area on May 27, 1944. Our group was equipped with P-51's. We were flying a group formation with my squadron on the right flank, and as we rendezvoused with the "big friends" (B-17's) at around 27,000 feet, we crossed over the bombers and started to make a lazy turn to the left. The group leader identified our bombers and then immediately someone called over the R/T that there was a large number of enemy fighters about to attack the bomber formation immediately in front of ours.

We released our drop tanks and turned sharp left to engage these fighters. At this point the flight I was leading was placed on the outside of the turn, and was therefore vulnerable to attack from the rear. Before I could look behind, my element leader, First Lieutenant Edward K. Simpson Jr. of Hampton, New Jersey, called out that four Me-109's were diving on our tails from five o'clock high.

My flight turned sharply into the Me-109's as we fell into a close string formation. The lead German was a sharp customer, but his attack was thwarted by our sharp turn. The four Germans pulled up and began circling with us.

At full throttle and rpm we were able to maintain our turn inside them. Climbing to 29,000 feet we equaled them and began to gain a little on them on each turn. The Germans decided to try something else. Turning east, three of them flew level at 29,000 while the number four man climbed as quickly as possible in the same direction.

Lieutenant Simpson and his wingman pursued the climbing Me-109. With my wingman, I continued to chase the other three enemy aircraft. They were at full throttle as we could see the black exhaust pouring from their engines. Our own throttles were clear to the firewalls, and we slowly crept behind the last German. Holding my fire until about 250 yards dead astern, I fired a short burst and got some good hits around the wing roots and fuselage.

More black smoke began to pour from his aircraft, only this time it wasn't exhaust. He rolled over on his back and flew upside down in an attempt to shake me, but I stayed level and fired another close-range burst. Chunks flew off and he burst into flames and began spinning lazily down to the deck.

We closed in now on the two remaining Germans, who saw us

coming. The leader pulled up sharply into a climbing turn, and his wingman rolled over and went diving for home. We cut across the leading German's climbing circle, which he tightened. I was forced to pull up sharply to avoid hitting this German, because he now reversed his turn and was pulling his nose up for a shot at my wingman, Lieutenant Skara. Skara threw his Mustang into a spin to avoid being shot, and as he descended the Me-109 followed him down. I followed. As I closed the range, the German broke violently into a climbing left turn and I had to pull up sharply again.

The German reversed his turn, pulling up steeply for a short burst at me. He was very close, and I could see the detail and color of his highly polished aircraft. Luckily, he couldn't get his nose high enough to get a shot at me. He stalled just before I did and as we both nosed down to gain speed I was again behind him.

Once more he pulled up into his tight left climbing turn. This time I throttled back slightly and stayed inside his turn. He saw that I wasn't going to overshoot him this time and he pulled almost straight up. Following, I was able to get in a long burst which connected in his cockpit and engine. He burst into flames and smoke, rolled slightly and then dove straight for the earth from 30,000 feet.

I joined up with my wingman and went home, where we learned that Lieutenant Simpson had destroyed the fourth German, with the pilot bailing out at 20,000 feet. The group had engaged the main enemy fighter attack, destroying twenty-three of them.

As any veteran combat pilot will testify, one of the cardinal sins of aerial combat is to forget about the enemy's friends. "Just as you have a wingman, so has the enemy. Just as you have squadron mates who are never far away if you keep your wits about you, so has the enemy. Just as you can turn toward these mates and have them take the leech off your tail, so can you be sucked into a similar trap by the enemy you are pursuing." So might any fighter leader of World War II have lectured his fledglings.

In the dynamic rough and tumble of aerial combat, the fighter pilot was often lucky enough to find an enemy who had forgotten everything except his target. Such an enemy was vulnerable. Major Robert M. Becker of Shattuck, Oklahoma, and Los Angeles, California, tells a story of such an incident in his combat career.

On Memorial Day, 1944, I was on a sweep deep in the heart of Germany when we met a large formation of fighters which were picking away at a group of Fortresses. Luckily, I found myself in good position to attack a twin-engined Me-410, whose pilot was really intent on the B-17 in front of him.

The job took only a matter of seconds. As I pulled off him there was *another* Me-410 in my sights, also oblivious to everything but the 20mm cannon fire he was pouring to the Fortress in front of him. A quick burst and he was aflame. With two down I felt it was time to pull up and get the sweat out of my eyes, but there was *number three* up ahead. Once again the German pilot was hammering the Forts and not watching his tail. It seemed incredible.

Lest I commit the same error as my victims, I took a quick look to clear my own tail. Then I got as close to this German as I could and let go with all six fifties. That put an end to him and to my own perfect day.

Major Becker is credited with seven victories over the Germans while fighting with the USAAF's 362nd Fighter Squadron in the ETO.

Some emphasis has been laid in this book on the importance to a fighter pilot of the knack of shooting at a moving target from a moving platform, all movement being in three dimensions. Some American pilots mastered this knack, although they were few in number. If they were also great pilots, they were almost certainly headed for big scores, unless they themselves were shot down, perhaps by one of the many outstanding German pilots who had made themselves masters of the difficult art of air-to-air shooting.

Colonel Walter C. Beckham of De Funiak Springs, Florida, was one of the American aces with outstanding shooting skill. He shot down eighteen German aircraft in less than six months of combat with the 353rd Fighter Group. Beckham was undoubtedly on his way to new records for American aces when an ultrasharp German in an Me-109 clobbered him on February 22, 1944.

Colonel Beckham spent the rest of the war in Stalag Luft III at Sagan, and at Moosburg. He was liberated by Patton's 14th Armored Division on April 29, 1945. Beckham would prefer to forget the mission on which he was downed, but there is one he does remember, a story of lightning inspiration under stress.

It was an attack on an Me-109. On overshooting him, it suddenly occurred to me that a barrel roll would put me back in firing position. It did. The puzzle to me has always been why this idea should suddenly occur in the excitement of a fight, and not during leisurely thought on the ground.

Another of the top-notch aces of the ETO was Lieutenant Colonel Duane Willard Beeson of Boise, Idaho. Filled with a great sense of adventure, Beeson enlisted in the RCAF in 1940 when he was only nineteen years old. He later transferred to the 71st Eagle Squadron in April of 1942 and to the USAAF in September of 1942.

Beeson flew Hurricanes, Spitfires, Thunderbolts and Mustangs in combat, which represented a fair range of fighter aircraft types. He shot down 19.33 aircraft, but was himself another victim of German flak in a low-level mission. He crashed and was taken prisoner, spending the final thirteen months of the war in Stalag Luft I at Barth, Germany. At the time he was shot down, Beeson was in a neck-and-neck race with Captain Don Gentile for the ETO fighter pilot top score.

Neat and meticulous in his dress, clean-cut, dark-haired and handsome, he epitomized the fighter pilot hero of World War II. He was a Lieutenant Colonel at twenty-six years of age. The Citation to his Distinguished Service Cross gives insight into his qualities and skill.

For extraordinary heroism in action with the enemy, 29 January 1944. Captain Beeson, while leading a flight of P-47 aircraft escorting bombers attacking Frankfurt, Germany, led his flight and his squadron down to engage enemy fighters harassing a formation of heavy bombers. As his squadron dived to the attack, Captain Beeson observed six enemy aircraft coming down on his squadron from above. Aware of the immediate danger to his squadron, accompanied only by his wingman, he turned into the oncoming aircraft. During the turn, an enemy fighter scored strikes on his tail-plane, impairing the operation efficiency of the aircraft. Despite this, and an unfavorable tactical position, he pressed home his attack against odds of three to one. The daring and vigor of his action scattered the opposing aircraft and permitted his squadron to proceed to the aid of the bombers. In combat ranging from 15,000 feet to 200 feet, Captain Beeson succeeded in destroying two of the enemy, and his heroism no doubt saved many fighters and bombers from damage and possible destruction. The unselfish bravery of Captain Beeson reflects great credit upon himself and the Armed Forces of the United States.

Beeson's tactical methods were along classic lines. Like the RAF's Bader, he had carefully studied the tactics of the great World War I pilots. He believed in keeping plenty of speed in his bounces. "The aircraft with speed has the initiative, because speed can be converted into altitude," said Beeson. He also had his own ideas about overshooting an enemy. "I think it's a good thing," he said. "Hold your fire until within range and clobber him in the last instant before you must break away. It's sorta like sneaking up behind and hitting him with a baseball bat."

A brilliant officer and pilot, Lieutenant Colonel Beeson remained in the USAF after World War II. In one of those strange quirks of destiny, Beeson passed away on February 13, 1947, from a brain tumor while on the way to Walter Reed Hospital. He is buried in Arlington National Cemetery. His unfortunate loss was typical in a way of many fighter pilots who, surviving several years of imminent death in the skies, returned to die in the United States in automobile accidents, freak aircraft crashes or from ill-health.

Lieutenant Colonel Louis Benne of Harrison, Pennsylvania, flew P-38's with the 49th Squadron of the 14th Fighter Group in the Mediterranean area, and is credited with five aerial victories. Benne thought he "had it made" when he was scheduled for what appeared to be a milk run on his 52nd mission. Due for rotation, he felt sure it would be his last mission. It was. The only problem being that Benne did not rotate back to the United States.

Although it was to be a milk run, we were awakened early and there was the usual rush to dress, get breakfast and get to briefing. My tour was actually over, as the rule was fifty missions and you went home.

We were providing close escort for heavies attacking Petfurdo, Hungary. Numerous groups would attack from different directions, dispersing the Luftwaffe's counter effort.

We were to cover the area north of the target, the most likely place for enemy action, and I felt uneasy at the briefing. I was leading the squadron and my own flight was very low on experience. The other three pilots had less than ten missions between them.

Over the target aircraft were called out at nine o'clock and six o'clock positions, and I radioed the squadron to drop belly tanks. The enemy consisted of about fifty Me-109's and FW-190's. "This'll be interesting," I thought to myself. "Fifty against fifteen P-38's."

We were soon in the thickest battle I had experienced. I found myself firing at an Me-109, got some hits and continued on around. I then noticed I was alone. Later I found out my number two man had trouble dropping his tanks and kept going down 11,000 feet before getting rid of them. Number three and four followed him, leaving me at 22,000 feet attempting to join the rest of the squadron.

I saw an Me-109 making a pass at another flight. I dove down and commenced firing from approximately five hundred yards to one hundred yards, and from thirty degrees to dead astern. I registered fatal hits and saw the enemy burst into flames. I turned toward the squadron again and found myself on the tail of another 109. I fired short bursts, and began to get angry at myself for not registering a fatal hit. Pieces and the canopy flew off the 109 when I myself was hit by another Me-109 behind me.

My right engine was shot out, the instrument panel shattered and the left engine was burning. I was also hit in the shoulder by fragments of a 20mm shell which exploded in the cockpit.

I snapped my airplane into a spin and had to leave it due to the fire. I bailed out and was captured by the enemy shortly afterward. The pilot who shot me down buzzed me a few times on the ground and later visited me in the hospital in Budapest. Through an interpreter he told me that I was not as fortunate as the pilot I was shooting at when he shot me down. He had bailed out and was flying again. He also told me that I was his thirteenth American victory, and that he had been flying Me-109's for six years."

Almost a year in prisons left Colonel Benne with the impression that his 52nd mission was the morning he should have "stood in bed."

Historians have little doubt that the almost incredible bungling of the Me-262 jet decisively assisted the Allies in winning the air war over Europe. The appearance of this revolutionary machine caused consternation among the Allied pilots. With a top speed of well over 500 mph and armed with the lethal punch of four 30mm cannon, the Me-262 was the kind of weapon that has turned the tide in wars of the past.

A comparable example of a lost military opportunity is hard to find. When these magnificent aircraft were placed in the hands of

Germany's great aces, they were a devastating weapon. Tangling with the Me-262 in the greatly inferior Mustang and Thunderbolt called for exceptional skill from the American pilots, many of whom were able to shoot down the jets.

Colonel George F. Ceuleers of Bridgeton, New Jersey, is among the pilots who downed an Me-262 while flying a Mustang. Colonel Ceuleers served with the 364th Fighter Group in the ETO and shot down 10.5 German aircraft. Like many of America's airmen, Colonel Ceuleers is not reluctant to discuss his experiences, and he is naturally proud of his triumph over the Me-262. The authors pieced the story together from combat reports, newspaper accounts and German versions of the incident.

Colonel Ceuleers had already flown a successful mission protecting a B-17 strike against Hamburg. His formation was homebound when Ceuleers spotted a formation of Liberators going in to hammer Hanover. Flying above an overcast, the Libs were having a rough time with eight German jets, which were slashing back and forth through the slow-moving American bombers with little opposition.

While Ceuleers watched, one of the German jets knocked down two of the Liberators on one pass with deadly bursts of its four 30mm cannon. Ceuleers immediately decided to go the aid of the embattled bombers. Disregarding the speed advantage of approximately 150 mph which the jet had over the Mustang, the American flight leader took his four P-51's into position for a head-on attack at 29,000 feet.

After the first successful attack, the victorious 262 broke off the action. The German pilot "poured the coal" to his machine, slanting his fast fighter downward for a hole in the clouds. Ceuleers saw he was being outdistanced, and decided not to try to beat the German for the cloud opening. Instead, he shoved the Mustang's stick forward and led his flight down through the overcast to intercept the jet. The race for the kill was on.

For 250 miles the German and the American raced over the German countryside, the jet marginally faster but the Mustang in the hands of a very determined pilot. The Mustang's manifold pressure shot up to seventy inches, nine inches in excess of the maximum allowed for war emergency power. Ceuleers kept going down. In level flight, he would have done nothing more than inhale the jet's exhaust fumes, but because of the overcast, the German pilot was loath to fly instruments. He played into Ceuleer's hands, for diving combat suited the American perfectly against the sleek German jet.

Because of its laminar flow wing, the Mustang could dive with almost any aircraft. Most World War II wings reached compressibility more quickly than the Mustang's, at which time a bubble developed in the air flowing over the wings. The aircraft would then become unstable and fall out of control.

For twenty minutes the two pilots raced, with Ceuleers slowly gaining. Little did Ceuleers know of the problem facing the German pilot. One of his Jumo 004 engines had failed and now the Mustang had a slight edge in speed and maneuverability. By now the Mustang's Merlin engine was almost leaping off its mountings, but as the chance for the kill came, Ceuleers poured even more power to the tortured engine. Screaming and howling with seventy-five inches of manifold pressure, the Mustang excelled itself for a few brief moments according to Ceuleers.

At five hundred feet over Leipzig, Ceuleers closed the gap. In full view of the startled and bolting citizenry below, the American poured six hundred rounds of heavy machine-gun fire into the jet. Fire belched from the German's right engine. Then the canopy flew off. The enemy pilot pulled his dying aircraft up sharply and released his safety belt, leveling out so that inertia would pop him clear and let him use his chute. Seconds later the Me-262 dived into the ground and exploded in a gout of flame.

Ceuleers eased back on his throttle and gratefully watched the manifold pressure subside. Expecting to find himself alone in enemy territory, he took a quick look around. Right behind him were the Mustangs of his own flight. They had clung to him throughout the long chase at speeds over 500 mph.

Colonel Ceuleers flew 103 combat missions, and now serves with the USAF in Hawaii. He was awarded the DSC, four DFC's, eleven Air Medals and the French Croix de Guerre. Although his victory over the jet was a classic, on another occasion he destroyed four Me-109's in one mission, a notable feat.

Lieutenant Colonel Donald H. Bochkay USAF is another of the American aces who brought down the Me-262 while flying the

Mustang. With 14.83 victories (14 plus .5 plus .33), Bochkay brought down *two* of the fabulous German jets. He is a pilot who believes in the right amount of confidence as a factor vital to success in aerial combat. "Overconfidence is as destructive as no confidence at all" is the way he summarizes his views.

Bochkay evidently brought the right amount of everything into the air on April 18, 1945, when he ran into an Me-262.

We flew deep in enemy territory, our mission being a fighter sweep into Prague, Czechoslovakia. Leaving the Blue Section, I spied an Me-262 climbing up toward the bomber track. I was at 32,000 feet with two flights of P-51D's. The German jet was about 12,000 feet under me, flying at a 90-degree angle when he passed me. I called him out and gave the command to drop tanks. I rolled over and firewalled everything I had, 3,000 rpm and around 70 inches of manifold pressure.

I leveled out on his tail indicating around 500. That would give me a good 150 mph speed edge over him. I ranged him on my K-14 and held off until I was 300 yards behind him. In perfect range, I pulled the trigger. All my shots hit his left jet engine, and about knocked it out of its frame. He split-essed as soon as I hit him and poured full kob to his good engine. Still having speed over the jet, I split-essed right after him. At 18,000 feet we were going straight down when my ship started to porpoise . . . it was hitting terminal velocity, and this was the fastest I'd ever traveled in an aircraft.

The Me-262 didn't leave me, and as we pulled out on the deck, still going flat out, he blew his canopy and started to get out. As he put his hands on the back of his seat, I let him have another full burst of API. The pilot disappeared into the cockpit and at the same time pushed full left rudder. At the speed we were going, his ship couldn't take it. The right wing snapped off, and then the whole tail. The jet exploded in the air before it hit the ground. I flew over the wreckage, rocked my wings and set course for home base.

Lieutenant Colonel Bochkay flew with the 363rd Fighter Squadron, 357th Group in the ETO. He flew 123 combat missions and his victories include Me-109's, Me-110's, FW-190's and two Me-262 jets.

Wartime letters from fighter pilots to their families are often revelatory of fighter-pilot thinking and attitudes. Lieutenant Grant M. Turley of Aripine, Arizona, served with the 78th Fighter Group at Duxford, and shot down six German aircraft before his death in combat. The following excerpts are from a letter Turley wrote to his mother, Mrs. Wilma F. Turley, and his wife, Katherine Ballard Turley, just twenty-five days before the young ace's final mission:

February 10, 1944

I am quite excited, for I finally fired my guns, have been bounced and have done some bouncing all in the same day. The final story was two Me-109's for Lieutenant Turley! We were bounced at 26,000 feet, and I broke (I'm an element leader now) with my wingman and managed to get on the tail of two Me-109's as they made a climbing turn away. They saw us coming and broke for the deck, with us on their tails. I shot one of them going down and then got a couple of short bursts into the other and he crash-landed burning.

Ten days later Turley became Arizona's first World War II ace, and he wrote:

I am tired—had a mission today and shot down my fifth Hun. I am an "ace," so they say. A lot of it has been luck, maybe a little skill. I have dreamed of being an ace, but now that I have succeeded it doesn't seem important any more.

On March 6, 1944, while participating in one of the first daylight missions over Berlin, Turley shot down his seventh German aircraft, only to fall victim to a German airman seconds later. He is buried in the U.S. Military Cemetery, Neuville-en-Condroz, nine miles southwest of Liège, Belgium.

The outstanding combat team of the ETO was undoubtedly the classic Godfrey-Gentile combination, which evoked much historic comment, both Allied and enemy. Captains Don S. Gentile and John T. Godfrey made their historic rendezvous as fighting partners after both had served as fighter pilots with the British forces.

Ohio-born Gentile got into the fray first by joining the RAF in July, 1941. By Pearl Harbor time, he was a Pilot Officer flying combat missions out of England. Transferred to the USAAF in August, 1942, he made his historic connection with Godfrey in the 336th Squadron, 4th Fighter Group.

Canadian-born Godfrey was raised in the United States, and after completing his high school education in Rhode Island, tried to join the USAAF as an aviation cadet. He was rejected. Like many other American aces who were originally rejected by the American forces, or who were washed out during training by misguided instructors, Godfrey headed for Canada. He was commissioned in the RCAF in October of 1942 and was sent to England. Godfrey transferred to the USAAF in April, 1943, and was an ace before his twenty-first birthday.

Like Bong and Lynch of Pacific fame, Gentile and Godfrey would change positions during a battle, taking it in turns to assault the enemy and protect each other's tails. Winston Churchill called them the "Damon and Pythias of the twentieth century," General H. H. "Hap" Arnold praised them as the greatest combat team of the war, and Herman Goering is alleged to have said that he would gladly give two squadrons for their capture.

The two aces were withdrawn from combat just when they were really getting hot, and sent home to stress the value of teamwork to the American people. The two pilots sold war bonds and were separated when Gentile was assigned to Wright-Patterson Air Force Base as a test pilot.

Godfrey returned to Europe, but things were no longer the same. He was shot down and captured by the Germans, an event which purportedly delighted Goering. Gentile was not allowed to return to combat, and was kept testing aircraft until well after the end of the war in which he had scored 19.83 aerial victories.

Called "Captain Courageous" by President Roosevelt, the dark-haired Gentile won the DSC, Silver Star and numerous other American decorations. His foreign awards include Britain's DFC. Like his Pacific counterpart, Richard Bong, Don Gentile was killed in a postwar aircraft accident while testing a Lockheed F-80 Shooting Star.

John Godfrey survived his internment by the Germans and two abortive attempts at escape, in either of which he might easily have been killed. He tried a third time. On this occasion, he made his way to the American lines near Nuremberg in April, 1945. As Major Godfrey he was placed on inactive status in January, 1946, and became a Rhode Island lace manufacturer and breeder of racehorses. He is credited with 16.33 aerial victories.

Before the twin financial charms of oil and ranching captured Lieutenant Colonel Richard E. Turner of Estes Park, Colorado, he was a successful fighter pilot with the 354th Fighter Group. He scored eleven victories over the Germans, but almost became a victory in the first fighter escort to Berlin on March 6, 1944:

The bombers aborted due to weather and a mid-air collision while still short of the target. A gaggle of sixty Me-109's jumped us from five o'clock high, out of the sun, hitting my squadron first. I called for the squadron to break into the Germans and I dropped my combat tanks. My engine quit before I could switch to the main tanks, and as I reached down for the switch, my wingman and the rest of the element thought I had been hit. They left me as my plane dived.

The engine recovered but my speed was low. As I looked around there was no squadron—but there were four Messerschmitts diving at me from five o'clock high. I chopped the throttle, dropped flaps, skidded to the left and almost stalled. The 109's flashed past, barely missing me. I cleaned up the flaps, opened the throttle and dove after them. I caught up with the Germans and as two winged over and split-essed away, I took the nearest of the remaining two and fired from about three hundred yards.

Hits sparkled behind his cockpit and at the left wing root. His ammunition in the left wing exploded and the wing snapped off. Canopy and pilot left the German machine right after the wing.

The second 109 had disappeared—behind me! I broke left, but he stuck, with height, speed and position. Feeling futile, I hesitated, waiting to dive and skid out of his line of fire when he opened up. He must have been out of ammo, because he did a quick wing-over and dove for home without firing. I felt real lucky.

After the war, commanding the 405th Fighter Group at Regensburg, Germany, I met one Kurt Mueller, who believes, as do I after comparing all records, that he was the pilot I shot down on that sixth day of March, 1944.

The top American fighter pilot of the Mediterranean Theater was Major John J. Voll of Goshen, Ohio. With twenty-one aerial kills to his credit it is likely that he could have become America's leading ace with a little additional opportunity. He ran up his twenty-one victories in just fifty-seven missions and seven months—an exceptional record for American combat pilots.

Voll shot down his first enemy plane on June 23, 1944, over Ploesti. A scant five months later, with twenty-one aerial victories, he was on his way back to the United States. He well remembers his last mission on November 16, 1944:

I chased a Ju-88 into a formation of Hun fighters in the Udine area. I got him okay and after five minutes or so of pitched battle, I had shot down two FW-190's, one Me-109, with a 109 and a 190 as probables and two more as damaged. I had all thirteen of them to myself. The confirmed victories gave me the lead in the theater with twenty-one.

To be called "The Whiz" was not an unexpected thing for Major William T. Whisner of the 352nd Group of the 8th Air Force, as it is a nickname he has had most of his life. The truth is, however, that he proved himself to be an absolute whiz, worthy to rank among the all-time great American fighter pilots.

Whisner ran up a string of 15.5 aerial victories in the ETO, and followed these up with 5.5 victories over the MIG-15's in Korea, giving him a total of 21 aerial victories in two wars. He is one of the "magic six" to become an ace in two separate wars.

Whisner is America's seventh jet ace and is unique among airmen in that he holds three DSC's. From his long combat career, The Whiz best remembers an incident over Belgium in January, 1945:

As we taxied out on the ice-covered strip for a New Year's dawn patrol, we became involved in Goering's last big air effort. As we neared takeoff position swarms of FW-190's came out of the east with Me-109 top cover. We leapt off right in the face of the 190's, which were flying at about five hundred feet. The commander, Colonel Meyer, was firing one of them before his gear was re-tracted. He subsequently attributed this feat to me, but since he was first off and first to fire, I am crediting this feat to the right man.

Twelve in number (P-51's), we were soon in a deck-level fight with about fifty enemy aircraft. Thirty seconds after takeoff I was firing into a 190 at one hundred yards range, altitude two hundred feet.

The 190 fell off on the left wing, hit the ground and exploded. I watched this a split second too long, for a 190 put six 20mm cannon shells into me, temporarily spoiling the fun. I shook loose from him and discovered that my only problem was a little oil on my windscreen. There were plenty of Jerries left to shoot at, and in the next half hour I managed to knock down another 190 and two 109's.

All the action took place right over the strip, and the low altitude made the confirmations quick and simple, making the action a fighter pilot's dream. When the action was over, the twelve of us had destroyed twenty-three enemy machines, without loss to ourselves. This was probably one of history's finest dogfights, and it is one which I will never forget.

Successor to Colonel Hubert Zemke in command of the 56th Fighter Group in August, 1944, was Lieutenant Colonel David C. Schilling, America's twelfth-ranking ace with a total of 22.5 German aircraft shot down. During the war, along with pilots like Don Gentile, Bud Mahurin and J. C. Meyer, Schilling got the full glare of publicity.

It is worth recording here that Colonel Schilling is one of the most decorated American fighter pilots, with a full range of awards, both domestic and foreign. The United States awarded him the DSC and one Oak Leaf Cluster, the Silver Star and two Oak Leaf Clusters, the DFC with ten Oak Leaf Clusters, and the Air Medal with nineteen Oak Leaf Clusters. The British DFC, the Belgian Croix de Guerre with Palm, the French Croix de Guerre and the Chilean El Merito are just a few of his foreign awards. He was killed in England in 1956 in an auto accident.

A distinguished American fighter ace who epitomized perhaps more than any other American airman the wartime accords between Britain and the United States was Wing Commander Lance Wade of the Royal Air Force. He was a Texan who exuded the fighting spirit for which his home state is justly famed.

Wade joined the RAF in Canada in April, 1941, and was commissioned Pilot Officer on May 23, 1941. Assigned to the 33rd Fighter Squadron in August, 1941, he entered combat with the Desert Air Force in North Africa shortly afterward.

He shot down twenty-five enemy aircraft in aerial combat and destroyed numerous aircraft on the ground. He was awarded the Distinguished Service Order and the DFC with two bars. Wade has passed into history as one of the leading RAF fighter pilots of World War II with an honored place in RAF annals although he is virtually unknown

today in the United States. His qualities are best summarized in the citation to his DSO, supplied through the courtesy of the Imperial War
Museum:

> Since being awarded a second bar to the Distinguished Flying
> Cross, this officer has continued to lead his squadron in operations
> against the enemy in the North African campaign and during the
> invasion of Sicily and the campaign in Italy. He has destroyed a
> further five enemy aircraft bringing his total victories to at least
> twenty-five enemy aircraft destroyed, and others damaged. An out-
> standing leader and fighter pilot, W/Cdr. Wade's great skill, cour-
> age and devotion to duty have largely contributed to the high effi-
> ciency attained by his squadron.

Wing Commander Wade lost his life over an Allied air base at
Amendola, Italy, in the accidental crash of his Spitfire. He was buried
in the military cemetery at Termoli on January 15, 1944.

Only eleven Americans in the history of aerial warfare shot down
more enemy aircraft than Wade. Like many Americans of World War
I who became aces in the service of the British or French, he never
transferred to the U.S. forces and is consequently omitted from all
official mention in America. Like many other Americans who ran up
substantial scores while in the service of the British or French, John
Malone, Stanley Rosevear and Frederick Libby being typical examples,
Lance Wade ran nowhere in the publicity sweepstakes. This book
should help rectify this and other unfortunate historical oversights.

5

☆ ☆ ☆ ☆ ☆

USAAF Aces of the European Theater of Operations (II)

AMID THE GRIMNESS and tension of war in the air, there was still room for humor and comradeship. Without the contrast and relief provided by these qualities, life in a World War II fighter squadron would have been too taut even for the strongest men. Sometimes when humor came, it was as riotous as the combat had been grim.

Lieutenant Colonel Henry W. Brown of Dallas, Texas, was the leading actor in a humorous chapter of accidents involving himself and his own squadron commander. Brown was the leading ace in the ETO with 17.2 victories when he was shot down over Germany. He made a forced landing in his crippled P-51 in a pasture. What followed was like a scene out of an Elliott White Springs novel or *The Dawn Patrol*.

Brown's squadron commander, Colonel Charles W. Lenfest of Boise, Idaho, himself an ace with five victories, landed his P-51 in the pasture close to Brown's machine. Lenfest's intention was to throw his parachute away, take Brown on his lap and fly the crowded Mustang back to safety. Lady Luck, unfortunately, was "out to lunch."

Lenfest's Mustang dug a wheel deep in the pasture mud while making a turn. Realizing his aircraft was hopelessly mired, Lenfest switched off, jumped out and shook hands with the mortified Brown. Arm in arm the two pilots swaggered off down a lane, waving farewell to the rest of the squadron milling helplessly overhead.

As they left the clearing, the two pilots failed to see Lieutenant Al White coming in low over the treetops, flaps and wheels down and ready for a landing. White landed and turned around at the end of the pasture, looking for his CO and flight leader, now long gone from the scene.

The rest of the squadron was now busily buzzing Lenfest and Brown in an effort to get them to turn back down the lane to the pasture. The two pilots failed to get the message, and Lenfest, infuriated, kept vigorously waving "go home" to his buzzing flock.

Over Al White's radio came the depressed conclusion of his squadron mates. "They don't see you, Al."

Concerned lest he, too, be captured, White gunned his P-51 and joined his buddies overhead for the flight home. Brown and Lenfest walked into internment.

The two-in-one Mustang trick was successfully used when Major Pierce W. McKennon of Clarksville, Arkansas, was shot down near Berlin in March, 1944. McKennon's wingman, Lieutenant George Green of Whittier, California, landed near him. Green dumped out his parachute and dinghy, let McKennon get in first, and then, using him for a cushion, sat in the major's lap and took off. They made it safely home, escorted by the entire 335th Fighter Squadron, and there was a hot time in the unit's Debden mess that night.*

Major McKennon was an ace with twelve aerial victories, and was considered to be one of the best pilots in Colonel Blakeslee's 4th Fighter Group. He was a man determined to be a fighter pilot, despite

* Another Greene, a Captain George B. Greene who is now a Major General in the USAF and currently stationed at HQ USAF in the Pentagon, Washington, D.C., tells a story of piggyback tests with the P-39 (Bell) in the Southwest Pacific. During the Coral Sea battles, it appeared the USAAF troops stationed in New Guinea might have to abandon their fields at a moment's notice, so every mode of possible transportation was investigated. Benny Greene made a test flight with a P-39. Tiny as the craft was, he squeezed a small mechanic into the area just behind the pilot's seat, took another pilot on his lap, and the three took off on a local excursion just to see if it could be done. Of course, all three were sans parachutes, and there wasn't an inch of spare room in the cockpit of that rear-engined pursuit plane. No doubt, Greene's outfit was extremely happy that they did not have to resort to such extreme measures at that time. There is no doubt, however, that the piggyback rescue or evacuation was accomplished in many types of aircraft during World War II. Various reports during World War II indicated that the Germans and the Japanese also resorted to the extreme of carrying two or more people in a single-seater fighter. On two separate occasions, two Japanese were seen to bail out from Zero aircraft during combat.

being washed out at Randolph Field in 1941. He joined the RCAF and switched over to the USAAF in September of 1942. McKennon survived World War II but was killed in 1947 while training a student pilot.

In all there were eleven other Browns beside Henry W. Brown who became American fighter aces in the Second World War. There was a Marine Corps Captain, a Navy Commander, an RCAF Squadron-Leader, and nine USAAF types including Henry W., who was the top-scoring Brown with his 17.2 victories.

Major Sam J. Brown of Tulsa, Oklahoma, was close behind Henry Brown with an ETO score of fifteen aerial victories. Sam Brown flew with the 31st Fighter Group, which boasted thirty-three aces in its ranks and a total of 571 aircraft destroyed. In such distinguished company, Sam Brown won free acknowledgement as the best all-around fighter pilot in the 15th Air Force. He is remembered to this day by those who flew with him for his standout ability to recognize enemy formations. One of his wingmen says of him: "Sam Brown could recognize the Luftwaffe's outfits and formations better than the Germans' own Adolf Galland."

Another highly successful Brown was Major Quince L. Brown of Bristow, Oklahoma. He is credited with 12.33 aerial victories in the ETO, and late in May, 1944, Quince Brown told pilot friends and newspapermen of one of his sorties in these words:

> We were flying into the sun when I spotted an aircraft quite a distance away that looked like a Mustang. I pulled on ahead just to make sure, and by golly, I got a big surprise as I sailed close over him. It was a 109. I pulled up in a steep chandelle, ran back down on the 109 from behind and gave him a few short bursts from about three hundred yards. As I pulled in closer he still didn't try to evade, and I could see my tracer banging into his wings and tail. Suddenly his nose went down and my shots splashed into the cockpit. He spun and burnt fiercely.

When asked what makes a good fighter pilot, Quince Brown was quick with his answer. "Teamwork! Plenty of teamwork!" He was another of the many outstanding combat pilots who was shot down while ground-strafing over Germany. Irate German civilians who captured this officer killed him a few minutes after taking him prisoner. His was a sad end, but rage knows no reason.

As a final statistical factor concerning America's World War II fighter aces named Brown, the twelve men accounted for 100.53 enemy aircraft in aerial combat. There were in addition many ground-destroyed machines.

Philosophers are fond of saying that in life things are not always what they seem. For fighter ace John Carder of Red Oak, Iowa, this proved to be the case when he downed what he thought was a Focke-Wulfe 190 over Germany on February 23, 1944. The aircraft was correctly marked with Luftwaffe insignia, and after some aerial hijinks, Carder triumphed over the 190.

Later in the day when his camera-gun film was processed and evaluated, Carder was shocked to learn from Intelligence that he had shot down not a FW-190 but a Republic P-47 Thunderbolt. Apparently it was a captured U.S. machine that the Germans were trying out in combat.

While it might surprise any World War II combat pilot to learn he had mistaken the sleek, slender FW-190 for the portly Thunderbolt, Carder's efficiency was not impaired by the incident. He shot down five German aircraft before being downed himself on May 12, 1944. On his second try, Carder escaped from prison camp in April, 1945.

Colonel Frank J. "Spot" Collins of Breckenridge, Texas, is among the aces who flew in both the Pacific and European Theaters in World War II. A stocky 190-pounder, Collins is a square-jawed, handsome man who has preserved into middle life the quick-thinking toughness that made him an ace. His nickname derives from a white spot about three inches in diameter in his otherwise black hair.

Still a pilot with the USAF and flying jets today, Colonel Collins could not isolate any one World War II combat incident in his career as standing out above the others. However, a combat report of Collins, written on May 27, 1943, yields the following excerpt:

I turned into an Me-109 and became separated from the rest of my flight in doing so. Just then, four 109's jumped me, but I managed to break under and evade them. I saw an Me-109 on one of the P-40's tails, so I turned onto the German's tail. He saw me, turned into me and as we passed head-on, I was so close above him I could see the Heine sitting in his cockpit looking up at me. He had been shooting at me and me at him. As he went by, I turned sharply onto his tail. For some reason, he did not evade. I gave him a long burst and he arched over slowly into a dive and hit the water.

This was Colonel Collins third aerial victory. After eighty-two combat missions with the 15th Air Force in the Mediterranean area, Collins was sent to the Pacific, where he served with a P-47 outfit near Okinawa.

During a strafing mission, Colonel Collins' Thunderbolt took a Japanese flak hit while howling along just a few feet above the water. Without knowing exactly how it happened, "Spot" recovered consciousness floating in the drink a few hundred yards from the coast of Kyushu. He hid behind a buoy in an attempt to avoid capture by the Japanese, but this effort was to no avail. The Japanese plucked the wounded pilot from the sea and incarcerated him in a bomb shelter without medical attention.

Emaciated and sick, he barely survived to the end of the war. When freed he gradually regained his strength, and he serves today as Commander of the Tactical Air Command's 31st Fighter Wing in Florida.

Colonel Glendon V. Davis of Parma, Idaho, shot down 7.5 German aircraft while flying with the 357th Fighter Group in England. Shot down himself on April 29, 1944, he managed a grand tour of the underground escape route, finally returning to the 357th on September 6, 1944. Colonel Davis tells a story that intimately involves another unknown American pilot. It typifies thousands of instances of one pilot saving the life of another, with the two men going their separate ways and never knowing each other's identity.

In escorting bombers on a mission to Munich in March, 1944, a box of our bombers some half a mile from my four-ship flight of F-51's called out that they were under attack by a large number of German fighters. Upon reaching them, I saw an F-51 from another group dive down from the bombers, followed closely by two Me-109's who were firing and scoring hits on the American machine.

With my flight I dove after them, calling to the F-51 to break, break, break, but he continued his near-vertical dive. At this time my entire flight was diving at full throttle. The last glimpse I got of

my airspeed indicator showed 475 mph. We drew up on our quarry
at approximately 8,000 feet, having started from about 25,000. By
firing and scoring hits at extreme range, I diverted one of the Me-
109's from the hard-pressed F-51.

The pursued American aircraft reached deck level and started a
circle to the left, followed closely by the remaining Me-109. The
other German was holding close above. I joined the circle in the
opposite direction, so as to get a head-on shot at the 109, whereupon
he broke and with his buddy started to retire.

Upon straightening out on their tails, I found my four-ship flight
in perfect formation on me. As I was preparing to fire on the nearer
109, he wobbled, winged over and went into the ground, evidently
as a result of previous hits. I gave the remaining 109 to my wingman, and after a full-throttle chase of some five miles over the
treetops, he shot him down.

This encounter stuck in my mind not just because we got two
enemy aircraft and saved one of our own, but because of the perfect
teamwork of my entire flight. We went through a full-throttle, near-
vertical dive followed by violent maneuvering on the deck, but
were still perfectly in formation at the end.

Colonel (then Captain) Davis was one of the P-51's most enthusiastic admirers, as well he might be after this incident which he relates:

We were climbing back to the bombers after an attack when I
saw five Me-109's coming down through a break in the clouds. We
let them get below us and then bounced them from above. On our
turn into them, my second element cut inside me and went after the
lead three 109's. I singled out the last one and he went for the deck.

While he was looking back at me, his aircraft actually touched
the snow-covered ground, but he pulled it back up and kept going. I
gave him a burst from three hundred yards, and saw strikes. He cut
his engine and began gliding for an open, snow-covered field.

I closed on him, firing all the way, and my bullets riddled his
aircraft. Just as I pulled off to avoid colliding, he exploded. Pieces of
his machine hit the top and leading edge of my right wing, *smashing
it flat.*

I struggled back up to 29,000 feet and came home by myself. I
owe my life to the excellence of American materials and workman-
ship, as the P-51 was a rugged aircraft. When it first was introduced
into World War II it was fast and agile, but its maximum altitude
left much to be desired. The P-51B model, however, could really
make height and this factor meant we finally had an aircraft that
could match either the Me-109 or the FW-190.

FLYING KNIGHT: Above, left, Maj. Richard Bong, flight leader of 5th Air Force "Flying Knights," scored 40 "kills" and won top decoration, the Congressional Medal of Honor. BLACK SHEEP: Above, right, USMC Maj. Gregory "Pappy" Boyington, CO of USMC squadron "Boyington's Black Sheep," which downed 61 planes in two tours of duty. DISTINGUISHED SERVICE CROSS: Below, Capt. Don Gentile, 19.83 victories, Col. Donald Blakeslee, 12.50 victories, congratulate each other after being awarded D.S.C.

RANKING U.S. ACE: Above left, Col. Francis Gabreski flew 1953 combat missions before capture by the Germans, became jet ace in Korea, is top living U.S. ace, with 37½ air victories. SIX IN TWO MINUTES: Above, right, Maj. Fred Christenson, one of the few ETO U.S. pilots to down 6 planes on one mission; did it in two minutes. TOP BRITISH ACE: Below, left, Group Capt. James Johnson, Britain's top ace, with 38 "kills" in World War II. MEDAL OF HONOR: Below, right, USMC Maj. James Swett scored 15½ victories, 7 on one mission, and won Medal of Honor.

TOP NAVY ACE: Above, Capt. David McCampbell, who downed 9 enemy planes and damaged 2 on a single mission, the American record, scored a total of 34 aerial victories. He is top Navy ace and a Congressional Medal of Honor winner. PACIFIC HIGH SCORER: Below, right, USMC Brig. Gen. Joe Foss, who in six weeks of service out of Guadalcanal downed 22 Japanese planes, including 16 Zero fighters.

NAVY AIRMEN: USN Capt. Paul Douglas Buie (center), who scored 9 "kills," with VF-16 pilots.

DOUBLE DECORATION: Above, right, Gen. Vandenberg decorates Col. David Schilling, one of the few to hold two Distinguished Service Crosses, and Col. William Ritchie. GENERAL'S CONFESSION: Below, 4-star Gen. Larry Kuter, reported to have told Jim Brooks, 13-victory ace, he would rather have been an ace than a general officer.

AMERICA'S ACE OF ACES: Brig. Gen. Joe Foss, who won Congressional Medal of Honor, is also ace in civilian life. He is former Governor of North Dakota and Commissioner of American Football League.

→ S.A.C Commander 1969—

DECORATED IN CHINA: Below, USAF Lt. Col. Bruce Holloway being decorated with the Air Medal by Brig. Gen. Claire Chennault in China, February 1943.

SHOWING OFF: Above, P-51 fighters of the 375th Squadron, 361st Fighter Group, based in England, in flight formation on way to target. No. 4 man flies early model P-51. NAVY FIGHTERS IN THE PACIFIC (below).

ADING HOME: Right, Curtiss P-40 "Sue" 51st Fighter Group heads for its home e in India after dropping 500-pound nb on Japanese supply base at Kamaing, ma, 1943. Below, Republic P-47N, long- ge model of Thunderbolt series, de- ed for and used mainly in the Pacific.

JAPANESE "JACK."

MESSERSCHMITT AND ITS DEMISE: Right, Messerschmitt ME-110 in flight. Below, Gun camera of Maj. Everett Stewart's Thunderbolt shows strikes he made on left wing of ME-110 before he stopped shooting to avoid hitting squadron mate Lt. Coleman, who finished the enemy plane.

German Focke-Wulf 190 in flight.

All photographs courtesy of Colonel Raymond F. Toliver

Courage is rightly esteemed a cardinal quality in the making of a fighter ace. A classic instance of a courageous bluff proving as effective as a battery of machine guns comes from the combat experiences of Lieutenant Colonel George A. Doersch of Seymour, Wisconsin.

After 148 combat missions with the 259th Fighter Group flying Thunderbolts, the then Lieutenant Doersch transitioned to the newly arrived Mustangs in May, 1944:

> I was at a rest home for a week while the transition was under way, and consequently had flown the Mustang only twice when I went on my first mission in the new aircraft. Escorting "big friends," we spotted eighteen FW-190's making a formation pass at a box of the bombers, so we positioned ourselves to be on their tails as they came off the first pass.
>
> As we closed on their tails, I hit a 190 and he went down burning. The remaining Germans split-essed to the deck. I attempted to follow, but as I still had some fuel in my fuselage tank [a critical weight and balance factor in the P-51], my aircraft refused to hold my line of sight properly.
>
> I finally closed and damaged another FW-190 and found in firing at him that all my guns except one had jammed. I lost my quarry trying to clear my guns. Being on the deck and now alone, I began looking for my outfit when I saw an Me-109 coming down nearby in a steep dive.
>
> I pulled in on his tail, lined up closely as he leveled out on the deck and pulled my trigger—all my guns were dead. I overshot him, and as I pulled up beside him he saw me and broke away. I pulled up in a gunnery pass at him and made a photographic pass, then another. After the second photographic pass, for some unaccountable reason the German released his canopy and bailed out.
>
> I went home full of my story, eager to tell the boys of two victories, one with guns and one with bluff. But they turned the tables on me when they told me that when I had lined up the first 190, the rest of my flight had broken into another gaggle of fighters. I had unknowingly engaged *all eighteen FW-190's alone*. The Germans, not realizing the limited nature of my attack, had turned and fled.

Now a B-47 pilot with the USAF, Lieutenant Colonel Doersch is credited with 10.5 aerial victories. He flew 419 combat hours in World War II.

The 9th Air Force in Europe produced far fewer aces than the 8th

Air Force, but it must be remembered that the 9th was the Tactical Air Force in Europe, and its pilots probably had more effect in hastening the war's end than those of any other U.S. command. Naturally, the fighter pilots of the 9th lost out in the publicity sweepstakes, but the deadly hazards of low-level flying were their daily business for years.

The troops on the ground are among those who will not forget the pilots of the 9th Air Force, who busily busted up trucks, locomotives, tanks, weapons carriers, armored cars, infantry strongpoints or anything else that needed the attention of their guns, rockets and bombs.

Generally, the pilots of the 9th Air Force did their work with top cover provided by high-flying Spitfires of the RAF or USAAF P-51's. The 9th Air Force proved to be the spawning ground for some of America's most accomplished pilots of fighter aircraft. Some of these men became aces, others did not. A typical case is Lieutenant Colonel John J. Kropenick of Newark, New Jersey.

"Krop" has over seven thousand hours of single-engine jet flying time, about four hundred hours more than his nearest rival and best friend, Lieutenant Colonel Robert C. Tomlinson. He cut his combat teeth with the 9th Air Force, but has only *one* enemy plane to his credit, an Me-109 he caught up with over Europe. Untold hundreds of trucks, parked guns and tanks fell before his guns, but the aerial targets simply did not come his way.

One 9th Air Force luminary who did make his ace ranking is Colonel Paul P. Douglas Jr. of Paragould, Arkansas. Douglas destroyed twenty-seven German planes on the ground and inflicted heavy damage on other ground targets. He proved he could also work "upstairs" by downing seven German aircraft.

Colonel Douglas wears decorations which adequately testify to his success in both major spheres of fighter piloting. He is one of the few Air Force officers to have been awarded the DSC twice. He has to wear two Air Medal ribbons on his tunic to accommodate his six silver Oak Leaf Clusters, each Cluster representing the award of five Air Medals. The British awarded Douglas their DFC in recognition of his services.

Reticent about his bold career, Colonel Douglas would only say: "All the aerial victories were exciting, but even more exciting were the close support missions we flew with the American First and Third Armies and with the British Army."

Another 9th Air Force pilot and one of the most colorful and controversial of America's airmen is Lieutenant Colonel William R. Dunn, of Minneapolis, Minnesota. Although he gained only 1.5 victory credits while serving with the 9th Air Force, Bill Dunn had previously been credited with kills while flying with the 71st (Eagle) Squadron of the RAF. There is a perplexing confusion between Dunn's wartime logbook credits and the credits that were transferred by the RAF to the USAAF when Dunn eventually changed uniforms in June of 1943. His is the case of a frustrated ace, with confirmation lacking in the official records to give him the necessary five confirmed victories.

The records at the present time, both Eagle Squadron and USAAF, credit Dunn with a total of 4.5 confirmed victories, thus keeping him out of the fraternity of aces. What makes Dunn controversial is the volume of contemporary material from his war days crediting him with up to 6.5 victories with the Eagle Squadron alone.

Regardless of the records, Bill Dunn has few equals among America's pilots as a soldier of fortune. His career is like something out of fiction, and his service as a fighter pilot was the crowning glory of his adventurous life. Schoolboys plunging into adventure books imagine themselves living in the kind of gung-ho world that was a reality to Dunn.

In 1934 he joined the U.S. Army as a private in the 4th Infantry, being then only seventeen. Discharged in 1936, he joined the Seaforth Highlanders Regiment of the Canadian Army. He went to England with this unit in April, 1940, and as a ground gunner shot down two Stuka dive-bombers in the Battle of Britain. Few if any American aces can equal this particular feat of Dunn's.

In December of 1940, Dunn requested pilot training when he heard there were openings. He was accepted, trained and commissioned and shot down his first German plane on July 2, 1941. When the majority of the American pilots left the Eagle Squadrons in September, 1942, to transfer to the USAAF, Dunn stayed on with the British for a further nine months.

In June, 1943, Dunn was transferred to the 53rd Fighter Group, 9th Air Force, USAAF, with later assignment to the 406th Fighter Bomber

Group. In the past he has worn four different military uniforms—U.S. Army (Infantry), Seaforth Highlanders (Canadian), Royal Air Force (British) and USAAF. His current service with the USAF makes it five.

He rose to Major in the USAAF during World War II and was promoted to Lieutenant Colonel in 1945. He served in both China and Iran in the postwar years, before being advised in 1949 that he had been passed over twice for promotion to Colonel and was being released from active duty. Undaunted, Dunn immediately joined the Strategic Air Command's 42nd Bomb Squadron as a technical sergeant. As a warrant officer, he is still serving with the USAF today.

One of the claims Dunn has made, which one day may well be proven, is that he was the first American fighter ace of World War II. He claims to have achieved this distinction on July 27, 1941, when he scored his fifth and six aerial victories in a wild battle over France.

Statistically speaking, the validity of his claim hinges on the confirmation of these two victories, which were evidently not regarded as confirmed by the RAF. Through German historical sources with which the authors have contact, it may prove possible to confirm finally not only these victories, but Dunn's unmistakable right to acedom. At the time of writing, this investigation is in process. Whatever the outcome of these efforts, colorful Bill Dunn contributes a lively classic of this encounter—his seventieth and last operation with the Eagle Squadron:

At 7:30 AM we took off from North Weald RAF Station to escort a group of Blenheim bombers for an attack on the steelworks at Lille. I was flying in the Red-Two position on the wing of Squadron Leader Woodhouse. The weather was beautifully clear and the sun showed indications of becoming very bright. This made it hard to see enemy aircraft high above the formation, since they would have the sun at their back, and in our eyes, during an attack on our bombers.

To allow me to see better into this type of sun, I carried a large fragment of a broken beer bottle, which was dark glass, attached to a cord. With this I could peer into the sun and aircraft would stand out almost black. More than once this system allowed me to detect the presence of the enemy in the sun. Sounds foolish, but it worked.

The squadron made rendezvous with the bombers at the appointed time. Other squadrons joined the formation as close cover and we of the Eagle Squadron took our place at high cover, weaving back and forth over the bombers at about 28,000 feet. Paddy Woodhouse and I pulled our Mark V Spitfires out on the right side of the formation where we could observe the bombers, about forty of them, and the complete escort of some one hundred Spitfires.

Far below was the ribbon of the English Channel, the French and British coasts and far to the north, Belgium and Holland. The scene was peaceful, just like a pleasure flight, but at the same moment I thought of scramble sirens wailing on German fighter fields, and pilots like us pounding across aprons to vault into their Me-109's.

Our formation crossed the French coast and we got our usual welcome of black flak bursts, most of it falling behind the bombers and leaving a long trail of dirty, menacing puffs in the sky. We fighter pilots were of no use when flak came up, since we could do nothing to protect the bombers from it. There was nothing for us to do but pull out to one side and let the bombers get the brunt of the shells.

Woodhouse was on the R/T telling everyone to look alive. Enemy fighters would follow the flak, and we all knew it. I was wearing a scarf of light wool that my family had sent me. After a few minutes of rubbernecking, the scarf began to chafe my neck raw, so I tore it off and threw it over the side of the cockpit. I watched it float down for a moment, and noticed we were well into France. We would reach the target in fifteen minutes.

I pulled my piece of beer bottle out of the map case and took a look at the area around the bright glow of the sun. Almost at once I saw a number of black dots climbing high above us. There were about thirty of them, enemy aircraft getting height and position for a bounce out of the sun. They no doubt figured their dive and speed would carry them right through our top cover and into the bomber formation without our getting too good a chance to shoot at them.

On the R/T I called, "Bandits, thirty-plus, one o'clock high." Other pilots saw them and the radio was soon squawking with warnings. Seconds later the Germans came streaming down through our top cover in a full-throttle dive.

They were the "Abbeville Boys," yellow noses and all. As they flashed through our formation on their way to get at the bombers, we poured the coal to our Spits and dove after them, hoping to catch them before they reached their targets. At first, wingmen stayed with their section leaders, but in a few moments all were involved in a milling battle, with each man fighting his own fight.

When Paddy Woodhouse rolled over after a flight of four Messerschmitts, I stuck with him. We fired everything we had, cannons and machine guns, and then Paddy took off after a 109 he had singled out and I started after another. I lost sight of Paddy then. The 109 I was chasing stayed with the other two aircraft of his flight and held a course towards the bombers.

I closed in to about one hundred yards and opened fire again. The deflection was nil, he was directly in front of me, and I could see the white trail of my tracers converging on him. Pieces of his aircraft started to fly off. The cannon shells were getting to him. Then his canopy flew off as he bailed out, the plexiglass structure almost hitting my Spit as it came whipping back in the slipstream.

I swung in on the second German, again firing both cannons and machine guns. Dimly I remembered seeing a painting of a rooster on the fuselage of the first 109 as it rolled over on its pilotless dive. I don't know why I should have remembered the insignia on the enemy aircraft at that particular time, but for some reason it stuck in my mind. I suppose I thought it odd that someone should use a rooster for his personal insignia since roosters are not noted for their flying skill.

Boring in on the second Me-109, I saw my bullets striking home, and a faint whisp of smoke wafted from the German's engine. The smoke suddenly turned into a white hot sheet of flame. He rolled over slowly onto his back and started down at a high rate of speed. Part of its tail broke off, and I last saw it far below me falling with a tumbling motion.

Then a Spit plunged past me at tremendous speed. Both its wings were torn off, leaving just the fuselage and the tail plane. The Spit was burning with a bluish fire reminiscent of a blowtorch. My face was wet with nervous sweat, my hair was soaking under my flying helmet, and I could almost hear myself gasping in my oxygen mask.

The fingers of my right hand felt numb, frozen, and I suddenly realized I was gripping the control column so hard I was cutting off the circulation in the hand. I relaxed my grip, quickly glanced in the rear-vision mirror, and satisfied that there was no German ready to squirt me up the tail, I pulled my Spit around in a tight turn after the third Me-109. This boy had seen me, and he started taking violent evasive action.

I closed to about seventy-five yards, and when the German pulled suddenly up into a steep climb, I got a good burst into his belly. He flicked over into a right turn, running straight across my sights. I fired another burst, and he began to smoke. I glanced into my mirror again and this time saw four Me-109's circling toward my tail.

I turned back to the 109 in front of me, which was now smoking heavily. I decided I had time to give him one more burst before the Germans behind me would be in a position to fire. After the burst I would break away and get to hell out of there.

Just as I pressed the gun button my aircraft lurched violently. My right leg bounced off the rudder bar and I banged my shin against the underside of the instrument panel. A streak of light shot through the cockpit by my hand, and the instruments on the right side of the panel shattered. I took a heavy blow on the head that snapped my face against the gunsight. Everything went black for a moment, but I was not knocked out.

I felt suspended in midair, swinging gently from side to side, like I was bouncing on a big cushion. My eyesight gradually returned, together with the rest of my senses and judgment. The first thing I saw was that the piece of beer bottle was laying against the top of the canopy over my head.

It seemed so damned funny, I laughed. Then I saw the earth spinning up toward me through the canopy, and as my mind cleared still more, I quickly grasped the situation. I righted the Spit, pulled up in a steep climbing turn, and looked behind me for the four 109's. The sky was clear, except for vapor trails far above me.

The altimeter showed six thousand feet, and, checking my compass, I turned onto a course for England, starting a gradual dive for the Channel, visible about fifty miles away. This dive would give me added speed. All I could think of was getting away. My fighting spirit was gone.

It occurred to me to check the Spit for damage. In the mirror I could see that the rudder had been badly shot up. Pieces of metal skin showed bent and jagged on the vertical fin. The tip of the right wing was gone, and a large hole about midwing left me no doubt that the guns on that side were shot out.

Two holes that I could see had penetrated the cockpit. The instruments on the right side of the panel were a jumble of twisted metal and distorted dials. Then I saw blood on the cockpit floor, and checked myself. I pulled my right leg into position to see its condition. It was numb, and I saw that the toe of my flying boot was shot off. While I examined the foot as best I could in the cramped cockpit of the Spitfire, I found my trouser leg was drenched in blood as well. I began to feel sick at my stomach.

Remembering that the Doc had told us to always turn on oxygen full blast if we ever got hit, I did this quickly and sucked in great gulps of the oxygen. It cleared my head a little. I was going to feel my head, but when I felt blood trickling down my neck I decided to let well enough alone. If I was hit badly I felt I would pass out from just knowing the wound was bad.

I weighed my chances of getting back to England. I checked the loss of blood and decided to bail out. I dumped the canopy, released my Sutton harness and started to climb out of the cockpit. Something seemed to tell me I was doing the wrong thing. The engine was running smooth, the wings were still on and the damn thing would still fly. I looked at the ground and thought about the months in prison camp, *if* I survived the parachute jump. I got back into the Spit.

I forgot to refasten the Sutton harness, and I reached the English Channel with nine hundred feet altitude. I sprayed the beach area with the last of my ammunition in the hope that it would discourage enemy ground troops from firing at me with small arms.

When I started out across the water I began to worry about coming down in the Channel, so I started squawking "May Day" on the R/T. Of course, I didn't know if I was being received by anyone. I didn't even know if the radio was shot out or not, but I kept squawking. About halfway across the Channel, two beautiful Spitfires pulled up beside me. The leader waggled his wings for me to follow him, and off we went toward the distant white cliffs of home.

They led me to Hawkenge field near Folkstone, where I made a straight in approach. When I selected "Gear Down" I wondered if they would extend, and if they did extend, would there be any tires. The gear light showed green, I dropped the flaps, and brought the Spit in on the newly mowed turf of the small field.

At one side of the field I saw an ambulance parked and a number of airmen standing nearby. I taxied over to the vehicle and pulled the Idle Cut-Off. Before the prop had stopped an airman climbed up on my wing and shouted in my ear, "You're in the wrong area—if you want fuel and ammo you'll have to taxi over to dispersal." I looked up at him and felt rage rise inside me.

"To hell with fuel and ammo. Goddammit, I've been shot!" He squinted into the cockpit, got a look at my bloody face and helmet, vomited and slid off the wing. They pulled me out of the aircraft and laid me on the grass in the shade of my Spit. Another airman called a Doc, who came running.

The Doc gave me a quick once-over, rolled up my sleeve, gave me a shot. In a few seconds I was so groggy, I didn't know what was going on. All I remember is asking the Doc not to cut off my boot. The boots were beautifully made of black leather and hard to come by. With this request, I passed out.

I awoke in a clean white bed in the Royal Victoria Hospital in Folkstone, my leg in a heavy cast, my head swathed in bandages. I had been there for thirty hours. My wounds were serious. The front part of my right foot had been shot off along with the toe of the boot. A piece of shell had hit me in the right leg and a machine-gun bullet had creased my scalp. I was in the hospital three months before getting a month's leave and reassignment to an OTU as a combat instructor.

Colonel Glenn T. Eagleston, who was born at Farmington, Utah, and calls Huntington Beach, California, his present home, was successful as a fighter pilot in two wars. In World War II he became one of the USAAF's most famous aces in the ETO with a score of 18.5 German aircraft destroyed in ninety-six missions. In nine months of jet combat over Korea, Eagleston shot down two MIG-15's to bring his total to 20.5 enemy aircraft destroyed in aerial combat.

Modest and friendly, "Eagle"—as he is known to his pilot friends —is exasperatingly modest about his combat career. His best day was October 29, 1944, when he shot down three Me-109's when leading the 35th Fighter Group across the Rhine. His account of the action epitomizes his modesty:

We were jumped by one hundred enemy fighters. We shot down twenty-three of them. We lost two Mustangs and only one pilot was killed. I got three 109's that day, which was my best day.

Now posted to the 2478th Air Reserve Sector at Long Beach Airport, California, Eagleston takes an active part in the affairs of the American Fighter Aces' Association, ably assisted in the social side of his duties by his attractive wife, known to the aces' fraternity as "Mrs. Eagle."

Multiple scores in a single aerial battle were not uncommon by 1945, but destroying four enemy machines in one encounter is an exceptional feat for any fighter pilot. Among the few who accomplished it was Lieutenant Colonel Francis R. Gerard of Lyndhurst, New Jersey, to whom it brought the award of the Silver Star. The action is recounted in a wartime letter written by Colonel Gerard:

Magdeburg—the great railway junction southwest of Berlin— has been a prime target for our heavy bombers lately. It's one of the main supply gates for the defense of Berlin.

Every time I read about Magdeburg being bombed again, I think about the mission I flew there. It was back in September, before the Russians began the big drive that has taken them so close to the German capital. Even then . . . long before Berlin was being threatened . . . we were hammering away at this strategic center.

On September 11, 1944, I was one of an escort of fourteen fighters flying protection for a formation of heavy bombers. Just before we reached the initial point of the bomb run, we saw two German fighters below us. We figured they were decoys, sent to draw us away from the bombers, so we ignored them.

Then we saw a formation of a hundred bandits . . . which is what we call German fighters. We dropped our external gas tanks and climbed for the sun.

The German fighters were in perfect formation. They made a wide turn and started to make a dead astern attack on the bombers. I was the first one in and started to spray them, but they wouldn't break formation. I concentrated on one of the 109's and blew him up with one burst. Then another 109 started to peel off toward the bombers, and I gave him a burst—and he went down, too.

About that time we were all in the middle of the bomber formation. They scored heavily on that one pass, shooting down fourteen bombers. In all there were about two hundred heavies in the formation. It was our job to try and keep the Germans from getting any more of them.

The Germans started to re-form for another attack, but we now broke them up. I got in the center and started shooting, but two of them got on my tail. I pulled a high, tight turn and a snap . . . and ended up on their tails. I closed on one and gave him two or three bursts. He blew up in my face. Then I gave the other one a short burst and he blew up, too.

In all, we shot down fifteen of them, and didn't lose any of our fighters.

Colonel Gerard is credited with eight aerial victories, all gained in the ETO in World War II.

The history of the air war is full of incidents where tragedy and comedy have played leading roles in matters of aircraft recognition. Captain George F. Hall of Greenfield, Missouri, and West Palm Beach, Florida, shot down six German aircraft in World War II, but most vividly remembers joining a Luftwaffe fighter formation by mistake:

Lieutenant Lloyd M. Langdon and I were watching a flight of what appeared to be friendly Spitfires. We saw the flight join up with another formation to make a gaggle of fifteen or so. Langdon and I were the only P-47 pilots around, and as we had been warned that Spits were in the area, we surmised that these must be the RAF aircraft.

I closed up on the right-hand corner man, however, and flew close formation on his right wing—for just a few seconds—just long enough to see that big black swastika on his fuselage!

I pulled back and slid in behind him and let him have it. Hits exploded all over him and pieces flew off in all directions. Down he went in flames as I slid over and got the next German in my sights. I pulled the trigger and he pulled up sharply and fell off to the left. Then I fired on another plane and it went down like a falling leaf with smoke pouring out of it.

I fired on a third and a fourth 109 before running out of ammunition, and got strikes on both of them. Langdon was doing okay, too, as he got one which exploded and I saw an object falling off another which he had hit. The object was either the canopy or the pilot bailing out. As we broke away, a flight of P-47's from another group came in.

For several years the Me-109 was the scourge of the skies over Europe. Before the advent of the P-51 Mustang there was no aircraft made which could hold its own against Professor Willy Messerschmitt's remarkable product *functioning in its own home skies*. As a result, Allied pilots had to develop tactics which could compensate for technical disparities. Cool common sense was often the best tactic of all, as illustrated in this story by Major Michael J. Jackson of Plainfield, New Jersey:

On Christmas Day, 1944, Jerry was making every effort to support the Battle of the Bulge. I had my squadron up on a sweep between Bonn and Frankfurt. Ground controller vectored us to a bogie, and while flying at 30,000 near Bonn we spotted numerous Me-109's at about 24,000. I maneuvered to get into the sun, and looking them over, saw they were flying the same battle formation we were flying, three flights of four aircraft each, almost line abreast.

I gave the order to drop tanks, and in a diving turn onto their rear gave instructions that I would take the man on the far end and each of my squadron was to "cue up" on the 109 corresponding to his own position. It was the prettiest sight a fighter pilot could ever wish to see.

Those poor German pilots never knew what hit them. My target blew up in front of me at 150 yards range. My wingman got his, and so on right down that beautiful line. All twelve Me-109's went down in pieces or flames on that one spectacular pass. After having been at the 109's mercy for so long during the war, it was a wonderful feeling to have been able to pull this off.

Major Jackson himself shot down eight German aircraft while flying with the 56th Fighter Group (Zemke's Wolfpack) in the ETO.

Youngest American ace in the ETO was Lieutenant Dale E. Karger of McKees Rock, Pennsylvania, who shot down 7.5 enemy aircraft, five of them before his nineteenth birthday on February 14th, 1944. Lieutenant Karger entered flying school in April, 1943, at eighteen years of age. He tells a memorable story of a brush with an Me-262 jet:

In 1944 after chasing an Me-262 for about fifty miles across Munich, he was leaving me far, far behind with his speed advantage. I was about to lose sight of him when, apparently thinking me long gone, he started a gradual turn to the left. I cut inside the circle, and when still not in range as far as my gunsight was concerned, I fired far ahead of his flight path. I was surprised to see immediate hits. The jet simply rolled over and crashed into some woods. Beside the thrill of downing a jet, this victory was also my fifth, which qualified me as an ace.

Major Wayne L. Lowry of Mason City, Nebraska, an ace credited with eleven aerial victories in the ETO, best recalls his encounter with "Germany's most uncomprehending pilot" whom he whimsically dubs "Mueller" in his story:

I sighted Mueller over Yugoslavia. As usual he was flying with his head up and locked, approximately a mile ahead of a large formation of American planes. [He was probably pacing the formation, giving speed and altitude information to flak units—Authors' note.] He had been there quite a while when I decided to investigate any Jerry who would be so stupid as to continue flying such a suicidal position for so long. I flew up alongside, half expecting it to be an American P-47 or P-51. The pilot looked right at me, not over thirty yards away. It was an Me-109, with the biggest swastika I have ever seen painted on its sides. I dropped back into position about a hundred yards astern, sighted my guns from dead behind and blew plane and pilot out of the sky.

"Mueller" was certainly very determined, but he became one of the eleven German aircraft downed by Major Lowry during his service in the ETO with the 325th Fighter Group of the 15th Air Force.

Top-ranking ace of the State of Missouri in World War II was Captain Raymond H. Littge of Altenburge, with 10.5 aerial victories over the Germans. Littge fought with the 352nd Fighter Group of the 8th Air Force, flying 391 combat hours in 91 missions.

Littge named one of his sons George Preddy Littge after the famous ace George Preddy of the ETO, whose unfortunate end has been recounted earlier in this volume. One of America's best fighter pilots, admired for skills and abilities that were not adequately reflected in his official victory credit total, Littge lost his life on May 20, 1949, near Maupin, Oregon, while flying an F-84 jet.

Prior to his death, Littge had hoped to write a book on his experiences as a fighter pilot. From his notes for this book the following narratives of aerial combat has been excerpted. The first concerns Littge's victory over an Me-262 jet.

We had finished a pass through the bomber formation. There was nothing funny about these jet jobs, but this one was having trouble with his landing gear. It kept dropping down and reminded me of a kid who was running away from someone, and whose pants kept dropping down. He was trying to fight, fly and at the same time keep working his gear up. This factor decreased his speed, and I was able to close and clobber him.

The Littge papers also include this account of a battle with the redoubtable Me-109's:

The tracers that lanced over my left wing told me that I had been singled out by one of the enemy pilots as his opponent. A quick glance at the 109 showed American flags on his canopy, and I quickly went into action—I wasn't about to be the next one to his credit. Sucking the stick back hard into my lap, I turned right. My turn was so tight I blacked out immediately. I gained a thousand feet after rolling out of my turn, and I had lost the Hun that had shot at me.

A Jerry came flashing down in front of me about five hundred yards away. He was in my line of flight, so I gave him a two-second burst. I didn't see any strikes. He'd been almost ninety degrees to me, so the two radii lead I had given him had not been enough.

As I swung again wide, looking for a Hun, I got the biggest thrill of my life. I had a ringside seat at the biggest dogfight I'd ever seen. Aircraft were everywhere. German and American both, spinning, rolling, diving, turning—and flashing where bullets and shells were striking home. A 109 was going down and another one was getting clobbered. One of our Mustangs was hit also and was spiralling earthward with smoke pouring out of it.

Tracers attracted my attention off to the left. A 109 was on the tail of a Mustang, with another Mustang on the tail of the 109 but with no possible chance of shooting him. The 109's 20mm shells were exploding behind the Mustang's tail, just a little out of range. A few more seconds and he would be in range. By the letters on the aircraft I recognized Captain "Tex" Sears and Lieutenant Ross as the pilots of the two Mustangs. Ross was in the one being shot at.

I made a diving pass at the Hun, hoping he would see me and break. He did! My pass was ninety degrees to him. We had him boxed in. If he broke left, I'd be sitting on his tail, and if he broke right, Tex would be on him in a minute.

The German decided to break into Tex and away from me. With altitude on him, I had no trouble in getting behind him. I let go a burst. Just before I fired he broke left and my bullets missed. His turn was very tight, and due to my higher speed he was off for home before I had turned around. His getaway was short-lived.

Tex and Ross were after him and behind him in nothing flat. He pulled the same tactics against them as he had against me and succeeded in getting away for a second time, but momentarily. In getting away from them, he flew directly in front of me. I slid down from above him and stayed there.

Closing on him, I commenced firing in earnest, although a little excited from the previous engagement. My three-second burst clobbered him and started coolant streaming out of his right wing. He decided to hit the deck. I hung on like a leech, firing occasional bursts but not seeing any hits as the chase led down to the deck.

The German pilot was determined to get home, judging by his evasive action. He kicked his aircraft first from one side, then to the other, skidding and sliding like a block of ice on a tin roof. The end came suddenly, as suddenly as the pursuit had begun. After three or four minutes we were eight miles west of Locker Lake. Here he started climbing for all he was worth.

With my higher rate of climb, I found myself directly below, which was *not* the place to be. He was badly hurt, so he probably never saw this advantageous position offered to him two or three times. Together we climbed to about six thousand, where he suddenly leveled off, and his canopy then flew off and came hurtling by my right wing. Then the pilot himself began bailing out. I fired again, holding the trigger down for a long burst. Strikes registered on the prop, fuselage and the wings. His aircraft started spinning and the fight was over. I watched the machine spin downward until it crashed into a railroad marshaling yard in a giant flash of flame and smoke. The pilot and his opened chute were not to be seen. He had no doubt been killed by the rain of bullets that surrounded his ship just before it started to spin.

The 56th Fighter Group shot down 679.5 aircraft in the ETO to lead all American units in this department. The group fought from April 13, 1943, until April 25, 1945, flying 19,391 sorties in this period. They lost 145 aircraft and suffered 150 casualties. The group produced a covey of aces, many of them among the ETO's most famous pilots. Gabreski, Schilling, Zemke, Robert S. Johnson, Gerald W. Johnson, Donovan Smith and "Bud" Mahurin were among the stellar performers passing through the 56th at one time or another.

The "name" value of these pilots and the publicity they commanded often tended to obscure the sometimes brilliant flying feats of other pilots in the 56th with only five, six or seven aerial victories to their credit. One such overlooked ace was Major Robert A. Lamb of Waldrick, New Jersey, who downed seven German aircraft and eventually rose to command the 63rd Squadron of the 56th Group in the ETO. Major Lamb contributes a narrative dealing with the protection of the bomber streams striking at Festung Europa. The scene is the sky above Emden, where, with eight Thunderbolts, Major Lamb's task is to protect a formation of B-17's and B-24's.

The bombers were in serious trouble when we made our rendezvous over Emden. About fifty Me-110's, M-210's and Ju-88's were sitting behind them, out of range of the 50-caliber tail guns, firing rockets into the bomber formations. At first glance it seemed that there were bombers going down everywhere. And sitting above us was a top cover of FW-190's and Me-109's–about 150 aircraft.

I called an attack on the twin-engined jobs, and in crossing over for the attack, two of my men collided in midair and exploded, reducing us to six. The moment we attacked the German twin-engined aircraft, the Germans entire top cover came down on us. We attacked in a rough six-abreast formation, and you could see the crisscross fire from the tail guns of the bombers streaking back past us.

The enemy twin-engined aircraft were in flights of five abreast and they all turned away from our bombers as we came in. I pulled up behind an Me-110 and opened fire at about three hundred yards, seeing hits primarily in the belly and wings. I saw flame break out of the belly as I crossed under. That one was finished.

I then saw a flight of five Me-210's at about eleven o'clock and slightly below. I pulled up gradually and opened up on the center ship. I saw his right engine explode and the right wing crumple. Two crewmen bailed out. Number two was gone.

The remaining four were diving at a steep angle now and it took a little time to get in range. I got another one in my sights and opened up. He veered away and increased his dive angle. I followed. I fired again and as I saw minor hits I ran out of ammunition. At the same instant I noticed we were very low over the water and as I started to pull out the Me-210 dove into the sea. I don't know whether I hit him in a critical spot or whether the pilot failed to see how low he was. In any event, number three was gone.

On return I learned that not only had we pulled the enemy away from our bombers, but also that the six of us had shot down fourteen and all of us got back. That day I was given confirmation of three enemy aircraft destroyed and was awarded the Silver Star.

To be credited with an aerial kill while the defeated enemy pilot was still firing at him is the unusual experience of William H. Lewis of Pasadena, California, now a Colonel in the USAF. He was flying with the 55th Fighter Group at the time of the incident.

The time is December, 1944, with Lewis leading a flight of four P-51's on an escort mission to Berlin:

Enemy aircraft were sighted approaching from south to north at 33,000 feet. There were thirty to forty Me-109's in the formation. I turned my flight to the south to engage the enemy with head-on passes. After the initial pass was made and the enemy formation had broken, I picked one Me-109 which was closest to me and pressed the attack so I could get into firing position.

After a series of turns the Me-109 split-essed and dove for the deck. As my aircraft was closing rapidly, I was able to roll and dive with such speed that upon completion of the roll I was directly behind the German by not more than twenty feet. The dive angle was close to eighty degrees. I fired.

The enemy pilot then reduced all his power with an abrupt throttle movement, and maintained his attitude in the dive. This forced me to choose between breaking off the attack or attempting to regain position by a similar reduction of power and lowering of flaps. I chopped the throttle, at the same time forcing the stick forward to maintain a steep dive attitude.

This maneuver evidently surprised the German, as he continued in front of me at very close range. Thinking I'd outsmarted him, I attempted to pull my nose up slightly to get into position for firing. Just as I did this, he repeated his previous maneuver, and before I could recover from overrunning, he was again behind me.

With air speed close to 500 mph and at an attitude of 75 degrees, I elected to break off the engagement. A severe loss of altitude had occurred, and I thought I was going to have difficulty pulling out of the dive. There was buffeting and severe vibrations, caused mostly by compressibility but helped by his shots hitting my wings and fuselage.

I pulled hard on the stick and noticed that I was blacking out at about 8.5 G's. My wingman called that I had gotten the enemy, so I released pressure and went into a steep turn. I saw the 109 spinning to the ground minus a wing. I believe it is unusual to receive credit for an aerial victory while being shot at by the pilot you defeated.

Colonel Lewis is credited with eight aerial victories in the ETO where he saw his Second World War service.

Colonel John H. Lowell, whose faith in the P-38 was dealt with earlier in this book, became an ace while flying with the 67th Wing's 364th Fighter Group. Colonel Lowell flew his first mission against the Germans on March 4, 1943, on the first fighter escort mission to Germany. He flew two combat tours and is officially credited with 7.5 victories. Now a roofing contractor in Denver, Colorado, Colonel Lowell best remembers a tussle with the redoubtable FW-190's:

Over Berlin we spotted a large gaggle of 190's about to attack. We dropped external tanks and turned into them. I was the first to fire, as I was in the lead, and the lead 190, my target, blew up. All hell broke loose then and every man in my group fired at the enemy that day. I lost two men but we got thirty-three confirmed. My third victory was a long-nosed 190 who took me down to the deck, although I was long ago ready to go home. I ran out of ammo. He was still going strong, and then in a very low pass at me he ran into a tree and blew up.

Colonel Walker M. "Bud" Mahurin of Benton Harbor, Michigan, is considered by the aces themselves to be one of the best combat pilots America has ever produced. No small part of his success is due to his outstanding ability as an air-to-air shot. He is credited with 20.75 aerial victories in the ETO, and one in the PTO. He added 3.5 MIG-15 jets in Korea, bringing his lifetime score to 25.25 kills in two wars.

Mahurin's career has been extensively publicized in the magazines, and during the war years in the popular press. A dashing, handsome man who epitomizes the hell-for-leather fighter pilot of movies, Mahurin could probably have made it in Hollywood as a romantic star had he not been successful as an aerial warrior.

He is an extremely intelligent man, with sharp, clear eyes that had much to do with his career as an ace. He could spot the enemy long before most other pilots, and he was an ardent advocate of tactical surprise in aerial warfare. "Hit 'em before they even know you're there" was one of his combat credos.

One story about Mahurin concerns his eagerness for kills during his race with another leading ace for top scoring honors in the ETO. The two outstanding pilots were flying together, with Mahurin flying as wingman to the other ace. Mahurin spotted a bandit, waited a few seconds and then dove after the German. After waiting several seconds more, an inordinate time lapse under the curcumstances, Mahurin called out the sighting. By this time, he was almost within range of the German and shot the enemy plane down immediately afterwards.

Incensed at Mahurin's infraction of the team rules, his CO was going to try Mahurin by court martial. They both went before a famous USAAF general the next day. The general greeted Mahurin with open arms.

A chill fell over proceedings when the general was informed of the pending trial of the overeager wingman. There was an awkward pause.

"OK, go ahead and try him," said the general to Mahurin's CO. "But you're going to look damned silly, as I just recommended him for the DSC."

As this incident shows, competition for scoring honors was often fierce, but it also served to maintain aggressiveness in the air, a factor that boded no good for the enemy.

Mahurin survived two wars and carved himself a permanent niche in the history of aerial warfare. In recent years, he has devoted much time to writing. His book *Honest John* is an account of his experiences as a prisoner of the North Korean Reds. He also turned his writing talents to good use as the first Publicity Director of the American Fighter Aces' Association.

Major Gilbert M. O'Brien of Charleston, South Carolina, flew sixty-nine combat missions with the 357th Fighter Group out of Boxted, England, and downed seven German aircraft. His most vivid recollection of aerial combat is of himself as the angriest fighter pilot in the ETO for a few brief minutes he will never forget. Escorting bombers, O'Brien's formation was jumped and a number of B-17's were shot down by a gaggle of perhaps thirty 109's and 190's.

Many B-17 crewmen had bailed out and at least three Me-109's were gunning our bomber crewmen while they were hanging in parachutes. This angered me beyond words. I got behind one of these Germans, pulled up to extremely close range and fired a short burst. The German pilot, hit and bleeding profusely, bailed out almost instantly and whipped past a few feet under my starboard wing. The Me-109 blew up in my face.

I immediately executed a wingover, fully intending to shoot the German pilot in his parachute, but instead I spiraled his falling body to the ground. His chute never opened. After seeing this guy actually shooting our people while hanging in parachutes, I felt this was my most satisfying victory.

Colonel Robin Olds USAF describes himself as an "Air Force brat," being the son of the late Major General Robert Olds. With his father in the service, Olds grew up without a real home town. He became a fighter ace in World War II with twelve victories over the Germans. Colonel Olds is married to movie star Ella Raines. Excitement ran high for Olds on August 25, 1944, when as a member of Zemke's group he took part in a wild melee over Germany. In breaking up a formation of 109's, Olds' flight scattered the German aircraft deckward:

I continued down after the gaggle and potted one from behind. Then a Mustang passed under me with one of Hermann's [Hermann Goering's—Aus.] boys hot behind him, so I rolled over to lend a hand. I forgot I was already on the verge of compressibility and didn't have much altitude left. I rolled back level and started to pull out, with the nose shuddering and trying to go steeper. Next my canopy flew off, and I really thought the war was over.

Using trim I managed to pull out right on the deck over a wheat field southwest of Rostock. That took all the starch out of one slightly clanked fighter pilot. I headed home. Looking round to check for damage, I saw the war wasn't over yet. There was an Me-109 about two hundred feet back and fifteen degrees angle off, and Hermann sure had the bit in his teeth.

That prop spinner looked like the Fourth of July and as large as a barrel. I horsed my P-38 into a resemblance of a left break, and immediately high-speed stalled. The thing just didn't want to fly with the canopy and a side panel gone. Hermann immediately overshot, and all I had to do was roll level and squeeze the trigger. It was his turn, and as the pieces flew off his ship, he leaped. This victory was confirmed by a latecomer from the rest of our group and made it three for the day for me.

Major MacArthur Powers of Inwood, Long Island, New York, served with the famed 11th Fighter Group of the RAF and gained 2.5 victories with the British. To these he added 5 more Germans after transfer to the USAAF's 324th Fighter Group of the 9th Air Force. His experiences include being shot down behind German lines in North Africa, with subsequent escape "thanks to one native and three camels."

Major Powers' most memorable experience has tragic overtones:

Over Cape Bon, North Africa, on Palm Sunday, 1943, we jumped some seventy-five enemy aircraft. Within the next five minutes I shot four Ju-52's into the water and added an Me-109 that tried to interrupt my party. We did not know that the Germans were evacuating their families from North Africa, although we subsequently had to assist in burial details, which made it a very hollow victory at best.

Long combat experience and intimate knowledge of the comparative strengths and weaknesses of one's own machine and that of the enemy often provided fighter pilots with exciting experiences. Colonel Carl W. Payne of Columbus, Ohio, flew Spitfires out of England in 1942. He was in the Dieppe raid and the escorting of the first American bombing raids in the ETO. Flying subsequently in the Mediterranean Theater he had many more encounters with the Focke-Wulfe 190, Professor Kurt Tank's answer to the Spitfire. He best remembers the invasion of Sicily:

While patrolling Gila Beach I spotted an FW-190 a few thousand feet above me. We had recently converted to Spitfire VIII's, and I knew that I had him trapped above me. There was no possible way for him to get away as I could out-climb him, out-run him and catch him if he tried to dive through. With this knowledge I caught him and shot him out of the first turn he made, and then watched him spin 14,000 feet and crash. The tables had turned since Dieppe [August 19, 1942] when the FW-190's hammered us and our Spitfires unmercifully, and always from above.

Colonel Payne flew 257 combat missions in World War II, over Europe proper, the Mediterranean area and in the Pacific in 1945. He is credited with seven aerial victories.

Colonel Donovan Smith of Niles, Michigan, was one of the best-known American aces of the ETO and the 56th "Wolfpack" Fighter Group. He was a far finer fighter pilot than his 5.5 victories might suggest, functioning more in the role of leader than spectacular scorer. His most memorable experience conveys something of the whirlwind activity of aerial combat:

We were over Emden on December 11, 1943, with Gabreski leading the 61st Squadron (sixteen P-47's). I was leading Blue Flight. We spotted twenty German fighters down around 28,000 feet, more than a mile below us, maneuvering to attack the bomber streams. As Gabby set the squadron up for the attack, two of the Jugs in my flight collided in a crossover turn. The flash of flame and loud explosion, together with the falling debris, was interpreted by Gabby as an attack by unseen enemy fighters and away we went.

We were in a near-vertical dive, and the sky seemed full of enemy aircraft in seconds. My wingman and I nailed two Me-110's carrying rockets and we damaged a Ju-88 in less time than it takes to tell about it. Aircraft were falling all over the sky.

As I attacked a single Me-110 I glanced over my right shoulder
to see all the cylinders in the radial engine of an FW-190. I broke
off my attack, gave my Jug full throttle and water injection, and
after three climbing left-near-vertical spirals was convinced I had
Baron Richthofen on my tail. Two more turns upward and I had
gained enough to hammer-head back on him and I started head-on
firing passes.

Two more vertical turns and I'd gained another ten degrees or
more, and this time as we passed nearly head-on he kept firing as he
passed me—which was confusing. I thought I'd lost my wingman in
the violent pull-ups. However, on what proved to be the final pass, I
tied the trigger down and saw hits on the "Baron's" cowling. Then I
saw tracers zip past my wingtip and I whirled to see my wingman
pull out from under my tail, where he'd been all the time. The 190
exploded in midair.

Colonel Everett W. Stewart is acknowledged freely by ex-subordi-
nates still serving with the USAF as one of America's greatest fighter
leaders. Hailing from Abilene, Kansas, Colonel Stewart commanded
the 4th Fighter Group at the end of World War II, and his record
includes 7.83 aerial victories gained while fighting with the 352nd,
355th and 4th Fighter Groups. He flew also in the Pacific with the 18th
Fighter Group in the dark days of 1941–1942.

In a letter to his father written from England on March 20, 1944, he
had this to say:

Last Saturday I finally achieved a goal I've had ever since I was a
kid. You probably remember when I used to read a lot of flying aces
magazine stories, etc.? Well, I've always wanted to be a fighter pilot
since then, and if I had to go to war, to be an ace. Saturday I got my
fifth one, an Me-109.

On Thursday I got my fourth, over the target area when four of
us scattered about thirty Me-109's before they could hit the bombers. We were fighting for almost the next two hours. I must have
been in at least ten fights myself, firing at six or more of them. They
were all fairly hard shots and I spent a lot of time watching my tail.
Several times I'd fire at one and then turn around to get at one
coming in from the rear, without seeing what happened to the first
one. I chased the last one all over the foothills and valleys, dodging
houses, trees and light lines. I hit him a few times and then ran him
through a high-tension line. . . . Finis!

No account of ETO fighter aces would be complete without a word concerning "The Hub"—Colonel Hubert Zemke, originally of Missoula, Montana. His name has already appeared many times in this book as the leader of the 56th Group, which has gone into history and legend as the "Wolfpack."

Zemke was the senior Allied officer at Stalag-Luft One at Barth, Germany, when "they stopped the fight" in 1945. He was shot down on December 16, 1944, with 17.75 victories to his credit and an unexcelled record as a leader of fighter formations.

"The Hub" was a professional airman, and attended the U.S. Army's flying school in 1936–1937 at Randolph and Kelly Fields. For two years he commanded his Wolfpack before being assigned in August, 1944, to command of the 479th Fighter Group. Four months later "The Hub" became the unwilling guest of the Germans.

The years have mellowed the erstwhile ramrod of the Wolfpack. Today he speaks of aerial combat as something that seems very far away. "They were all easy," he says, "once I hit them." But a little conversation with old fighter pilots soon finds "The Hub" making wings out of his hands and banking steeply above the bar with the best of them. At these times, something of the fierce energy of the World War II fighter leader reappears, a glimpse of the boldly determined man who used to talk like this:

> A fighter pilot must possess an inner urge to do combat. The will at all times to be offensive will develop into his own tactics. If your enemy is above, never let your speed drop and don't climb, because you'll lose too much speed. If you're attacked on the same level, just remember you can outclimb him. Beware of thin cirrus clouds—the enemy can look down through them but you can't look up through them. Don't go weaving through valleys of cumulus clouds, either with a squadron or by yourself. The enemy can be on your tail before you know it.
>
> When popping down out of a cloud, or up, always do a quick turn and look back. You may have jumped out directly in front of a gun barrel. When attacked by large numbers of enemy aircraft, meet them head-on. In most cases half of them will break and go down. Handle all those remaining in an all-out fight until you're down to one—then take *him* on.
>
> If there are twenty aircraft down below, go screaming down

with full force to pick out the most logical target at the point of firing. Then pull up to a good altitude and develop an attack on one of those remaining enemy pilots who had been shaken out of his helmet by your sudden onslaught.

I stay with the enemy until he is destroyed, I'm out of ammunition, he evades into the clouds, or I'm too low on gas and ammo to continue. When you have your squadron with you and the enemy has so much altitude you never would get up to him, stay below and to the rear of him—he'll be down.

Learn to break at the proper time to make a head-on attack—the enemy doesn't like it. Don't run. That's just what he wants you to do. When caught by the enemy in large force, the best policy is to fight like hell until you can decide what to do. . . ."

With those few words copied from a 1944 peptalk to American pilots under his command, it is time to leave Zemke and the ETO. The skies over Europe provided the bulk of the opportunities in World War II for American fighter pilots to join the fraternity of aces. In those days, the Air Force was part of the Army, and there were those who said that the greatest enemy of the Army was the Navy, and vice versa. It is time to look at the different aerial war fought by the U.S. Navy's fighter aces of World War II.

6

☆ ☆ ☆ ☆ ☆

U.S. Navy Aces of World War II (I)

THE BLOW STRUCK by Japan at Pearl Harbor had as its objective the destruction of the U.S. Pacific Fleet, or at least its temporary reduction to impotence. For this bold stroke, carried out at what was in those times a phenomenal distance from the home islands, the Japanese deserted naval gunfire in favor of naval aviation.

The force, power and effectiveness of this revolutionary blow shocked the opponents of American naval aviation into embarrassed silence. The sheer dynamism of events suddenly elevated naval aviation to a position of primacy in the Pacific war. In a very large measure, the outcome of the whole Pacific conflict turned on which nation would produce the most aircraft carriers—or sink the most of the enemy's.

The stroke that almost drove America to its knees simultaneously provided naval aviation with a stimulus and drive that twenty years of peacetime bumbling could never have equaled. Politicians who had hacked at naval budgets and condemned aircraft carriers in the halls of Congress now insisted that they had "always believed in the aircraft carrier," and joined their colleagues in voting huge appropriations for their construction.

The development of naval fighter planes was immediately seen as a fundamental key to the conquest of the Japanese. When it turned out that the existing Grumman Wildcats were not adequate to cope with the Zero, all the stops were pulled out to get more and better aircraft to the U.S. carrier forces. The magnificent Grumman Hellcat, which first appeared in action in the Marcus Island area in 1943, was one result of this production drive. The rugged and durable Vought Corsair soon followed.

Fighter aviation in the Navy had little tradition on which to draw. Until the Battle of Balikpapan in 1942, the U.S. Navy had not fought even one surface action in the twentieth century, let alone established any combat tradition or experience for its fighter pilots. David Ingalls of World War I was the only U.S. Navy fighter ace at the time of the Pearl Harbor attack, although several other Americans had become aces in the Royal Naval Air Service in the First World War.

By war's end in 1945, after three and a half years of tremendous growth and technical development, the U.S. Navy had 329 new fighter aces to relieve David Ingalls of his solitude. And the oceans of the world had never seen such power as that contained in the mighty U.S. task forces that dominated the Pacific and relentlessly hunted down the last vestiges of Japan's naval power.

The Navy aces fought a different kind of war to their army counterparts. Functioning mainly from aircraft carriers and operating for the most part over the ocean, they faced the problems of exacting navigation and the always-tricky carrier landings in addition to the hazards of confronting the enemy.

The U.S. Navy pilots had to face in their Japanese foes some of the world's most experienced combat pilots. Highly skilled and thoroughly trained, many of the Japanese naval airmen had years of combat experience over China.

The Zero fighter was superior to the equipment initially available to the Americans, and the skill of the Japanese pilots in the early months of the war accentuated this technical superiority. The Japanese machine had a considerable psychological impact on the Americans, who were accustomed to thinking of Japanese technology in terms of the inferior trade goods with which Japan had flooded the world's prewar markets. The Zero provided a rude awakening from this concept.

Aiding the Japanese pilots in the first period of the Pacific war was the tide of victory on which they rode. Japanese military and naval power had sprawled across the Pacific, crushing all resistance in what seemed like an unstoppable drive for victory. The brunt of the battle in these grim early days was borne by a relatively small group of professional U.S. Navy pilots. From their ranks came the greatest naval fighter pilot of all time—Captain David McCampbell.

An Annapolis-trained Navy professional (class of '33), McCampbell spent a brief time out of the service in the middle thirties before returning to become a naval aviator at Pensacola in 1938. He served with both the Pacific and Atlantic Fleets aboard the famous carriers *Wasp, Hornet* and *Essex*.

The bulk of McCampbell's combat was with Air Group 15, and his score of thirty-four enemy aircraft shot down is in some ways hardly an adequate testimony of his qualities and skill, even though no other naval fighter pilot came near his score. He was a superb shot, a brilliant leader and a top tactician.

He holds the American record for the largest number of kills on a single mission, with nine confirmed and two probables on October 24, 1944. Today, Captain McCampbell is the leading Navy ace of all the wars, the top living Navy ace, and the number two living American ace, but his nine confirmed kills on one mission is a feat unequaled by any other American pilot, living or dead, Army, Navy or Air Force.

This spectacular mission is also the most memorable combat experience of the distinguished Captain McCampbell:

Indubitably, the most exciting action I had in combat occurred during the battles of Leyte Gulf in the Pacific. On my first flight on the morning of October 24, 1944, I was launched from the U.S.S. *Essex* with a group of seven Grumman Hellcats to intercept an incoming raid of a hundred-odd Japs. This was the second and last time I was to take part in a "Fighter Scramble," primarily because my job as Air Group Commander did not normally demand that I engage in this type of combat. Also, after the action, our Admiral said to me, "It's all right this time, but don't let it happen again."

We intercepted the raid at a distance of about twenty miles from the task group. This incident met the highest expectations of my fondest hopes and dreams of favored combat conditions. Due to my experience in the previous four months of combat, plus the luck of the Irish, I was able to exploit the situation. Without attempting to describe the action in detail, suffice it to say that I just did what came naturally to one who had spent many years training for just such an occasion.

My wingman and I accounted for fifteen definitely destroyed. I was credited with nine shot down and two probables. Not a single plane got through to attack our ships.

After following the decimated formation nearly all the way to Manila, we returned to the vicinity of the task group, exhausted of ammunition and near fuel-exhaustion, to witness the agonized maneuvering of our ships under attack by a second raid, which caused mortal damage to the U.S.S. *Princeton.* I landed aboard the *Langley*, since it had the only clear deck in the task group that could take me, and I had barely sufficient gas to taxi out of the arresting gear.

When the final tally was in, the small flight of seven planes I had led were credited with twenty-seven enemy planes destroyed and an additional eight planes probably destroyed. We had only superficial damage, largely as a result of flying through the debris of exploding enemy planes.

In addition to the Congressional Medal of Honor, Captain Mc-Campbell was awarded the Navy Cross, the Silver Star, the Legion of Merit, the DSC and the Air Medal.

Some units of the U.S. Navy did not split or share victory credits. Through a gentleman's agreement, the victory was credited to the pilot among the several destroying the enemy machine who had the least number of kills.

Frequently, a leader and his wingman would both fire at a target, and as in the case of McCampbell on several occasions there was doubt as to who actually knocked the enemy down. McCampbell often gave the victory credit to his wingman, and bore a reputation for generosity in this regard.

Many other leading U.S. Navy aces followed this practice, since it proved to be a morale-booster for combat pilots who sometimes did not get to shoot at the enemy at all on many operations. Had Mc-Campbell not been such a team man, it is certain his score would have been much higher.

Commanding VF-16 aboard the U.S.S. *Lexington* was Captain Paul D. Buie of Nashville, Georgia, an ace with nine confirmed victories and the following standout memory of combat in the Pacific:

On November 23 and 24, 1944, the U.S.S. *Lexington* was part of a carrier task group covering the invasion of Tarawa in the

Gilbert Islands. The *Lexington* was operating between Tarawa and Mille to prevent Japanese air interference with landing operations.

About noon on the twenty-third, the *Lexington* radar controller vectored my twelve-plane Combat Air Patrol to a fighter pilot's dream position four thousand feet above and up-sun of a twenty-one-plane parade formation of Zekes. The position was perfect for coordinated high-side and overhead attack. We are sure we got seventeen Zekes and we think we got all twenty-one of them.

Action was initiated at 23,000 feet and carried down to 5,000 feet chasing stragglers. In this action, Ralph Hanks bagged five Zekes.

Same time, same place, next day the twenty-fourth, my twelve-plane formation was again on CAP and vectored to intercept another Jap flight of twenty Zekes and two Bettys. This time the CIC misjudged altitude of the enemy, and action was begun with Jap fighters having a 2,000-foot advantage. We met, but could not prevent the Japs' first firing pass, but they never got another chance.

Action began at 23,000 feet, carried up to 28,000 and then worked down to about 5,000. In this action we got thirteen for sure and think we bagged nineteen. We lost no planes on the twenty-third, and one on the Japs' first firing pass on the twenty-fourth for a certain ratio of thirty to one in the two days of fighting.

Lieutenant Richard L. Bertelson called the U.S.S. *Cabot* home in 1944–1945 while reaching his ace ranking with five aerial victories. Hailing from Minneapolis, Minnesota, Bertelson has one special recollection of aerial combat:

Ten of us were striking an airfield on a small island north of Okinawa in April of 1945. We had just recovered from a run, and as my leader and I were top cover, I looked back and then up into the sun. There must have been at least thirty Zeros pouring down on us. The lead Zero was opening up on my section leader, so I swung into him, fired, blew him up and the dogfight started.

After a wild melee in which I was lucky enough to shoot down two more, the Nips had all been shot down or had made off.

Lieutenant Bertelson flew eighty-eight missions in World War II.

The Pacific war had its share of oddities, among them a novel kill scored by Lieutenant Commander Roger A. Wolf of Fort Collins,

Colorado. He recorded a notable first for the Navy by using his hulking Coronado patrol bomber as a fighter.

Returning from a mission, Wolf looked down and spotted a Jap Betty bomber cruising serenely along about two hundred feet above the ocean. Wolf eased his lumbering machine into a stern chase position on the Betty. The Coronado's guns roared and the Betty, aflame from wingtip to wingtip, cartwheeled into the ocean in a spectacular kaleidoscope of steam, spray, smoke and debris.

Commander Wolf survived World War II, but was killed on October 1, 1955 in the crash of a jet fighter while taking off at El Paso, Texas.

Commander Hugh N. Batten of Huntington, West Virginia, is credited with seven aerial victories in the Second World War. His most vivid combat memory is of chasing Zeros in the murk near Okinawa, during his service aboard the U.S.S. *Essex:*

On April 16, 1945, near Okinawa, while on CAP we intercepted nine Zeros in low visibility. After the lead section of our flight attacked, I took my section in and my wingman and me each knocked down a Zeke. First section lost contact due to the restricted weather, but they could see planes burning and falling in the murk. By the time they would reach the spot, we would then be far enough away that they could not see us. The first section confirmed seven kills for us.

My plane was shot up a little, and badly damaged when I flew through the blast of an exploding Zeke. I had four victories and my wingman three. Then on the way home we spotted a Zeke down low. Diving down I pulled the trigger—only to find I had just two shots left. I pulled aside and my wingman made the kill to even the score at four Zekes each. All the victories were further confirmed by my gun-camera film. My wingman was Lieutenant Commander Samuel J. Brocato, and we both got the Navy Cross for this mission.

This same aerial battle stuck prominently in the memory of Batten's wingman, Sam Brocato, who also ended World War II with seven confirmed aerial victories:

We were intercepting a nine-plane flight of Zeros, each of which was carrying a 500-pound bomb externally. We approached undetected from astern and splashed the four trailing Zekes before the others knew we were there. The remaining Zekes jettisoned their bombs and joined battle.

The section maintained its integrity during the chase which followed through flipper turns, loops and Immelmanns and in and out of the overcast. During one maneuver we looped up into the overcast to shake two Zeros from our tail and emerged diving at the bottom of the loop to find ourselves on the tails of the Zekes. The Japanese pilots had unintentionally pulled their loop tighter and inside ours. By shifting from offensive to defensive tactics as the situation demanded, and containing the dogfight in a localized area, we were able to destroy four more Zeros. The ninth Zeke either escaped into the clouds or fell victim to a large flight of Corsairs that came on the scene. Batten and I each destroyed four Zeros.

Lieutenant Commander Norman R. Berree scored nine aerial kills in World War II, and was present at the historic "Marianas Turkey Shoot." His recollection of this encounter in June, 1944, crams a lot of action into a few telegraphic words:

Eight of us in Hellcats intercepted mucho Jap aircraft. Made an overhead run on a Judy, exploding it at close range. Flew through the explosion, was able to knock down two other Zekes before my ammo was expended.

Having a new pilot on his first combat operation for a wingman often caused experienced pilots some apprehension. Captain John Blackburn found that he had no cause to worry about his neophyte wingman in the combat he remembers best:

We were flying high cover over a dive-bombing strike at Rabual in February of 1944. I led a four-plane flight of Corsairs which got seven kills over Zekes and Hamps, and broke up a significant portion of the opposition to the bombing strike. The bombers were unharmed and there was no damage to any of our fighters. My four kills were seen by my wingman—a pilot on his first combat mission.

Captain Blackburn is credited with eleven aerial kills in World War II.

That a Pennsylvania mountain boy can make good as a Navy fighter pilot is attested to by the career of Lieutenant Commander

Foster J. Blair of Stroudsburg, Pennsylvania. Blair downed five planes while fighting in the Pacific with numerous units, including VF5 and UC39, aboard such well-known carriers as the *Saratoga, Independence, Belleau Wood* and others.

> As leader of a section of four Wildcats during the invasion of Attu [May, 1943] we sunk a Jap landing barge on one pass with our 50-caliber guns. It was loaded with about ninety Japs who were going to land behind our troops on the east arm of Holtz Bay. I feel this contributed to the saving of more U.S. troops, and was therefore more memorable to me than any of my individual victories.

Commander Paul J. Bruneau is known among the fraternity of U.S. aces for the novel means by which he became an ace. At the controls of a ponderous patrol bomber he shot down five Japanese fighters while serving with the 7th Fleet. These amazing victories required a wealth of airmanship, yet Bruneau does not discuss them today as anything memorable or remarkable. He best recollects one of his victories near Truk:

> While attacking a Jap merchant ship escorted by two gunboats fifteen miles east of Truk, I was taken under attack by four Zekes. The attack lasted about twenty minutes, during which one of the Zeros was shot down. My aircraft was moderately damaged, and one of my crew members was severely wounded, but there was no difficulty in returning the 650 miles to Green Island.

Anyone with even a fleeting knowledge of aerial combat is aware of the sitting duck target that a patrol bomber represents to a cannon-armed fighter, let alone four fighters. Paul Bruneau is one of America's most unusual fighter aces.

When Lieutenant Johnnie J. Bridges of Shelby, North Carolina, took his gear aboard the U.S.S. *Saratoga* he little realized that he would return from the Pacific Theater as a Navy ace, with six confirmed victories to his credit. He best remembers an air battle on December 15, 1944, when his division was flying high cover for an attack on Manila harbor:

We were at 17,000 feet when sixteen Oscars came out of the sun. For several passes, during which the advantage was with the Japs, we held our own, but we expected the division below us to come and help. They'd lost us. We were operating in sections and were executing a big Lufbery circle for defense, working our way toward a big cloud east of Manila.

One Oscar got anxious and joined the circle to get in a shot, but was quickly hit himself and dropped away belching smoke. We were too busy to confirm whether he crashed or not. Slowly we inched our way to the cover of the cloud. Credit for bringing us back, and with us the photos we had taken of the Manila raid, goes to Lieutenant (j.g.) Robert S. Barton of Washington, D.C., who was killed a few days later. This was the best and most exciting battle of my career, even though there were no kills confirmed.

One of the hard-case pilots of the American Volunteer Group in China was Lieutenant Commander Edwin S. Conants. At least, that is the name he took when he joined the Flying Tigers. Transferred to the Navy later, Conants ran into trouble when his ace qualification was published, and the Navy began looking for his name in its records. His real name was, and is, John Francis Perry, but the Navy decided in 1945 after straightening the mess out, to let Perry stay in the books as Conants. He is credited with six confirmed victories.

The U.S. Navy came back from near extinction in the Pacific in 1941 to the point where day after day U.S. Navy planes swept over Japan proper. Such an assault on the enemy's home skies made a vivid impression on Commander Robert C. Coats, an ace with 9.5 confirmed kills against the Japanese:

My division was launched from the Hornet with a flight of about sixty F6F/F4U fighter-bombers to deliver 500-pound bombs and rockets against the Kanoye airfield complex in the Kagoshima Bay area. This was the final daylight launch of the day.

The flight proceeded through broken clouds and below a solid overcast for about 200 miles to the target area, where the lower overcast became solid with a base about 8,000 solid through to about 12,000 feet. The flight initiated attack on a time estimate and in rebuttal of a heavy flak concentration.

My division was composed of three F6F's, each loaded with six 50-caliber machine guns and one 500-pound general purpose bomb. My number four man was an airborne dud and did not accompany the flight. Just prior to following in the attack, my number three man tallyhoed a bogey, and we broke off to attack the airborne enemy. The number three man initiated the attack, obtained strikes on the enemy's outer wing panel and turned the enemy machine into my section.

It was a George, and my wingman and I got strikes in the fuselage and engine section, and started him smoking and then burning as he dived into the overcast. We did not follow as the number three man tallyhoed a second Jap plane. We stayed in this clear area between the two overcast layers and fired on about ten enemy aircraft, all singles.

Undoubtedly, they had evacuated the lower area because of our heavy strike on the Kanoye complex. After exhausting the enemy above the overcast, we dived through to deliver our bombs. In the dive, we saw a flight of five Zekes, joined in the traffic pattern around Kanoye West.

We dived into them, but at the speed and angle of attack could not stay with them for other than short bursts. We regrouped, and then number three man again spotted a bogey, a Tony, north of the field. He attacked and followed him down for a sure kill.

We proceeded to Kanoye East and dropped our bombs, my wingman and section leader making this run sans ammo. I ran out of ammo on the final part of the run. Despite two hits sustained on this run my wingman was able to continue back with us, and at last light we turned back for a night landing aboard the *Hornet*. We had scored damaging hits on every enemy we fired on, and had all of them at least smoking. Because they dived into the overcast, we could not claim definite kills.

What made this encounter memorable was the manner in which my wingman, then Lieutenant (j.g) G. J. Foster, and my section leader, then Lieutenant (j.g.) W. T. Colvin, so completely and perfectly executed this mission. They were rookies when launched from the *Hornet,* but returned as veterans.

In the same vein, the first fighter sweep over Tokyo etched itself indelibly in the mind of Henry K. Champion, of Fighting Squadron 9 aboard the U.S.S. *Essex* and U.S.S *Yorktown:*

I was on the first fighter sweep over Tokyo at daybreak on February 16, 1945. We were the first fighters to invade Japan proper and our mission was to destroy enemy aircraft in support of the pending Iwo Jima landings.

The sky in the sector to which I was assigned was jumping with

Japanese planes of all types. There were at least fifty of their machines and a similar number of Hellcats in this one little ball of air, all locked in deadly combat. With my wingman I shot down the first Jap we came to, and later I exploded another in midair. . . .

Henry Champion ended the war with five victories over the Japanese to his credit. He was also a prolific destroyer of aircraft on the ground, in strikes that he asserts were far more dangerous than the air-to-air combat that made him an ace.

Even the most enthusiastic advocates of air power in the prewar years were skeptical about the value of naval aviation. The tendency was to write down the aircraft carrier as a vulnerable and clumsy weapons system of dubious value. These concepts were a far cry from the mighty sweeps of Navy fighters, 1,200 at a time, that drummed in over Japan in the last days of World War II.

This setting provides the most vivid combat memory of Lieutenant Robert A. Clark, of Hartford, Connecticut, who is credited with seven aerial victories against the Japanese. His story is a classic of its kind:

At 0700 March 14, 1945, I was flying wing on Lieutenant Charles Weiss as part of a twenty-plane Hellcat sweep over airfields in the vicinity of Kure, Japan. The sweep was only a small part of a vast attack on the Kure Naval Base that day, with over 1,200 carrier-based aircraft involved. Our job was to keep enemy aircraft from rising against the dive-bombers and torpedo planes headed for the basins and anchorage to destroy what was left of the Jap fleet.

It was a bright, cold morning and as we approached the Shikoku coast, we flew over snow-covered ground. I remember Mt. Fuji being visible far away, and as we flew in close formation at thirteen thousand feet, we took in the beauty of the scene. We also thought of the hail of flak we would have to face in attacking the three airfields assigned as our targets.

The idea of vigorous aerial opposition didn't occur to us because of the repeatedly poor showing of the Japanese in meeting previous attacks. We figured that with the number of planes we had in the air this morning, they probably wouldn't even show a head.

But just a few minutes later, crossing the coastline over Shikoku, and with our tactical radio channels silent, two flights of about thirty-five planes each approached us on the same level from twelve o'clock. We paid them no special attention—until they pounced on us like hawks. Then Charlie himself yelled into the mike, "Hey, fer cats' sakes! Those aren't sixes [F6F's], *they're Japs!* Everybody weave! Weave! ... *Weave!*"

The divisions broke off to meet the attack, and just as Charlie turned tightly in a dive to the right, two Japanese fighters came up in a sweeping turn to meet us head-on. They were flying in tight section, firing as they came.

In a split second, Charlie was gone from in front of me, and I bent around in a tight-G turn to the left, looking for the rest of the Jap planes. At that moment, a Zeke came right across my path from left to right, in a climb, and I punched off a mad burst at him, twisting to hold the sight on him as he passed.

His canopy shattered as he went by about a thousand feet away, and he started to burn just behind the engine. He rolled off in a steep spiral, and I inverted to follow him down, but the whole plane was ablaze now. Just as I was completing my roll-out I heard a loud bang in the wing section of my own plane. I didn't bother to check what it was, but snapped into a split-ess and dove for the deck.

I pulled back up in a tight recovery and nearly blacked out from the high-G, suddenly finding myself at 13,000 feet again. I sneaked a quick look at the wing and saw a hole near the tip ... not big enough to worry about.

Just then I caught another Zeke maneuvering in lazy turns in front of me, and as he zigzagged past the sight I started firing on him. One of his landing-gear wheels came down and he dropped his flaps on me. I had to chop my throttle to practically nothing to stay with him ... firing all the time. Pieces flew off his plane and zipped past me, and just as I overran him, his whole plane was engulfed in a ball of fire.

By now the radio was a scrambled jabber of pilots screeching for help and yelling advice to each other. I noticed about three thousand feet above us a circle of Jap planes apparently loafing through the fight, but I soon saw their game. They'd formed a Lufbery circle World War I style, and were waiting until a Hellcat got on some Jap's tail. Then they'd jump him in section and shoot him down, and return to the upper circle for another crack at "Glumman airplane."

This tactic worked, because we lost eight of the twenty Hellcats in that fight. One Hellcat went screaming by me in a plunging dive with his belly tank on fire. Someone was yelling on the radio, "Drop it! For God's sake, drop it—yer on fire!" The sky was a flaming kaleidoscope of burning airplanes, flashing insignia and lacing tracer. Four or five chutes floated gently downward.

The entire Hellcat flight had been broken up by the Jap attack, and the fight had become a series of individual duels over a wide area of the sky. Out of ammo and without a partner, I noticed a Tony trailing me. I lunged for the coast and the task force, knowing that the Tony was only good for 330 knots at best. I made a long, flat, running dash at near max speed and lost him after a few minutes.

After getting back to the *Hornet*, we rendezvoused the survivors of our ill-fated sweep. We had lost eight. We had accounted for twenty-one Japanese aircraft, and also discovered that our dive-bombers and torpedo planes had excellent success at the Kure Base with minimum losses. Charlie had parachuted and was taken prisoner by the Japanese, as were several others.

Five aerial victories in one mission came the way of Lieutenant Commander Kenneth J. Dahms of Winnebago, Minnesota. For this pilot it was the "Okinawa Turkey Shoot," as he succinctly records: "Twelve of us tangled with forty-seven Japs . . . we shot them all down." An average of four kills per U.S. pilot in one combat encounter is good in any league. Commander Dahm finished the war with 7.5 victories credited.

Lieutenant Commander John W. Dear, while an ace with 7.5 aerial kills to his credit, is more noted for his unusual ability at destroying Japanese aircraft on the ground. The unofficial records kept of this activity attribute fifty-two ground kills to Dear, but nightfighting provided him with an unforgettable experience:

On July 4, 1944, at 0030 I was part of a five-pilot nightfighter unit attached to the U.S.S. *Hornet*, which had just participated in the occupation of the Marianas. Admiral Marc Mitscher ordered Carrier Division Five, which included the *Hornet*, to go north and make a sneak attack on Chi Chi Jima, a sister island to Iwo Jima in the Bonin Group. Admiral "Jocko" Clark relished this assignment, because the islands had been untouched up to this time.

Two nightfighters, Lieutenant F. L. Dungan and myself, were assigned the job of going in on the islands the night before for the purpose of drawing fire and locating gun positions, keeping the Japs awake and nervous, and locating and identifying any ships there for the bombers due to strike shortly after dawn. It was not thought that any planes were stationed on the Japanese-held island.

Buck Dungan and I were launched by catapult at 0030 and flew blacked-out formation until we were near the target. Then we separated to make sector search with radar for ships that might be in the vicinity. There were none.

Buck beat me back to the island, and had already started his run to draw fire . . . and *did he draw it!* I never saw more tracer ammunition erupt from one concentrated spot before or since. Fortunately, those Japs had no electronic aiming devices, so they were firing in a pattern hoping that we would fly into a projectile. We made scores of runs but were not touched.

In the predawn light around 0430 I spotted ships streaming out of the harbor by the dozens. One of these was a destroyer, off to one side of the main force and somewhat isolated. I decided to use the last of my two 500-pound bombs on it.

I made a glide-run from about eight thousand feet, pulling up at about two hundred feet . . . and missed by about fifty feet. As I pulled up, Buck let out a yell for help. He had three planes on his tail. After spotting him, I started a frantic climb up to meet him. He had them, all right (or vice versa), and he was trailing them behind him in an "S" pattern like a kite tail. They were Zekes on floats and while they were over twice as maneuverable as our F6F's, they had only small guns.

Buck brought them head-on toward me, and evidently caught them by surprise. I knocked off two of them almost as fast as you can say "one . . . two." The third turned too quickly for a shot, but Buck got him on the way back. In the next furious half hour, the air seemed saturated with little float planes. Buck downed four of them, and I got one more in the air and one on the water when he tried to run for cover in a secluded inlet. The Jap ack-ack knocked down one of their own aircraft as well while Buck and I were chasing it.

As the sun began to rise, the air cleared magically, and we thought we had routed them completely. We went about the business of charting the ships that were pouring from the harbor. While I was intent on this, a flash went by my canopy. I swung around to look, and there was a Jap not more than one hundred feet behind me filling me full of 6.6 bullets. Before I could elude him in a vertical dive, he had shot out my hydraulic system, radio, gun chargers and had punctured my oil line.

Sheer instinct, I guess, told me how to get back to the fleet eighty miles away, but I got there. Because of the urgency of the situation I had to land aboard the *Yorktown*—the only carrier in a position to land me immediately. As soon as I hit the deck my engine froze from lack of oil.

Buck got nailed the same way, in an almost identical experience with another Jap, and landed with a bullet in his shoulder.

In numerous experiences related already in this book, aggressiveness proved to be one of the fighter ace's greatest psychological weapons. From running with the Japs in hot pursuit, Lieutenant Eugene Valencia, USN, dramatically turned the tables on his foes by turning directly into them. Six Zekes chased Valencia in his Hellcat for miles and miles. Although the Japanese machines were fast enough to keep up with Valencia, they could not hit him.

Valencia suddenly turned around and drove his Hellcat furiously into the Jap formation. Three Zekes exploded in midair before the American's fire. The dramatic change of odds and Valencia's obvious determination to take on the rest of them completely demoralized the remaining three Jap pilots. They bolted in terror from the lone Hellcat.

Valencia emerged from World War II as an ace with twenty-three aerial victories. Still dark-haired and handsome today, he has made considerable efforts to collect and preserve valuable historical material pertaining to aerial combat. Valencia is a vice president of the American Fighter Aces' Association. We will meet him again later.

A flight commander in Fighting Squadron 5 aboard the U.S.S. *Yorktown*, Lieutenant Commander Robert W. Duncan of Marion, Illinois, finished World War II with seven aerial victories. His combat report after an attack on Truk tells of a wild melee with the redoubtable Zeros:

I spotted about ten Zekes coming at us out of the sun from about twenty thousand feet. We began at fourteen thousand. My section and Merrill's began to weave. One Zeke started an approach at me; he was coming in from about ten o'clock with good position for a high-side run, but instead he elected to flip over on his back and approach upside down. Immediately I turned in and under him where he couldn't pull through me.

He managed to hit Burnett's plane aft of the cockpit and shot away a piece of his elevator. As the Zeke passed over us I turned toward him and caught him as he recovered with a long burst at four o'clock low. He began to burn. Another Zeke recovered right then almost in front of me. . . . I got off a tail shot, but missed.

This Zeke then turned back toward me and as he passed, I turned, got on his tail with a short burst and set him on fire. Now a Zeke was trying to get on *my* tail from eight o'clock above, but I turned into him and we began several violent scissors maneuvers toward each other. He fired short bursts at me twice, but was behind each time. He then decided to break off and forget the whole thing, and started to glide towards some clouds at four thousand feet.

I caught him at eight thousand, however, and closed fast, firing as I came. He burst into flames as I overran. I blacked out when I pulled up, and then I climbed to 8,000 again, where yet another Zeke was coming head-on. We were still well apart when he started firing—a short burst. I opened up on him and just as it appeared we might collide he rolled over on his back and I pulled up. Banking sharply, I started swinging around to get at him again. But I'd probably killed the pilot as he slowly began a gliding right-turn spiral and finally crashed.

An immaculately executed "bounce" is the outstanding combat memory of Navy ace Willard Ernest Eder of Buffalo, Wyoming. Commander Eder ended the war with six aerial victories to his credit, and brought off his classic bounce on March 18, 1945:

I was leading the fighter cover for a strike by bombers on Omuta, Kyushu. My division of four planes was flying highest cover. About thirty miles short of the target we spotted a sixteen-plane gaggle of mixed Jap fighters lining up for a pass on our bombers below. We slid in behind the enemy planes and closed the gap, wondering whether we could get close enough to blast them before being spotted.

We got into firing range unseen. We all opened fire simultaneously, and the tremendous hail of fire knocked down seven Japs and damaged another before they could scatter. I destroyed one Rufe and one Tojo, and also damaged one Tojo in this sixty-second engagement.

Almost thirty-six years of age when he entered aerial combat for the first time, Captain James H. Flatley, Jr., was an "old man" as fighter pilots are measured. Nevertheless, the years since his 1929 graduation from Annapolis served more to put a patina on his skills than to diminish them. Jim Flatley shot down 6.5 Japanese planes in World War II, no doubt flown by far younger men than he.

Originally from Green Bay, Wisconsin, Captain Flatley served during the Second World War with VF-2, VF-42 and VF-10. He was

one of the trained professional Navy pilots who held back the Japanese
tide in 1942. Like many other pilots of this period, his most unforgettable combat experience is connected with the surprise impact of the
Zero on American airmen:

My most unforgettable combat experience was shooting down a
Zero in the Battle of the Coral Sea on May 7, 1942. It was my first
encounter. We were astounded at the Zero performance, having had
absolutely no intelligence about them. I attacked three by myself.
They outclimbed and outmaneuvered my Grumman F4F3, but they
could not stay with me in a dive with an aileron turn.

General Claire Chennault, as mentioned earlier, had sent warnings
from China about the formidable performance of the Zero. This intelligence, however, never found its way to the American pilots who had
to face the Zero in the first days of the Pacific war.

Francis M. Fleming of Portland, Oregon, saw service in the Pacific
with Air Group 16, and is credited with 7.5 aerial victories. Two of
these kills were gained in Fleming's first combat mission, from which
he vividly recalls the prowess of the Japanese pilots:

In November, 1943, we were flying just north of the Gilberts in
a position to intercept Jap planes coming down from the Marshall
Islands. I was one of twelve Navy Hellcats on CAP at 15,000 feet.
We found our bogey in a perfect intercept with about 2,500 feet
altitude to our advantage.

The planes were Zeros, and there must have been twenty-
twenty-four of them. We made a coordinated attack and completed
the pass before the Jap pilots knew there were any other planes near
them. This was my first aerial combat!

The first Jap I fired on just kept flying straight ahead, smoking
heavily but not burning. I had to recover from my initial dive and
was not able to follow him to see what happened to him. This plane
was classified as a probable.

After the first pass, the wildest dogfight you ever saw erupted.
My wingman got separated from me after the first pass, and when I
located him, he had a Zero hot on his tail, pouring the fire to him. I
swung in behind the Zero and was just ready to open up when the
Jap spotted me on his tail.

He maneuvered violently and left my wingman's tail. I was real
close to him, and in a good firing position. I had hardly touched the

triggers when the Zero disintegrated immediately in front of me. I had to dodge violently to avoid flying into the engine from his plane.

Then I found I was not alone. A Zero was on my tail and closing fast. I took violent evasive action but he stuck with me, because the Zero was much more maneuverable than the Hellcat at speeds less than two hundred knots. This cat-and-mouse maneuvering went on for what seemed like an eternity, with the Jap and me trying to second-guess each other. He was fighting to get into firing position on me, and hadn't fired a single round yet, with me trying to get the hell away from him.

It dawned on me that these guys were not the easy prey that I had allowed myself to believe. The private dogfight was getting a little wearing, and my desire for self-preservation was becoming stronger and stronger. I decided to pull a little maneuver that I had learned from an old World War I combat pilot, whose name escapes me now.

I shoved everything forward to get as much speed as possible, straightened out a little and went into a shallow dive to get speed quicker. When the Zero began to follow and close on me, I started a turn to the left and stayed in this turn, allowing the Zero to cut across the turn to where he figured he had me and was about to open fire.

Then I made as tight a turn to the right as possible at this higher speed. The Zero could not follow the right turn because of the high control forces. I chopped my throttle and turned back to the left, finding myself behind him.

I closed on him and opened fire. He burned, losing one wing and then the other, and went straight in from about 12,000 feet.

The most successful fighter division in the U.S. Navy during the Second World War was led by Lieutenant Eugene Valencia, whose routing of four Zeros by aggressive action was related earlier. A part of VF9 aboard the U.S.S. *Yorktown*, Valencia's division was famed throughout the Pacific Fleet as "Valencia's Flying Circus." Because of its tactics and outstanding successes against the Japanese, it was also known as the "mowing machine."

Valencia assembled his elite unit in the United States after returning from his first tour in the Pacific as a fighter ace. He sought outstanding pilots and marksmen who could also enthusiastically give their all to teamwork and to the implementation of the tactics that Valencia had conceived.

With James French, Harris Mitchell and Clinton Smith, Valencia wrote his unforgettable success saga in the Pacific. All four men ended World War II as aces.

Today the former Lieutenant James B. French dusts crops in Bakersfield, California. The harvesting machinery on which he looks down from the air while pursuing his hazardous calling may well put him in mind of the "mowing machine" of which he was once a part. From the stirring days when he scored his eleven aerial victories, Jim French retains one special memory:

> I was leading the section on April 17, 1945, with Lieutenant E. A. Valencia leading the division when we engaged about forty Jap fighters at fifteen thousand feet. We shot down six of them before they got out of auto-lean [Mixture control setting usually goes to full rich when you go into combat—Aus.] After that it was tough going for ten to fifteen minutes and the four of us began to realize we could not keep them all cornered for long. We called for assistance—which came—and the Japs bolted. We were low on gas and could not chase them. Valencia had shot down six for sure with one probable and one damaged. His wingman, Lieutenant H. E. Mitchell, had clobbered three. I shot down four and my wingman, Lieutenant C. O. Smith, had three.

Not for nothing was it called the "mowing machine," and its fifty confirmed victories stands as a U.S. Navy division record.

The same action stuck fast in the memory of another participant, Valencia's wingman, Lieutenant Harris Mitchell. Here is his account of the battle:

> Date: April 17, 1945
> Time: Approximately 0900
> Place: East of Okinawa
> While flying CAP with two divisions, whose calls were Ruler 4-1, -2, -3 and -4 and Ruler 6-1, -2, -3, -4 over a destroyer that was called Bright Boy, we received the following message:
> "Ruler 4-1 and 6-1, this is Bright Boy—victor 320 degrees, angels 20, Buster."

This is self-explanatory except for Buster, which designated a power setting for fast cruise.

We were at the time circling the destroyer at five thousand feet
and immediately started to climb toward twenty thousand and on a
heading of 320 degrees. Approximately three minutes later, Bright
Boy called us and told us to orbit, because he'd lost the Bogie from
his radar screen. A few seconds later, Bright Boy called again and
the message was a little disappointing for 6-1:

"Ruler 4-1 resume Vector 320 degrees, angels 20, Buster, *Small
Bogie* ahead sixty miles. Ruler 6-1 return to Bright Boy, Orbit
Angels 10."

With this information we assumed that one or two enemy planes
were trying to sneak through our radar screen for a Kamikaze attack. With our division of four planes, we had them outnumbered
two to one, which would make it comparatively easy for us to
destroy them if we ever made contact.

Eager for the kill, we climbed steadily to twenty thousand feet
and settled down to a fast cruise of about 250 knots. Ten minutes
elapsed and off in the distance, barely visible, we spotted what we
thought was a small bunch of planes. The contact report was made:

"Tallyho! Ruler 4-1, small bogie ahead 12 o'clock, down thirty
miles."

We closed our formation a little and all eyes were glued on the
enemy formation. As we approached them, they blossomed from a
small speck to something bigger. Another sighting report:

"Bright Boy, this is Ruler 4-1. Change my tallyho. Ten planes."

The odds were no longer in our favor, yet we were still confi-
dent, though more concerned than we had been at first. You could
tell by the stern expressions on the other pilots' faces that each had
gone over and over his check-off list and that all was in readiness.

As the distance kept closing, the enemy formation grew and
grew. This time, another change of sighting report, with a tinge of
urgency:

"Bright Boy, this is Ruler 4-1. Change my tallyho to 25. Send
help."

That was the last tallyho before the attack, which we carried out
as we had always planned, trained and hoped for and which we
never in our hearts really expected to be able to use.

We came in high with the sun to our backs and the green and
brown camouflaged Jap fighters with their big bright "meatballs"
were clearly visible. They weren't even aware of our presence until
the first two of them exploded violently in the midst of their formation.

At that moment, they all seemed to jettison their bombs at once.

We picked the top planes first and as soon as one would burst into flames, we would have another in our sights. For ten minutes or so we zoomed in and out of that formation.

We kept on the offensive continually, protecting each other when necessary. We were beginning to have trouble keeping the swarms of Jap planes in check when Ruler 6-1, the second division, arrived on the scene.

We rendezvoused, and before departing for our home base on the *Yorktown*, we counted eight parachutes still coming down. Our total score was fourteen Jap fighters destroyed, nine Jap fighters probably destroyed and six damaged. The total was reckoned at thirty-eight, and remarkable as it may seem not one enemy bullet pierced any of our planes.

There is no doubt that "Valencia's Flying Circus" will be a part of Navy lore for generations to come.

Mutually mistaken identity in the air, humorous sometimes in retrospect, proved to be a petrifying experience for a surprising number of America's fighter aces. Lieutenant Commander Robert W. Shackford of Medford, Massachusetts, had this experience and will carry the stark memory of it all his days. He calls it his "most fortunate victory" among the six with which he is credited:

On June 19, 1944, while on a search mission for the Jap fleet, I flew about two hundred miles—almost a solid hour—with a plane about a thousand feet above me that I thought was one of ours. While searching the sea, I took a long look up at this aircraft and got a real jolt to find it was Japanese. I shot the plane down, and it was a case of mutually mistaken identity.

Many of the American aces in Europe had similar experiences, of which this book will contain several examples. All the pilots involved consider the sudden discovery of an "enemy wingman" to be the best known recipe for grey hair—getting it, that is, not getting rid of it.

If an enemy in aerial combat makes a cardinal tactical blunder, it is tantamount under the dynamic rules of war in the air to his giving an opponent in a street fight a free crack at his chin. A Japanese formation leader presented an incredulous Commander Samuel L. Silber with just such an opportunity:

On January 1, 1944, my squadron escorted bombers and torpedo planes on an attack on Kauieng. As the bombers entered their final push-over I led my fighters over them. Just at this point we were attacked by numerous Zekes.

As I turned into my section leader on a weave maneuver, the leader of a Jap flight *turned away from me*. He exposed almost his entire flight to me and my wingman. I shot down three Zekes in the time it takes to make a tight 360-degree turn.

My excellent wingman, Ensign Robert Beedle, also got one. Three days later on another attack on Kauieng, Beedle and I were again attacked by numerous Zekes, but without getting any free shooting as on the previous occasion. I was wounded and Beedle was shot down. He was movie-star William Holden's brother, and was very much like the character Holden portrayed in the *Bridges of Toko-Ri*.

Sam Silber is credited with seven aerial victories. He hails from Baltimore, Maryland.

Hanging on tightly to an enemy's tail has always been a fundamental in aerial combat. This principle was evidently emphasized strongly in the training of Lieutenant Commander Warren D. Skon of St. Paul, Minnesota, for on his first aerial encounter it meant a great deal to him:

My first victory was my first sighting of an enemy aircraft in June of 1944 off the coast of Guam. I followed the Jap Zero into a split-ess, which he had taken as an evasive maneuver. He was slippery and agile but I stayed right with him. When he leveled off just above the waves, I doubt if he knew I was still there. I let him have a burst and he burned, snap-rolled twice and plunged into the water.

Lieutenant Commander Skon is credited with seven aerial victories.

Two and a half years of combat with VF-11 and a powerful will to win brought seventeen aerial victories to Lieutenant Commander Charles R. Stimpson of Salt Lake City, Utah. This pilot's aggressiveness was a legend among those who flew with him. His story modestly veils this all-important trait of the fighter ace:

While on CAP over the Hornet on October 14, 1944, a large group of bogies were picked up on our radar and we were vectored onto them. We were just completing our first carrier strikes on Formosa and the Japs were really out in strength to get us.

When my division leader's radio became inoperable, I assumed the lead of the two four-plane divisions. We intercepted the attacking Jap force of sixteen Zekes plus a number of bombers about seventy miles from the *Hornet*. In that battle I destroyed five confirmed and three probables.

The exciting part for me was that with only eight planes we met and totally defeated a numerically superior force and prevented a full-scale attack on our carriers.

As in so many instances in the history of aerial warfare, aggressive spirit was the key to aerial superiority in the battle Commander Stimpson relates.

For numerous aces, the most memorable combat experience is not a victory of their own, but rather an occasion on which they were the subject of an enemy victory. Commander James S. Swope of Killeen, Texas, falls into this category. His own ten aerial victories have not stuck in his memory as vividly as his narrow escape from Japanese guns:

On June 16, 1943, over Henderson Field, Guadalcanal, we engaged an estimated 105 Jap aircraft. While working on some Aichi dive-bombers, I had the misfortune to become engaged singly with a Zero. The F4F is certainly no match for the Zero, but I found it could take a hell of a lot of punishment and still fly.

I couldn't get a single lick in at the Zeke, but my F4F took two explosive 20mm cannon shells and close to forty 7.7mm bullets. Three cylinders were blown off the engine but I evaded the Jap and still flew that battered F4F 20 miles back to Fighter One strip and the scrap heap.

Despite the passage of the years, pride in a job well done still fills Commander John Carlos Cleves Symmes, living now in Lima, Peru. Credited with 10.5 aerial victories in the Pacific war, he sums up his memories of the conflict as follows:

The record I like best is that no Navy Fighter Squadron I was with ever lost a bomber, or torpedo pilot escorted by us to enemy fighter action. I am proud to share that good feeling with all the men of those squadrons. For those fighter pilots who did not get back, it represents something concrete and well worth fighting for, since it was one of the primary missions of the fighter pilot to see the bombers safely through. In spite of all the baloney written about fighter pilots, the kind of achievement that gives me such pride is indicative of the teamwork without which the war could not have been won.

On the combat side, my best victory was over Guam one day when my division got away from me chasing enemy fighters after my water injection failed. [Water injection is the mechanical injection of water into the cylinders of an airplane engine, which allows an engine to produce a great deal more power without breaking down due to detonation—Aus.] I had detailed the lead as I had no radio.

I was completely alone and lagging badly when I was jumped by an element of Japs from above. I was able to hold my nerve until they were committed by their speed, then pulled up into them. As the first Jap overshot and dove below me, I flipped over into a dive behind him, figuring I would at least get him before his buddy got me.

I shot into him, and although he didn't burn or explode, I undoubtedly shot out his hydraulic system, because a wheel dropped and eventually his engine quit. All the while, we were in a twisting, vertical descent tail chase. The Jap finally went in on Orote Peninsula, and I leveled off on the deck, dodging as best I could through light ack-ack fire. To my surprise, the Jap number two man had gone, probably scared by his own side's flak, I guess.

Control of the air was not easily won from the Japanese in the early months of the Pacific war. Hard-flying, dogged and persistent Navy pilots had their hands full, as did Commander Stanley W. Vejtasa of Circle, Montana, during the Battle of Santa Cruz. On October 26, 1942, Vetjasa flew Combat Air Patrol for no less than nine hours and fifteen minutes:

> Flying F4F's from the *Enterprise*, we were in a savage battle when our Task Force, consisting of *Enterprise, Hornet, South Dakota* and escorting curisers and destroyers, was attacked by hordes of enemy fighters, dive-bombers and torpedo planes. I succeeded in shooting down seven enemy planes in one flight, which is a good indicator of the number of targets available to our fighters.
>
> *Enterprise* was hit, and our own surface ships had to sink the heavily damaged and helpless *Hornet*. They were grim days.

Commander Vejtasa is credited with eleven aerial victories in World War II.

Commander John M. Wesolowski of Detroit, Michigan, was presented with a rare personal opportunity to return the "sneak punch" of Pearl Harbor against two unsuspecting Japanese. His experience shows how pure luck, fused with shooting skill, can bring aerial victories. Wesolowski is credited with seven aerial victories over the Japanese, but these are the ones he remembers best:

> At Guadalcanal, early in the battle, I took off for a dusk alert. I got separated from my flight in the overcast at twenty thousand feet so I let down by myself when the alert was over, and found myself just behind eighteen Jap fighters at five thousand feet.
>
> Making one pass at the last two planes in the formation, I destroyed them both with about seventy-five rounds of ammo fired. I ducked back into the overcast and returned to Guadalcanal unscathed.

A proud navel aviator is Captain Robert A. Winston (Ret), who commanded VF-31 aboard the U.S.S. *Cabot* in World War II. While under his command, this squadron shot down sixty-four enemy machines without loss, either operationally or in combat. A Pensacola graduate (class of '35) Bob Winston saw sixteen of his original thirty-two pilots in VF-31 become fighter aces. Winston himself best remembers a true triple that came his way near the Palau Archipelago:

> At sunset on March 31st, as Task Force 58 returned from the mining of the Palau Archipelago, I was flying CAP and sent by radar to an unidentified bogey seventy-five miles west of the task force.
>
> It was a formation of twelve Judys in the dusk, and I attacked, leading my four Hellcat division. I got the leader and both his wingmen in one pass—less than ten seconds. My wingmen destroyed the remaining nine aircraft for a grand slam. They proved to be the *first* contacted Judy *kamikaze* dive-bombers.

As the fighter pilots of the U.S. Navy, with the aces in the van, gradually rolled back the Japanese tide, a new era of naval strategy and tactics was opened. The dominant role of airpower in determining control of the seas became a naval fact of life rather than a revolutionary theory. Thus, the fighter aces of the Navy did much more for their country and their era than conquer the enemy in the air. The latter task, however, proved long and costly, and provided a generation of Navy fighter aces with the most memorable experiences of their lives.

7

☆　☆　☆　☆　☆

U. S. Navy Aces of World War II (II)

BY THE AUTUMN OF 1943 the balance of the Pacific air war had tipped against the Japanese. The Americans had superior aircraft and communications, and had the necessary experience, tactics and confidence to keep the Japanese in check. Although the Japanese pilots were aware of this decisive change, it in no way diminished the fanatical bravery with which they fought.

In the intervening years, the angry defiance of some of the Japanese pilots has gained almost legendary status. But behind the legend lies the incredible reality, as experienced by Lieutenant Commander Rober E. Murray:

On October 16, 1943, Task Force 38 was under a night attack by Japanese bombers from Formosa. The cruisers *Houston* and *Canberra* were both torpedoed and had to be taken under tow. Two carriers were dispatched from the task force to escort them away from Formosa, and I was on the U.S.S. *Cabot* with VF-29 flying F6F's.

About 1200 the next day, we were still only 180 miles off the coast. There eight of us up on CAP when CIC got a large bogey on the screen, coming in for the disabled ships to finish them off. There were between seventy-five and eighty Jap planes—fighters, twin-engined bombers and single-engined torpedo bombers. We intercepted them about thirty-five miles from the force.

Our eight F6F's shot down twenty-seven of these Jap planes and fighters scrambling from our carriers got another five, for a total of thirty-two. I shot down four myself, consisting of one Zeke, a twin-engined Francis and two Jill torpedo bombers.

As I went by one of the Jills just before it hit the water, the Japanese pilot stood up in the cockpit and *shook his fist at me.* He was still shaking it when his aircraft went in.

Lieutenant Commander Murray is credited with 10.33 aerial victories.

A similarly defiant Japanese pilot is the dominant figure in the unforgettable combat experience of Lieutenant Michele Mazzocco Jr. of Peekskill, New York.

During the Okinawa battle, swarms of Jap aircraft were dispatched from Kyushu on suicide missions against the U.S. Fleet, then operating in support of the Okinawa invasion. Contacts of our CAP's with the enemy units were numerous, and in one such contact I engaged a Jap Zeke in a dogfight at approximately eighteen thousand feet.

My plane was an F6F Hellcat, and because of good radar interception, I was able to fire a short burst into the Zeke before being detected. He was smoking badly, and I expected him to go down at any moment, but instead he climbed sharply and opened fire on me.

We both knew that he would not make it back to the home islands, that it was just a matter of time before he went in. But he was going to fight to the last. During the dogfight, about fifteen thousand feet of altitude was lost and somehow or other we ended up in a head-on run.

I had the choice of either meeting him head-on or turning and offering him the best shot. I decided to trade shots. We were both scoring hits on one another. Then I noticed that this Jap wasn't going to veer off, and that a collision was not only inevitable, but planned by him.

I waited until the last possible moment, my heart in my throat, then pulled up hard and to the right. His left wing came through the bottom arc of my prop and debris flew all over the sky. The concussion was tremendous, and jarred to the bone, I lost control of my plane for a moment that seemed like an eternity.

When I recovered, I could see him spinning slowly down toward the sea. The Jap plane was blazing and minus a large portion of the left wing. My wingman checked my plane and told me my belly tank had taken most of the punishment in the collision. I managed to jettison it and made an emergency landing on the carrier. Mr. Grumman surely built a tough one when he built that Hellcat. God bless him.

In addition to the brush with death he relates and 6.5 aerial victories credited during the Pacific war, Lieutenant Mazzocco's distinguished career includes dropping a bomb on the giant Japanese battleship *Yamoto* and sinking a Japanese submarine with rocket fire.

One rugged Japanese pilot also provided Commander Richard J. Griffin of New York City with his most memorable combat experience:

I engaged in a dogfight with this Jap pilot at eight hundred feet and two hundred knots airspeed. This boy really knew his business. After three or four scissors maneuvers, none of which gained any angular advantage for either of us, my air speed was dropping rapidly, and it was only a matter of time before my adversary would be in the saddle.

However, we were so closely matched that neither of us could gain the advantage, until another Hellcat made a pass at the Jap. Being alert, the Jap flicked to counter, and that gave me the opportunity to fire and get strikes. He bailed out at about two hundred feet.

I really appreciated that Jap pilot's professional ability. This was my sixth or seventh victory, and by that time I was concerned by the manner in which an enemy was downed, such as "sloppy" or "clear."

Commander Griffin served with VF2 and is credited with eight aerial victories.

For many aces, their first aerial combat is the most memorable. This is the case with Donald Gordon, now a U.S. Navy Captain commanding aircraft carriers, but in the Battle of Santa Cruz on October 29, 1942, a fledgling fighter pilot who learned much:

I was launched at 0700 as part of an eight plane CAP to defend the task force from aerial attack. My station, in company with Ensign Gerald Davis, was over the U.S.S. *Enterprise*.

At approximately 0750 I was instructed to take a heading to intercept incoming bogies. Soon three Jap dive-bombers were sighted. We initiated an attack on them just before they commenced their bomb run on the *Hornet*.

Closing in, I fired and observed something fly off the first Jap machine I fired at. I shifted my sight to the right wingman, and saw a small fire start in the rear cockpit. This fire went out when I quit firing.

At this time I was in a vertical dive and the AA was heavy, so I pulled out and watched the dive-bombers continue their attack. No bombs were seen to drop. One of the dive-bombers plunged into the *Hornet*, hitting the carrier forward of the island. The other two dive-bombers crashed into the water nearby. I did not claim either as a victory.

After clearing the AA area, three more Jap torpedo aircraft were sighted low near the water. Davis and I made a run. I fired too soon, but closed, and one torpedo bomber crashed into the water, another jettisoned his "fish" and we lost the third.

A short time later, a Zero was seen making a run on one of our F4F's. I was in good shooting position and pulled the trigger. Four rounds popped and then the guns quit. I was out of ammo, and so was my wingman. But my few shots and the presence of our machines had forced the Jap off the tail of the F4F.

We returned to the *Enterprise* to rearm, but a new Jap attack waved us off. Ensign W. Redding joined me and saw a torpedo-plane attack coming in on the task force. Although out of ammo, I made a head-on pass at one of the torpedo planes and in avoiding me, he dug a wing in the water and crashed. I claimed two torpedo planes destroyed, and one probable.

It was my most exciting mission, and I learned three vital things about air fighting:

1. Only fire when in range
2. Conserve your ammunition
3. Continue after your quarry until you are sure it is a kill.

Captain Gordon was educated at the University of Kansas, and ended the war with seven aerial victories to his credit.

What did the well-trained U.S. Navy pilot do when his guns jammed? He kept firing. At least, that is what Lieutenant Commander Willis E. Hardy did when he was chasing kamikazes in 1945:

Flying an F6F Hellcat off the *Hornet* on April 6, 1945, on our second mission, my wingman and I encountered a swarm of kamikaze-bent Japs north of Okinawa. Some very violent maneuvering on my part had jammed my ammo belts in the cans, and by the time I was on my fifth Jap of the afternoon, only one gun was firing—and that only one round at a time each time I would kick the charger button.

The fifth Jap was finally flamed after twenty minutes of the "line-up, get off one round-break-recharge" routine. My score for the mission was one Zeke, two radial-engined Judys, and two Vals. My wingman got three more and stuck with me the whole time giving mutual defense.

Commander Hardy hailed originally from Corning, California, and spent his World War II service with VF-17 flying off the U.S.S. *Hornet*. He is credited with seven aerial victories, and holds the Navy Cross.

Fighter pilots who hailed from Texas invariably wound up with the "Tex" nickname, and Commander LeRoy E. Harris of Brownwood, Texas, was no exception. An Annapolis man (class of '39), "Tex" Harris flew with VF-2 and VF-10 during World War II. Credited with twelve aerial victories, his most vivid combat memory is of the first carrier aircraft attack on Manila, September 24, 1944:

I led the fighter escort for the *Hornet* (CVA-12) group attack on shipping and installations about Manila Bay. We caught the Japanese with their kimonos down, and had no opposition. After covering the bombers and torpedo plane attacks, we strafed Jap auxiliary shipping which filled the bay.

Then, starting home, some several flights of Tonys jumped us. I led my division into them, instructing the others to stay with the bombers. I got one Tony and the others two in the first pass. Tonys dove for the deck, and we followed.

Caught another shortly afterward and destroyed him at one hundred feet, running out of ammo in the process. I broke off and commenced rendezvous. I found the second section, also without ammo, being attacked by three Tonys. I called them and told them to head for home while my wingman and I made a head-on pass at the Japs.

Luckily, on our first pass the Japs broke and ran—but so did we. Just before landing I discovered the last two feet of my left wing tip had been mangled by an explosive shell.

Aerial combat was not the only tough part of Navy flying in the Pacific, a fact well illustrated by the most memorable war experience of Lieutenant Commander Everett Hargreaves, originally from Saskatchewan, Canada. His narrative provides an insight into the tension and excitement of a naval air mission in wartime:

It is difficult to pick out any one flight and say that it was the best or most exciting, especially after a lapse of years. They were all flights of duty, and we took the assignments as they came, such as the late-afternoon launch of eleven fighters, twelve dive-bombers and nine torpedo-bombers from the U.S.S. *Hornet* west of Guam.

The strike group headed for the enemy fleet, which had been sighted for the first time in a year and a half, as I remember. I was flying in the fighter escort, but we were all carrying 500-pound bombs for maximum striking power. The bombs could be dropped in case enemy air action started, but we carried the bombs all the way in.

Flying west into the sun, we passed the given point of sighting with no contact, and flew on for approximately one hundred miles before our strike group made the contact. AA shells began to appear immediately, and by the time we reached our pushover point, you could see the flashes on the ships below. They were sending up the heaviest concentration of flak we'd seen up to that time.

The attack was made just at sunset, and I think that dive was about the longest I ever made, if not in actual altitude certainly in time—for the hail of enemy tracer lacing with your own was not a sight to soothe the nerves.

After getting rid of our bombs, we grouped again in the graying dusk and headed for home, with every pilot thinking of the instructions we had received when we were standing the nightfighter watch. "If launched before midnight, bail out when you get low on fuel, for the admiral will not take a chance of putting the carriers into the wind long enough to land you aboard and give the Jap Betty's their chance at the fleet."

Certainly they were not going to carry that instruction through with so many planes in the air, not only from the *Hornet*, but all the other ships too, even though only the old Navy men were probably the only pilots experienced in carrier landings at night.

The dusk gradually died, and the darkness set in. Over water, with no reflection of city lights on the horizon to help brighten the sky and give you checkpoint assistance on your navigation, a moonless night and the black sea below made the prospect of a safe return for you seem very remote.

To add to the tension, every one of us knew that flying those extra miles to the target had put us at the extreme end of fuel supplies. It was not long before I heard the first radio call from a buddy. He had no juice left and was being forced down to that black, fathomless depth below.

I automatically leaned my fuel mixture just a wee bit more, hoping that my old battle-worn plane was not quite such a gas eater.

Every few minutes we heard some other pilot call the flight leader that he was going in. By the time we sighted the wakes of our own fleet below, the radio was so filled with distress calls that you couldn't hear the landing instructions given by the carriers.

My fuel indicators gave me much more leeway than some of the pilots reporting in, so I stayed high above and circled, to try and give some of the other pilots a chance to land first. The carrier decks were clear, but not for long.

Many of the inexperienced and harried pilots were crashing into the barriers. It was a grim and nerve-wracking sight. Then Admiral Mitscher gave his historic order. "Turn on the lights," he said, accepting the risk of Jap subs getting our fleet.

Landings now speeded up. When it looked like I could join the traffic circle without ten others all at the same time, I started in and got a "cut" on the first pass. I taxied forward and was spotted.

Just as I was climbing out of the cockpit, I saw the plane captain drop everything and bolt. He had a good reason. What turned out to be the Air Group commander making the last landing of the night came barreling through the only remaining barrier. Flames started to shoot out of his ship, which swerved to my side with the roll of the ship. For a moment, I wondered if I'd come through the rest of the operation only to get it on the *Hornet*'s deck.

The rampaging aircraft finally settled on top of the port gun mount, a few scant inches from going over the side. It was a glum ship to come back to, for only a handful of planes landed. It brightened as we sat relaxing over a cup of coffee, for the teletype started to give the information on pilots who had landed on other ships. Before the day was out, all our squadron had been accounted for.

Hargreaves is credited with 8.5 aerial victories in the Pacific. Today this Navy ace follows a more prosaic calling in peacetime America as a bank examiner in Milwaukee, Wisconsin.

With twenty-four victories scored in the Pacific Theater, Commander Cecil Elwood Harris of Cresbard, South Dakota, is the Navy's second-ranking fighter ace. He flew fighter cover for the North African landings in 1942, and then went to the Pacific to serve with VC-18, VF-36 and VF-18. Commander Harris is an extremely modest man, and his story of what he considers his "most timely" victory epitomizes his self-effacing character:

My most timely mission was when I was assigned to a search mission one day. There were four planes in the group, each assigned to guard a different sector and escort a bomber. The weather was overcast as we took off, and while making a turn around the carrier just below the clouds, two enemy aircraft dropped down through the overcast just ahead of me, and very close to the fleet.

They started their run immediately, and I closed on the leader, shot him to pieces, then turned to get behind the second Jap. Luckily, I shot it down before it reached the bomb-release line. Both planes fell flaming harmlessly (to our fleet) in the water amidst the ships, and I continued my assigned mission.

Service as a fighter pilot with a Fast Carrier Task Force in the Pacific resulted in nine aerial victories for Thomas Switzer Harris. Odd conduct on the part of a beaten Japanese pilot stuck in his mind:

It was just north of Okinawa. My wingman had damaged a Tony and in the melee we had become separated from the flight. I got behind the Tony and poured some lead into him. Finally a small fire started under the engine nacelle, and then his engine froze.

The Jap plane started down in a gentle glide toward Okinawa. I kept firing, trying to make the fire spread. To my amazement, the Jap pilot climbed out on the left wing, but held on *with his head and shoulders still inside the cockpit.*

While watching this drama, I ceased firing. It was incredible. The pilot looked almost like a midget, and what his intentions were I'll never know. Perhaps he wanted to ride the plane down to a lower altitude before bailing out for fear of being shot in his parachute.

However, I intended to burn the plane, and when I aimed and shot at the left wing tank, some of my tracers appeared to hit him. At least, this is the way it appeared to me at the time. The Jap pilot let go and went hurtling past me looking like a bundle of rags, his chute streaming behind him. It never opened. The plane never burned very fiercely and I refrained from wasting any more ammunition on it.

Tom Harris stayed in the Navy after the war, and served with the Navy's first carrier jet squadron in 1948, with later service as an Exchange Pilot with the Air Forces Air Defense Command 33rd Fighter Interceptor Wing. In 1954 he resigned his Navy commission to enter test-piloting work for a commercial concern.

Lieutenant Charles H. Haverlund Jr. returned from the Pacific

Theater and service on the *Enterprise* and *Lexington* with an indelible memory not so much of his own experience or achievements, but of Lieutenant (j.g.) Douglas Baker, one of the Navy's top fighter pilots:

> The most exciting aerial victory I can recall was not one of my own, but the first victory of many by the late Lieutenant (j.g.) Douglas Baker [sixteen aerial victories]. Doug had all the prime requisites of a fighter pilot, and combined his many outstanding abilities as an aviator with the uncanny ability to see and identify aircraft long before they were sighted by anyone else in the flight.
>
> These attributes were all coordinated beautifully by Doug around the first of October, 1944. I was flying on his wing, when, as happened so many times later, he sighted Jap fighters and initiated an attack.
>
> My own excitement over a first encounter was apparently not shared by Doug, as his perfectly executed run and short firing burst had his target spinning in flames almost instantly, while I chalked up a clean miss on my own target.

Haverland is credited with 6.5 aerial victories, despite his marksmanship on this occasion.

When the kamikazes hit the U.S.S. *Bunker Hill*, Commander Rogers R. Hedrick was aboard the stricken carrier as Commander of Air Group 84. He considers himself lucky to be alive after this incident, which claimed the lives of 104 of his personnel. Hedricks ran up twelve aerial victories himself in the Pacific, and recalls a wild melee over Bougainville:

> I led a flight of six Corsairs on station as high cover CAP over Empress Augusta Bay, Bougainville, against thirty-six Jap fighters which were acting as cover for one hundred Jap bombers attacking our amphibious forces. Our medium andlow CAP fighters had intercepted the bombers as we took on the Jap high cover.
>
> The ensuing dogfight lasted thirty-five minutes. Pilots and observers aboard ship later reported seventeen burning aircraft had come plunging through the overcast, but we claimed only five kills, due to so many of our damaged targets disappearing into the low deck clouds, most of them on fire. All the Jap planes were driven off, leaving our lower CAP flights free to successfully hit and repulse the Jap bomber attack.

Rarities among America's fighter aces are *night* aces. Commander William E. Henry of Bakersfield, California, is one of these rare birds, having scored six of his ten aerial victories at night. One of these night encounters he remembers well:

My most exciting victory was my first night intercept, which I completed on an Emily. I scored immediate hits, and after setting fire to his port engine, I pulled out to the port quarter to avoid debris if the Nip plane exploded. Then a port turn by the Jap pilot put me close abeam—with the Jap's engine fire dying out.

The rear gunner immediately saw me and cut loose at very close range, but did not score a hit before I retired beyond the limit of visibility.

It was easy to keep track of the Emily, for although the fire had gone out, a bright glow remained. As I pulled astern of the Jap to do the job right, the fire started up again before I could get in another burst, and the Emily went into a starboard spiral and crashed into the water.

If you fly with Trans World Airlines you may find yourself in the care of Navy fighter ace Kenneth G. Hippe of Peoria, Illinois. A Reserve Commander, Ken flew with VC-13 in the Pacific and is credited with five aerial victories. He is one of the few American fighter pilots to become an "instant ace" by scoring all five kills in one mission:

October 24, 1944. We took off on a CAP and intercepted a Lilly, a twin-engined Jap bomber, over Leyte Gulf. Luckily, I shot it down. I was directed by radar to intercept a raid coming in, and got four out of this big formation of Lillys. Only one of this complete formation of twenty-one bombers was unaccounted for by the rest of my division and the others who joined the scrap. It all took place in ten minutes. I was flying an FM-2, and just happened to be in the right place at the right time.

When Lieutenant Charles W. Huffman of Rockville, Missouri, bounced some Zekes after a radar interception, he was hardly prepared for what followed:

On October 15, 1944, while attached to VF-14 on the U.S.S. *Wasp*, my division was flying a CAP over the task force. We received a vector and another division was assigned to follow, as numerous bogies were reported. I was a wingman on the division leader, but he was having radio trouble so he passed the lead to me.

I took the next few vectors and radar placed me about three thousand feet above and about nine o'clock from fifteen to twenty Zekes. I announced contact with the enemy to the ship and proceeded to attack with the other seven planes following.

"I set the lead aircraft on fire from close behind, probably about four hundred feet. Just as I stopped firing, the Jap plane seemed to stop in midair and exploded. As I flew through the flames and pieces of the aircraft, I could feel the heat in the cockpit.

After getting in the clear, and while checking my engine instruments and controls, I realized someone was shooting at me. I turned around and saw two Zekes sitting about five hundred feet behind me with all guns firing. After some hectic maneuvering I finally got away from them and with the fight over, I returned to the ship.

There were half a dozen holes in my right wing, but the major damage was to the flaps, ailerons, elevators and rudder, which all had to be changed. The heat from the exploding Jap aircraft had scorched the paint and left the fabric in ripples on the flaps.

The controls were unfit for further service and I felt real lucky to have eluded the other two Japs in view of this. This was my most exciting combat flight.

Huffman survived the war, and is credited with six aerial victories.

Wheat and cattle ranching at Palouse, Washington, are a far cry from piloting a fighter in the Pacific war. Lieutenant Commander Elvin L. Lindsay made the transition successfully, however, and while he ranches quietly today he has this memory of more violent times:

After completing a recce flight over Nielson Field near Manila, six of us in Hellcats headed north to look for targets. As we approached Clark Field, we spotted fifteen enemy planes making a rendezvous around their base.

For one terrible instant a heavy hand clutched my heart—we were only six against fifteen, with several new-type fighters among their planes. But we approached unseen, and slashed into their flight with such fury that three of their planes went down on the first pass.

In defensive formation we continued to pick off singles in a series of dogfights until thirteen Japs were down with no loss to us.

Back on our carrier, our skipper demanded, "What the hell do you mean letting two planes get away like that?"

Lindsay's final score was eight aerial victories in the Pacific, gained while flying with VF-19.

Commander Charles Mallory is credited with eleven victories by the Navy, one more than he himself claims. This kind of anomaly occurs sometimes when the pilot cannot take time from combat to actually watch a wounded adversary crash, and someone else confirms his victory at a later date.

Mallory fought with VC-30, VF-36, VF-18, and VF-151 off the U.S.S. *Intrepid*. The big carrier was part of a task force providing fighter cover for bombers attacking Manila on September 21, 1944. Mallory was aboard, and had an exciting day:

It was late afternoon, and the sky was clear except for scattered white cumulus clouds at five thousand feet. I was assigned top cover for the group with six F6F's at eighteen thousand feet.

The fighters began their nervous weave, and it seemed to intensify as they picked up speed approaching our target, Clark Field. The air had been full of Jap fighters all day, and we expected to be jumped at any moment. I played a hunch, and signaled for my top cover group to start climbing as we passed the last range of mountains and started across the green fields of central Luzon. A few minutes later we were at 24,000 feet, as our dive-bombers and torpedo planes started their attack.

At the same time, numerous enemy bogies were spotted, and the lower fighter cover became engaged with Jap fighter planes which outnumbered them two to one. There were calls coming over the radio fast and furious. "Look out, Frog, there are two Tonys behind you!" "Break, break!" and so on.

Meanwhile, at 24,000 feet I started a circle around the field. Just when I felt we were missing the big fight below and was getting set to go down, my wingman, Lieutenant (j.g.) Beatley called "Poncho!"—he'd spotted twenty-four Jap fighters, five miles away, ten o'clock low. They were in tight formation and flying toward us at about 20,000 feet.

I called for the attack, but instructed my group not to lose our altitude advantage, and to be prepared for a defensive fight. I rolled into a dive with the other planes spread out in pairs, and we hit the enemy before they had time to spread.

On my first pass I lined up a Tony in my gunsight, squeezed the trigger, and saw tracers eating into the other cockpit. I pulled up just as he exploded in a ball of flame. The next few minutes were a free-for-all. My planes kept their altitude and covered each other very well. My wingman had his guns shot out in his first pass, but he stayed with me and covered me just the same.

Suddenly I looked down and saw one of our fighters about 5,000 feet below the rest of us, boxed in by five Tojos. It was only a matter of seconds before he'd be shot down. I called for a break and went into a dive.

The Jap fighter shooting at the F6F was only about a hundred feet behind, and I placed the pip of my gunsight in front of the F6F to compensate for lead. As the range closed to firing distance, I squeezed the trigger and saw the Tojo buck and roll over with flames spurting out all along his side.

In the pull-up, my plane shuddered and my air speed dropped off to 180 knots. I looked to the rear and saw a Tojo sitting on my tail. My left elevator had been shot away, my wheels were hanging down, and big holes were being blown in my wings where the 20mm cannon shells were exploding.

With what control I had left, I twisted into a dive, then pulled up, as if I were going to split-ess—but instead, flew on my back. The Tojo thought I was going to pull through the split-ess and rolled with me, but he pulled on through. I righted my plane and headed for the nearest cloud, and took a heading for the coast.

Two of my group joined me at the coast, and all six had joined up when we reached the carrier. All six planes were badly damaged, and two pilots were wounded. All of us landed OK, but my plane never flew again. My plane captain counted sixty-seven holes, but my Grumman had brought me safely home. It was quite a day. I was credited with five kills for the day.

A reluctant Navy ace is Lieutenant Commander Lee Paul Mankin of Mammoth Springs, Arkansas. Mankin claims only four aerial victories, and hesitates to take credit for the fifth victory because he chased the enemy plane into the water without firing a shot. Among other famous ships of the Pacific war, Mankin called both the *Saratoga* and the *Enterprise* home. He best recalls a battle over Guadalcanal, for which he had an audience:

Above Guadalcanal with VF-5 I was confronted by two Zeros. Fortunately, one gave up and the other made a wrong turn, which put me behind him. With only one 50-caliber gun working I centered his cockpit in my sight and let go. I followed him up a steep climbing right turn, and at the very top of the climb he exploded into flames.

Five minutes later I landed at Henderson Field, and the reception I received from the Marines on the ground was more than adequate reward for the sweat I'd just experienced. Those Marines were an appreciative bunch of men. This victory stuck in my mind because it was a straight fighter-against-fighter battle, and I had often wondered how I would fare in such a situation.

One of the U.S. Navy's famed formations in World War II was Fighting Squadron 3, under the command of Lieutenant Commander Edward "Butch" O'Hare. Until his death at the hands of a gunner in a Japanese bomber, O'Hare proved himself an inspiring leader, and many of the Navy's top fighter pilots passed through O'Hare's VF-3 during their careers.

Lieutenant Commander Richard H. May was among the Navy aces who served with VF-3. Credited with six aerial victories, May carries a memory with him that gives the uninitiated the true flavor of aerial combat and provides a pang in the solar plexis for the initiated:

Eight Hellcats were catapulted from the U.S.S. *Langley* early one morning during darkness to sweep the Truk area for enemy fighters, and to coordinate and protect friendly bomber attacks. Truk was swarming with planes, as it was a highly fortified Jap base. Our task group was given orders to neutralize Truk at all costs.

Our fighters were supposed to rendezvous with two hundred other task group fighters from other carriers in our group. Due to miserable weather conditions, our eight were unable to locate the main attack group. The eight of us under the leadership of the skipper headed for Truk alone—it was some 150 miles due east.

The eight of us were split into four sections of two planes each. I led the second section behind the skipper. Lieutenant (j.g.) John Pond, a Tennessee boy, was flying my wing position. Approaching Truk at sixteen thousand feet, Lieutenant Hills, an RCAF veteran, leading the last section suddenly tallyhoed a large gaggle of bogies at eight thousand feet. These bogies were flying southeasterly over the enemy group of islands. We counted forty-three Zekes and Tonys in the formation.

The skipper signaled attack. We dove on the unsuspecting Japs below, and the element of surprise was with us. No doubt radar had alerted the enemy to our main general attack, and this was the first group of enemy fighters climbing for altitude.

We were ten minutes ahead of the main flight of task group fighters, so these climbing enemy planes were taken by surprise. Diving at full power we were on them before they spotted us. I picked out an enemy division leader, leading a flight of four Zekes in the middle of the formation, allowing plenty of mils in the gunsight for the deflection shot of about forty-five degrees. John Pond drew his bead on the enemy division leader's wingman.

At a thousand yards we opened up with our six 50-caliber wing guns, blasting those two Japs into eternity. The entire enemy formation scattered as we tore into them. They broke up into sections and singles, climbing vertically in panic to gain precious altitude. My section bore down through swirling fragments of enemy aircraft at high speed. We recovered quickly, pulling as many G's as possible, heading straight back up—recovering altitude and at the same time rolling back toward the enemy.

The sky was full of diving, twisting, exploding and burning aircraft. The fear that oppressed me most was of collision. Zeros were everywhere, milling, looping and blazing. John Pond was expertly handling his controls to stay with me in the gyrations and aerobatics necessary to get back on the enemy. We dove, twisted, rolled, split-essed, recovered, pulled into eye-popping, brain-blurring turns in the effort to get the necessary lead in gunsights to drive our 50-caliber bullets home.

Rolling out of a half-wing-over, I gave a Tony a long burst, smoked him, pulled back on the stick, and headed down toward the sea in a hurry to pick up more valuable flying speed. Not a moment too soon. A flaming enemy fighter went hurtling past the cockpit, missing me by but a few feet. He was a victim of one of my buddies, but he almost took me out with him.

By this time the fight had become a sort of aerial alley brawl. Planes were blowing up, burning and disintegrating all over the sky. Chutes were mushrooming. It seemed to me to last about an hour, but actually it lasted only a few minutes. The battle had been fiercely fought, but it ended as abruptly as it had begun. One minute the sky was full of Jap planes and the next minute it was empty. The enemy—those that were still healthy—had scattered.

The record accredited our lonely eight Hellcats with twenty-three confirmed kills and eleven probables. John Pond confirmed two aerial kills and one probable. The record credited me with three confirmed kills and two probables in this battle.

FIVE DOUBLE ACES: Above, five USAF jet aces in Korea. From left: Capt. Lonnie Moore, Col. Vermont Garrison, Col. James Johnson, Capt. Ralph Parr, and Maj. James Jabara (also below), who became America's first jet ace on May 20, 1951.

SOLITARY CONFINEMENT: Left, USAF Col. Walker Mahurin, who scored a total of 24.25 "kills" in World War II and Korea, was shot down over Korea May 13, 1952, and held in solitary confinement until released on Sept. 6, 1953. In earlier photo Col. Mahurin (below) poses next to a World War I-vintage aircraft.

KOREAN ACE: Right, USAF Brig. Gen. Royal Baker scored 16 "kills," 13 of them in Sabre jets, and was 21st U.S. jet ace. COMING IN: Below, F-86 Sabre jet about to land after completing mission in North Korea.

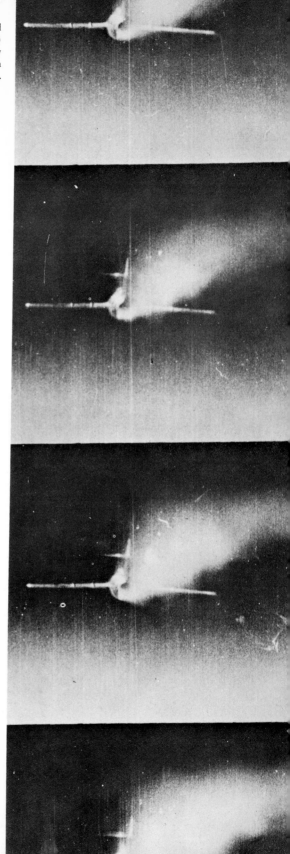

COMPARISON TEST: After reassembly and ground checks, a captured MIG-15 (left) is taxied down runway for take-off by USAF test pilot. Performance of MIG, flown by 5 USAF pilots, was below that of F-86.

BREAK LEFT!: Four F-86 Sabres (left) turn sharply to left over Korea, probably just before heading toward MIG Alley and a rendezvous with the enemy.

FLAMING MIG: Right, 4 stills of gun-camera film showing MIG-15 "kill."

MEETING OF ACES: Above, Eddie Rickenbacker, 26 "kills" in World War I, and Maj. Frederick Blesse, 10 "kills" in Korea, discuss relative merits of the SPAD and the Sabre. Above, right, from left: Vermont Garrison, Glenn Eagleston, Francis Gabreski and James Jabara at first meeting of American Fighter Aces Association in San Francisco, 1960. Below, right, three of America's top aces hold the American Fighter Aces Association insignia. From left: USN Cdr. Eugene Valencia (23 "kills"), USAF Maj. James Brooks (13 "kills" and USMC ace Joe Foss (26 "kills").

ASSOCIATION OF ACES: First meeting of American Fighter Aces Association, September 1960.

This wild encounter over Truk was by far the most exciting action experienced by me in five hundred hours of combat flying time.

Hamilton McWhorter III of Athens, Georgia, ran up twelve kills in the Pacific in World War II, taking part in such actions as Tarawa, Saipan and the Marshall Islands landings. Commander McWhorter earned five DFC's and seven Air Medals. His story tells how he earned one of these decorations:

I was flying an F6F as section leader in escort for a bombing and torpedo strike on Truk on February 16, 1944. As the SBD dive-bombers were pushing over into their dives, I saw three fighter aircraft about two miles away turn toward us. At that distance, and head-on, they looked very much like friendly F6F's. However, my wingman and I turned into them, "just in case."

I was not positive they were enemy aircraft until they were within three thousand feet or so, then I saw they were painted orange and black. They were in loose left echelon, the leader apart from the other two. I rolled into them, turning on to the tail of the first of the two wingmen, my wingman lining up on the leader.

My wingman, Lieutenant Bud Gehoe of Wilkinsburg Manor, Pennsylvania, shot the leader down just as I fired on the number two man. My target burst into flames and I pulled over to the third plane, who was still maintaining the most perfect formation possible.

He exploded almost the moment I touched the trigger. The elapsed time between shooting down the two planes was perhaps five seconds, and counting my wingman's kill the combat had not lasted over ten seconds.

Commander McWhorter still serves with the U.S. Navy.

Many pilots have speculated on what the Japanese might have accomplished in the Pacific war had their otherwise able Zero not been such a tinder box. The tough, durable Hellcat and Corsair could often take the Zero's best punch and keep flying as though nothing had happened. Rarely could the Zero survive the accurate blast of six 50-caliber guns. Sometimes, as some of the aces in this book have recalled, one gun, or even *one bullet* was enough to score a flamer.

Such a one-gun encounter with a Zero came the way of Navy ace

Horace B. Moranville, of Guide Rock, Arkansas. In Lieutenant Commander Moranville's view, it rolled aerial combat back to World War I for him for a few brief minutes:

> During a fighter battle over the Philippines, I had shot down two Jap fighters when my guns jammed. I left the fight to try to clear my guns. After several tries I was able to get one gun working, and just as I did so, I spotted a lone Jap plane racing low over the ground.
>
> I decided I'd better try and get him before he saw me, so I made a dive on to his tail. I opened up with my one gun, and after a very few rounds he made a sharp turn, drug his wing on the ground and crashed.

Moranville's luck was not always quite as good as this. He was shot down himself in January, 1945, over Indo-China, and spent four months as a POW. He is credited with six aerial victories.

The Zero did not have self-sealing fuel tanks, and as a consequence a hit in the fighter's tanks usually sent the Japanese pilot to join his ancestors. The violent flammability of the Zero became a legend among Pacific pilots, but if you talk about "fragile Japanese aircraft" to Lieutenant Commander Marvin R. Novak, he will tell you this surprising story:

> The most memorable combat experience for me was a fifty-mile chase of a Betty during the Marianas campaign. With a division of four Hellcats we caught and shot up a Betty cruising not more than ten feet above the water. We four Hellcat pilots loaded the Betty with 50-caliber slugs from highside, level, rear and frontal attacks. There was no opposition and we could afford the time for careful aim. We poured a fantastic volume of lead into that one bomber, expending all our ammunition.
>
> Finally, there were only one or two guns still firing. Twenty minutes had gone by. Then the Betty, almost as though from the sheer weight of the lead we had pumped into it, slammed into the water amid mountainous flames and debris.

Lieutenant Commander Novak hails from Manitowoc, Wisconsin, and spent his World War II career mainly with VF-14. He is credited with five aerial victories. His experience with the Betty shows that not *all* Japanese aircraft were easy to shoot down, and nor were any of them a sure thing.

An elite inner cadre of Japanese fighter pilots were superior air-to-air shots. A favorite tactic of these Japanese fliers was to get any American machine to enter either a loop or a Lufbery circle and try to out-turn them. This situation was made to order for the light Japanese machines, and they were often able to lure green American pilots into this trap.

The favorite grandstand shot of the Japanese was to shoot an American plane down precisely from the top of the loop. Many Japanese pilots have been seen to enter a vertical Lufbery, sometimes known as a squirrel-cage loop, passing up several opportunities for shots until the precise moment that their enemy was pulling through the top of the loop. Then—blast!

The Japanese pilots of the early days in the Pacific had few equals in aerobatic flying, and their numerical and technological superiority at that time allowed them to indulge in fancy feats of this kind. As the war progressed, such things occurred less and less frequently.

By 1943 the Japanese were committing younger and younger pilots with less and less experience. The habile veterans gradually were reduced in numbers. The Japanese attempted to compensate for the declining skill of their pilots with fanatical indoctrination in bushido. However, the latter proved to be no match for the skill, training and mounting technical superiority of the Americans.

Lieutenant George Pigman Jr. of New Orleans, Louisiana, had an experience while flying with VF-15 that emphasizes the importance of the men on the ground to those in the air:

Every plane you shoot down is a new and exciting experience: it is impossible to say which is really the greatest thrill. But the victory which I remember best occurred over Formosa in 1944. We had heard about a new Japanese fighter called the "Tojo," which looked like the P-47, carried 20mm cannons and heavy armor plate.

Naturally, it was not as maneuverable as the Zero, but it was supposed to be quite a plane, and in this encounter, I suddenly saw one coming at me head-on. Never will I forget those flashing guns blazing at me, although it lasted only a few seconds.

I knew my guns were scoring, and so were his. As he went under the right wing, I pulled up and to the left. The Tojo was

burning, and the pilot was bailing out. This encounter was just one
of the many instances of the contribution made by nonflying personnel. There had been no airmanship, tactics or anything like that.
All I had to do was sit still and pull the trigger.

Because those on the ground had provided me with a reliable
aircraft whose performance was perfect that day, the Tojo went
down. There were other times when the skill and the experience of
the pilot meant the difference, but on that occasion the credit
should have gone to someone other than me.

Pigman ended the war with 8.5 victories to his credit, and today is
an attorney in New Orleans.

Ralston Murphy Pound Jr. of Charlotte, North Carolina, racked up
six aerial victories while flying with VF-16 off the *Lexington* and with
VF-150 off the *Lake Champlain*. He best remembers the "Marianas
Turkey Shoot."

We encountered the Jap fleet near our fleet while covering the
Saipan landings, and had a field day in one of the war's most colorful
battles. The Japs lost over four hundred planes that day to Navy
aircraft, with very slight loss to us.

I had flown two four-hour combat patrols, starting before daybreak, without making contact with the enemy. Our planes had
been shuttling between our fleet and the enemy fleet all day, and late
in the afternoon, the air group commander (Commander Ernie
Snowden, USN) asked for someone to fly wing on him to follow
the action.

We joined up after takeoff, and headed where our planes were
engaged with the enemy. We had flown about an hour before we
located the action, and as we flew around observing, a Jap plane
made a pass at us.

Commander Snowden took chase, and made his first kill. During
the action I lost contact with him and found myself in the middle of
several of our planes chasing a Judy bomber. I tried a side pass and
the Judy started a half-spin. I followed his maneuver, and ended up
looking straight at him from the right side about fifty feet away. I
was so close that I could see the pilot and observer clearly.

I opened up with all guns, and as I fired, a ball of flame belched
out of his engine. I flew through the fireball, and broke off my run.
As I rolled, I saw the Judy's engine quit and he started a gentle glide
to the ocean, about four thousand feet away.

All the planes around were making passes on the sitting duck, but I had done the damage, and since neither pilot nor observer tried to get out, or fired a shot after my run, I was credited with the victory. The Judy didn't burn, but kept gliding until it hit the water. Several boys from my squadron saw the action and confirmed the kill. I later joined up with the group commander and we landed safely, with his first plane and my sixth to our credit. I flew a total of twelve hours that day. I was one tired guy, but very happy.

Lieutenant Commander Luther D. Prater of Lexington, Kentucky, served appropriately enough aboard the U.S.S. *Lexington*—with VF-19. His eight aerial victories include one of the most harrowing experiences that can come the way of a carrier pilot—attempting a landing without an arrester hook:

Sixteen of *Lexington*'s fighters were launched before dawn for the first fighter sweep on southern Formosa. Upon arrival over the airfields in our assigned area, we were attacked by an estimated forty Japs fighter planes. In the battle, most of our planes were separated, and each time I spotted a Hellcat two or three Zekes would be jumping him.

I finally got behind a Zeke that was firing at the squadron commander. I closed to about six hundred feet and opened fire. The Jap plane exploded with the first burst and crashed in flames. Thirty seconds later I saw a Zero coming at me head-on. I pulled my plane up and opened fire, the second and third bursts slamming into his engine. He flamed and crashed.

Shortly afterward, while the squadron commander and I were strafing parked planes on a small airstrip, he crashed and was killed. After three more strafing runs, I was able to contact three of our planes in the area and started climbing out to rendezvous with them. Three Zekes jumped me at six thousand feet, and I managed to duck into some cloud.

When I came out of the cloud I spotted one of these three Zekes and made an immediate attack. I chased him down to treetop height, and there finally hit his engine. His plane exploded and crashed. After joining three of our planes we all proceeded to the carrier for a landing.

During the landing approach, I discovered my arresting hook had been damaged and would not extend. After circling the carrier for about ten minutes I was given the alternative of landing in the drink or landing on the carrier "the hard way"—with no hook.

On my first approach, I managed to land aboard without damaging the plane or myself, and was without doubt the happiest man in the Navy when I climbed out of that plane.

In Denver, Colorado, there's a building contractor named Vincent A. Rieger. Building was not always his business. During World War II he served as a fighter pilot aboard the U.S.S. *Cabot*, and became an ace with five aerial victories. He well remembers June 11, 1944:

Fighter Division 4, of which I was number two man, accompanied by Divisions 2 and 6 was assigned a sweep against fields on Saipan, Tinian and Rota—all islands of the Marianas group. We went in low to avoid radar detection, and forty miles out, eight of us started climbing to act as top cover.

A 12,000-foot overcast kept us at 11,000 feet. Upon arrival we found the fields below us being well beaten up by waves of our carrier aircraft. We thought we'd caught the enemy by surprise. Then tracers spurted past in front of my eyes. *We'd* been surprised instead.

I swiveled round and saw several Zekes coming straight down through the overcast, making overhead runs on us. We dropped tanks, spread out to scissor and I saw a Zeke flatten out directly behind Lieutenant Turner, my division leader. Turner turned towards me and I turned toward him, which gave me a head-on shot as the Zeke turned with Turner. This was a mistake for the Jap. My first burst exploded him in midair. I narrowly avoided the debris of his plane.

A second Zeke, following my first kill, lost heart and started to bolt. He put himself in perfect position as I pushed over, gained speed and closed and fired, setting him on fire. The fight was now almost over, except for a Hellcat that was obviously in trouble with a Zeke sitting on his tail.

I got over to him, knocked the Zeke down, and discovered the Hellcat was our number three man, Lieutenant Conant, who had had his canopy shattered by Jap fire and was bleeding about the face and neck from cuts. I led him to our rendezvous point and we flew back to our carrier and landed OK.

Lieutenant Roy Warrick Rushing of McGehee, Arkansas, was flying as wingman to top Navy ace David McCampbell when these events unfolded:

On the morning of October 24, 1944, our task force was off the coast of Luzon. Most of our Air Group were out on strikes, and six of us who had been on an earlier mission were on standby alert. Among us was Commander David McCampbell, our top ace, and I was his wingman.

As the morning advanced, our radar picked up a large bogey coming from the Philippines and we were scrambled. They were Jap dive-bombers with several layers of fighter cover. Most of the fighter escorts were carrying bombs, too. McCampbell and I took advantage of clouds to get above the Japs, who were stacked up to 24,000, while the remainder of our flight was ordered to strike the dive-bombers, which were coming in at 15,000 feet. McCampbell and I discovered our quarry consisted of about forty fighters and twenty dive-bombers.

We immediately went to work, and in the course of the next thirty to forty-five minutes we managed to break up their force and chase them back to Luzon. We turned back because we were running low on gas and ammo, but could not be taken back aboard because the deck was not clear.

McCampbell was lower on gas than any of us and had to be taken aboard another carrier. The rest of us sweated it out and then were taken aboard our own ship, the *Essex*. McCampbell destroyed nine on this mission, and I was credited with six.

Lieutenant Rushing is credited with thirteen aerial victories and four probables during his World War II career, bad film in his gun camera and lack of full confirmation no doubt depriving him of the extra victory credits. His service with VF-15 is a cherished memory as he goes about his work today as an industrial engineer in McGehee, Arkansas.

Just as the U.S. Navy had taken the brunt of the first blow against America by the Axis, so was it the U.S. Navy that took the final swipe at Japanese air power on August 15, 1945. The last confirmed aerial victory of World War II is credited to Lieutenant Commander Thomas H. Reidy of North Field, Illinois. This historic victory is not likely to be forgotten by Tom Reidy:

On the morning of August 15, 1945, I led a sixteen-plane fighter sweep to the Tokyo Bay area. Mission was to destroy airborne aircraft, and if none were sighted, to attack Atsugi airfield near Tokyo.

At 0540 hours and while about fifteen miles offshore, I sighted a Jap reconnaissance bomber (Myrt) headed toward the fleet. His mission was probably recon or kamikaze, or both. One pass and I'd shot him down.

I proceeded on towards Tokyo when, at 0545, I received a coded message saying the war was over. I had shot down the last Jap of World War II, and was awarded the DFC for my final and tenth victory.

Thus ended the contribution of the U.S. Navy's fighter aces to Allied victory in World War II.

8

☆　☆　☆　☆　☆

Fighter Aces of the U.S. Marine Corps

PILOTED with the dash and élan that is traditional with the U.S. Marine Corps, Marine fighter aircraft were a vital part of the American campaigns in the Pacific in World War II. Marine fliers not only harried the Japanese in aerial combat, they also lent their strength to the work of the "mud Marines" with energetic close-support flying.

The aggressive spirit that is essential to the making of a Marine found adequate outlet in aerial combat. The USMC claimed and was credited with 2,355 aircraft shot down in air-to-air combat. To this figure must be added the untold hundreds of Japanese aircraft destroyed on the ground by Marine fighter pilots.

The spearhead tasks of the Marine Corps in the Pacific war ensured that Marine fighter pilots were in the van of the action. These flyers wrote many glorious chapters in Marine history during the dark days of Guadalcanal and Midway Island, as well as in the later campaigns after the turn of the tide. Marine aviation produced not only outstanding fighter pilots, but some fabulous characters as well.

One Marine who will pass into folklore as well as hold his place in formal history is Colonel Gregory "Pappy" Boyington. Unsurpassed by any other American fighter ace for sheer color, flamboyance and fighting skill, Boyington ended the war with twenty-eight aerial victories to his credit.

Boyington scored twenty-two of these victories while flying with Marine Corps units in the Pacific. The remaining six kills he gained while flying with Chennault's Flying Tigers in China. This has created a perennial controversy as to who is the top-ranked Marine fighter ace of World War II, and arguments about it invariably erupt whenever buffs gather.

Joseph Jacob Foss is credited with twenty-six aerial victories, all of them gained with the Marine Corps. Few fighter pilots can match the career of this ace for either distinction or diversified service to his country. Foss entered public life after World War II, and subsequently became Governor of South Dakota, as well as a Brigadier-General in the Air National Guard.

Because of this career and background, Foss is regarded as the all-American boy of Marine Corps aviation. Most of the quasi-official material circulated about him refers to Foss as the Marines' top ace, and for purists there can be no doubt that he is entitled to this honor.

Boyington, on the other hand, has always been something of a black sheep, and for a long time the Marine Corps did not seem able to make up its mind whether Boyington belonged to them or not. He destroyed more enemy aircraft in combat than any other Marine pilot, and this distinction cannot be taken from him.

Suffice it to say of the Foss-Boyington statistical comparison that both were outstanding fighter pilots, and both provided the wartime press with morale-building feats. Both men have become historical personalities in their field.

Boyington immortalized himself and the gang of outcast, rambunctious pilots he led as the "Black Sheep" Squadron. Because he was older than most of the men with whom he flew, and also because he was their leader, they came to call him "Pappy."

The name stuck, and through the years has become as well known to the public as that of any American flyer who ever lived. Boyington's prowess in downing Japanese aircraft brushed off on the Black Sheep Squadron. However abrasive Boyington's ways might have been to Marine commanders who went by the book, his squadron shot down more Japanese aircraft than any other operating in the Pacific.

In his own way, "Pappy" got the job done, even if his plain speaking, frankness and insobriety made him seem less than a gentleman to his wartime critics. The last word on "Pappy" Boyington will come, of course, from "Pappy" Boyington. His best-selling book *Baa Baa Black Sheep* tells his whole story and is as good a tale of a reluctant hero as can be found.

Pappy's own view of heroes is a jaundiced one—"Show me a hero and I'll show you a bum." Because of his own fierce battle with himself, a struggle as strenuous as any he engaged in during his combat flying years, Boyington is no doubt sincere in this view, but it is certainly less than true of many quiet men whose stories appear in this book.

Boyington's "Black Sheep," scattered now to dozens of different trades and towns, still remember their old boss with a special kind of affection. Even Boyington's decision to run for Congress (he was defeated) brought the following irreverent but typical comment from one of his Black Sheep:

"Well, old Pappy has tried everything else, and there he is right down at the bottom of the barrel—running for Congress."

Thus did Boyington set the stamp of his personality on those he led. To them, he can never be anything else but the wild man he was in his Pacific days, a flying and shooting demon who more closely epitomized the hell-for-leather fighter pilot of fiction than any other American pilot of World War II.

As a pilot Boyington was superb. A wrestler in his college days, he made good use of his powerful neck muscles in out-turning his Japanese foes, using this development as a built-in G-suit. Pappy was a crack shot and blessed with an almost psychic acumen in combat that saved his life on many occasions.

It is appropriate here to quote another of Boyington's "Black Sheep," one who belongs to the fraternity of fighter aces. Major Robert W. McClurg of Coshocton, Ohio, fairly expresses the kinship between all "Black Sheep" when he says: "The fact that I was the wingman of Pappy Boyington means more to me than medals—by far." Bob McClurg is credited with seven aerial victories, and remembers what it was like to fly with Boyington's VMF-214:

I was flying wing on Pappy when we took off from Vella Lavella on October 18, 1943, to escort SBD dive-bombers over Kihili Air Base, Bouganville. Our mission was to knock out fresh new Jap fighter planes that were now ready for operation, and the fighters under Pappy were to protect the SBD's while they bombed the Jap fighter fields.

When we got over the target area flying at 28,000 feet, my Corsair developed a magneto flash and the engine conked out. The prop windmilled and I lost considerable altitude. Just at that moment the dive bombers were peeling off to lay in their eggs on Kihili. The Jap Zeros jumped our fighters from about 30,000 feet from behind a huge thunderhead. At the same time the new Jap fighters were taking off from Kihili Field to intercept the SBD's as they came in on their bombing run.

Meanwhile I was fighting to start my engine again. It would cut on and off momentarily, and it was running very rough when I got down to 2,500 feet. I was figuring on a water landing and was looking for an offshore area so I could be picked up by the Dumbo or Black Cat rescue PBY.

Then ahead and below I spotted two Zekes flying formation and climbing for altitude, and I quickly figured I had a good chance to take one of the slant-eyed boys with me. I closed in on the rear Jap in the two plane formation, and at 2,000 feet on a stern run set him blazing.

They'd been flying a loose formation, and the rear plane was quite a bit behind, so I assumed the leader never saw me get his wingman, who by this time was almost down to the drink and still blazing. As I pressed my attack home on the leader he saw my tracer instantly, and pushed over to break away. Even though my engine was running rough as hell, the guns still functioned OK and the leader now rolled over and burned all the way down to the water.

By now I was down to five hundred feet and flying like crazy for friendly water. I was able to nurse the plane well away from the Jap-held land, and when I was about to attempt a water landing my engine cut back in again and took me home to base. The kills on these Japs were confirmed by an Army flyer who was flying low cover that day. He saw the whole thing and told the Intelligence officer. I got the DFC for this action.

On the following day, October 19, 1943, Bob McClurg again went into action as Pappy Boyington's wingman and tells this story:

It was a volunteer strafing raid on Kihili, and I remember adding up the scores of our division members as we took off in pouring rain and darkness. There was Pappy with over twenty Jap kills and me with my seven in one section, and Chris Magee and Don Moore with nine and three kills respectively in the other. We had over thirty Jap planes to our credit, as a division.

Pappy led us directly to the target, and in our haste to get at it Pappy separated from us. Chris Magee and I strafed nine Jap planes on the strip at dawn and beat up a couple of gun emplacements. They fired shore battery guns at us, trying to have us fly into geysers of water because we were too low for AA fire.

Pappy strafed Kara airfield by himself and a Jap sub as well. I was lucky I came back as I just missed flying into the signal tower on Kahili. I got the DFC for this operation also.

In scoring his twenty-six aerial victories, Joseph J. Foss had innumerable brushes with death. His most memorable encounter was his first, which he recalls in these words:

My first encounter was probably the most stimulating of all I engaged in. I made several errors and the Good Lord let me get by with them. One was to concentrate on one opponent and not notice who he was with. As a result, I got him, and his three buddies gave me the works.

I made a dead-stick landing on Henderson Field as his friends chased me to the very ground. I came in a little hot and almost ran into the palm grove. There were more than 250 places where some of their lead had pierced my aricraft and not me.

During the battle for Guadalcanal in November, 1942, Foss almost died by drowning as a sequel to an aerial battle with superior Japanese forces. Foss downed three enemy aircraft, but sustained some engine hits in the process that crippled his Wildcat and forced him into the ocean.

As his machine plunged into the water, the cockpit canopy slammed shut, and as the Wildcat began to sink fast, Foss found the canopy jammed by the impact. The desperate pilot struggled in vain with the latch, while the ocean closed over the aircraft. Finally, just as the water was coming up to his chin, Foss popped the latch and the canopy slid back.

Dragged to the surface by the combined pull of his parachute pack and his Mae West, which he inflated once clear of the sinking Wildcat, Foss now faced a long swim to the nearest shore, the island of Malaita.

Half-drowned and exhausted, he was eventually picked up by an Australian sawmill operator.

After the securing of Guadalcanal in 1943, Foss was returned to the United States with twenty-six aerial victories to his credit. He was awarded the Congressional Medal of Honor. Foss' standing as an ace and hero was used for morale and training purposes by the Marine Corps. He did not get back to the Pacific for his second tour of duty until February of 1944, and did not add to his score.

As previously mentioned, the postwar years saw Joe Foss successful in both politics and business. He is an esteemed figure among the fraternity of fighter aces, and was the first President of the American Fighter Aces Association.

The seventh-ranking fighter ace of the Marine Corps is Lieutenant Colonel Marion E. Carl, who is credited with 18.5 aerial victories. Lieutenant Colonel Carl is one of the heroic band of Marine pilots who helped turn the tables in the Battle of Midway Island. At that time, Carl was serving with Marine Air Group 22, the unit which sacrifically attacked the raiding Japanese Zeros with obsolescent Brewster Buffalo fighters and a handful of Wildcats.

Carl survived this epic battle and found himself not long afterward at "the Canal," site of much Marine glory. He best remembers this incident from a hectic combat career:

In September of 1942, while lowering my landing gear in the pattern at Henderson Field on Guadalcanal, a Zero jumped me. I pulled up the gear and headed for an antiaircraft battery. The Zero pulled away, so I took after him.

He reversed very quickly and started to meet me head-on, then he pulled up very steeply. I stood my Wildcat on its tail, and caught him just as he passed over with a ninety-degree deflection shot. He exploded not far off the beach. I still have the oxygen bottle from that enemy plane—the only thing that floated in.

Colonel Carl's decorations include two Navy Crosses, five DFC's and fourteen Air Medals. He is still serving with the Marine Corps, and in the postwar period added peacetime feats to his illustrious record as a fighter ace. Among other achievements he has held both the world's speed record and the world's altitude record.

The nightfighter ace is one of the rarities among the 1,300 or so American fighter aces. This distinction belongs to Major Robert Baird of Los Angeles, California, a Marine fighter pilot who got his night eye in over Okinawa early in 1945. He shot down three Bettys, one Jake, one Frances, and one Nell at night while flying with VMF(N)-533. He tells this story:

On night CAP I was vectored onto a bogey, a Frances, and splashed him. However, I was so close to him that when he blew up, the explosion covered my Hellcat with oil. Then I was vectored to another bogey, a Betty this time, and had to look out the side to see him because of the oil on the windshield.

It was a duel lasting three minutes or so, and we exchanged numerous shots. Finally, mine must have got to him because he started spinning and I saw him blow up in the darkness below me.

Only six American fighter pilots have become aces in two wars involving the United States.* The Marine Corps has a representative in this elite group, Lieutenant Colonel John F. Bolt. During World War II Bolt served aboard the U.S.S. *Black Island* and won six aerial victories. In Korea, Bolt became the only Marine Corps ace of the Korean War and the only Marine Corps jet ace when he downed six MIG-15's. During his Korean duty, Lieutenant Colonel Bolt was attached to the USAF's 39th Interceptor Squadron and flew forty-two missions.

Lieutenant Dean Caswell of the Marine Corps was flying off the U.S.S. *Bunker Hill* in the Pacific when he entered an unforgettable aerial battle:

April 26, 1945, in the Okinawa campaign we were providing air cover 150 miles north of Okinawa for three radar picket destroyers. A vital part of the radar warning net of Vice Admiral Marc A. Mitscher's famed Task Force 58, these destroyers had been having fits as a result of kamikaze attacks.

Action began with my three F4U Corsairs vectored toward a bogey coming in high. Up we went for the enemy, clawing for altitude at full throttle. There was a bad haze that got worse as we

* The first American fighter pilot to become an ace in two separate wars is probably Major Albert J. "Ajax" Baumler, who scored eight kills in the Spanish Civil War and is credited with five kills in World War II as a pilot with the 10th Air Force in the Far East.

gained altitude, and we couldn't see a thing. We were high, on oxygen, and it was extremely cold up there.

"Many bogies dead ahead, twelve miles," rasped the controller's voice in our headphones. If we couldn't see any better than this, we were going to miss them. Everything was a dirty yellow haze. We heard a "Tallyho" from nearby friendly planes and almost immediately saw aircraft going down in flames about two miles to starboard. It was quite a show.

Suddenly I felt my stomach tighten and I got an ominous feeling of hostile presence. We had run right smack into twenty to twenty-five Jap fighters in the haze. We were no longer spectators enjoying someone else's flamers.

Initially we tried to fly by the book, but things got screwed up awfully fast. The lead F4U did a split-ess after a Zeke and I was left with the third man of the flight, First Lieutenant John McManus, USMC. You might say we were left holding the bag, the bag being a sky full of Zekes and Tonys.

Things happened fast. I was on their tail. Then they were on mine. Some of those Japs were good pilots. Round and round, tight, high-G turns and milling confusion. In this melee I steadied on a meatball target and it exploded in orange flames as I pulled the trigger.

This was not a new feeling, for I had done it before, but each time my exultation barely overcame the paralyzing fear that grips the vitals when you are fighting overwhelming odds. There were plenty of targets. The Japs were going round and round and we were in the middle. The battle sorted itself out into that kind of thing.

Mac got one, and I saw it flame out of the corner of my eye. I got another one. We began to weave, Mac and I, protecting each other, until I got caught between two fires, a Zeke in front and a Tony in back. In much less time that it takes to say it, my six 50-calibers blew the Zeke apart and Mac got the Tony hugging my tail.

We again pressed the attack. Our only salvation lay in aggressiveness and in keeping the enemy confused, and confused they were now. They had lost seven aircraft in as many minutes and were in danger of shooting each other down in their efforts to get at us. All their losses had been huge, terrifying flamers, those colossal gouts of fire that so often ended the lives of Japanese pilots.

In the haze, these livid firebursts were heightened in effect. It probably tipped the balance in our favor that they did not get us and yet the two Corsairs, full of fight, kept coming at them and scoring flamers.

Mac and I continued to hustle, and our shots were soon snap bursts at fleeing Japs. We actually turned the rest of them for home, with my Corsair riding herd on two Zekes. I put one of them in my sights and drew a blank. No ammo. I signaled to Mac and he took over, sending another Jap down in flames.

Caswell ended the war with seven aerial victories. Originally from Banning, California, he new lives in Edinburg, Texas.

James Norman Cupp of Red Oak, Iowa, scored thirteen aerial kills in World War II while flying the famed Hellhawks Squadron (VMF-213). He best remembers what happened right after the first F4U Corsairs were delivered to his outfit. The time: September, 1943. The place: The Solomon Islands.

We were on our way to patrol over Vella Lavella on September 17th when the news came from our ground controller that a large bogey was heading down our way. The sky was dotted with puff clouds that stretched up to eighteen thousand feet, and as leader of a four-plane division, I figured that the enemy aircraft would be riding just over the top of them.

We started to climb towards the southern tip of the island, dodging clouds all the way. We nosed through a hole and saw a massive formation of dive-bombers plowing in about five miles away from us and at the same level.

The same instant I looked up and saw a string of eight Zeros zigzagging across the sky and less than a hundred feet above my head. We turned over on our backs and headed for cover, while radioing the Japs' position and course. The Zeros saw fit not to follow, so, after a few thousand feet, we hauled up to try it again.

The second section lost a little ground in this maneuver. As we headed along a parallel course to the bombers, looking for another hole in the overcast to poke through, there was quite a lot of air between our first and second sections. However, it was not long before we saw our opening and headed through it.

This time the string of Zeros were looking straight down their guns at us, and we quickly repeated our "breakaway" maneuver. This time we were followed. This mistake the Zeros made was to get in between the two sections. As my wingman and I headed for lower altitude, Avey and Stewart of the second section were on the other end of the string blasting away merrily. It did not take long to whittle down the odds to "even" and the remaining Zeros left my tail for safer places.

In the meantime the Jap bombers were getting on their target. By the time we again gained our altitude, we found most of them in their dive and only a few left upstairs for us. We had a speed advantage and as we came from behind we chopped our throttles and sat there. We could almost reach out and touch them as our six guns on each plane opened up.

The one I was on looked like a toy suddenly thrown to the floor. Pieces started flying from it and suddenly there was nothing there. In the distance, I saw one already in his dive, and for some reason I was determined to get him at all costs. All that was possible at the moment was to follow him down and avoid as much of our own AA fire as possible. I was glad to note that Stewart, my wingman, was still with me.

We leveled off right over the water and began to sidle over to our target. My eyes had been so focused on the one plane that I was suddenly surprised to see another bomber flying alongside the first, and another—and another. I looked around and found the whole area covered with them. We'd followed our man to the rendezvous where all the planes completing their runs were assembling in formation for the return trip to Kahili airfield on Bougainville.

I pulled back on the throttle to keep from overrunning them and started in. It was almost pathetic to see their efforts to avoid destruction. They were already less than ten feet off the water, and all they could do, apart from firing the gun in the rear seat, was to skid from side to side.

I came upon one with a very earnest desire to live. He threw his plane around with all his might and it was hard to keep my bullets going into him. First the gunner slumped over and next the engine started to burn. In an instant the whole plane was a flaming torch skidding across the water.

I pulled up and crossed over the top of Stewart and came down again. The bomber ahead of me was jerked around and I came closer without firing. The closer I came, the more violent his maneuvers became, until finally one wing dug the water and he crashed. I pulled up, crossed back over Stewart and continued on up the line.

It was disheartening to find that their gas tanks were bullet-proofed and flamers were rare, but we did well in spite of it. Everytime I turned back to look over the course, I could see a Jap plane hit the water. I was able to count three of Stewart's, though it was hard to keep track of him. Four of mine hit the water but we passed over most of them so fast it was impossible to watch the effect.

We were nearing the head of the column and had just finished off one together when my little world started falling apart. A 20mm shell came through the tail and exploded the CO_2 bottle back of the seat. The noise scared the hell out of me. Another came over my head and hit the accessory section just back of the engine. Another knocked a hole in my left wing, carrying my flap away.

By this time I had gathered enough presence of mind to turn around and look for the trouble. Trouble there was, and plenty. Four Zeros were sitting a thousand feet above and behind me, getting set to take turns at me. When I saw their altitude advantage, the fire of hope dimmed. Stewart had pulled ahead and did not respond to my radio.

Undaunted, I pressed on the sending button, hurriedly gave my position and shouted for help from anybody. With those holes staring at me from my fuselage, I was sure that I could not stay in the air long. I would have ditched then and there, but I did not relish the prospect of being strafed while swimming around in the sea.

The alternative was to shove the throttle home, just on the off-chance something remained of the engine. It did. That beautiful, faithful greyhound of a plane leaped like a bat out of hell. I was on a heading rough toward home at the time, and the Japs must have been too low on fuel to risk a chase away from their own base. They made no effort to follow.

I landed at Munda without flaps or brakes. Only a trickle of oil was getting to the engine, and most of it had leaked out. The skin of the plane was sieved with small-caliber holes in addition to the gaping ones that sent me scampering home. My life was charmed that day.

There is good reason why Jim Cupp's experience conveys a remarkable sense of immediacy. Like many other fighter pilots, he wrote down his experiences during the war. He very kindly provided the foregoing passage from an unpublished manuscript of aerial combat with the Marine Corps, written in 1943–1944.

Lieutenant Colonel Jack E. Conger, Marine ace from Des Moines and Orient, Iowa, not only picked on Japanese aircraft, shooting down ten of them, he also tackled Japanese destroyers. He sank two destroyers in concert with three other Marine pilots in the Solomons. In 1944 he sank another destroyer in the Palaus.

Conger emerged the victor in a Solomons air battle after making highly unorthodox use of his aircraft. He tells the story of what must surely be one of World War II's strangest aerial victories:

In October of 1942 I was at Guadalcanal, and was involved in a dogfight with a Zero. I finally got myself into an advantageous position on his tail, but on pressing the trigger found I was out of ammo. I didn't like the idea of breaking off and giving him the chance to get on my tail.

I decided to ram this Jap and I used my propeller like a buzzsaw. It cut the Jap plane into two pieces. My aircraft went into a violent spin and I was afraid to bail out for fear of being swiped by the tail section. My plane hit the water and miraculously I was able to get out. After inflating my Mae West I saw the other pilot, the Jap, in the water about a hundred feet away.

A few minutes later a boat with some Marines and Coast Guardsmen aboard came out to pick me up. We then tried to get the Jap pilot in the boat also, but he was completely unwilling. While trying to fish him out of the water with a grappling hook the Jap pulled a pistol and tried to shoot at us. Luckily the pistol misfired, probably due to dampness. We clouted him unconscious with the boat hook and pulled him aboard.

Guadalcanal was the site of an aerial battle on December 12, 1942, involving Major Jefferson J. DeBlanc of St. Martinsville, Louisiana:

We dove from five thousand feet to intercept Jap twin-engined Betty bombers making torpedo runs on the fleet off Henderson Field. We had to dive through our own AA fire, and two of our planes were shot down in the process. There were twenty-five Bettys. I managed to shoot down two before they reached the fleet and smoked a third, sending him veering off course. With all the steel that was flying round and by that time only fifty feet off the water, I was fortunate, through God, not to get any "arrows" in the F4F-3.

Major DeBlanc holds the Congressional Medal of Honor and is credited with nine aerial victories in World War II.

The eleventh-ranking Marine Corps ace, with fourteen aerial victories to his credit, is Archie G. Donahue of Texas City, Texas. Now a Lieutenant Colonel in the Marine Reserves, Archie sells real estate and insurance, and well remembers this incident from a distinguished combat career:

I was credited with five kills in one battle at Okinawa, but my most exciting victory was my first Zeke off Guadalcanal. Lieutenant

Hughes and I were escorting several bombers to attack a Jap battle-wagon. A flight of nine or ten Zekes came down at us to break up our formation. I blew up the lead Jap with a lucky short burst. The rest of them then quit and left us alone.

There were no further attacks from the air, but this incident and the subsequent storm of AA fire from the Jap battlewagon and its escort made this the most exciting mission of my career.

Also a Lieutenant Colonel in the Marine Reserves is Frank Carl Drury, an ace who flew with VMF-212 and VMF-113 in the Pacific during World War II. Drury scored six aerial victories, five of them during the Solomons campaign. He best remembers this one:

We were on a predawn patrol and joined combat over Rekata Bay, San Isabel Island. Eight of our F4F's were dogfighting float-equipped Zeros below two thousand feet and in almost total darkness. They used running lights and we did not, but it was still pretty "hairy." One Zero shot down another Zero that morning in a case of mistaken identity. When I got into firing position on one of the Japs I found only one of my guns firing, but it was enough. He flamed and plunged into the ocean.

Frank Drury was not done with combat flying when Japan surrendered. He flew again with VMF-331 in Korea for eight months before returning to civilian life as a citizen of Danby, Missouri.

Bill Farrell of Gardena, California, flew in two wars with the Marine Corps. In Korea, Bill flew in the ground-attack role by day with VMF-311 and by night with VMF(N)-513, destroying over fifty-two trucks and aiding the general dislocation of North Korean logistics. In World War II, he accounted for five Japanese planes in aerial combat while flying with VMF-312. His most vivid recollection is of a thrilling pursuit:

In May, 1945, while attached to VMF-312 at Kadena on Okinawa, three squadron mates and I were on Combat Air Patrol thirty miles north of Okinawa. We were relieved on station, but before leaving for home base we took one more tour of our patrol area. Cloud coverage was about nine-tenths, and a formation of thirty-five Zekes, Tojos and Vals were spotted through breaks about a thousand feet above us and on a collision course.

Their formation was a V of V's, and our formation of four pulled into rear position and started firing. In the ensuing ten minutes' dogfight, which passed from ten thousand feet down to water level, fourteen Japs were confirmed destroyed and three others probably destroyed.

I witnessed the destruction of one of our Corsairs—the pilot was lost—but I personally accounted for the Zeke that exploded him.

I followed this fellow for four thousand feet to the water, in a dive in which every time I would fire my guns he would pull out of range as my aircraft slowed. I finally started him burning as we leveled out on the water.

His sudden slow-down caused me to close to such a near wing position I could see the frightened expression on his face as he spotted me. He was trying to climb out of the cockpit through the flames, but his aircraft hit the water and exploded violently.

In this fight I shot down one Tojo, two Zekes and one Val and shared another Val. I also probably destroyed another Zeke for a total of 4.5 destroyed and one probable. My grand total for World War II was five destroyed and one probable, as I had shared the destruction of another Val a few weeks previously.

Dewey F. Durnford Jr. of Columbus, Ohio, flew with VMF-323 in World War II and scored 6.33 aerial victories. His forty-nine missions in that war were followed by seventy-six missions with VMF-311 in Korea and sixty more missions as an exchange pilot with the USAF in F-86 Sabrejets. While flying Sabres, Durnford was credited with a shared kill of a MIG-15, bringing his total victory credits to 6.83. His outstanding combat memory is of an action in World War II:

While flying number three in a flight of Corsairs covering the invasion of IeShima, our flight was vectored to a picket ship that was under attack. I first spotted this DD smoking badly from a direct hit near the bridge, and as we approached, I saw a Jap Lily bomber commencing another run.

Firing from six o'clock high I flamed him and he crashed about eight hundred yards short of the DD. Ten minutes later we spotted another bomber and our flight was now down to the leader and myself, the remainder having returned to Kadena for various reasons. The leader, finding his guns jammed, made feinting runs while I closed to fire. On the first pass I smoked the port engine, and as I pulled away my own cockpit began to fill with smoke.

The Jap tail gunner had been pouring it to me and I immediately figured he had hit my aircraft. When I opened my canopy to bail out, the smoke cleared instantly and I suddenly realized that it was the bomber's smoke. I strapped back in and started back toward the burning bomber when the Helen released a Baka.

This was the first of these new weapons to be observed in this area, and I was properly amazed. The Baka spun into the water and I closed on the Helen, blowing the port engine off. Then the wing came off and he plunged into the sea in flames.

The lively sky above Guadalcanal was the setting for this combat experience recollected by Lieutenant Colonel Kenneth DeForrest Frazier of Burlington, New Jersey:

On October 3, 1942, while flying over northern Guadalcanal with a flight of F4F's led by Captain Marion Carl, we engaged a superior number of Zeros. In a brief engagement, I shot down two Zeros before my plane was struck by 20mm cannon fire from a Zero that slipped in behind me while I was occupied with one of my victims.

My engine stopped and fire broke out in the forward section of the aircraft. I dove through a large cloud to shake my attacker, and then bailed out. While I was floating down under my parachute I was shaken out of my skin by the sight and sound of tracer bullets whizzing past within inches of my head.

My attacker had followed me down and was strafing me in my parachute. After a few seconds of this, which seemed like a terrifying eternity, a lone F4F piloted by Lieutenant Colonel H. W. Bauer (now deceased) closed in on this strafing Zero and drove him off trailing a large column of black smoke, despite the fact that Bauer had only one or two guns operating. I made a successful landing in the ocean several miles from the northeastern tip of Guadalcanal, was picked up by an American destroyer two hours later and returned to Henderson Field none the worse for wear.

Lieutenant Colonel Frazier is credited with 12.5 aerial victories in World War II.

Lieutenant Colonel Kenneth M. Ford of Whittier, California, shot down five aircraft in the Pacific to become a Marine fighter ace, and then returned to the fray in Korea in 1952–1953 as a helicopter pilot. He had this experience over the Russell Islands in World War II:

As wingman I followed my section leader from the main formation toward the Jap Zero horde over the Russell Islands. A Zero turned into my section leader's tail, and I shot him down in flames. The section leader continued on by the Jap force flying in the opposite direction, and as I was then right next to the Zeros with no chance to escape, I turned into the center of their force.

This probably saved my skin. There was such a rush of Jap planes trying to get on my tail for the kill that they got in each other's way, and I got in some good shots on the rest of them before the rest of the Corsairs joined the battle.

Practically every ace would echo the sentiment expressed by the Marines' Colonel Julius W. Ireland in his most memorable combat experience:

In January, 1944, while over Rabaul, I became separated from my wingman and found myself in the unenviable position of having a Zero firmly positioned on my tail. Unable to shake him, he just about had me boresighted when a lone Navy F6F appeared from nowhere and blew the Jap out of the sky.

I am positive that had he not appeared at that exact moment, I would not be here today, taking this opportunity to thank that unknown Navy pilot for saving my life.

Colonel Ireland is credited with five aerial victories, and has had a distinguished career with the Marine Corps. He now calls Baltimore, Maryland, his home.

Major Thomas H. Mann, Jr., of Sullivan and Graysville, Indiana, is credited with ten aerial victories, and well remembers four of these kills and the subsequent events:

While flying with VMF-121 at Guadalcanal on November 11, 1942, we had an 0900 scramble for a bogey. It turned out to be ten ACHI-99 dive-bombers escorted by Zeros. It was my last flight at the Canal.

We followed the dive bombers and I shot down my first at five thousand feet, my second one as it released its bomb in the dive, my third in retirement and the fourth in retirement about five miles northeast of Savo Island. Right there I was hit and shot down by my next target, an ACHI-99, who was ably assisted by a flock of Zeros.

I spent the next ten hours in the drink, swimming for the shore.

Then for the next six days I lived with natives on the northernmost island of the Florida group. They returned me to Tulagi in their war canoe on November 18, 1942.

One of the Marine Corps pilots who resigned his commission in 1941 to join the Flying Tigers is Lieutenant Colonel Edmund F. Overend of Portland, Oregon, and Coronado, California. Like many other aces who entered World War II this way, he cut his combat teeth over Rangoon, and found the experience the most exciting of his combat career:

My first mission was by far the most exciting, and took place on December 23, 1941. That day was my first day off in quite a while, and dressed in civvies with a shirt and tie, I was on my way to town with my good friend Charlie Older.

When the alarm went off we ran to the field and took off in two P-40's, primarily to get them off the field and avert their destruction. But as we climbed away we looked up and saw two formations of about fifty Bettys with fighters escorting them. I aimed a long distance ahead of them to pick up altitude and finally made a poor head-on run, being a little off course.

Their turret gunners were no better than I was and no damage resulted to either Charlie Older or me, so I dove deep and came up underneath the formation. I closed in to about fifty feet, firing all the way, and finally the right engine started to burn on the plane I was working on. It drifted out of the formation and started to go down.

Being green, I followed it to make the kill sure instead of letting it go and getting some more of the Bettys. I finally struck the turret gunner and he went down over his guns. At this point the bomber went into a steep dive, and in excitement and elation at having splashed it, I dived steeper and steeper with it. Finally, the P-40 being a good deal more streamlined than the Betty, *I found myself passing it.*

I pulled away sharply with Oscars hard after me. I evaded them and returned to base. Although I saw plenty of action after that day and my technique improved considerably, it was never matched for sheer excitement and that dry feeling that reaches from the throat to the navel.

Lieutenant Colonel Overend is credited with nine victories in World War II.

The Charlie Older mentioned by Overend in his story is Colonel Charles H. Older of Los Angeles, California, another Marine Corps pilot who volunteered for the Flying Tigers after resigning his commission. Older shot down 10.25 aircraft with the AVG, and then knocked down eight more after transferring to the 23rd Fighter Group in the 14th Air Force, for a total of 18.25 victories in World War II.

Older was trained as a pilot as a Marine Aviation Cadet at Pensacola, Florida, in 1939–1940 and served with the First Marine Corps Fighter Group in 1940–1941 prior to signing up for the AVG. Older survived the war and now practices law in Los Angeles, California. He also handles the legal affairs of the American Fighter Aces Association.

It was the misfortune of many highly trained and eager fighter pilots sometimes to fly numerous missions without getting even one shot at the enemy. Captain Robert B. See had the unusual experience of finding both combat and victory on his first combat mission.

> On a fighter sweep over Rabaul, New Britain, I was flying tail-end Charlie in another squadron, as three planes in my division had had to turn back. I just joined up with the first three-plane division I found.
>
> Sixty F4U Corsairs led by Pappy Boyington encountered approximately 140 Zeros and Tonys over Simpson Harbor. That melee was the wildest of all dogfights. I had all I could do to stay with it, and I didn't get a single good shot until I spotted a lone Zero pulling a tight chandelle to evade a pursuing Corsair.
>
> He was going slow and a set-up, so I dove on him. When I fired, I expected six 50-calibers to blaze out, but only one gun fired intermittently. Now I could visualize an unhappy ending to this otherwise perfect bounce, with the Zero turning on my tail and gunning me. But I kept boring in on him, and suddenly the left wing of the Zero ignited into a ball of flame.
>
> I was astounded to see the Zero fall off in a steep spiral and crash into the sea. As he went in, the impact set off a phosphorus wing bomb he was carrying, which produced a dense white cloud of billowing smoke.

Captain See flew with VMF-321 and is credited with five aerial victories.

There's a considerable contrast between flying fighter combat with the Marines and owning a chain of haberdashery stores, but Harold E. Segal of Chicago, Illinois, and Woodmere, New York, is an ace who enjoys the contrast. In World War II, Harold Segal attained the rank of Marine Major and shot down twelve Japanese aircraft. He will never forget July 11, 1943:

I was flying wing on Jim Swett on an eight-plane patrol mission over Kolobangara. This mission was near completion, two planes returned to base with engine trouble and Swett sent the other four planes back. He and I were to stay only a few minutes longer.

Just as we turned to start back to base, Swett spotted bogies, forty bombers and a horde of escort Zeros both high and low. Swett headed directly for them, and, although my engine was acting up, I followed. As we headed for the bombers, Zeros attacked us and one came between Swett and me. A fast three-second burst and there was one less Zero.

Following Swett, I tried to hit one of the bombers, without success, using about one hundred rounds of ammo. Diving away, I almost escaped, but one Zero had me wired and riddled my plane with holes from nose to tail. I managed to climb away toward some clouds, but saw ten Zeros below and dove on them. In one run I managed to flame two of them.

Then all hell broke loose, and I was shot at from every angle by the Japs, finally going down into the water, where the Japs strafed me as I swam and ducked under the water during each of their passes. I waited until they ran out of ammo or got low enough on fuel to pull out, and then I climbed into my life raft. Thirty-six hours later a destroyer picked me up.

Harold Segal's leader on this mission, Jim Swett, is another distinguished Marine ace. He is now Lieutenant Colonel James Elms Swett of Seattle, Washington and San Mateo, California, and has 15.5 Japanese aircraft to his credit. Swett shot down seven Japanese dive-bombers, with another as a probable, in a single fight over the Solomons on April 7, 1943, a feat which brings him close to Navy Captain David McCampbell's one-mission record of nine confirmed kills.

Although the archetypal Marine has perhaps been somewhat over-drawn by Hollywood, the Corps has produced innumerable rugged, dashing and fearless heroes. It also produced one of the most modest in the person of Major Franklin C. Thomas, Jr.

Credited with nine aerial victories in World War II and bearing a high reputation among his fellow Marine pilots as a combat flyer, Thomas was asked to relate his most exciting combat experience for this book. His reply is a model of frank modesty:

Most exciting experience? All my combat experiences were exciting. Hell—I was scared to death the whole time.

More than this Thomas would not say about his combat career, which extended from December, 1942, to March, 1944. The records say that he was shot down and so badly wounded in his final battle that he required nine months in a hospital to recuperate.

Colonel Donald K. Yost of Princeton, New Jersey, is credited with eight aerial victories as part of a distinguished career that includes command of VMF-111 at Samoa in 1942 and of VMF-121 in the Solomons from December, 1942, to February, 1943. Later, as Air Group Commander of MCVEG-4 aboard the *Cape Gloucester* he scored his eight victories. His first victory, unclaimed, made the deepest impression on him:

This was on the afternoon strike of December 23, 1942, while my squadron was providing close fighter support for eleven SBD's bombing Munda Airport, New Georgia, from Henderson on Guadalcanal. As the bombers approached their push-over point to dive on the airfield, Zeros appeared at all altitudes as the eight P-39's between fifteen and twenty thousand feet, the eight F4F's below fifteen thousand feet, and the eleven SBD's were jumped simultaneously by about fifty Zeros.

The four P-38's flying high cover at thirty thousand feet were unaware of the presence of the Zeros. Communications were bad between planes of our own squadron and practically nonexistent with the Army Air Force units. Hence, it was pretty much a free-for-all.

As my flight started down with the SBD's, my wingman spotted a Zero off to the side and above and went after it. My radio call to him to stay with me was unanswered, and he was not heard from again. I continued down with the SBD's, believing my other planes were following, but as I attacked six Zeros making a pass at the SBD's I found I was *alone*.

After one pass, I found the six Zeros above me and in position to make runs at me. They took it in turns. While five stayed in position above me, one Zero would make a pass, fire, do a slow roll and pull up to the tail end of the other five. Then another would make his firing pass. It was just like we used to practice gunnery runs, and the way I was set up they were likely to get me eventually.

While the Japs were making their runs, I maneuvered to cause full-deflection shots—then as they pulled out and started up, I would fire on them. I was rewarded by having two in succession burst into flames and disappear. The Jap leader maintained position but did not make runs, thereby keeping me set up for the other Jap pilots. I was at such a disadvantage that if two Japs made simultaneous passes they would probably get me, so I looked around for friendly planes or a cloud to jump into.

There were no friendly planes, but there was a cloud about a mile away and above me. Figuring that the Jap leader was waiting for a good straightaway shot and that he would be on me immediately if I tried to climb for the cloud, I set myself in a position whereby he could come down on me from behind, but I never took my eyes off him.

He started his Zero down, and when he was well committed and closing fast, I turned into him and fired, with which he immediately broke off, and I bolted for the cloud. Just before I reached the safety of the cloud, tracers went smoking past me to the right and left and slightly above my wings. I snapped over quickly to evade this fire and apparently ducked under the engine of a Zero, for I saw it pass above me and to my left just before I got up to my cloud.

In the cloud I climbed to ten thousand feet and when I came out of it I turned back toward Munda to look for friendly planes. I stayed close to the clouds that usually hang over the center of the islands in the South Pacific in the afternoons. I saw plenty of milling planes, but could not recognize any friendly ones. I was about to turn back toward the Canal when far below me I spotted eleven SBD's heading for home. Behind the last SBD was a Zero, closing in with another Zero to the right and above the first.

Figuring I didn't have time to hit the wingman and get to the lead Zero before he shot up the SBD's, I passed by the top Zero and squeezed the trigger as I closed on the tail of the lead Zero. The thin, futile sound of only one outboard gun firing followed my trigger squeeze. As I fired, the Jap pulled up in a steep wingover, with me following part-way, but I broke off and ducked into the bottom of a cloud, figuring his wingman would be on me.

When I came out of the cloud I charged all my guns and found them all functioning perfectly. Again I could see no friendly aircraft, so I headed for home alone. I was the last plane on the whole mission to get back to base. My wingman was never found, and

from the story pieced together it appears he shot down a Zero but
was shot down by another Zero while doing so.

Several days later when they got time, the pilot and gunner of
the tail SBD came over to the squadron to thank the pilot who shot
the Zero off their tail. According to their story, the Zero completed
his wingover burning, and plunged into the sea. I had not reported
that plane and did not later report it as it seemed unimportant at the
time.

Epitomizing the unquenchable Marine spirit is the fourth-ranked
Marine ace of all the wars, Lieutenant Colonel Kenneth A. Walsh,
credited with twenty-one aerial victories. He has the rare distinction
among Marine aces of having received his pilot's wings while still a
private.

Walsh joined the Marine Corps as a private in 1933, and by sheer
ability and persistence won assignment to flight school. He began his
aviation flight training as a private and flew as an enlisted man until
1942, when he was commissioned. A wild aerial battle in which he took
part on August 30, 1943, was the most significant of several bold deeds
which won him the Congressional Medal of Honor.

After taking off with his fellow pilots of VMF-124 to escort B-24
bombers raiding Kahili airfield on Bougainville, the supercharger of
Walsh's Corsair failed. He was cursing his ill-luck in having to abort
the mission when he spotted our newly operative airstrip on Munda.
He dove his ailing Corsair with all speed for the strip.

When Walsh piled out of his plane, he was met by Major Jim
Neefus, CO of the advanced airstrip, an officer with whom Walsh had
served previously. Neefus immediately granted his urgent request for
another aircraft, and Walsh vaulted into the cockpit of a Corsair sitting on scramble alert. The ace was back in the air within ten minutes,
racing full throttle after the bombers.

With an ideal thirty thousand feet of altitude, Walsh caught up
with the bombers just as they were being bounced by a swarm of
Zeros. Streaking in from astern at just the right angle and with perfect
timing, Walsh threw the Japanese fighter attack on the bombers into
confusion.

In the fierce battles that followed, the aggressive Marine shot down
four Zeros before being shot into the sea off Vella Lavella by a concen-

tration of the Japanese planes. Plucked from the ocean by Seabees who had seen him crash, Walsh was back flying combat from Henderson Field within three days. For this spirited mission and other feats of arms in the air, Kenneth Walsh was awarded the Medal of Honor. He retired from active duty February 1, 1962, and is presently residing in Santa Ana, California.

A valiant Marine ace who did not survive World War II was the colorful Robert M. "Butcher Bob" Hanson. This skilful aerial fighter entered the Second World War with a background of experience few Americans his age could equal. He was born in Lucknow, India, the son of missionary parents, in February, 1920.

Educated by turns both in the United States and India, Hanson at age 18 was heavyweight wrestling champion of the United Provinces in India. On his way back to America in 1938, Hanson included a bicycling trip through Europe in his plans, and was a spectator to history in Vienna during the *anschluss*. Four years later, Hanson was making history in the Pacific as a Marine First Lieutenant and a fighter ace of formidable skill.

Lieutenant Hanson is the third-ranked Marine ace and is credited with twenty-five aerial victories. His feat in shooting down twenty of these machines in only six consecutive flying days is probably un-equaled by any other American pilot. On January 24, 1944, Hanson brought down four Zeros after battling them alone over New Britain. Three weeks later, Hanson's meteoric career was over. His plane crashed into the sea during an escort mission over Rabaul.

Hanson was awarded both the Congressional Medal of Honor and the Navy Cross, among other awards, for his feats in the air. The Navy made a more permanent memorial to Hanson in the form of a de-stroyer, named the U.S.S. *Hanson* in honor of the Marine ace.

Two other Marine aces who also became Medal of Honor winners are Major John Lucian Smith and Lieutenant Colonel Harold W. Bauer. Both aces won their spurs in the bitter battles around Guadal-canal in the August-September-October period of 1942.

Major Smtih was twenty-eight years old and the Commanding Offi-cer of VMF-223 during this period. He provided his men with leader-ship by example, personally shooting down sixteen Japanese planes between August 21 and September 15, 1942. His squadron scored eighty-three kills during this same period. He is credited with nineteen aerial victories in World War II.

Annapolis-trained Harold W. Bauer was thirty-four years old in the dark days of 1942, an "old man" as fighter pilots go. He went into the air in the Guadalcanal battles and shot down four Japanese fighters on October 3, 1942.

Two weeks later, Bauer led twenty-six planes on a 600-mile over-water ferry flight. Just as he was successfully completing this mission, Bauer saw a squadron of Japanese aircraft attacking the U.S.S. *Mc-Farland*. Alone and with his fuel almost gone, Bauer hurled himself onto the attacking Japanese planes, destroying four of them and demoralizing the remainder with his aggressive attack. He is credited with eleven aerial victories in World War II, eight of them on two missions. Bauer's father, John T. Bauer, resides in Fort Collins, Colorado.

The Marine Corps made a tremendous contribution to victory in the Pacific, both in the land battles and in the skies. The Marine Corps uniform was worn by 120 aces, and among them shot down 985 of the 2,355 enemy aircraft accredited to the Marines in aerial combat. These Marine aces added a new dimension and great splendor to the illustrious traditions of the elite Marine Corps, and two of them, Foss and Boyington, have become living legends.

9

☆ ☆ ☆ ☆ ☆

The Enemy Aces

AMERICA'S FIGHTER ACES won their laurels against skilled and determined foes. The Americans were made to fly and fight hard for their glories. No story of the American aces is complete without some record of the men they flew against, especially in World War II, the period of America's greatest engagement in aerial warfare. Many of the enemy aces were superlative airmen, whose careers are full of surprises and exceptional feats.

The German aces of World War I have been adequately covered in dozens of historical works on the subject. Detailed studies of the major German air fighters of that war are still periodically appearing. Suffice it to say of them that when the Americans finally got into the air in 1918 in their own units, the American flyers faced an experienced, determined foe mounted on better aircraft. Nor was this all.

Backing the German aces by 1918 was a four-year-long tradition of aerial fighting. Not only were there great individual aces, both living and dead, as examples to the German pilots, there was the hard-won knowledge of how to fight in the air. The lessons learned and taught by Boelcke and Richthofen were every bit as potent in the making of the German pilots as was the urge to equal or excel the achievements of Immelmann, Udet or Goering.

Against such opponents, the raw Americans did surprisingly well, as history now records. By war's end the Americans had rolled up an impressive ratio of victories to losses, which is history's endorsement of the qualities and skills of the Americans.

World War I is an open book as far as aerial warfare is concerned. There is hardly anything concerning the major aerial combatants that cannot be quickly and easily learned by studying published material. In World War II, a completely different set of circumstances prevailed, which has had as one of its effects the astounding lack of information about enemy combat pilots, both German and Japanese.

There was the hated Nazi regime on the one hand, and the conceivers of the Pearl Harbor assault on the other. Propaganda techniques, using the modern devices of radio and mass publicity, permitted little mention of the enemy as being even human. The Japanese in particular were looked on as something but little above the savage. Where Richthofen, Boelcke and Udet could have read about themselves in British and American newspapers in World War I, the American pilots for the most part hardly ever knew the name of an enemy ace during the whole of World War II.

Japanese procedures aided the total anonymity in which the Japanese aces fought as far as the Americans were concerned. Japanese tradition could allow only dead heroes. To the Japanese military caste of that day, the idea of publicizing the aerial victories of Hiroyoshi Nishizawa, their greatest ace, was unthinkable.

Equally unthinkable to the Japanese military was any special recognition for fighter aces generally, such as that accorded by the Allies and the Germans to their air heroes. Only in March, 1945, when the final collapse of Japan was imminent, did the Empire announce a special citation for two air fighters, Soichi Sugita and Saburo Sakai. Sugita was credited with eighty aerial victories, and Sakai, now the most successful living Japanese fighter pilot, with sixty-four.

The ironclad Japanese caste system saw the outstanding fighter aces fight through most of the war in noncommissioned rank. When after sixty aerial victories and eleven years as a combat pilot, Saburo Sakai became an officer in the Imperial Japanese Navy, he set a record for rapid promotion.

These restrictions of caste and tradition united with the wartime propaganda of the Allies to leave the Japanese fighter aces in almost total obscurity. They were as little known to the people they defended as they were to the Allied pilots they flew against. This situation, while almost incredible to Westerners, in no way detracts from the accomplishments of the Japanese aces in aerial combat.

The Japanese naval pilots in particular were put through a training as rigorous and exacting as any in the world. An example is the box-like structure with telescopic-looking openings to the heavens used for eyesight development. Inside the box, for untold hours, the tyro pilots peered through the tube-like openings. Their eyesight became so enhanced that they could see stars in the daytime.

The Japanese were trying their combat wings over China for many years before World War II. While they seldom bumped into any notable opposition, they gained invaluable experience in real shooting warfare in the air, and the confidence that developed from this became an intangible asset of enormous value.

The Japanese pilots who swept over Pearl Harbor and through the Philippines and the Far East were outstanding combat pilots by any estimate. They were standouts in both aerobatics and in air-to-air shooting, the latter skill bringing them many early victories.

The tactics used by the Americans in the early days of World War II played right into the hands of the Japanese pilots at the controls of their Zero fighters. At this time, the Zero had no equal for close dogfighting. Since all combat pilots in those early days were trained for this kind of battle, with the traditions of World War I lying heavily upon them, the Japanese knew many triumphs.

The Zero's 20-mm cannon, maneuverability and lightness were an unpleasant surprise for all the Allied pilots who met it in early combat. In the well-trained hands of Japan's "first team," the Zero had its heyday in the Pacific in 1942, battling the Grumman Wildcat F4F, the Bell Airacobra P-39 and the Curtiss P-40.

The American carrier pilots had to rely on superior tactics and teamwork until the later and better Hellcat came to hand in the summer of 1943, from which time the whole aspect of fighter combat over the Pacific changed decisively to Japan's disadvantage. With the introduction of the F4U Corsair, the P-38 Lightning and the P-47 and P-51, Japanese airpower was gradually crushed.

The greatest of all Japanese fighter pilots both by aerial victories credited and the estimate of his own Japanese contemporaries was Hiroyoshi Nishizawa, who survived in the Zero even against the much better American equipment that flowed into the battle. The Japanese pilots called Nishizawa "The Devil," for no other term could convey as well the way he flew and scored his victories.

Big at five feet eight inches for a Japanese, the cadaverous-looking Nishizawa was a withdrawn, aloof and reserved man who deliberately avoided the society of his fellow pilots. In this respect, he was not unlike the unsmiling grim French ace of World War I, Georges Guynemer, who turned into a ferocious demon the moment he entered the cockpit of a fighter plane.

In the air, Nishizawa could make a Zero do his bidding as no other Japanese pilot ever could. Part of his own will power seemed to break off and fuse with the aircraft, so that in his hands the design limits of the machine meant nothing. He could enthrall to the point of rapture even hardened Zero pilots with the unmatched vigor of his aerobatic flying.

One of the coterie of Japanese fighter aces who flew with the Lae Wing in New Guinea in 1942, Nishizawa was riddled with tropical diseases and often racked with dysentery. He seemed to drop these ailments and infirmities like a cloak as he sprang into his Zero, for once aloft his legendary vision and skills showed no evidence of his almost constant sickness.

Nishizawa has been credited with 103 aerial victories, a total that is perhaps disturbing to anyone accustomed to the much lower scores of the American and British aces. Nishizawa, however, flew right through the worst of the war, and was the kind of pilot and marksman who got kills almost every time he went into combat.

No one who flew with him doubts that he shot down over one hundred Allied aircraft. The disservice done to history by propaganda is graphically illustrated by the fact that despite this pilot having downed over a hundred American-flown aircraft, he was not known by name until long after the end of World War II. He bears the rare distinction of being the only enemy pilot in the Second World War to score over ninety kills against Americans.

Nishizawa was piloting an unarmed twin-engined transport plane on October 26, 1944, taking a load of pilots to pick up some Zeros at Clark Field in the Philippines. The lumbering machine was intercepted by U.S. Navy Hellcats, and even the invincible Nishizawa's skills were useless. The Hellcats made a few runs and the transport crashed in flames, taking "The Devil" to his death.

Ranked second among Japanese fighter aces was Naval Air Pilot First Class Shoichi Sugita, credited with eighty aerial victories. Sugita also fought right through the war until the final months, when U.S. fighters began sweeps over the Japanese home islands. At this time, Sugita was flying the Shiden (Lightning) fighter, considered to be the equal in the hands of a competent pilot of any Allied fighter.

On April 17, 1945, Sugita was strafed while taking off at Kanoya, his Shiden bursting into flames to become the ace's funeral pyre.

When human bravery and endurance are mentioned in connection with combat flying, it is impossible to ignore the career of Lieutenant Saburo Sakai, the greatest living Japanese fighter ace. Credited with sixty-four aerial kills, Sakai was in combat from prewar days in China right through to the Japanese surrender in 1945. One of his early World War II kills was the B-17 of U.S. air hero Colin Kelly, or at least so say the Japanese now.

His story has been vividly told in *Samurai*, the book he wrote in collaboration with Fred Saito and the distinguished American aviation historian Martin Caidin. The world of aviation buffs that has honored the RAF's legless ace, Douglas Bader, can hardly turn its back on Sakai. The courageous Japanese flew through the latter part of World War II with only *one eye*. Comparable examples of personal courage are rare, since eyesight is so vital an element in the survival of a combat pilot.

After one fierce encounter with Navy SBD's over Guadalcanal, Sakai flew back to Rabaul almost completely blinded and partially paralyzed. This 600-mile flight is one of the outstanding epics of fighter pilot survival. He recovered from his wounds and despite the loss of his right eye returned again and again to combat.

It is barely credible that this one-eyed fighter pilot, on the very eve of Japanese capitulation, took up his Zero *at night* and with another Zero shot down a U.S. B-29. He has in *Samurai* frankly attributed his survival to the poor air-to-air shooting of a number of American pilots who had him cold during his four years of combat over the Pacific.

Lieutenant (s.g.) Naoshi Kanno was a fighter pilot who gained fame tackling the B-17, an aircraft whose bulk, structural strength and firepower terrified many Japanese pilots. Kanno's score of fifty-two

aerial victories includes twelve B-17's. The same diving and rolling
attack from dead ahead that was later used by the Germans* against
the B-17 was first perfected by Kanno early in World War II in the
South Pacific. He was shot down and killed during the final defense of
Japan.

The Japanese fighter pilots could boast of at least one surpassing
"character" in their ranks, Lieutenant (j.g.) Temei Akamatsu of the
Imperial Japanese Navy. He was everything, and much more, than the
wildest fighter pilot of fiction has ever been depicted as being. To
the Imperial Japanese Navy, he was a "black sheep" and an incorrigible
nuisance. To the young ladies of Japan, Akamatsu was a hero to be
adored. To his fellow fighter pilots, Akamatsu was a flying enigma—a
breaker of rules who nevertheless amassed a formidable total of aerial
kills.

It was not uncommon for his squadron mates to see Akamatsu
literally reeling across the apron to his fighter, waving a sake bottle as
he went. With a disregard for regulations that seems incredible in the
austere Imperial Japanese Navy, Akamatsu declined to attend pilot
briefings. Word of imminent operations was conveyed to him by special runner or telephone in order that he could wallow in the brothel
of his choice until the last possible moment. At takeoff time he would
come steaming on to the airfield in an ancient jalopy, yelling like a
banshee and fighting drunk.

Akamatsu was broken in rank again and again. After ten years in
the Navy he was a Lieutenant, (j.g.), almost a record in itself. His wild
habits on the ground, which made him a living legend, were duplicated
in the air, together with some extremely shifty piloting and an outstanding tactical skill. These attributes in combat were so highly developed and valuable that they permitted Akamatsu the rein he was
given by his superiors.

Akamatsu demonstrated his flying skill superbly at the controls of
the heavy, hard-punching Raiden fighter, developed to battle the B-29.
With a top speed of 400 mph, the Raiden was a dead loss in aerobatics.
Almost any other fighter could out-turn it, and it was as tricky to fly

---

* The Germans credit Major Julius Meinberg (fifty-three victories while flying
with JG-53 and JG-2) with devising and executing the first head-on attacks against
the B-17 and B-24 daylight bombers over Europe.

in combat as any aircraft ever built by any of World War II's combatants.

Notwithstanding these grave technical handicaps, Akamatsu took on the formidable Mustangs and Hellcats many times in the Raiden, and he is known to have shot down at least ten of these superior fighting machines in aerial combat. His boasting and swaggering on the ground did not prevent him from maintaining a healthy and objective respect for the superior American machines aloft. Only in this way could he possibly have survived repeated combat with them, let alone emerge the victor many times.

Akamatsu is one of the few top Japanese fighter pilots to survive World War II. Credited with fifty aerial victories, he is in the restaurant business in Kochi, Japan.

A daring and aggressive pilot, Flying Warrant Officer Kinsuke Muto hacked down no fewer than four of the massive B-29 bombers. When these aircraft first appeared, the Japanese had barely recovered from their shock at the strength and fighting power of the B-17 Fortress. When the B-29, with its tremendous speed and firepower, carried the war to the Japanese home islands, it was a moral victory for America from which the Japanese never really recovered. Muto was one of the few pilots to gain multiple kills against the B-29.

The fearless Muto piled into an obsolescent Zero in February, 1945, and took off alone to tangle with twelve F4U Corsairs strafing Tokyo. The American pilots could hardly believe their eyes. "One good burst into a Zero and it'll explode" had been the experience of the Americans. This time, the shoe was on the other foot.

Flying like a fiend, Muto flamed two Corsairs one after the other with short bursts, demoralizing and disorganizing the remaining ten American pilots. The Americans regained their composure and started taking turns at the audacious Zero. Muto's brilliant aerobatic flying and aggressive tactics kept him aloft and unscathed until his ammunition was exhausted. By that time, two more Corsairs had gone down, and the remaining American pilots knew they had run into one of Japan's best. Navy records show that these four Corsairs were the only American losses over Tokyo that day.

By 1945, the Zero was virtually outclassed by all the Allied fighters pressing in on Japan. Muto was still flying the Zero in June, 1945, during the final phases of the war. He was shot down while attacking a Liberator. A few weeks more and Muto would have survived World War II.

The Japanese confirmation rules for victories were similar to those of the Allies, but were very loosely applied. As a consequence, many of the Japanese scores could be questionable. Due to Japanese desire to minimize weight, they did not carry gun cameras in their Zeros, and did not have this valuable filmic evidence to support their claims. There is, however, little evidence of any exaggeration or false claiming of victories. Since no medals, citations, promotions or publicity were given for fighter pilot prowess, there was no motive for inflating totals.

The Japanese pilots, for all their valor and the unquestionable brilliance of their top men, were ground down by an enemy that gradually gained all the advantages. The American pilots were mounted on better aircraft from the time the Hellcat and Corsair appeared. They also had better teamwork, superior communications and the all-out support of their nation. In the final months of the war, the Americans were numerically superior even over the Japanese home islands.

All the skill, courage and experience in the world could not turn such a tide. In view of this, the continued fighter sorties by Japanese pilots, virtually to the final shot of World War II, were born of an admirable never-say-die spirit vital to success in aerial combat.

The Japanese had a host of pilots with twenty kills or less, many with twenty to thirty kills, and a diminishing number on the higher rungs of the ladder that led to Nishizawa, Sugita and Sakai. Typical of other top Japanese pilots and their scores were:

NAVAL AIR PILOT FIRST CLASS KENJI OKABE, 50 (7 in one day with the Lae Wing)

LIEUTENANT TOSHIO OTA, 50

LIEUTENANT WATARU NAKANICHI, 55

LIEUTENANT YASUHIKI KUROE, 51

American pilots who flew against both the Japanese and the Germans in World War II generally consider the Germans to have been superior to the Japanese. Those who flew longest over Europe speak of the top German fighter pilots not just with respect—they consider them the best pilots of World War II, bar none!

This estimate buttresses one of the most remarkable and little known facts of the air war. The top ten German fighter pilots between them destroyed 2,588 Allied aircraft! This staggering figure has not been happily received on the Allied side. The sheer magnitude of the achievement certainly invites skepticism, if the feats of the Allied aces are made the sole basis for judging the feasibility of the German scores. America's top ten fighter pilots in World War II, for example, scored a fraction over 302 kills, or not quite 12 percent of the comparable German record.

In the years following the Second World War, skepticism about the achievements of the German fighter pilots found another ally in the continuing hatred of the Nazi regime. United, these two factors have served to obscure historical facts of some significance in the history of aerial combat. The only sensible approach to the activities of the German pilots is to consider the *facts* and not adopt the utterly unjustifiable view that because the Allied aces did not register such large bags of enemy aircraft, therefore the Germans did not.

It is a historical oddity that every student of aerial warfare knows the names of Richthofen, Udet and Boelcke, and yet the names and deeds of their descendants in World War II remain almost a total blank. Germany did have a Richthofen in World War II in the person of Lieutenant Colonel Erich Hartmann, credited with the amazing total of 352 aerial victories. Hartmann's score is more than four times as great as that of World War I's "Red Knight," yet Germany's greatest World War II ace is hardly known outside Germany today, almost a generation after the war's end.

Most of the German pilots were sportsmen. So were their Allied opponents. In the heat of battle, sportsmenship often went by the board in the desperate, milling kaleidoscope of kill or be killed, but only briefly. Composure was soon regained, if only because a hot head is a luxury a fighter pilot cannot afford. On both sides, aerial combat was like a hunt. The hunt was for other aircraft, piloted by other hunters.

During the unfolding of World War II, the Germans had to do far less hunting for their quarry then did the Allied fighter pilots. For most of the war, the Germans had their targets come to them. The course of the war and Germany's commitments gave Luftwaffe fighter pilots opportunities to gain experience and score aerial kills that were denied to the Allied pilots. Very little reflection is needed to show the truth of this.

There was the gigantic Russian front, ablaze from mid-1941 to the end of the war, and extending from the Baltic to the Caucasus. All along this unprecedented front, German air power worked in general accordance with the overall military plans. It was on this front that most of the Luftwaffe pilots cut their combat teeth and ran up large scores against the enormous swarms of aircraft hurled into the battle by the Russians.

Beyond the Baltic was the Far North and operations against the Allied convoys. The Luftwaffe's Polar Wing probably functioned under the most difficult and grim conditions of the war, but almost nothing has been recorded in English-language historical works concerning this unit.

Once the Allied effort turned Germany's juggernaut at El Alamein and Stalingrad, the Germans fought ever afterward on the defensive. For the fighter pilot, the defensive role favors both high scoring and pilot survival. The pilots were sure of finding plenty of targets, and if shot down, would land in their own territory and live to fight again.

The Germans had the tremendous defensive task of tackling the Allied bomber boxes. From 1942 onward, with mounting power by day and by night, Allied bombers pounded the Reich continually. Each of these bombers was a target to German fighter pilots operating over their own territory. The Allies carried the air war to Germany, and everywhere the German pilots flew they had an abundance of targets—hundreds of targets—a situation that applied to the Allies only in isolated and brief situations, such as in the struggle for Malta and the Battle of Britain.

The Germans would have been very poor airmen indeed if they did not score dozens of aerial victories under such circumstances. Since German fighter pilots were not withdrawn from combat for morale purposes or for assignment to training duties, as was the case with most of the leading Allied aces, it is obvious an elite corps of high-scoring German aces had to emerge. The experience of aerial warfare that came the way of these men is unrivaled by the pilots of any other nation.

The members of this elite, tactically formidable and brilliant marksmen to a man, were very rarely outflown by any individual Allied pilot pitted against them. Nevertheless, most of them were shot down many times, for aerial combat in the later years of the war saw the Germans outnumbered on all fronts. Even these elite German pilots were snowed under in the end by the avalanche of Allied machines sent against them. Indicative of their skill is the fact that seven of the top ten German aces survived the war!

Objective investigation, free of the antagonisms that prevailed in World War II, reveals the efforts of many of the individual German pilots to have been Herculean. A substantial number of the top men, right to the end, persisted in flying and fighting even though they were frequently shot down themselves. The historical facts of missions flown, planes destroyed and actual aerial combats engaged in make an absorbing statistical story. When the facts are allowed to speak for themselves, there can be no doubt that the German fighter aces of World War II belong in history with their illustrious predecessors of the 1914–1918 conflict.

Many German fighter pilots flew between 1,000 and 2,000 missions during the war, joining in combat from 800 to 1,400 times. On the Allied side, the most active fighter pilots flew between 250 and 400 missions. One American pilot with 254 missions actually fired his guns at an airborne target only 83 times, and this may well be the best record of any American pilot. By this measure alone, the German pilots had far greater opportunity for accumulating large scores, for with experience came guile, cunning and finesse.

In gaining his 352 aerial victories, which establish him as the leading fighter ace of the world and of all time, Major Erich Hartmann flew 1,425 missions. Many times Hartmann flew from two to seven missions a day, often entering combat on every mission. He was involved in more than 800 actual aerial combats.

The Germans show the thoroughness in their statistical methods that characterizes their nation. The Luftwaffe separated missions from actual combats. The latter were termed "rhubarbs" in Luftwaffe slang. Here are a few of the official figures for "rhubarbs" engaged in by German fighter pilots:

FIRST LIEUTENANT BUSCH, 442
MAJOR ROLF HERMICHEN, 629
CAPTAIN FRIEDRICH GEISSHARDT, 642
MAJOR KLAUS MIETUSCH, 452
CAPTAIN EMIL LANG, 403
CAPTAIN EBERSPÄCHER, 298

Staggering as these figures are, they are typical of what might be termed the "average" German fighter ace. None of the pilots named is even in the top ten German aces.

Criticism of the German pilots' scores quickly loses ground in the realm of objective research. Greater opportunity produced these large victory totals, and so did the German practice of letting a good air-to-air shot and ace pilot fly as long as he wanted.

The leading aces of the RAF in the Battle of Britain built up substantial scores during that defensive encounter. They were subsequently deprived of the chance to build up these totals as the war moved back across the English Channel and deep into occupied Europe. Their Spitfires did not have the range to keep in contact with the enemy as the Germans were thrown back.

Had ace pilots like the RAF's Johnny Johnson and Sailor Malan been able to meet the Luftwaffe on Battle of Britain scale throughout the war, it is a fair conjecture that they would have run up massive victory totals. They might also *not* have survived, for continued fighter combat demanded constant exposure to the imminent threat of death that is part of the fighter pilot's life.

By the time American fighter strength built up in the ETO, a long flight deep into Germany usually preceded any engagement with enemy fighters. The top American aces flew only for a short time compared with the leading Germans, and when the Americans built up large scores by Allied standards, they were usually grounded by their higher commanders.

Twenty years after these events, it should be possible to pay the German pilots their due. Attempts to vitiate their feats *as airmen* by slapping the Nazi label on them now serve no useful historical purpose. With the overwhelming majority of German pilots, it is fair to say that their primary love was flying and aircraft and that politics and patriotism were secondary. The love of flying is a common bond uniting all fighter pilots, and it transcends regimes, politics and the temporary hatreds of wartime.

Broadly speaking, there were two classes of German pilots in World War II—the brilliant and the mediocre. There was no middle class of pilot, probably because of the tremendous erosion of their numbers before they gained wide experience. Those who survived the attrition became masters of aerial warfare, able to hold their own in any company.

These differences in German fighter piloting skill probably account for the days of phenomenal scoring sometimes racked up by some American aces. Sometimes the top Americans could score three, four or five kills in a single mission. Other days, the same pilots in the same aircraft would meet the identical type of German aircraft they had knocked down with ease in previous encounters. To their dismay and chagrin, they would find a master of aerial combat at the controls of the enemy machine.

Gabreski, Mahurin, Blakeslee and Zemke all had the experience of bouncing a German aircraft with everything in their favor, only to wind up with a draw. Sometimes they were lucky to get a draw. Colonel Robert S. Johnson had just such an experience, and owes the fact that he is alive today to the armor plate behind his cockpit. After running afoul of a particularly habile German pilot, Johnson's Thunderbolt was so full of holes it could hardly fly. The German pilot, ammunition exhausted, gave the thankful Johnson a friendly wave and flew away. The German reportedly requested confirmation of a kill because he did not believe that Johnson's weaving and soggy P-47 could possibly fly more than a mile or two.

The German ace list is far too large a document for reproduction here, but suffice it to say that the Germans were meticulous with their statistics and highly conservative in their procedures. Certain aspects of German scoring methods need clarifying, because the impression is widespread that the German victory totals were exaggerated for propaganda purposes. A thorough investigation has permitted no such conclusion.

A German pilot usually had more difficulty in confirming a victory satisfactorily than his opposite numbers in both the USAAF and RAF.

The Germans also operated under a somewhat more rigid system than those employed by the Allies. The Luftwaffe system worked as follows:

1. One aircraft shot down, definitely confirmed by gun cameras or by one or two other eyewitnesses, gave full single credit, regardless of the number of engines powering the enemy aircraft. A claim could be made only if the aircraft was seen to disintegrate in the air, catch fire in the air, be abandoned by its pilot in the air, or seen to crash on the ground.

2. There were no "shared" kills as with the USAAF. Where more than one pilot contributed to the downing of the aircraft, the pilots involved had to decide between themselves which *one* of them was to get *one* credit for the victory. If the pilots could not come together for any reason, such as their belonging to separate squadrons or failure to agree, then none of the individuals involved got any victory credit. The Luftwaffe *unit* concerned would add one victory credit to its historical records. "One pilot, one kill" was the invariable scoring rule of the Luftwaffe system.

3. There was a points system for the award of medals and decorations which had no counterpart in the Allied scoring procedures.

The German points system was in effect on the Western front only, and for the purpose of decorations points were awarded in the following manner:

Single-engined plane destroyed	1 point
Twin-engined plane destroyed	2 points
Three-engined plane destroyed	3 points
Four-engined plane destroyed	3 points
Twin-engined plane damaged	1 point
Three- or four-engined plane damaged	2 points
Final destruction of a damaged twin-engined plane	.5 point
Final destruction of a damaged 4-engined plane	1 point

The Germans also set great store by the ability of a fighter pilot to separate individual Allied bombers from the box formations in which they flew. Thus, a German pilot could not win points for damaging an

Allied bomber unless he separated it from the box—that separation known to the Germans as *Herausschuss.*

That this "points for decorations" system, with all its ramified and intricate rules, has been confused with the normal victory confirmation procedures is obvious from much inaccurate material previously published about German fighter pilots' scores—most of it critical. A practical example of the two systems as they worked during the war will show how the confusion has arisen.

Suppose it is early 1943, at which time forty points were required to qualify a fighter pilot for the Knight's Cross of the Iron Cross. Our hypothetical pilot, *Oberst* Fritz Flugmann, has already shot down and confirmed twenty-two single-engined fighters (twenty-two points), five twin-engined bombers (ten points) and two four-engined bombers (six points). *Oberst* Flugmann is an ace with twenty-nine kills, but he has thirty-eight *points*—not enough for his Knight's Cross.

Next day, Flugmann takes off and damages a B-17, separating it from its box formation, and accomplishes the final destruction of a second B-17 damaged previously by another German pilot. Oberst Flugmann now has forty-one points, enough for his Knight's Cross, but he is credited with thirty kills after reconciling the aerial battle with other pilots and getting victory credit for one of the bombers.

This point-decoration system was used only on the western front, because the Germans believed it was easier to shoot down Russian fighters and bombers on the Eastern front than to down Mustangs, Thunderbolts and Mosquitos in the West. They considered the mighty Allied bomber streams, with their lethal volumes of protective fire and hordes of accompanying fighters, to be a far tougher proposition than Soviet air power.

Although the point-decoration system for the Russian front was therefore not in effect, the kill-confirmation rules were the same. Late in the war, there were pilots on the Russian front with over one hundred confirmed victories who had still to receive the Knight's Cross awarded for forty points won in the West.

Within the ranks of the German pilots themselves, there is a subtle distinction between Russian front and western front victories. A pilot with one hundred kills against the Americans and British stands higher by far in the pilots' own hierarchy of achievement than the pilot with two hundred victories against the Russians. The Germans generally recognize that this distinction is due to the superior pilot material faced in the West, rather than to any other factor.

In fairness to the German pilots who fought on the Russian front, it should be recorded that they continually faced odds, after 1942, in the air of up to twenty to one. The output of fighter aircraft by the Soviet aircraft industry during World War II was enormous, and that, together with aircraft shipped under Lend-Lease, enabled the Russians to enjoy a wide margin of numerical superiority. Unfortunately, pilot quality was generally inferior to the Germans as was the Russian tactical sense in the first years of the war.

German pilots in Russia fought under conditions of hardship and difficulty which had no parallel in the West until the final days of the war. These fighter pilots had more than their share of the dangerous ground-to-air action, flying close support missions in support of the Wehrmacht. Their lot became harder as the Russians gradually made up their early deficiencies and their flying skill and aircraft improved. The top Russian ace* scored sixty-two aerial victories against the Germans, which indicates that not everything was easy on the Russian front.

The various grades of Iron Cross awarded to the German fighter pilots should perhaps be briefly explained, since it was for this decoration in the main that the points system was instituted.

At first the Iron Cross was given in two classes, the First Class being a single Iron Cross without ribbon. The Second Class was worn on a black ribbon and hung on the winner's tunic breast. During World War I a special order of the Iron Cross with Golden Rays was created and awarded only to Marshal Hindenburg and Marshal Bluecher.

In World War II Hitler revised the awarding of the decoration. He created two classes of the Iron Cross similar to the old, but changed the ribbon colors to black, white and red, the official Reich colors since 1871. Hitler also created a higher order, the Knight's Cross of the Iron Cross.

The Knight's Cross was referred to as the *Ritterkreutz* and was worn around the neck of the winner. It is a larger medal than the First

* Ivan Kojedub

and Second Class Iron Cross. Even higher decorations were soon required to recognize exceptional deeds. Accordingly, three higher grades of the Ritterkreutz were adopted. These were, in ascending order, the Oak Leaves (*Eichenlaub*), the Crossed Swords on the Oak Leaves (*Eichenlaub mit Schwertern*) and the Diamonds on the Crossed Swords and Oak Leaves (*Eichenlaub mit Schwertern und Brillianten*).*

No precise equivalents exist between the decorations of one country and another, but an extremely rough comparison of the Oak Leaves with Swords and Diamonds would be with the American Medal of Honor or Britain's Victoria Cross. Only twenty-eight Germans won the Diamonds award in the period 1939-1945.

With characteristic flamboyance, one final grade of Iron Cross was created especially for Hermann Goering. This was the Great Cross of the Iron Cross, a gross article awarded only to appease the *Reichsmarschall's* vanity. This bauble was draped around his neck on a huge ribbon and hung there like a cowbell.

One other special version of the Diamonds award was presented to Colonel Hans-Ulrich Rudel, commander of the Stuka-equipped unit SG-2 "Immelmann." The tenth man to win the original Diamonds award, Rudel was given a golden edition of this decoration nine months after winning the Diamonds award.

Erich Hartmann is the top fighter ace of Germany and the world, with 352 confirmed aerial victories. He survived the war. Today a handsome, vigorous and friendly man of forty-one, he is a Lieutenant Colonel in the new German Air Force. Appropriately enough, he was the first commander of the new Richthofen Wing, JG-71, and has recently been transferred to Bonn as a Tactical Evaluation expert.

Hartmann is of middle height, with a thatch of flaxen hair, and with quick blue eyes that miss nothing, be it the fleeting expressions on his interviewer's face or a passing pretty girl. Seventeen years ago Erich Hartmann was a boyish-looking captain in the Luftwaffe, the

---

* These decorations were awarded to winners regardless of branch of service. Galland was the first to win the Swords award, followed by Moelders, Oesau, Lutzow, Kretschmer, Rommel and 145 others. Moelders, Galland, Marseille, Hermann Graf and Rommel won the Diamonds award in that order, followed by only twenty-two other winners.

scourge of the Russian front and the compiler of the most amazing record of victories in the history of aerial warfare.

Although not a big man, Hartmann is possessed of remarkable physical strength. In World War II he used this valuable asset of the fighter pilot to wrench his Me-109 around on to the tail of his enemies, frequently overstressing his machine, but even more frequently and more importantly, sending his foe plunging to earth in flames.

His skill in air-to-air shooting has become legend, and it was the predominant factor in making him the fabulous ace he became. A fellow pilot of Hartmann's tells of the time when Hartmann's flight was closing in on some Russian fighters from astern. Hartmann flicked off a cannon shot to range on the enemy, and the single shell whacked fairly into the Russian machine and blew it up. As this kind of thing happened again and again, pilots spoke in awe of the young ace's marksmanship wherever they gathered together.

Hartmann flew 1,425 *einsatz*, as the Germans called them, and took part in over 800 "rhubarbs" in his career. His 352 kills included many days and missions with multiple kills, his greatest single mission score being six Soviet machines downed on August 24, 1944. This total was made up of three Soviet-built P-2's, two YAK-9's, and one American-built Airacobra. This same day was his biggest day, with 11 victories in two missions, and on the second mission he became the first man in history to score 300 kills in air-to-air combat.

That Hartmann's skills were applicable only against Soviet aircraft is an unfounded contention. Certainly it is not borne out by his unusual feat in flying against the Americans. Over Rumania, in two missions on one day at the controls of his beloved Me-109, Hartmann shot down five American-flown P-51's.

As the symbol of his separation from his sweetheart Ursel Paetch, Hartmann painted a bleeding heart on his Me-109. Flying this machine and shooting down Russian aircraft in droves, he became the most feared airman on the Eastern front. The Russians knew him as the "Black Devil of the Ukraine." The morale value of his presence on any section of the front was in every way comparable to that of Baron Richthofen in World War I.

Hartmann was shot down no less than sixteen times himself, most of the time making forced landings. Three times he was knocked down by the flying debris of Russian aircraft that his guns had blown up under his very nose. On September 20, 1943, the day of his ninetieth victory, he was shot down and belly-landed behind the Russian lines. After four hours as a virtual Russian prisoner, he escaped and got back to the German lines.

Not once was Hartmann wounded. The major disaster of his life did not come until after the war had ended. As commander of Group One of JG-52, operating from a small base near Strakonitz, Czecho-slovakia, Hartmann knew the Red Army would overrun his unit within a few days. He ordered the base destroyed and with all personnel marched westward into the arms of an advanced tank unit of the U.S. Army.

But orders had already been given that Germans fleeing from the Russians were to be turned over to the Red Army at the first opportunity. In this way, the Russians finally got their hands on the pilot they hated and feared.

Trial in a Russian kangaroo court, some outlandish Soviet justice and ten and a half years of incarceration in Soviet prisons followed. Many times Hartmann was offered his freedom if he would spy for the Russians or join the Air Force of East Germany. Refusing all these appeals, Hartmann stuck it out, and was finally freed in 1955 to return to his wife in Germany.

Starting all over again, he learned once more to fly jets, having checked out in the Me-262 in World War II. This time his tutors were Americans. He was at Luke AFB in Arizona a few years ago, mastering the intricacies of the latest jet fighters. He has become a successful leader in the new German Air Force and a valued ally in the defense of the West.

The world of combat flying has only one other member of the exclusive "300 club," Major Gerhard Barkhorn, with 301 confirmed aerial victories. All of Barkhorn's victories were gained on the Russian front. Slightly taller than Hartmann at about five feet nine inches, Barkhorn is as dark as Hartmann is fair. Dark brown hair and olive complexion throw his penetrating blue eyes into vivid relief.

Barkhorn was graduated as a Luftwaffe pilot in 1939 and was assigned to the famous Richthofen Wing. He was later sent to the Russian front. He downed his first enemy plane in June, 1941, and from this time on, the victories came thick and fast. On the Russian front, like all fighter pilots, Barkhorn flew multiple missions and scored multiple kills on many days.

His most successful mission was on June 20, 1942, when he shot down four Russian aircraft in one mission, and on his biggest single day he recorded seven aerial kills. Transferred to JG-6, the "Horst Wessel" Wing, Barkhorn converted to jets when this unit became the Jet Wing. He flew only two missions in the Me-262 and scored no kills.

On the second of these missions, Barkhorn was attacking an American bomber formation when his right engine failed, and he was promptly set upon by a covey of eager Mustangs. On one engine, the Me-262 was a little slower than the Mustang, and the American pilots knew it. Barkhorn drove his crippled jet for a clearing and a crash landing, opening his canopy just before he touched down. The bumpy belly-landing slammed the canopy shut, almost breaking Barkhorn's neck.

He flew in 1,104 actual combat missions, with between 1,800 and 2,000 "starts." Barkhorn was shot down nine times, wounded twice and bailed out once. He survived the war as Germany's second-ranking fighter ace. In 1955, only 36 years old and possessed of a vast store of combat experience, he joined the new German Air Force. He now commands an F-104 training wing at Novenich, Germany.

In Munich, Germany, and sometimes at Palmdale, California, a vigorous fair-haired German colonel acts as F-104 Project Officer. He is Gunther Rall, the third-ranking Luftwaffe pilot of World War II, with 275 confirmed aerial victories. His combat flying experience covers a wide spectrum.

Rall fought against France and England in 1939–1940, then against Rumania, Greece and Crete in 1941. From 1941 to 1944 he flew on the Russian front. In late 1944 he returned to the air wars over Germany proper, all this experience involving him in over eight hundred "rhubarbs."

Rall was wounded three times and shot down several times. On November 28, 1941, in a day encounter, his aircraft was so badly shot up that he was unable to land it without a crash. His back was broken in three places and he was not given any hope for a return to combat flying. But after nine months of hospitalization, Rall's health and strength returned, and he went back into the air again.

Defending Berlin in 1944 from the American air assault, Rall collected a permanent souvenir of the USAAF. Thunderbolts boxed him in over the German capital, shot up his rudder controls and removed his left thumb with surgical cleanliness. Rall bailed out, recuperated in a few weeks, and returned again to the shambles.

Another of the top aces who learned to fly jets in World War II, Rall took his refresher course on jets at the same time and place as Erich Hartmann. He was promoted Colonel in the new German Air Force in 1961.

Lieutenant Otto Kittel, known to his comrades as "Bruno," was only five feet five inches tall, but he was a good enough air fighter to become the fourth-ranking fighter ace of the Luftwaffe with 267 aerial victories. Quiet, serious and shy, the dark-haired Kittel was the antithesis of the popular conception of a fighter ace.

When Kittel was originally assigned to JG-54, his superiors soon concluded that he would quickly join the great horde of German fighter pilots who were shot down before they could make a single kill. "Bruno" was an incredibly bad marksman. Hans Philipp and Walter Nowotny, among others, carefully tutored Kittel and brought the little man's shooting eye in. Once he mastered the principles of air-to-air trajectories, Kittel rang up an impressive string of victories.

Sent to the Russian front, he became the fifth German fighter ace to exceed 250 aerial victories. His experiences included a forced landing behind the Russian lines and fourteen days in a Soviet POW camp. In battle with IL-2 dive-bombers,* Kittel was hit by cannon fire and went down in a flat glide through a hail of flak to his death in a fiery crash.

Although he ranks as Germany's fifth fighter ace, Major Walter Nowotny was one of the most famous German aces of World War II outside Germany. He ranks with Galland and Mölders in foreign popularity, and his name was one of the few to drift across the lines during World War II to be discussed in Allied messes as Boelcke and Richthofen were in World War I.

---

* The Stormovik dive-bombers would form into a Lufbery defensive circle when attacked by Luftwaffe fighters and took a fairly high toll.

Nowotny was esteemed among the German fighter pilots as few men ever have been. For all his daring and skill in the air, Nowotny was a charming and friendly man on the ground. He joined the Luftwaffe in 1939, aged eighteen. Like Otto Kittel, he was assigned to JG-54 and flew a number of combat missions before he conquered his buck fever and found his shooting eye.

On July 19, 1941, he scored his first victory over Oesel Island in Estonia, following it up with three additional kills before sundown. On the same day, Nowotny was given a first-hand view of the other side of the hill, when a determined and skilful Red pilot shot him out of the air and into the drink. It was dark by the time Nowotny paddled his rubber raft to shore.

"Nowi," as he was affectionately called by his comrades, was a legend in his own lifetime. A captain at twenty-two, he had scored 250 aerial victories before his next birthday, and was the first pilot of any nation to reach this almost incredible total. He was the eighth German soldier to receive the Iron Cross with Oak Leaves, Swords and Diamonds.

An outstanding leader, tactician and pilot as well as a standout marksman, "Nowi" scored many notable successes in the difficult art of aerial fighting. General Adolf Galland gave Nowotny command of the first Me-262 fighter unit at Achmer, near Osnabrück. With 255 victories to his credit, Nowotny took off to defend the base from Fortresses, Mustangs and Thunderbolts intent on its obliteration, already whirling overhead as Nowotney left the ground.

He sailed into the bombers and knocked down three of them in quick succession. Then one jet engine failed. Only a few thousand feet up, Nowotny was immediately tackled by American fighters. What actually happened in the ensuing few minutes is not known, but it is thought that Nowotny's remaining jet engine may have sucked in one of the many birds that abounded near Achmer.

In any event, the Americans caught Nowotny and scored hits. Moments later he crashed thunderously into the earth at the end of a screaming dive. In the wreckage lay a piece of the ace's *Brillianten* award from his Iron Cross.

The Luftwaffe's sixth-ranking ace, Wilhelm Batz, almost spent World War II in a training command. In 1942, after repeated and energetic requests for transfer, Batz finally forced his way into combat from the dreary task of instructing new pilots. He was sent to Russia and quickly promoted.

Of this period, Batz says today, "I got my promotion to squadron-leader far faster than my experience or victories permitted, because we were suffering such heavy losses of our trained officers." Those losses and his modest five victories so depressed Batz that he seriously considered withdrawing from fighters and going back to training command. Nothing would come right for him.

"I realize now that I was a mass of inferiority complexes," he says, "which I lost in the Crimea, and from that time on I was successful."

Batz piled them up starting then, and ended the war with 243 confirmed victories, gained in 445 rhubarbs with the enemy. His best day came in the summer of 1944 over Rumania, when he downed fifteen fighters* and fighter-bombers while flying three missions in one day. In 1956, aged 40, Willi Batz entered the service of the new German Air Force.

Already recorded in this book is the feat of U.S. Navy Captain David McCampbell, who shot down nine Japanese aircraft, with two more as probables, on one mission. The all-time record holder for multiple victories is Major Erich Rudorffer, the seventh-ranked German ace of World War II.

In a wild seventeen-minute engagement on November 6, 1943, Rudorffer shot down thirteen Russian aircraft, one after the other. This feat was no accident for Rudorffer. He was an absolute master of aerial gunnery, and the Germans themselves consider that he had only two equals in this respect—Erich Hartmann and Joachim Marseille. Multiple kills became Rudoffer's specialty.

His demonstrated abilities in aerial gunnery were not confined to the Russian front. In Africa on February 9, 1943, Rudorffer downed eight British aircraft on a single mission. Six days later, he shot down seven more British aircraft in two missions. Transferred to Russia in June, 1943, Rudorffer rang up more multiple kills.

On August 24, 1943, he scored eight victories in two missions. On

* Only two other pilots have exceeded this record day's bag. Marseille shot down seventeen aircraft in three missions in Africa (in JG-27 commanded by Colonel Edu Neumann) and Captain Emil Lang shot down eighteen Russians in three missions on the Eastern front.

October 11, 1943, seven kills in one mission. His record thirteen kills in one mission came on November 6, 1943, and on October 28, 1944, he downed eleven Russian aircraft in two missions. His World War II score is 222 aerial victories, and like the majority of the leading German aces, he survived the conflict.

In all the Luftwaffe there was no more friendly, outgoing, and warm personality than Colonel Heinz Bär (pronounced "bear") the eighth-ranked German ace of World War II. A generous, genial, light-hearted soul, Bär was one of those men born to the air. In 1928, aged 15, he began his flying career on his own initiative, joining a gliding club at a time when military aviation was denied Germany under the Versailles Treaty.

Bär earned a private pilot's license in 1930 and joined the air force, intending to get flying experience on all types of aircraft so he could then fly for Lufthansa, the German airline. The European situation did not permit him to realize this ambition. When World War II broke out he was among the first German fighter pilots in action, gaining his first victory over a French-flown, American-built Curtiss P-36.

In the struggle for France and the Battle of Britain, Bär added seventeen more victories, flying at the time with one of Germany's greatest pilots and commanders, Colonel Werner Mölders. Posted to Russia in 1941, Bär had run up 103 victories by February, 1942, and for these feats had been awarded the Knight's Cross with Oak Leaves and Swords.

Transferred to Sicily, he commanded a fighter wing in the epic battle for Malta, and by the end of that struggle his score stood at 175. He became the CO of the Udet Wing, the 3rd Fighter Wing, defending the Reich. Later, as one of the top aces, he was selected to join the elite JV-44, flying the Me-262 under the command of General Galland. In this role, he became a jet ace, with sixteen kills at the controls of the Me-262. He might be considered tied for top jet honors with America's Captain Joseph McConnell Jr. of Korean fame.

Ending World War II with 220* aerial victories, Bär was another ace who could look back on fifteen to eighteen occasions when he was himself a victory. Several times wounded, he finished up in a POW camp. After his release, he found his wartime eminence a liability. As a

* Of Bär's victories, one hundred twenty-four were British and American.

"militarist" he was barred from all worthwhile positions, but in 1950 got a good break when he was put in charge of sport flying in West Germany.

After surviving enemy guns and six full years of war in the air, the likeable Bär was killed in 1957 while demonstrating a light plane. He was one of the outstanding pilots and personalities of German aviation, and was widely mourned.

To outline the careers of Germany's fighter aces is impossible in this book. The authors have in preparation a volume devoted entirely to these pilots, of which these few comments can be considered no more than a glimpse. Even a glimpse would be incomplete without mentioning several more German fighter aces whose scores put them nowhere near the top of the list, but whose contributions to German fighter aviation parallel the work of some of the American aces.

With Rudorffer and Hartmann, Captain Joachim Marseille was one of the three leading marksmen produced by the Luftwaffe. To quote General Galland, "Marseille's career was meteoric." Joining the Germany Army at twenty, he learned to fly at twenty-one and flew combat for only two years. When he was killed in action in North Africa on September 30, 1942, he had amassed 158 aerial victories.

He lifted deflection shooting to the level of personal virtuosity, and gained all his victories in the Me-109. He flew on both the Western front and in North Africa. Above the arid wastes of the western desert, Marseille found rare glory. With Field Marshal Rommel he was one of the most famous German warriors of the North African campaign, in which he gained 151 aerial victories.

Like Hartmann and Rudorffer, Marseille could do terrible damage to enemy formations and still land with plenty of ammunition remaining. When he fired, he hit his target. On one occasion, he brought down six aircraft in succession using only ten 20mm cannon shells and 180 rounds of machine-gun ammunition from each gun.

Covered in glory and at the zenith of his fame, Marseille took off in an experimental Me-109 on a fighter sortie, his hopes high that the specially souped-up aircraft would bring him fresh victories. Shortly afterward, his fighter thumped into the desert floor seven kilometers south of Sidi Abdel Rhaman, and Marseille was no more.

The true cause of his death seems obscure. The Germans say his plane caught fire, and, on bail-out, Marseille hit the rudder and was killed. Perhaps it was a British pilot who took the virtuoso's measure, but whatever the cause, his death was a demoralizing blow to the fading hopes of the Luftwaffe in Africa.

Marseille bears the historical distinction of having shot down more British aircraft than any other German pilot, and he had the rare qualities of color and personality that make a man and his deeds legendary.

The Germans had adequate opportunity to develop outstanding nightfighter pilots, and those who survived the fierce pilot attrition of this kind of warfare became masters of the art. Major Heinz-Wolfgang Schnaufer was the top scoring nightfighter pilot of the war, with 121 victories. The British called him "The Night Ghost of St. Trond." He lived through the war and all its hazards only to lose his life in an auto accident in France on July 15, 1950. He won the Diamonds award for his wartime exploits.

Lieutenant Colonel Helmut Lent ranked behind Schnaufer as a nightfighter pilot, with ninety-seven confirmed victories. He also had ten day kills, but these are insignificant compared with his night exploits. Lent cut his combat teeth in Poland in 1939, and transferred to nightfighters in May, 1941. By June, 1944, he had over a hundred victories to his credit, and tackled the Lancasters and Halifaxes that were Germany's nocturnal nemesis.

Lent was wounded three times and survived untold dozens of eerie night battles, only to die following a crash with three other flyers from his unit, NJG-1. Lent lingered for two days after the crash, but it proved impossible to save him and he died on October 7, 1944.

Among the fighter pilots of every nation there emerge those who are fitted for higher leadership. Three German fighter aces are outstanding in this way, although their scores do not rank them anywhere near the top. They are Adolf Galland, Werner Mölders and Johannes Steinhoff.

Mölders was originally turned down on medical grounds when he applied for flying training early in 1935. After rigorously exercising to make himself fit, he passed his medical, only to be dogged throughout his flying training by nausea, headaches and vomiting. He determinedly concealed these conditions, became a flight instructor and had the opportunity for real aerial combat. He went to Spain in April, 1938, with the Condor Legion.

When Mölders joined Jagdstaffel 3 in Spain, he found Adolf Galland in command of this unit. Galland was cool to Molders at first, but before long was reporting that Mölders was "an excellent officer, and a splendid pilot with brilliant and precise leadership."

In May, 1938, Mölders took over command from Galland and began his climb as a leader and dominant figure in the history of combat flying. He ran up fourteen kills in Spain, which made him the leading German ace in that conflict. It is worth noting here that Americans Frank Tinker and A. J. "Ajax" Baumler also became aces in Spain —on the opposite side to Mölders!

Mölders played his part in the development and adoption of the famed "finger-four" fighting formation adopted by the Luftwaffe and later copied by the Allied nations. He had the rare ability to discern and correctly translate into tactics the basic changes wrought in aerial warfare by the advent of the all-metal, low-wing monoplane.

Due in no small measure to Mölders, the Luftwaffe broke away from the First World War concepts, which had only limited application in the new era. Thanks largely to him, the Luftwaffe entered World War II with fighter tactics that were second to none.

By October of 1940 he had scored forty-five aerial victories over the RAF as CO of JG-51. By the first half of 1941 he had reached one hundred kills, and this dismaying news found its way across the English Channel. It was a certain indication that on the German side the Second World War was going to produce some substantial aerial victory totals.

After service in Russia, Mölders was killed in the accidental crash of a Heinkel 111 near Breslow. He was flying to Berlin to be in the Honor Guard at the funeral of World War I ace Ernst Udet. On Mölders' death, his former CO in Spain, Adolf Galland, who was now serving under Mölders, was promoted General of the Fighter Arm.

General Galland fought a soldier's war. A combat genius, he shone as well in both the planning and tactical phases of fighter operations. His passages at arms with the florid Goering and his passionate differences with both Goering and Hitler over the employment of the fighters adequately demonstrated his courage.

Galland's war career is a further example of the value to the Allies of Hitler's astrologically-inspired notions of strategy and tactics. Had Galland had a free hand, there can be little doubt that the whole pattern of the air war in the ETO would have been different.

His mounting anger with his superiors as he watched them send Germany down the drain, drove him to extremes of challenge and confrontation. In the end, he was relieved of his command in January, 1945.

Galland formed JV-44, a jet fighter unit, after his dismissal. JV-44 was made up of seasoned aces of his own choosing plus a few of the younger pilots. The unit was to take the Me-262 into combat as a fighter, a course which Hitler deplored and fanatically opposed. Hartmann, Barkhorn, Bär and Steinhoff were among the superlative pilots originally chosen for this elite unit.

For a brief time, Galland knew again the feeling of air superiority, if only in a local way and with no power to change the war's course. Two or three years earlier, a dozen such units might well have turned the tide—a bitter reflection for Galland.

While Galland is known more for his activities as a leader than as a fighter ace, his personal score of 103 aerial victories places him among the foremost German airmen. All his victories were scored against the British, French and Americans, and include 31 Hurricanes and 47 of the fabled Spitfires.

The special qualities and skills that made Colonel Johannes Steinhoff one of the outstanding tutors and leaders of the World War II Luftwaffe rightly place him in the historical company of Mölders, Galland and the other ace leaders. As a Luftwaffe colonel during the war, Steinhoff exhibited powerful attributes of initiative and independence. These qualities were essential to successful leadership in those times because of the often crazy edicts issued by Hitler and Goering about the employment of fighter units.

The late Hans-Otto Boehm, until his death in 1963 the greatest living authority on German fighter aviation, said of Steinhoff: "An outstanding *individual,* who often acted contrary to orders and independently, especially in Italy as Commander of JG-77." Steinhoff is credited with 176 aerial victories, 27 against the Western Allies and 149 on the Eastern front. Six of his victories were scored while flying the twin-jet Me-262. A superlative leader, Steinhoff tutored many pilots on their first combat missions. Lieutenant Walter Krupinski, 196 kills, scored his first while flying as Steinhoff's wingman.

After service on the Channel front in the Battle of Britain, in Russia, North Africa and Italy, Steinhoff was a colonel in a jet fighter unit in the final months of the war. He was severely burned in the takeoff crash of an Me-262 on April 18, 1945, and was hospitalized for two years, undergoing numerous skin grafts in this time.

In the nineteen-fifties, Steinhoff was one of the leaders selected to form the command nucleus of the new German Air Force. He took an American refresher training course on jets in 1955–1956, and is now a major general. As this is written, Steinhoff is serving in Washington, D.C., as the German Air Force military member of the NATO staff, and it is freely predicted that he has a long career in high command still before him.

This outline of the careers of a few of the enemy aces who opposed America's airmen shows that the Americans did have interesting counterparts "on the other side of the hill." In both Germany and Japan there were outstanding pilots, incredible "characters," superb marksmen and men who shone in leadership. The enemy aces won the statistical war in terms of individual victory totals, but factors over which they had no control put them on the losing side.

Today the antagonisms of the past are gone. Met in person, the enemy aces are friendly human beings, and contacts between the erstwhile combatants are continually broadening. To have flown combat is an unforgettable personal experience that unites all such men around the world in one of the most elite of all fraternities. Be they Japanese, Germans, Italians, British or Americans, fighter aces are a race apart, survivors of a surpassing adventure that is unlikely ever to be repeated.

Very little is known to this date about the Japanese fighter aces. Almost every attempt to contact official source in Japan has been rebuffed or ignored. The Japanese believe it is still too early to recognize and publicize their successes against an enemy who is now their principal ally.

Similarly, the German people are extremely slow to recognize their World War II heroes. Highly sensitive over being duped by the Nazi regime, the Germans have quietly soft-pedaled accolades to the fighter pilots.

General Galland, publicly accused by Hitler and Goering of being responsible for the Allied bombers' destruction of Germany, was removed as the commanding general of the fighter arm and given command of a "service test" fighter interceptor (Me-262) squadron late in the war. No doubt Hitler and Goering meant this assignment of a general to command only a squadron as a demotion. Galland accepted it as a challenge and set out to prove his theory that an Me-262 squadron was worth ten conventional squadrons. After the war the ambitious Galland traveled to South America where he engaged in business. When the new German Air Force was formed after the war, this emigration to South America was misinterpreted by the high command and Galland was not invited back into the Air Force, although he is recognized by most of the professional airmen as the *real* potential existing in Germany today.

The authors queried General Galland in 1963 regarding the methods of confirmation of kills used by the Germans. Since so many Americans, including aces and general officers of the U.S. Air Force, have the mistaken impression that only our own American aircraft actually used the gun camera for evidence of victories, we thought it best to investigate the facts. The evidence proved that it was more difficult for a Luftwaffe pilot to get a confirmation than it was in many American units. And one of the most interesting facets of this problem came to light in Galland's reply, printed here by kind permission of General Galland, the German fighter pilots' organization's periodical *Jägerblatt*, the late Hans Otto Boehm, who served as its editor, and Hans Ring of Munich, who was serving as associate editor:

*The Use of Cameras in German Fighter Aircraft**
Adolf Galland

Our friend and member Colonel R. F. Toliver, USAF, informs us that in the United States the odd impression prevails that only American fighters had cameras in their planes.

* *Jägerblatt*, Frankfurt a.m., March 1963, p. 10.

The first installation of a camera was effected in 1940, just before the real battle for England began, at the instigation of a war correspondent, Mr. Bermer, in my Me-109 E-4 in France. His intention was purely one of propaganda. The first results were soon available and immediately showed that the tactical and technical evaluation opened a broad field which extended beyond the confirmation of a downing. I immediately informed the Inspector of the Fighter Pilots—Major Apfel. They took up the matter and demanded that cameras be installed in all fighter planes. This was never carried out completely because of the additional expense and the shortages, but it was set up as a goal. The cameras were issued as standard equipment and, of course (insofar as they were available), were claimed by the more successful fighter pilots. Built into the "surface nose" [Flachennase] wing tip, synchronized with weapons, but already operable during the approach. The German Air Ministry immediately set up an office to evaluate the films of the aerial battles carefully, not only with regard to success or failure, but also tactically and technically; in other words, ranging from the downing report to the ballistics, angle of fire, effect of ammunition and fuse effect [Zunderwirkung], etc. As a "GdJ" I had cut up downing training films especially against four "Mots" and made them available to the units as "Wrong-Right-Best." Many hundred downings by German fighters were thus recorded. Most of the copies of the films that survived ended up in England, as far as I know. Due to the increasing shortage of material, however, the unit soon received only an evaluation and not a copy.

In 1944, when film cameras became even scarcer than fighter planes, we installed the cheap Robot camera, provided with a stepping relay operated by a spring. This way we got three pictures per second, which was quite adequate. As late as 1945, I myself photographed Me-262 Robot downings, which photographs I wouldn't mind having again, that is, with 4 x Mk-108 (3cm) and R4-M rockets, which confirmed* the simultaneous downings of two Marauders.

* General Galland's 103 victories include 7 scored while flying the Me-262.

10

☆ ☆ ☆ ☆ ☆

Aces of the Korean War

WHEN NORTH KOREA planned and launched its invasion of South Korea, Uncle Sam was asleep at the switch. A country the size of the State of Florida was ready and willing to risk war with the United States in its determination to communize South Korea. Soon, behind the euphemism of a United Nations "police action," war between America and North Korea was a reality. When the conflict began, America's air strength was barely equal to the burdens suddenly thrust upon it.

The pathetic unpreparedness of the United States for both great world wars was reproduced in 1950. All the deadly processes of the nineteen-twenties and-thirties were repeated, in a greatly compressed fashion, between 1945 and 1950. In the minds of politicians authorizing appropriations, the fresh memory of America's awesome military strength in World War II became a substitute for the real thing. "What America has done before it can do again, if required," was the belief. Meanwhile, American air strength dwindled.

The Air Force that had grown by 1945 to two hundred combat wings was reduced by drastic disarmament to forty-three wings. The fighter pilots who had made America supreme in the skies went back to flying civilian desks. The battle-tested fighter squadrons were disbanded, their aircraft junked or parked to await slow decay in America's southwestern deserts. On top of it all, the approach to the jet age became as slow, awkward and stumbling as the original approach to the aeroplane prior to World War I.

KUDOS FROM THE FUEHRER: Above, Hitler decorates members of his military command, 1943. He shakes hands with Walter Krupinski, 196-victory ace. Next in line, to Hitler's right, is Erich Hartmann (also below), the world's top ace, with 352 "kills."

TOP GERMAN ACES: Above, left, from left: Maj. Prinz zu Sayn-Wittgenstein, 83 night victories; Maj. Hartmann Grasser, 131 "kills"; Maj. Walter Nowotny, 258 "kills"; Maj. Gunter Rall, 3rd-ranking fighter ace in the world, with 275 "kills." WORLD'S TOP ACE: Left, Hitler decorates Hartmann in 1944. A FRIENDLY MEETING: Above, from left: Col. R. F. Toliver, Cadet McCormick and Lt. Col. Hartmann at U.S. Air Force Academy, May 30, 1961.

DISCUSSING OLD TIMES: Above, left, Col. Gerhard Barkhorn, 301 victories; Col. Toliver; Col. Herbert Wehnelt, 36 victories and Col. Walter Krupinski, 196 "kills." Below, left, Col. Krupinski talks with American ace, Col. Herb Zemke, 17¾ victories, as Col. Hartmann listens, in a photo 'aken at Büchel Air Base, Germany, May 1961. MESSERSCHMITT IN FLIGHT: Above, Messerschmitt ME-109. A HIT: Below, the passing Messerschmitt-410 had nearly scored another "kill" when this picture was taken. The hole in the wing near the identifying H symbol on the B-17 is from cannon shot.

TOP OF THE LUFTWAFFE: Above, meeting of top officials of the Luftwaffe at Le Touquet, 1940. NUMBER-TWO ACE: Maj. Gerhard Barkhorn (right), German Air Force, world's number-two ace, with 301 "kills."

20TH ACE: Below, left, Col. (now Maj. Gen.) Johannes Steinhoff, Luftwaffe ME-262 Wing Commander, the 20th-ranking ace of the world, with 176 "kills." CONTROVERSIAL ACE: Below, right, Hans Joachim Marseille, whose disputed record is officially confirmed to include a total of 158 victories. GERMAN FIGHTER PILOT MEMORIAL: The Memorial to the Fallen Fighter Pilots of World War II (over), erected at Geisenheim by the German Fighter Pilots Association.

The Germans had been the first to make jet fighters operational, and had even used manned rocket-powered fighters during World War II. America reacted to this threat in the war years by launching a jet program of its own. When the Axis collapsed in 1945 and the challenge of actual war was removed, jet fighter development began to dwindle. By 1946, the Lockheed F-80 jet was being produced only slowly. The first tactical unit to receive this machine was the 412th Fighter Group at March Field, California. The complete conversion of this unit to jets was not accomplished until late in 1946.

The Air Force began to undergo a complete transformation in equipment, personnel and command. Reserves were released from active duty and the Air Force was reduced almost to skeleton status. The continual reduction of American air strength led the Department of Defense to lodge some of the strongest protests ever presented to the Congress and the President. Despite the clear lessons of the past, until the Korean debacle came, the American body politic proved almost impervious to warnings that dwindling American airpower was an invitation to aggressors.

Asia had always been the poor relation of Europe in American military and political thought. The "Germany first" policy of World War II reinforced this concept, and following that struggle military planners concentrated mainly on the possibility of a European war with Russia.

Russia was also recognized as an Asiatic power, but in the postwar years, Soviet aims had been ostensibly directed at bolshevizing Eastern Europe and a further spread of the communist regime to Western Europe through intrigue and other agencies. Korea decisively altered all the expansive thinking that had been done along these lines.

At the time of the invasion of South Korea in June, 1950, Air Force units in the Far East were being converted slowly to jet aircraft. Tachikawa AFB and the battle-tested Clark AFB in the Philippines became the junkyards for the once superb P-51 Mustang. As the jets flowed out to the squadrons, the Mustangs came back to be scrapped.

Forsaken, neglected and growing in numbers in the junkyards, the Mustangs suddenly became worth their weight in gold with the North Korean irruption into South Korea. The P-51 had few equals for the important ground-support role. They were rushed back into top condition and were used to punish the thousands of ground targets offered by the North Korean military forces.

At the controls of a Mustang, Major Louis B. Sebille became the USAF's forty-third winner of the Congressional Medal of Honor. Leading a squadron of P-51's of the 18th Fighter Bomber Wing, Major Sebille was hit by ground fire directed at the formation by an armored car or tank. Sebille's wingman could see that the major was wounded, as his Mustang began weaving and Sebille could be seen struggling to sit upright. His cockpit canopy was covered in blood.

Sebille knew he was mortally wounded. His voice came crackling over the radio, "I'm going back to get that bastard!" He turned around and drove his Mustang, all guns thundering, into a concentration of Red troops and vehicles. Sebille's last act caused heavy enemy casualties, and was as brave a thing as any American fighter pilot has ever done.

Korea became primarily a theater of air-to-ground combat, the fighter-bomber pilots flying innumerable missions against ground targets. In the beginning, the Reds showed little comprehension of the decisive influence of airpower on ground operations such as theirs. Their supply columns and convoys were frequently hacked to pieces from the air.

In response to the ensuing anguished appeals of the Red high command, the first communist jets appeared over Korea. Dogfights were the order of the day once more, this time at near sonic speeds. Aerial combat and its heroes were soon again filling the pages of America's newspapers and magazines.

The straightforward stories of aerial combat between the Soviet-built MIG-15 and the American Sabrejet concealed the wider importance of these aerial battles. Without the American jets to protect them, the slower, older Mustangs and other ground-support aircraft would have been at the mercy of the communist jets. For the infantryman facing the swarming hordes of North Korean and Chinese solders, the "police action" would have assumed a different character in the absence of close air support.

First Lieutenant William G. Hudson shot down the first communist aircraft in aerial combat. Flying a P-82, Hudson overtook a propeller-driven YAK-9, a product of the Russian aircraft industry, and downed it with some accurate gunnery. The ubiquitous Mustang could be considered present on this historic occasion, since the P-82, later to be designated the F-82, consisted of two Mustangs joined together by a stubby midwing about ten feet long.

The first communist jet fighter was shot down by Lieutenant Russell J. Brown, on November 8, 1950. Brown was mounted on an F-80, and his victory over the Russian-built MIG-15 is believed to be the first confirmed victory in an all-jet aerial dogfight.

America's first jet fighter ace was Major James Jabara, of Wichita, Kansas. Jabara scored his first MIG-15 kill on April 3, 1951, and followed it up with one more on April 10 and one April 12. Ten days later the fourth MIG went down under Jabara's guns. Two more kills on May 20 made him an historic ace—America's first in the jet age.

Returned to the United States for special duty and many accolades, Jabara was anxious to return to combat. He returned to Korea at his own request in January, 1953 and scored nine additional kills against the MIG-15's. He ended the Korean conflict as the second-ranking jet ace of the United States, with an all-time total of 16.5 enemy aircraft destroyed in aerial combat.

Jabara's total is made up of 15 Korean War victories and 1.5 victories gained in the ETO during World War II. Two additional World War II victories were never confirmed. The top-ranking living jet ace, Jabara is today an honored figure among the fraternity of aces, and he is an official of the American Fighter Aces' Association.

The "sanctuary" beyond the Yalu River, the often impenetrable political factors swirling around the Korean conflict, and the remoteness of the country from the United States created problems for the American fighter pilots that their forebears in First and Second World Wars had never had to face. The new tools of trade, the jets, sent aerial warfare into yet another phase, as different from World War II as that conflict had been from World War I.

These differences are well described in a letter written to Colonel Toliver, co-author of this book, by Colonel Robert P. Baldwin of Los Angeles, California. Colonel Baldwin was CO of the 51st Fighter Interceptor Group in Korea in 1953. He summed up the new mode of aerial combat this way:

Air-to-air combat at 45,000 feet is something entirely new to World War II vets. The old razzle-dazzle, ham-fisted fighter pilot is out. Now it's accurate, precision, feather-touch flying. If you get clumsy it costs you valuable speed, altitude, position—maybe your fanny! The MIG's have a tremendous weight advantage, being at least 3,000 pounds lighter than our F-86. The only way we can overcome that advantage is to fly at speeds where the drag ratio is the deciding factor.

The F-86 matches the MIG-15 on the power-drag scale anywhere above the .8 mach reading. So the unwritten law is "If you don't have .8 or better, don't look for a fight." That, plus taking advantage of the very few bad characteristics of the MIG, accounts for most of our success.

The MIG is prone to snap in a right-hand turn, and it loses considerable maneuverability around .95 mach. Flying our F-86 is no snap either, and staying in formation is rough. You maintain position by playing turns and altitude—and you never reduce power.

From Colonel Baldwin's description, it is clear that in Korea as in the other great conflicts, the skill and ingenuity of the fighter pilot in exploiting his enemy's weaknesses bulked large in the achievement of acedom. Also obvious is that the enemy machines were well worthy of the respect of America's fighter pilots. Colonel Baldwin became a jet ace in Korea and is credited with five aerial victories.

When the opposition became too rough for the communist pilots, there was always the haven beyond the Yalu River, to which the Red pilots often bolted with the Americans in hot pursuit. The idea was to knock the fleeing Red pilot down before he reached the river and thereby gained "sanctuary." Not even in the most primitive days of aerial combat was there ever a situation quite as queer as that prevailing around the Yalu.

The story of such a chase is told by Major Frederick C. Blesse of Richmond, Virginia, who destroyed ten enemy aircraft in aerial combat over Korea:

Leading a flight of two F-86's, I spotted several MIG-15's. They split up when we pressed our attack, and we finally singled out one and got him. We made a wide circle and started home, but another single MIG bounced us. The next four or five minutes we looped, rolled and finally got a snap at him from about thirty-five degrees angle off at 1,500 feet distance.

He began to smoke, and pulled up vertically, ruddering into a spin. He spun, with my wingman and me following around the outside, from 15,000 feet down to 4,000 feet, where he began firing his cannon to reduce his nose weight. I was ready for him, when at 1,800 feet he neatly recovered in a direct heading for the Yalu River.

I moved in, taking the regular high side approach shot. Pieces of his fuselage and tail flew off, followed by his canopy. Fire began to trail the MIG, but he still wouldn't bail and kept driving for the Yalu. I dropped back to the six o'clock position and gave him another burst. Out of the cockpit he came, so close I had to turn hard left to avoid him. I didn't realize that my two kills this day made me the leading ace with six MIG victories and an LA-9 kill. I then ran the string to ten kills, which held the lead until February, 1953, when Colonel Royal Baker got his eleventh kill.

Major Blesse flew the F-86 in scoring all his victories, although he flew 67 missions in Mustangs between November, 1950, and February, 1951, with the 18th Fighter Bomber Group. Blesse thus had his share of the low-level strafing work, and he also flew 35 missions in the F-80 jet as well as his 121 Sabre missions.

The Colonel Royal Baker mentioned by Blesse is now Brigadier General Royal N. Baker USAF, a distinguished Texan who flew fighters in both World War II and Korea. Baker flew 160 combat missions in British Spitfires during World War II with the 31st Fighter Group. He is credited with 3.5 aerial victories in that conflict.

Brigadier General Baker shot down his fifth enemy aircraft in Korea in November, 1952, thereby becoming the USAF's twenty-first jet ace. Another eight enemy aircraft fell to his guns in Korea, including one LA-9. His lifetime score is 16.5 aerial victories for both the wars in which he flew. The 45-year-old ace is a career officer in the Air Force, and his decorations include the Silver Star, Legion of Merit, forty Air Medals and the French Croix de Guerre.*

The same shooting skill that made outstanding aces in World War I

---

* Only one other pilot has been awarded more than the forty Air Medals held by Baker. Lieutenant Colonel Clyde B. East, 12 Victory World War II ace, of Chatham, Virginia, has garnered forty-two of these awards. Colonel James E. Hill has thirty-nine Air Medals.

and World War II was also required in Korea. The jets, for all their speed, did not alter this fundamental of aerial warfare. Most pilots of the Korean War speak in awe and admiration of the marksmanship of one particular pilot—Captain Manuel J. Fernandez of Key West, Florida.

As the third-ranking jet ace with 14.5 victories over MIG's to his credit, Fernandez ran up this score between September, 1952, and May, 1953, in 125 missions. Significant indeed is Fernandez' prior appointment as a gunnery instructor at Nellis AFB in Nevada, his last duty in the United States prior to going to Korea. His long study and practice of the mechanics and art of aerial gunnery paid off handsomely in combat.

Captain Fernandez well remembers this incident:

I was approaching the Yalu River with a flight of four when the radar people warned us of bandits in the area. My squadron commander was leading the second element and was forced by aircraft malfunction to return to home base. I was also unable to jettison my left tank. I was trying to shake it off when I found my element was just underneath forty-odd MIG's.

Two enemy aircraft were approaching from my left, and I turned in behind them. They started a high-speed turning dive, pulling away, so I tried a burst on the leader—and saw strikes on his fuselage. He began smoking and slowed down. His wingman turned up and into the sun and disappeared. I gave the wounded MIG two more short bursts and saw good strikes.

Then the enemy wingman came slicing down out of the sun and joined formation on his smoking leader. I banked slightly and fired a short burst at the wingman. The bullets hit his nose section and exploded his ammunition.

The wingman broke sharply to the right, and then reversed. His canopy came off and the pilot baled out. I was still close to the original MIG and I closed in to two hundred feet and fired a long burst. This caught the MIG in the bottom of the fuselage. Flame came whipping back from him and I was forced to break to the right. The pilot was slumped over the controls, and I broke off the attack to return home.

Captain Harold E. Fischer of Lone Rock, Iowa, flew 105 missions with the 8th Fighter Bomber Wing between March, 1951, and December, 1951. After a short rest in Japan, he returned to Korea for 70 missions in Sabres. With ten victories he became a "double MIG" ace, but his second tour of duty was destined to last until May 31, 1955. Shot down during a rhubarb with the MIG's, Fischer was captured by enemy ground troops and hustled north of the Yalu to captivity.

Fischer was held as a POW long after the majority of captured Americans were released. He finally regained his freedom two years after the end of the Korean War. Fischer's most vivid combat memory is of his fifth aerial victory, the one that made him an ace:

Radar vectored my flight into four MIG's. The number two man of the MIG flight panicked when we bounced them, and his three fellow pilots zoomed for altitude. I went after the number two MIG, who nearly stalled and then began a long dive.

I latched on at great distance. Intermittent bursts from my guns finally started to hit him, stopping his engine and setting him on fire. I gradually closed at low altitude, and pulled alongside to see why he did not bail out. The pilot was struggling with his canopy, which was jammed, and he could not eject. Finally, he tried to ram me, and then crashed with his aircraft. This victory made me an ace.

The hitting power of the Sabrejet's armament was often the cause of much criticism. Many of the World War II fighters had a heavier punch than the Sabrejet, one of them being the first operational jet fighter, the German Me-262. While much of the criticism of the Sabre's armament seems justified, Captain Cecil G. Foster of San Antonio, Texas, tells a story of the Sabre's guns in his most memorable combat experience. Foster was flying as element leader on September 26, 1952, in a flight of four Sabres when the incident took place:

My flight leader initiated a bounce on two MIG-15's, and as I turned to protect him, I was bounced by six MIG's. We entered a scissors maneuver, and everyone was firing at everyone else at ninety-degree angles. With my first burst I scored lucky hits on both the MIG leader and his wingman. The leader exploded instantly. This was a real surprise, as we were at forty thousand feet and MIG's seldom burned or blew up at this extreme altitude.

The wingman was also hit and smoking, and fire began to show. The pilot ejected as I was positioning for my next pass. To my knowledge, this is the only time two MIG's have been shot down with a single burst from a Sabre—a burst of only one second's duration.

Captain Foster's experience is reminiscent of Colonel "Hub" Zemke's recollection of his aerial battles—"They were all easy *once I hit them.*" Cecil Foster is the twenty-third American jet ace, with nine MIG-15's to his credit.

To be nicknamed "Hoot" is the inevitable fate of most fighter pilots named Gibson. Captain Ralph Duane Gibson of Mt. Carmel, Illinois, is no exception. Five aerial victories in Korea over MIG fighters put "Hoot" Gibson into the fraternity of fighter aces.

Gibson's account of combat action with the 4th Fighter Group tells of a fleeting opportunity seized in lightning fashion:

On June 18th, 1951, a bright summer day, I was flying my thirty-fifth Sabre mission to the Yalu. It was routine, flying cover for F-80's and F-84's on a fighter bomber sweep. I was leading an element on my squadron commander's right.

We were forty miles out of the Yalu when contrails were sighted ahead, moving toward us. We counted at least thirty-six MIG's. We were eight in number. We dropped tanks and made a 270-degree turn to the left. During the turn, I flew high cover for the flight, where I met a flight of the MIG's one of them passing within ten feet of my aircraft. At 600 mph, ten feet is mighty close!

As we completed the turn, my CO was on a MIG's tail, and the MIG's wingman was maneuvering to get behind the CO. I called and said that my wingman and I would get the second MIG. We turned in to the attack.

My wingman, leading the turn, fired two long bursts into the MIG. The enemy jet burst into flames before I could fire on him, and spun off burning, to crash a few seconds later. When my wingman and I rolled out on a southerly heading, I saw a MIG drop into position behind my friend. I shouted to him to "break left" as I came in on the MIG's tail, firing bursts as I came.

On the first burst the enemy reversed his turn, but I easily out-turned him, closed to about five hundred feet and opened up on him again. He made evasive turns, and I fired again, getting numerous hits around the wing root and cockpit. Flames streamed from his speed brakes and he crashed to the ground.

Rolling out of this fight, my wingman and I ran into yet another

MIG. He was higher and in front of us, coming in from our ten
o'clock position. We made a hard turn into his attack and closed to
five hundred feet. I fired one burst into his right wing root, and the
whole right wing flew off his aircraft. He went in immediately.

"Hoot" Gibson stayed with the USAF, and today is the leader of
the U.S. Air Force aerobatic team, the Thunderbirds, flying out of
Nellis AFB, Nevada.

One of the best-liked members of the fraternity of American
fighter aces is Colonel James K. Johnson of Phoenix, Arizona. Johnson
is also one of the Air Force's finest contemporary leaders. Small, dark
and dapper, Johnson does not have a single grey hair in his head,
despite aerial combat in two wars. A remarkably handsome man with
an impish sense of humor, "James K.," as he is often called, is as
brilliant socially as he has been in aerial combat.

Johnson shot down the only German aircraft he tangled with in
World War II and became a "double MIG" ace with ten aerial victories in Korea. The citation to his Distinguished Service Cross is a
fitting testimony to his qualities and skill:

> Colonel James K. Johnson distinguished himself by extraordi-
> nary heroism in connection with military operations against an
> armed enemy of the United Nations as pilot of an F-86 type air-
> craft, 4th Fighter-Interceptor Wing, 5th Air Force, on June 30,
> 1953. On that date, Colonel Johnson was leading a flight of four
> F-86 aircraft deep within enemy territory when a flight of twelve
> enemy MIG aircraft were sighted at 35,000 feet. Colonel Johnson
> immediately initiated a forceful attack, and concentrated on de-
> stroying one of the enemy aircraft. Closing on the single MIG,
> Colonel Johnson held his fire until he was within 1,200 feet, at
> which time he scored numerous hits on the wing and fuselage of the
> enemy aircraft. To assure that he did not lose his tactical advantage,
> and with full knowledge of the potential danger from other MIG's
> in the enemy flight, Colonel Johnson continued the attack.
>
> With unswerving singleness of purpose, Colonel Johnson began
> firing from a range of six hundred feet, continuing his devastating
> barrage until he was only fifty feet from the enemy aircraft, at
> which time it began to burn and disintegrate. Only then did Colonel
> Johnson turn to face the fire of the other MIG's. While expertly
> maneuvering to escape the attacking enemy aircraft, Colonel John-
> son experienced a loss of engine power, which later proved to be the

result of damage caused by debris from the destroyed enemy aircraft. In spite of this handicap, Colonel Johnson valiantly turned to
attack the enemy MIG's, and by superb airmanship and aggressiveness, outmaneuvered them until they withdrew from the area.
Colonel Johnson then brought his disabled aircraft back to base.
Through his intrepidity, in the face of the enemy, and by his high
personal courage, outstanding professional skill and devotion to
duty, Colonel Johnson reflected great credit upon himself, the Far
East Air Forces and the USAF.

There have been some notable examples of deflection shooting
mentioned in this book. Generally forbidden to fighter pilots are snap
shots at hundred degrees deflection. The spirit of the fighter pilot,
however, is by nature that of a gambler, and sometimes when presented with such temptations the pilot is unable to resist. Off goes a
hundred-degree deflection shot, sent on its way with a liberal charge of
wishful thinking. If Lady Luck lends her caress to the affair, spectacular results may follow.

A classic instance forms the outstanding combat memory of Major
Clifford D. Jolley of Cleveland, Ohio, who flew with the 4th Group in
Korea:

On August 8, 1952, while flying top cover for two groups of
F-80's in the area of Anju, my wingman and I were bounced by two
MIG's from six o'clock. I called for my wingman to break hard left
so I could clear his tail. The MIG's pulled up hard. I called a fast
reverse and fired broadside at one as he flashed past me—*and my
shots set him afire!* The pilot baled out. This gave me my fifth
victory and made me the USAF's eighteenth jet ace.

Teamwork was indispensable to survival over Korea. The advent of
the jet, the high-altitude combat, flashing speeds and radar assistance
from the ground, and the lone-wolf fighter pilot was no more than a
historical curiosity. The commander of jet formations had to be more
than ever a thoughtful and alert aerial general.

Throwing firsthand light on these matters is Colonel George L.
Jones of Vero Beach, Florida, commanding officer of the 334th Squadron of the 4th Fighter Group from July to October, 1951, and of the
51st Fighter Group from November, 1951, to March, 1952. Colonel

Jones is credited with 6.5 aerial victories in Korea and his story vividly illustrates the planning required for a successful jet fighter mission:

During one phase of the Korean conflict, it was noticed that the communists were able to identify our Sabrejets approaching the target area early enough to get set for the attack. By the time we arrived in "MIG Alley," the enemy pilots usually had a five to ten thousand foot altitude advantage.

On March 29, 1953, our group was committed to make a fighter sweep through North Korea to the Yalu River. On this particular day, seeking to surprise the enemy pilots on their initial climb out, I obtained permission from the group commander to take off with a flight of four aircraft ten minutes before the main mission. Strict radio silence was maintained as we taxied out and took off. Shortly after we became airborne, my number four man had to abort the mission. I signaled the number three man to escort him back to base. With my wingman, Major Wendel Brady, I continued on as planned.

As we approached the combat area, we could hear the radio transmissions from the main mission as they were taking off and joining up ten minutes behind us. Then I spotted six MIG-15's streaking across the river in a climb. This was what we were looking for. I called Brady and told him to drop his external tanks and follow me. We were then at about 39,000 feet, indicating about .83 mach.

As the lead element of MIG's swept in front of us, I turned in behind them and started my attack. As I began coming up behind the nearest MIG my wingman called out, "There's a MIG above you and to your left who looks as though he's going to attack." I told Brady to keep an eye on this MIG and call out if the MIG got into firing position on me.

I was now slowly overtaking the MIG I had picked out to attack, and since I was gradually closing in on him, I decided to hold my fire until within point-blank range. The MIG wingman now became extremely aggressive, and two or three times started to turn in to make an attack. Each time he would start in, Brady would turn into him in such a way that if the MIG wingman continued his attack, Brady would end up right behind him. The MIG would therefore withdraw from that particular attack. All the while, I continued to close in on the lead MIG.

When I got 1,400 feet behind the MIG and 500 feet below him, I pulled back on the stick and closed to a position directly behind him at a range of 800 feet. We were now at 42,000 feet. As soon as my sight pipper settled into position, I squeezed the trigger and saw a heavy concentration of hits on the MIG. Debris flew off his aircraft and he decelerated rapidly.

My aircraft was closing in on the slowing MIG so fast that I was afraid of running into him. As soon as I lifted my finger from the trigger, I discovered a loss of engine power, due to compressor stall. Smoke, oil and hydraulic fluid entering my air intake aggravated this condition. When the compressor stalled I was in the middle of the smoke left by the blown-up MIG. I couldn't see where I was going and was concerned with running into debris. I threw the stick over to the left side of the cockpit, retarded the throttle and started a steep dive to break the compressor stall and regain power.

Usually stalls like this can be broken quickly. But at 25,000 feet my engine had not regained power and I began debating whether to pull out of the dive and try gliding to the coast. I decided to take it down to 20,000 feet, and if the engine didn't catch by then, to pull up and join the local glider club.

At 20,000 feet, the engine regained power. What a reassuring feeling it was. I started to climb back up, but now the engine appeared to be running rough and my airspeed was much less than it should have been. Running a quick check, I found my speed brakes were extended. I had automatically put them out to slow down when collision with the MIG was imminent. I'd put them out with such force that I'd stripped the plastic button from the speed brake control switch. With some difficulty, I could still actuate the control, and immediately the aircraft began to accelerate.

My canopy was coated with hydraulic fluid and oil from the exploded MIG, but on looking through some clear spots I could see that my wingman had stayed with me all this time. Brady told me that during the entire fight the MIG wingman had made many attempts to turn in on me, but that he had kept him off while I made the kill. When his leader was blown up and I was groping around with my stalled engine, the MIG wingman tried again, but was once more forced to pull up by Brady and was lost from the fight entirely.

Later, as we headed back from home base, I kept thinking to myself, "Teamwork is the answer—teamwork and confidence."

The intelligent use of radio silence, backed up with this kind of teamwork, put the aerial warfare of Korea in a different category to that engaged in by the pioneers of World War I. Yet it should be observed for historical purposes that the entire past of aerial warfare is contained in its present. If the pilot of today's flashing jets stops to think about it, Raoul Lufbery, Eddie Rickenbacker and their like are in a sense flying with him. Their experience and know-how are part of what he has been taught as a pilot. The inflammable crates of World War I, with all their lessons, are contained in the sleek machines of today.

A tradition that threaded its way through all three conflicts was the "victory roll." A slow roll or barrel roll performed at low altitude over the pilot's own airfield, it came to signify success in aerial combat. Eventually, the tradition demanded one roll for each enemy aircraft downed.

The tradition originated in World War I but was by no means a universal practice. The more daring and exuberant pilots introduced the victory-roll idea and occasionally performed it in World War I, usually on special occasions. The majority of World War I pilots, however, took a different view of things. They were so glad to see their home airfields, and so eager to get safely down on them, that they had neither the energy nor the taste for risky low-altitude maneuvers. Their flimsy, "ground-hungry" crates no doubt induced a healthy aversion to too much victory rolling.

The maneuver was nevertheless the kind of dramatic highlight in which fiction writers have always reveled. It became a special favorite of screen writers. The victory roll was prominently featured in numerous flying films and stories, in the grand era of such aerial swashbucklers between the wars. Thus World War II's future pilots were extensively exposed to the victory roll during their growing years, and many came to regard it as a hallowed tradition of combat flying.

These pilots naturally carried the tradition of the victory roll to a much more general application in World War II than it had ever enjoyed in World War I. The vastly improved performance and design of World War II aircraft also made the maneuver more feasible, assuming that superior aerobatic skill was being employed. It was here that tragedy permeated the tradition.

Many fine combat pilots of World War II were possessed of indifferent aerobatic ability, frequently owing their combat success more to marksmanship than flying skills. The execution of a victory roll, at altitudes from ten to 100 feet above the runway, called for considerable aerobatic skill, especially when multiple kills demanded multiple rolls. The tragic historical fact is that many American fighter pilots plunged to their doom in attempting victory rolls. Pilot error frequently found a potent partner in unsuspected battle damage in victory-roll crashes.

In Korea, the victory roll appeared less frequently than in World War II. F-86 Sabres returning from combat at the Yalu were usually extremely low on fuel on reaching home base, and victorious pilots seldom took the hazardous chance involved in making the roll. Korean War pilots were also a more seasoned breed, frequently with a World War II career behind them. Getting combat film to the lab took precedence with them over emulating Errol Flynn and Richard Barthelmess.

In the classic pattern of the pursuit pilot is the most memorable combat experience of Captain James H. Kasler of Indianapolis, Indiana. Captain Kasler's fourth and fifth aerial victories came together on May 15, 1952:

> I was leading a two-ship element near the Yalu River when I spotted three MIG's at about 1,000 feet altitude. I split-essed on the lead aircraft and opened fire at 1,200 feet, closing to about 100 feet and pulling up on the MIG's wing. I could see the pilot sitting in a ball of flame. The MIG banked to the right and struck the ground, leaving a wide trail of fire.
>
> I looked out to the right and saw another MIG firing, with Albert Smiley,* my wingman, as his target. I bent around after the MIG and called Smiley to break. Smiley had been so intent on watching the MIG I'd downed that he had failed to see the MIG getting on his tail. The MIG overshot Smiley and dove for the treetops. The Red flak was terrific at this time, the gunners apparently not giving a hoot whether they hit the MIG or not.
>
> I chased the MIG about fifty miles on the deck until we reached the sea. He pulled up sharply in an Immelmann, and as he started down again, I scored a burst. By this time, I'd closed in to about five hundred feet, and as we came down out of the loop we were over the mud flats.
>
> With the haze over the coast, it was impossible to distinguish ground from sky. I didn't realize I was in any danger until the MIG

* First Lieutenant Albert Smiley was credited with three victories over MIG-15 aircraft while flying with the 335th Squadron in Korea.

splashed into the mud. We were both doing between 550 and 600 mph, and were still in a sixty-degree dive when the MIG hit.

As the fountain of mud and water shot up where he went in, I dropped my dive brakes, chopped the power and grabbed the stick with both hands. For a few seconds that seemed like years, I thought I was going to join my opponent in the mud. Then I saw the nose come back above the horizon. I don't know exactly how close I came to the mud, but I would estimate it at ten feet or less—not much of a margin for safety at 600 mph.

Captain Kasler is credited with six aerial victories. He flew with the 4th Fighter Group, the stellar fighter outfit in Korea.

Serving with the 4th at the same time as Kasler was another jet ace, Major Thomas Latshaw of Amarillo, Texas. Latshaw was flying his second-to-last combat mission in Korea when he became the fourteenth jet ace on May 4, 1952. His story reveals how easy it is even for an ace to be downed in aerial combat if his wingman goes astray:

It was my ninety-ninth mission at a time when only one hundred missions were allotted to an individual. I had four kills at the time, and was determined to make the most of any chance I might get to have a fifth kill.

We entered the combat area at an altitude that placed us just under the contrail level, about 35,000 feet. Maintaining radio silence and punching off the drop tanks when they were dry, we continued to search for a likely bounce. We spotted a flight of four MIG's at 25,000 feet. To the rear of the flight of MIG's and stacked up approximately 4,000 feet were four more MIG's. More flights of MIG's were stacked up above these in and above the contrail level.

My element leader also had four MIG's at this time, and was eager to enter the fray. Diving to the attack on the MIG's in the van of the formation, we dropped dive brakes so as not to overshoot them, and I selected the number two man flying on the left side of the MIG formation.

I opened fire at approximately 2,500 feet range, and hoped to score an easy and rapid kill before the MIG's behind and above us could dive to the attack. The MIG I was firing on, however, broke down and to the left at the same time that my element leader overshot the MIG he had selected.

I followed the MIG down, firing and scoring successive strikes until we were approximately 2,000 feet above the ground. He pulled up and I immediately began to lose out. Realizing I had my dive brakes still out, I closed them and began closing in on the MIG. At this time my wingman disappeared, and as I prepared to pour some more fire into the MIG, I spotted tracers arcing across my canopy. I looked up. A MIG and his wingman went flashing over me. They were so close I could still hear their cannon firing.

Since they'd dived on me from above and had a high airspeed, while mine was low, they overshot and slid almost a mile to the outside of my flight path. Taking advantage of their error, I began firing at the MIG once again. Just as my tracers sped toward the MIG, I noticed additional tracers intermingling with mine. I made a rapid check, and found a MIG firing at me from seven o'clock.

Things were getting hot, so I rapidly got back on the gunsight and fired at the MIG in front of me, lighting him up this time. The pilot ejected. In the meantime, the MIG at seven o'clock had found the range and put a cannon shell through my left wing tank. I had to take violent evasive action to get rid of him.

Captain Leonard William Lilley of Washington, D.C., shot down his fifth MIG-15 on November 18, 1952, to become America's twenty-second jet ace. A West Point graduate, Captain Lilley accounted for seven MIG-15's before being returned to the United States in February, 1953, for reassignment. He was yet another of the luminaries of the 4th Fighter Group, and his story of jet combat over Korea, to quote him, will "hold up any bar in the Air Force."

On September 4, 1952 I was flying close support on fighter bombers, who were bombing the main supply route leading south from Sinuiju, North Korea. First Lieutenant Drury Callahan was my wingman. While heading north at 18,000 feet, just under an overcast, we passed eight MIG's in a staggered-V formation, heading south.

We immediately swung south and fell in trail with this formation. The MIG's started to turn right, and this enabled us to close to effective firing range. Still unobserved, we closed to within 1,500 feet of the lead MIG. I opened fire, and the MIG burst into flames and started to dive straight ahead. We pursued, firing all the while.

As we dove, four MIG's chandelled to the left, and three pulled up to the right. In short order, we were nicely boxed in. The four from the left came whipping in just as the flaming MIG pilot ejected. We broke hard into them. This set us up for three MIG's on the right, who then came in firing.

We continued our turn to the left, managing to keep this turn tight enough for the MIG's to fire out and never hit us. However, the original four now repositioned themselves and took up a firing position right where their three pals left off. Our turn carried us right to the deck. By this time, the MIG's were firing at us from head-on, from ninety-degree angle-off, and from our six o'clock position.

Just as our fuel reached the point of no return, the seven MIG's all broke off and pulled up into the overcast. With a new lease on life we headed for our home base, 160 miles to the south. Minutes later we arrived, limp and exhausted, but with a story that would hold up any bar in the Air Force.

To illustrate the background of a remarkable fighter ace, whose successful career he predicted, Colonel Raymond Toliver, co-author of this book, takes over in the first person for a few paragraphs.

At San Bernardino, California, in 1946 and 1947 I had many opportunities to bounce and be bounced in mock aerial combat by a National Guard pilot who really appeared to be a "hot rock." This ANG pilot was the best and most aggressive I have ever met, and eventually a meeting on the ground was held in order to let me meet this character face-to-face.

He was Major Robert John Love, Canadian-born and close to my idea of what a fighter pilot should be. He turned out to be just as good in real combat as these previews indicated, and it came as no surprise to me to learn that in four months and fifty-two missions with the 4th Fighter Group in 1952, Bob shot down six MIG-15's to become the eleventh USAF jet ace.

The two stories of Bob Love's Korean experiences in this book are to my mind classics of fighter pilot's talk and jargon. You can almost see him banking his jet, palms of his hands down, and sadly needing yet another hand to show how the enemy pilot flew.

Major Bob Love now speaks for himself:

This was one of those "max effort" days when we managed six aircraft up out of the squadron on a cover mission. These birds, F-86A and F-86E, were tired "A" models up through the middle of the "E" series. Our flight of four was to cover west to east, south of the "creek" from the Yellow Sea and meet my two-ship element working east to west from the Mizu area.

I was flying a tired "A" with another on my wing, flown by a pilot who always aborted opposite Cho-do Island on the way in, and today was no exception. Lieutenant Ted Campbell was spare, and filled in on my wing with an "E" when my first boy dropped out. We held radio silence, driving to Mizu and turning west at 27,000 feet, just south of the creek. We were under an overcast, in haze, with about two miles' visibility.

I punched off the tanks and watched Ted clean up. I checked Ted's area to the south and east (left wing) and then checked my own five o'clock position just in time to find seven MIG's breaking hard on us from the north and level. Had we been five seconds later, they would have passed in front of us ninety degrees off north to south.

Their drops (tanks) were already fluttering down, so I called a hard right break into them, and once I saw the lead MIG driver, an instructor type, was washing through badly in his turn, I called a hard reverse back into him. We met about ten degrees off. I am sure Ted didn't hear the reverse call, as his reverse was delayed just long enough for the MIG to latch on behind him.

At this time, I noted the MIG instructor type's students were still in their turn to the west, and rather wide in "flock" formation. I reversed the third time and followed the MIG on Ted, turning my six o'clock to the students. I spent the next four minutes and several thousand feet of altitude trying to catch that full power "E" Sabre and the MIG in some real rough crossed-needle 360-degree turns. At times, I felt Ted would have to shake the MIG without my help, as when I managed to trim on the inside, Ted would reverse and leave me again on the outside, running out of breath and strength.

I fired short bursts of tracer, trying to scare the MIG off, but the range was letting the tracers burn out. Each few seconds we would meet the Students, in string, head-on, around these five- and six-G turns. We'd worked down to around 15,000 feet when Ted could no longer read me due to plugged ears, and pulled up to the west in a climbing turn. Ted at this time was convinced he'd lost the MIG, but broke down and to the east when he heard my call.

During the entire rat race the MIG fired at Ted, but failed to score a single hit. Once I could fly the tired "A" under the first line, I caught the MIG in close range with two bursts after this climbing turn. The canopy and engine doors left the MIG and the driver continued a slow turn from south to east.

In his hard, fast break to the east, Ted received only part of my call to "reverse and pick us up at three o'clock." He reversed and disappeared under me to the south toward "Long Dong." The MIG reversed in these few seconds, and with no canopy, engine doors gone, dumping fuel and belching smoke, he stuck the nose down slightly and headed east. He fired the rest of his ammo, and simply pulled hard over the top.

Following him, I was once again on the first line (no elevator deflection) and lost him as he pulled up into the sun. I managed to trim around somewhat of a pullup. I climbed into the sun until reading 170 knots, and being once again in the middle of the Students, I went out the bottom, joined with Ted farther south and back to home plate.

I never saw the lame MIG after his break upward. A photo Joe with an 86-escort flight from 334th Fighter Interceptor Squadron witnessed the scrap and confirmed the MIG as splashed. I felt this MIG driver was one of the better types, and mach-wise, his MIG could give an "A" model Sabre trouble. This was one of those scraps at low altitude and working downhill, where a few muscles, a G-suit and those hours of rat-racing with your buddies pay off.

The ebullient Bob Love also writes of another encounter with the MIG's:

Once airborne and on combat frequency we picked up the first flights calling MIG's out and shooting in general. Being off late, and to catch the MIG's before they turned north again, we maintained a flat, fast climb up the west coast, turning right (east) and paralleling The Creek on the south side. It sounded a little quiet over the horn, and it appeared the MIG's were about to leave the scraps east of us and go home. We dropped tanks. At about 30,000 feet we met the first two "early returns" almost head-on. These boys were going slightly more down and in a westerly direction.

We broke left and on to their tails, when we were bounced by two more from about three o'clock high. These latter two fired and broke up hard from west to south. Continuing on up, our element three and four latched on to these second two MIG's and chased them all the way up to where only a MIG would operate. Both these MIG's were damaged.

"Jumpin' Bob" (Second Lieutenant Bob Straub) and I continued on a NNW heading after the first element of MIG's. We couldn't close enough to fire until the MIG's started a slow turn to the south. I threw in two short bursts and the wingman bailed, almost hitting Jumpin' Bob's bird. The element leader had broken head up and to the north as we continued our turn south. Incidentally, the MIG wingman's hot seat functioned perfectly, as he separated from the seat on slipstream contact and his chute blossomed at once.

"Junior Bob" (Lieutenant Bob Campbell) of our element three

and four had moved to the inside of our turn south and called, "Break left and cover me, I've got one cold." We broke hard left, and three MIG's in an uneven string had passed under us to the east, ninety degrees off. As we completed the hard turn, I was able to tell Campbell he was covered and detect which of the string he intended to chop up. Campbell made a four o'clock pass on the number two MIG, cutting the bird in half. Number three MIG slid on to Campbell's tail. I shook this MIG with a short burst and called a hard up and right break to Campbell.

The number three MIG I'd hit finished in true Hollywood fashion, looping east to west at eight thousand feet altitude. I flew slot man on this boy, hitting well through the first half of the loop, firing out inverted. Dumping fuel, parts and debris, and smoking badly, the MIG continued on through the first half of a Cuban eight, but neglected to pull out.

During this acro show, Jumpin' Bob was in element, and as I completed firing out he yelled, "Break left!" I had just rolled right side up. One MIG came in from four o'clock and almost rammed the element. Bob didn't waste time calling this left break again, as he had a flight of four MIG's firing from seven o'clock at him. He could hear the cannons in the pit.

We continued our hard left break to the south, and were clear of MIG's in twenty seconds. Their top cover almost worked. Low over the water we checked our birds for hits. . . . There were none. Our damage was one jammed gun on each side of my aircraft due to G's and heat. We had knocked off three MIG's in less than two minutes.

On this mission, all three pilots with Bob Love were also named Bob. They had to work out a call sign appropriate to each pilot. Bob Love for radio purposes became "Old Bob." His wingman Bob Straub* was "Jumpin' Bob." The number three man, Lieutenant Bob Ferber, was "Ferb" and the number four, Lieutenant Bob Campbell, was plain "Bob" or "Junior Bob." Novel names were used, to quote Bob Love, "because with plugged ears and 5-G's on the man talking, Able, Yellow and Purple all sound the same. But a name like Jumpin' Bob could be understood under all but the roughest conditions."

For readers who might be wondering if Bob Love was using some strange foreign language in his unexpurgated combat accounts, this is "fighter talk." Strange terms unfamiliar to the "ground lubber" will be

* Lieutenant Robert L. Straub was credited with two MIG's destroyed in Korea.

found in the Glossary of Fighter Slang in the Appendix. With its aid, Bob Love's classic accounts can be easily translated.

Major Bob Love keeps his hand in today with the California Air National Guard's 196th Fighter Squadron at Ontario, California. He is still professionally associated with aviation as an official of Northrop Aviation in California.

There appeared from time to time in the ranks of the "MIG Drivers," as Bob Love would call them, combat pilots of formidable skill and tenacity. Their identity remains a mystery. An encounter with such a pilot forms the outstanding combat memory of Lieutenant James F. Low of Sausalito, California:

We were on a fighter Sweep over North Korea in the vicinity of Suiho Reservoir on December 18, 1952. My wingman and I were cruising around thirty thousand feet when two MIG's appeared at two o'clock level about five miles away. We closed in on them, and they split, one going high, the other low. They were camouflaged with brown and green spots. It looked best to jump the MIG that had gone low, since the other one had turned away and seemed to care nothing for his buddy's fate.

My wingman was in a better position for a bounce, so I told him to take the MIG. Little did we know that we had tangled with a honcho [A topnotch fighter pilot—Aus.] We closed in, my wingman getting to within five hundred feet of the MIG, but he was unable to draw any lead on his target. The MIG was pulling a high-G load constantly, and my wingman's bullets were falling uselessly behind the enemy machine.

I told him to quit firing until he had lead, but he had target fixation and soon fired off all his ammunition. All this time I was flying his wing and keeping his tail clear. Finally he screamed, "Yellow Three, you better take him, I'm out of ammo!" I slid down on the MIG's tail while my wingman slid high.

I tried pulling lead on this MIG, and squeezed off a couple of bursts, but I also underled him. I concentrated now on getting the necessary lead before firing again. The enemy pilot continued his evasive maneuvers, and could that guy fly? First rolling under and split-essing, we ended up "on the mach" about a hundred feet off the deck. He wound round hills and mountains reversing and trying to shake me. With no success at this, he started a chandelle, trying to outzoom me, but I cut him off in the turn and stuck with him.

Finally he relaxed a little and I caught him with a short burst in the tail section. He continued to turn, but I hit him with another good burst in the engine and wing root. He blew his canopy and I thought he'd bail, but I waited and waited, fighting to stay above and behind him. He had a dead engine and was decelerating, so this was difficult to do.

Then he pulled straight up, firing, hoping to catch me overshooting. He didn't. As he rolled over I caught him dead center with a long burst. He never pulled out of the dive, and crashed thunderously about ten miles east of the reservoir.

Jim Low was the only Second Lieutenant to become a jet ace in the Korean War. He ended the conflict with nine confirmed victories over the Red jets. The skill of the enemy pilot in this and other instances reported by American aces serving in Korea raises some interesting questions, and has given rise to much speculation. The "honchos" encountered in Korea may have been soldiers of fortune from European countries, Soviet Russian "volunteers" or just simply Chinese who had learned their trade well. The Red pilots of the Korean War remain one of the riddles of combat aviation's colorful history.

While it is true that the modern jet jockey flies in far greater comfort than his predecessors of the First and Second World War, and also requires less physical effort to maneuver his aircraft, combat conditions sometimes suddenly returned Korean jet pilots to the era of helmet-and-goggles. Colonel Winton W. "Bones" Marshall well remembers his unwelcome return to open cockpit and tearing slipstream:

The 4th Fighter Wing was intercepting a large formation of Red TU-2 bombers, escorted by LA-9 and MIG-15 fighters. Their mission was to wipe out our United Nations island holdings which were supporting radar installations and rescue operations. They were going to strafe and bomb these installations into oblivion. Led by Colonel Benjamin Preston* and Colonel Harrison Thyng our attack completely broke up their formation and caused them to abort the mission.

I was lucky enough to get one LA-9 and one TU-2 and damage another of the bombers. Following one pass, I was hit head-on by the cannon fire of an LA-9, which made a large hole in my wing and shot off my canopy. The shell that hit the canopy went on to hit and demolish my headrest, throwing my head up against the instrument panel and cracking my helmet.

* Colonel Preston shot down three MIG's and an LA-9 in the Korean war.

I usually lean far forward when I fly, or I would have probably had my head blown off. Shrapnel from the shell damaged the cockpit interior and sieved my parachute, which was a package of tatters. My wingman, Lieutenant Honaker, one of the finest fighter pilots I have ever flown with, shot down the LA-9 immediately, and then escorted me for a cold trip home. It was forty below zero at that altitude in the middle of a bitter Korean winter.

I was not sure whether the aircraft was going to continue to run, but the F-86 is one of the best aircraft I have ever flown and it brought me safely home.

Colonel Marshall hails from Beverly Hills, California, and for the action described was awarded the Silver Star and Purple Heart. In the Korean War he destroyed 4.5 MIG's, one LA-9, and one TU-2 for a total of 6.5 confirmed aerial victories. He is another ace from the 4th Fighter Group in that conflict.

Captain Ralph Sherman Parr, America's thirty-fourth jet ace, was another pilot who saw plenty of Korea's abundant air to ground action. He flew 165 missions in F-80's prior to his transfer to the 4th Fighter Group. Once in a position to prove his worth in air-to-air combat, he quickly proved his mettle. In forty-seven missions in the Sabre he downed ten enemy aircraft—nine MIG's and one IL-2. His most memorable aerial encounter reveals how poor enemy shooting can often deliver a fighter pilot from the jaws of death:

While on combat patrol in North Korea and flying at 42,000 feet, I spotted a flight of MIG's at extremely low altitude. I made a vertical diving attack, in which I lost the remainder of my flight. At 3,000 feet I selected the leader of a sixteen-ship formation of MIG's. They spotted me.

As the fight began, right on the deck, my gunsight failed. By using extreme close range firing, I was able to destroy two MIG's and damage a third. My aircraft sustained no damage—an incredible thing. *No fewer than seven MIG's fired themselves out of ammo at my aircraft*, at ranges from *five to six hundred feet* during this battle. The remainder of my flight intervened and the MIG's bolted for the Yalu.

Ralph Parr, who joined the USAAF as a flying cadet in 1942, is a career USAF officer. Only ten other fighter pilots besides Parr ended the Korean War with ten or more aerial victories. This officer also bears the historical distinction of scoring the final aerial victory of the Korean conflict. He shot down an IL-2 near Hoha-dong less than twelve hours before the Armistice on July 27, 1953.

Colonel Harrison Reed Thyng of Barnstead, New Hampshire, is America's sixteenth jet ace and belongs to the illustrious "inner six" who became aces in both World War II and Korea. He has probably shot down a greater variety of enemy aircraft than any other ace, for his World War II kills include German, French, Italian and Japanese aircraft. To these he added five of the Soviet-built MIG's in the Korean War.

Colonel Thyng's most memorable victory once again involved the Yalu River and the strange situation pertaining there:

I was flying an F-86E up over northern Korea early in the spring of 1952. I was flying top flight at 45,000 feet up and down the Yalu, covering a fighter-bomber strike in the Sinuiju area.

MIG-15's started taking off from Antung, and as they came across the Yalu, they were immediately engaged by other flights of my group (the 4th). The battle had just started when I saw six MIG's cornering one of my F-86E's. With my wingman, I dove down to eight hundred feet and gave the MIG leader a short burst after getting on his tail.

Naturally, as he had just taken off, his tanks were loaded with fuel and my burst hit him in the tank located just behind the cockpit. The low altitude was very conducive to explosion and burning, and the MIG partially exploded and headed quickly for Antung. He made a fiery crash in the middle of his own airfield, and disrupted all further action from that field for the next few hours. I believe the morale of the Reds must have been severely shaken when this pilot went in under their very noses, as he was the leader of the attacking MIG formation.

The top jet ace of the United States is Captain Joseph McConnell Jr. of Dover, New Hampshire, who is credited with sixteen MIG-15's. Captain McConnell was sent to the Far East Air Force in August, 1952, and assigned to the 51st Fighter Interceptor Wing in Korea, flying the Sabrejet. He did not win a victory until January 14, 1953, when he brought down his first MIG-15.

From then on, Captain McConnell was "hot," in fighter pilots' parlance. With 106 missions and 16 victories to his credit, he returned to the United States in May 1953 after a brilliant combat career. Like Richard Bong, John Herbst, Buzz Wagner and numerous other famous fighter pilots who survived aerial combat, McConnell was killed in an aircraft accident. He was testing a new and more powerful model of the Sabre that carried him to glory when he crashed and was killed on August 25, 1954.

The only other pilot in the history of aerial combat to score sixteen confirmed kills while flying a jet is the late Lieutenant Colonel Heinz Bär of the Luftwaffe in World War II. He and Captain McConnell might be considered tied for world primacy as jet aces.

The U.S. Navy found history repeating itself in the Korean War, when it produced only one ace in the conflict. Lieutenant Guy B. Bordelon gained his fifth aerial victory on July 16, 1953, less than two weeks before the Armistice. Although naval air power made a mighty contribution to the UN struggle in Korea, Navy fighter pilots did not have the opportunities to grapple with the enemy air force that came the way of USAF units. Just as David Sinton Ingalls was the U.S. Navy's only World War I ace, Guy Bordelon bears the same distinction in the Korean struggle.

The Marines produced only one ace in the Korean War, Lieutenant Colonel John F. Bolt, who was attached to the USAF's 39th Interceptor Squadron. As with the Navy, the role of Marine aviation in Korea was largely confined to close-support flying, with little or no opportunity offered the pilots to tangle with the MIG's. Lieutenant Colonel Bolt is the Marines' only jet ace and, as mentioned in Chapter Eight, is the only Marine to become an ace in both World War II and Korea. He is credited with six victories in each conflict for a lifetime total of twelve aerial victories.

In July, 1953, the Korean police action ended in armistice. Aggressive patrols to the Yalu were replaced with the interminable bickerings of the peace table. The aces of the Korean War passed into history, their names etched in the immortal records of aerial combat beside those of their predecessors.

Forty new jet aces were produced by the Korean War, consisting of thirty-eight Air Force aces, one Navy ace and one Marine Corps ace. Numerous other American pilots became aces as a result of combining their Korean scores with World War II credits. American aces from World War II increased their victory credits in Korea without actually attaining their second "five down" in the latter conflict. John C. Meyer (24 World War II, 2 Korea), Glenn T. Eagleston (18.5 World War II, 2 Korea) and Walker M. "Bud" Mahurin (20.75 World War II, 3.5 Korea) are among the famous aces in this category.

Less than 10 percent of the USAF pilots credited with aerial victories in Korea became aces, a fact which again illustrates the elite nature of acedom. Those who did become aces accounted for 36 percent of the enemy aircraft shot down during the war. Enemy losses in aerial combat totaled 893 aircraft, which serves to illustrate the smaller scale of aerial combat in Korea compared with W W I and W W II.

There has been a tendency both in and out of military circles to deprecate the role of fighter aircraft in the Korean conflict. Somewhat unrealistically, the cost of the Yalu patrols by jet fighters has been estimated more in terms of dollars than tactical factors. Not uncommon in some military quarters today is the statement that U.S. jets shot down only 841 MIG-15's, and that this cost so many millions of dollars or so much per aircraft and that it was "expensive."

Aside from the fact that all war is expensive folly which only an all-around improvement in human nature can eradicate, there is considerable danger in such intellectualizing about fighters in Korea. Their contribution must be evaluated in terms of the overall struggle and their influence upon events.

What would have been the consequences of having the 841 enemy MIG-15's setting upon the UN close-support aircraft—the B-26's, P-51's and other obsolescent machines? The fearful devastation of enemy supply systems wrought by the UN command's World War II aircraft governed the whole unfoldment of the ground war. The Sabre umbrella kept the Red jets in check, and allowed the UN forces to utilize the residue of Allied airpower from World War II in a manner out of all proportion to its age.

Korean War pilots, whose combat missions were normally limited to 100, had the benefit of well-controlled policies governing rotation, rest and recuperation. USAF personnel serving in Korea were entitled each six weeks to three days' temporary duty in Japan. They could also choose the station in Japan at which they would spend the three days.

This procedure, although sometimes modified, was fairly standard throughout the conflict. It was quite a contrast to World War II conditions, where the primary factor governing the rotation of fighter pilots was the number of missions flown. Each air force in World War II set its own requirements for the number of missions. These requirements were then varied to suit the dynamics of the particular theater of operations.

In World War II, the availability of replacement pilots and aircraft, the terrain over which the pilots had to fly and fight, calibre of opposition, attrition rates, and the number of missions involving actual combat were some of the factors governing pilot rotation and rest and recuperation procedures. Depending on the air force with which he was serving, the World War II fighter pilot could count on flying from thirty-five to 150 missions before being sent back to the United States or to the rear areas.

Korean War pilots could frequently get a few fast days in Japan by ferrying tired F-86 Sabres back to the repair depot in Japan. After their rest period, they ferried restored Sabres back to their combat station.

Occasionally, outstanding combat pilots might have their tours extended from 100 to perhaps 120 or 125 missions. Even these extensions were frequently curtailed before completion. Generally speaking, there were just too many fighter pilots in the USAF who needed the combat experience, and this resulted in fairly strict adherence to rotation policies.

Many pilots in the Korea fracas never completed 100 missions before returning to Japan to complete their overseas tour, or before returning to the States. There were also numbers of pilots who could not adapt themselves to the taxing requirements of jet tactics, maneuvers and procedures. These men were weeded out as rapidly as possible.

In Korea, many pilots senior in age and grade were allowed to take part in a limited number of missions (usually no more than thirty-five) to give them firsthand combat knowledge. These were officers whose specific assignments in the USAF would benefit from such familiarization. The average Korean War jet fighter pilot flew fewer than 100 combat missions.

After Korea, Uncle Sam did not again trustfully disarm as he had done twice before to his own subsequent detriment. World conditions and especially the Korean fiasco demonstrated the need for raw power in being. Drawing-board aircraft and missiles, or memories of what America did in World War II and could do if called upon again, were now recognized as feeble answers to the challenges of the space age.

Fighter plane development, even if downgraded somewhat in the transition to missiles, has not again sunk into quite the hapless state of neglect that prevailed between the world wars. Nevertheless, some of the most energetic devotees of air power have inclined in recent years to take a narrowing view of the air weapon.

As this is being written, the latter-day deprecation of naval airpower is following similar trends to those of the nineteen-twenties and-thirties. Whereas in earlier times it was the aircraft carrier that came under criticism, even from airpower advocates and pioneers, today the super-carrier is the subject of similar controversies. The trend is very powerful in contemporary American military thinking toward extremely narrow, specialized uses for the aircraft of the future.

Many fighter pilots and aces, although long separated from their own days of combat and glory, remain deeply concerned about the changing role of airpower. In most gatherings of aces, these matters are given more than passing attention. While some of the discussions generate more heat than light, there can be no doubt of the sincerity and depth of concern shown by America's air heroes for their country's future.

Should there be a third world conflict, such as might have erupted over the Cuban affair or which may erupt in the near future in Asia, it seems certain that there will be a fourth generation of fighter aces. If hostilities do not break out for another decade or so, then America's airmen may well perform quite different tasks to the aerial combat of the past.

The fighter pilot, it seems, is being metamorphosed into the space-craft pilot. America's first orbital astronaut, Colonel John H. Glenn USMC* is a former combat fighter pilot whose experience as such was

* Glenn scored three kills over MIG-15's in Korea.

invaluable to him as an astronaut. The late Captain Iven C. Kincheloe Jr.* was a jet ace of the Korean War who died while applying his skills to the first manned flights to the edge of space.

Technology moves forward in seven-league boots. What vehicles will be devised for manned flight within the next decade few men can accurately predict. Perhaps a fleet of X-15 type aircraft will exist then. Possibly Dyna-Soar will point the way. Maybe the "space fighter" concept of British designer Barnes Wallis will come to fruition. He has put his half-century of successful design skill behind a new craft that will take off by jet from regular runways, fly by jet to the fringe of space, fold its wings and vault into space by ramjet—all under pilot control! It is possible also that some kind of electrical propulsion will revolutionize our whole conception of travel above the earth.

The potential development in terms of military hardware is fantastic to contemplate. But without the same qualities of courage, daring and ingenuity; skill, steadfastness and devotion to duty that have been the traditional possessions of America's fighter aces, the new battles of space exploration and development cannot be won. The machines of the future will be different. The human qualities epitomized in the fighter ace are the eternal properties of the human spirit, ever striving for conquest over mankind's physical environment.

America's 1,300 knights of the air have passed into history, and if all aerial combat as we have known it is to vanish, at least America's military glories have been enhanced by the fighter ace. He gave his country a new kind of folk hero, born in and fitted to the technological era of the twentieth century. His exploits and individualistic traits have brightened the military records of the age, and kept alive, however faintly, the last vestiges of knightly chivalry.

---

* Kincheloe scored five kills in Korea. On the fiftieth anniversary of the USAF, Kincheloe, the ace and test pilot, took Captain Frederick Libby, first American to down five planes in aerial combat, for a flip in a modern jet fighter. The veteran Libby, then in his late sixties, took over in the air and flew the jet like a pro. On landing, Kincheloe announced, "The old boy is as good as he ever was."

Tops and Firsts

First American to Shoot Down Five Enemy Aircraft in World War I
CAPT. FREDERICK LIBBY (shot down 10 as an observer in RFC)
First American Ace of World War I
CAPT. ALAN M. WILKINSON (19 victories)
First American Ace to Serve with the AEF
CAPT. RAOUL G. LUFBERY (17 victories)
First American AEF Ace of World War I
CAPT. DOUGLAS CAMPBELL (6 victories)
Top American Ace of World War I
CAPT. EDWARD V. RICKENBACKER (26 victories)
Top American Ace with Foreign Government (World War I)
CAPT. STANLEY C. ROSEVEAR, RFC (23 victories)
First American Ace of World War II
CAPT. CYRIL D. PALMER (RAF) (5 victories)
First American USAAF Ace of World War II
LT. BOYD D. "BUZZ" WAGNER
Top American Ace of World War II
MAJ. RICHARD BONG, USAAF (40 victories)
Top Navy Ace World War II
CAPT. DAVID McCAMPBELL (34 victories)
Top Marine Corps Ace World War II
LT. COL. GREGORY BOYINGTON (28 victories including 6 scored with the AVG in China)
COL. JOSEPH J. FOSS (26 victories, all with USMC)
Top American Ace with Foreign Government World War II
WG. CDR. LANCE WADE (RAF) (25 victories)
Most Kills in a Single Mission
CAPT. DAVID McCAMPBELL USN (9 confirmed; 2 probables)
Top American Ace of Pacific Theater of Operations World War II

MAJ. RICHARD BONG (40 victories)
Top American Ace of European Theater of Operations (World War II)
COL. FRANCIS S. GABRESKI (31 victories)
First American Ace of Korean War (1950-1953)
CAPT. JAMES JABARA (May 20, 1951) (15 victories)
Top American Jet Ace of Korean War
CAPT. JOSEPH McCONNELL (16 victories)
First American to Score an Aerial Kill in Korea
1ST LT. WILLIAM G. HUDSON (F-82 pilot shot down a YAK-11, June 27, 1950)
First Jet-to-Jet Kill of Korean War and First Jet-to-Jet Kill in History
1ST LT. RUSSELL J. BROWN (F-80 over MIG-15, November 8, 1950)
Top Living American Ace
COL. FRANCIS S. GABRESKI 31.0 World War II
                           6.5 Korea
                          ─────
                          37.5 Total victories
First American Ace of Two Wars
MAJ. A. J. "AJAX" BAUMLER 8.0 Spanish Civil War
                           5.0 World War II
                          ─────
                          13.0 Total victories

American Aces with Twenty or More Victories—
All Wars

			World War I	World War II	Korea	Total
BONG, RICHARD L.	Maj.	USAF	—	40.00	—	40.00
McGUIRE, THOMAS B.	Maj.	USAF	—	38.00	—	38.00
GABRESKI, FRANCIS S.	Col.	USAF	—	31.00	6.50	37.50
McCAMPBELL, DAVID	Capt.	USN	—	34.00	—	34.00
JOHNSON, ROBERT S.	Lt. Col.	USAF	—	28.00	—	28.00
BOYINGTON, GREGORY	Lt. Col.	USMC	—	28.00	—	28.00

			World War I	World War II	Korea	Total
MACDONALD, CHARLES H.	Col.	USAF	—	27.00	—	27.00
RICKENBACKER, EDWARD	Capt.	AEF	26.00	—	—	26.00
FOSS, JOSEPH JACOB	Maj.	USMC	—	26.00	—	26.00
MEYER, JOHN C.	Col.	USAF	—	24.00	2.00	26.00
PREDDY, GEORGE E.	Maj.	USAF	—	25.83	—	25.83
HANSON, ROBERT M.	1st Lt.	USMC	—	25.00	—	25.00
WADE, LANCE C.	Wg. Cdr.	RAF	—	25.00	—	25.00
MAHURIN, WALKER M.	Lt. Col.	USAF	—	20.75	3.50	24.25
HARRIS, CECIL E.	Lt.	USN	—	24.00	—	24.00
ROSEVEAR, S. C.	Capt.	RFC	23.00	—	—	23.00
VALENCIA, EUGENE A.	Cdr.	USN	—	23.00	—	23.00
WETMORE, RAY S.	Capt.	USAF	—	22.59	—	22.59
SCHILLING, DAVID C.	Col.	USAF	—	22.50	—	22.50
JOHNSON, GERALD R.	Lt. Col.	USAF	—	22.00	—	22.00
KEARBY, NEEL E.	Maj.	USAF	—	22.00	—	22.00
LAMBERT, WILLIAM C.	Capt.	RFC	22.00	—	—	22.00
ROBBINS, JAY T.	Lt. Col.	USAF	—	22.00	—	22.00
CHRISTENSEN, FRED J.	Capt.	USAF	—	21.50	—	21.50
DAVIS, GEORGE A., JR.	Maj.	USAF	—	7.00	14.00	21.00
VOLL, JOHN J.	Maj.	USAF	—	21.00	—	21.00
WALSH, KENNETH A.	Maj.	USMC	—	21.00	—	21.00
WHISNER, WILLIAM T.	Maj.	USAF	—	15.50	5.50	21.00
EAGLESTON, GLENN T.	Col.	USAF	—	18.50	2.00	20.50
ALDRICH, DONALD M.	Capt.	USMC	—	20.00	—	20.00
GILLETTE, FREDERICK W.	Capt.	RFC	20.00	—	—	20.00
LYNCH, THOMAS J.	Lt. Col.	USAF	—	20.00	—	20.00
MALONE, JOHN J.	Capt.	RN*	20.00	—	—	20.00
WESTBROOK, ROBERT B.	Lt. Col.	USAF	—	20.00	—	20.00

* Royal Navy

American Aces of World War I

AEF—American Expeditionary Force
FFC—French Flying Corps
RFC—Royal Flying Corps (British)
*—Lafayette Escadrille

Name	Home Town	Rank	Service	Victories
BADHAM, WILLIAM T.	Birmingham, Ala.	1st Lt.	91 Sq AEF	5.00
BAER, PAUL F.	Fort Wayne, Ind.	1st Lt.	103 Sq AEF*	9.00
BAIR, HILBERT L.	New York, N.Y.	1st Lt.	RFC	5.00
BAYLIES, FRANK L.	New Bedford, Mass.	Lt.	FFC*	12.00
BEANE, JAMES D.	Concord, Mass.	1st Lt.	22 Sq AEF	6.00
BENNETT, LOUIS B.	Weston, W. Va.	1st Lt.	40 Sq RFC	12.00
BIDDLE, CHARLES J.	Andalusia, Pa.	Maj.	13 Sq AEF*	7.00
BISSELL, CLAYTON L.	Kane, Pa.	Capt.	148 Sq AEF	5.00
BROOKS, ARTHUR R.	Framingham, Mass.	Capt.	139 Sq AEF	6.00
BUCKLEY, HAROLD R.	Aqawam, Mass.	Capt.	95 Sq AEF	5.00
BURDICK, HOWARD	Brooklyn, N. Y.	1st Lt.	17 Sq AEF	7.00
CALAHAN, LAWRENCE K.	Chicago, Ill.	1st Lt.	85 Sq RFC	5.00
CAMPBELL, DOUGLAS	Mt. Hamilton, Calif.	Capt.	94 Sq AEF	6.00
CASSADY, THOMAS G.	Spencer, Ind.	Capt.	28 Sq AEF*	9.00
CHAMBERS, REED M.	Memphis, Tenn.	Maj.	94 Sq AEF	7.00
CLAY, HENRY R., JR.	Fort Worth, Tex.	1st Lt.	148 Sq AEF	8.00
CONNELLY, JAMES A.	Philadelphia, Pa.	Lt.	FFC*	8.00
COOK, EVERETT RICHARD	Germantown, Tenn.	Capt.	91 Sq AEF	5.00
COOK, H. WEIR	Indianapolis, Ind.	Capt.	94 Sq AEF	7.00
COOLIDGE, HAMILTON	Boston, Mass.	Capt.	94 Sq AEF	8.00
CREECH, JESSE O.	Washington, D.C.	1st Lt.	148 Sq AEF	8.00
CURTISS, EDWARD P.	Rochester, N. Y.	Capt.	95 Sq AEF	6.00

Name	Home Town	Rank	Service	Vic-tories
D'OLIVE, CHARLES R.	Cedar Falls, Ia.	Lt.	93 Sq AEF	5.00
DONALDSON, JOHN OWEN	Washington, D.C.	Capt.	85 Sq RFC	8.00
EASTERBROOK, ARTHUR E.	Amsterdam, N. Y.	1st Lt.	1 Sq AEF	6.00
ERWIN, WILLIAM P.	Chicago, Ill.	1st Lt.	1 Sq AEF	8.00
FURLOW, GEORGE W.	Rochester, Minn.	1st Lt.	103 Sq AEF	5.00
GEORGE, HAROLD H.	Niagara Falls, N.Y.	1st Lt.	139 Sq AEF	5.00
GILLETTE, FREDERICK W.	Baltimore, Md.	Capt.	RFC	20.00
GRAY, CHARLES G.	Chicago, Ill.	Capt.	213 Sq AEF	5.00
GRIFFITH, JOHN S.	Seattle, Wash.	Capt.	60 Sq RFC	9.00
GUTHRIE, MURRAY K.	Mobile, Ala.	1st Lt.	13 Sq AEF	6.00
HAIGHT, EDWARD M.	Astoria, N. Y.	1st Lt.	139 Sq AEF	5.00
HALE, FRANK L.	Fayetteville, Ark.	Capt.	85 Sq RFC	18.00
HALL, JAMES NORMAN	Colfax, Ia.	Capt.	FFC	6.00
HAMILTON, LLOYD A.	Burlington, Vt.	1st Lt.	17 Sq AEF	9.00
HAMMOND, LEONARD C.	San Francisco, Calif.	Capt.	91 Sq AEF	6.00
HARTNEY, HAROLD EVANS	Pakenham, Ont.	Maj.	1 Sq AEF	6.00
HAYES, FRANK KERR	Chicago, Ill.	1st Lt.	13 Sq AEF	6.00
HEALY, JAMES A.	Jersey City, N. J.	Capt.	147 Sq AEF	5.00
HOLDEN, LANSING C.	New York, N. Y.	1st Lt.	95 Sq AEF	7.00
HUDSON, DONALD	Kansas City, Mo.	Capt.	27 Sq AEF	6.00
HUFFER, JOHN W. F. M.	(Born) Paris, France	1st Lt.	FFC	7.00
HUNTER, FRANK O'D	Savannah, Ga.	1st Lt.	103 Sq AEF	8.00
IACCACI, PAUL T.	New York, N. Y.	Capt.	20 Sq RFC	18.00
IACCACI, THAYER A.	New York, N. Y.	Lt.	22 Sq RFC	11.00
INGALLS, DAVID SINTON	Chagrin Falls, O.	Lt. USN	213 Sq AEF	5.00
JONES, CLINTON	San Francisco, Calif.	2nd Lt.	22 Sq AEF	8.00

Name	Home Town	Rank	Service	Victories
KEATING, JAMES A.		Maj.	49 Sq RFC	6.00
KINDLEY, FIELD E.	Gravette, Ark.	Capt.	148 Sq AEF	12.00
KNOTTS, HOWARD C.	Carlinville, Ill.	2nd Lt.	17 Sq AEF	6.00
KNOWLES, JAMES	Cambridge, Mass.	1st Lt.	95 Sq AEF	5.00
KULLBERG, HAROLD A.	West Somerville, Mass.	Lt.	1 Sq RFC	16.00
LAMB, DEAN I.		Lt.	4 Sq RFC	5.00
LAMBERT, WILLIAM CARPENTER	Ironton, Ohio	Capt.	24 Sq RFC	22.00
LANDIS, REED G.	Chicago, Ill.	Capt.	25 Sq AEF	10.00
LARNER, G. DeFREEST	New York, N. Y.	Capt.	103 Sq AEF*	8.00
LIBBY, FREDERICK	Sterling, Colo.	Capt.	25 Sq RFC	14.00
LINDSAY, ROBERT O.	Madison, N. C.	1st Lt.	139 Sq AEF	6.00
LUFBERY, RAOUL G.	Boston, Mass.	Maj.	N–124 FFC*	17.00
LUFF, FREDERICK E.	Cleveland, Ohio	1st Lt.	25 Sq AEF	5.00
LUKE, FRANK	Phoenix, Ariz.	2nd Lt.	27 Sq AEF	18.00
MAGOUN, FRANCIS P.		Lt.	1 Sq RFC	5.00
MALONE, JOHN J.		Capt.	Royal Navy	20.00
MATTHEWS, ALEXANDRE	Louisburg, W. Va.	Lt.	84 Sq RFC	5.00
McARTHUR, JOHN K.	Everett, Wash.	2nd Lt.	27 Sq AEF	6.00
McCLURE, DAVID M.	Pittsburgh, Pa.	1st Lt.	147 Sq AEF	6.00
MEISSNER, JAMES A.	Brooklyn, N. Y.	Maj.	94 Sq AEF	8.00
MILLER, EWART S.	E. Palestine, Ohio	1st Lt.	139 Sq AEF	5.00
MILLER, ZENES R.	Evanston, Ill.	1st Lt.	148 Sq AEF	5.00
O'NEILL, RALPH A.	Nogales, Ariz.	1st Lt.	147 Sq AEF	5.00
OWENS, J. SIDNEY	Baltimore, Md.	2nd Lt.	139 Sq AEF	5.00
PACE, W. J.		Capt.	RFC	5.00
PARSONS, EDWIN C.	Springfield, Mass.	Lt.	N–124 FFC*	8.00
PETERSON, DAVID McKELVY	Honesdale, Pa.	Maj.	FFC*	5.00
PONDER, WILLIAM T.	Mangum, Okla.	1st Lt.	103 AEF*	6.00
PORTER, KENNETH L.	Dowagiac, Mich.	2nd Lt.	147 Sq AEF	6.00
PRINCE, NORMAN	Prides Crossing, Mass.	2nd Lt.	N–124 FFC*	5.00

Name	Home Town	Rank	Service	Victories
Putnam, David E.	Brookline, Mass.	1st Lt.	139 Sq AEF*	12.00
Ralston, Orville A.	Lincoln, Neb.	1st Lt.	148 Sq AEF	5.00
Rickenbacker, Ed V.	Columbus, Ohio	Capt.	94 Sq AEF	26.00
Roberts, E. M.	Duluth, Minn.	Lt.	60 Sq RFC	7.00
Robertson, Frank A.	Oakland, Calif.	Lt.	29 Sq RFC	6.00
Robertson, Wendel A.	Fort Smith, Ark.	Lt.	139 Sq AEF	7.00
Rogers, Bogart		Capt.	32 Sq RFC	5.00
Rose, Oren J.	Kansas City, Mo.	Capt.	92 Sq RFC	16.00
Rosevear, S. C.		Capt.	201 Sq RFC	23.00
Rummel, Leslie J.	Newark, N.J.	1st Lt.	93 Sq AEF	7.00
Schoen, Karl J.	Indianapolis, Ind.	1st Lt.	139 Sq AEF	7.00
Seerley, John J.	Chicago, Ill.	1st Lt.	13 Sq AEF	5.00
Sewall, Sumner	Bath, Me.	Capt.	95 Sq AEF	7.00
Springs, Elliott White	Lancaster, S.C.	Capt.	148 Sq AEF	12.00
Stenseth, Martinus	Twin Valley, Minn.	Capt.	28 Sq AEF	6.00
Stovall, William H.	Stovall, Miss.	1st Lt.	13 Sq AEF	7.00
Strahm, Victor H.	Bowling Green, Ky.	Maj.	91 Sq AEF	5.00
Swaab, Jacques M.	Philadelphia, Pa.	Capt.	22 Sq AEF	10.00
Thaw, William	Pittsburgh, Pa.	Lt. Col.	N-124 FFC*	5.00
Tipton, William D.	Tarretsville, Md.	Capt.	33 Sq RFC	5.00
Tobin, Edgar G.	San Antonio, Tex.	Capt.	103 Sq AEF	6.00
Todd, Robert M.	Cincinnati, Ohio	2nd Lt.	117 Sq AEF	5.00
Vasconcells, Jerry C.	Denver, Colo.	Capt.	27 Sq AEF	6.00
Vaughn, George A.	Dongan Hills, N.Y.	1st Lt.	17 Sq AEF	13.00
Veil, Charles Herbert	Big Run, Pa.	Capt.	N-150 FFC*	5.00
Vernam, Remington DeB.	New York, N.Y.	1st Lt.	22 Sq AEF	6.00
Warman, C. T.	Philadelphia, Pa.	Lt.	RFC	15.00
Wehner, Joseph F.	Everett, Mass.	1st Lt.	27 Sq AEF	5.00

Name	Home Town	Rank	Service	Victories
WESTING, F.	Philadelphia, Pa.	Lt.	RFC	5.00
WHITE, WILBUR WALLACE	New York, N.Y.	1st Lt.	147 Sq AEF	8.00
WILKENSON, ALAN M.		Maj.	48 Sq RFC	19.00
WILLIAMS, RODNEY D.	Waukesha, Wis.	1st Lt.	17 Sq AEF	5.00
WRIGHT, CHESTER E.	Cambridge, Mass.	1st Lt.	93 Sq AEF	9.00

Fifteen or More Victories

Rickenbacker, Edward V.	26.00
Rosevear, S. C.	23.00
Lambert, William Carpenter	22.00
Gillette, Frederick W.	20.00
Malone, John J.	20.00
Wilkenson, Alan M.	19.00
Hale, Frank L.	18.00
Iaccaci, Paul T.	18.00
Luke, Frank	18.00
Lufbery, Raoul G.	17.00
Kullberg, Harold A.	16.00
Rose, Oren J.	16.00
Warman, C. T.	15.00

American Aces of World War II

USAF—United States Air Force or United States Army Air Forces
USN—United States Navy
USMC—United States Marine Corps
AVG—American Volunteer Group (China)
RAF—Royal Air Force
RCAF—Royal Canadian Air Force

Name	Home Town	Rank	Service	Victories
ABERNATHY,				
ROBERT W.	Pulaski, Tenn.	Capt.	USAF 8 AF	5.00
ACKERMAN, FRED F.		Ens.	USN	5.00
ADAMS, BURNELL W.	Chester, Ill.	1st Lt.	USAF 5 AF	7.00
ADAMS, CHARLES T., JR.	Denver, Col.	2nd Lt.	USAF 15 AF	6.00
ADAMS, FLETCHER E.	Ida, La.	Capt.	USAF 8 AF	9.50
ADAMS, ROBERT H.	Pomeroy, Wash.	Capt.	USAF 5 AF	5.00
AINLAY, JOHN M.	Santa Monica, Calif.	1st Lt.	USAF 12 AF	8.00
ALDRICH, DONALD N.	Chicago, Ill.	Capt.	USMC	20.00
ALISON, JOHN R.	Gainesville, Fla.	Lt. Col.	USAF 10 AF	6.00
ALLEN, CALVIN D., JR.	Hufford Woods, Ill.	Maj.	USAF 15 AF	7.00
ALLEN, DAVID W.	Belvedere, Calif.	1st Lt.	USAF 5 AF	8.00
ALLEN, WILLIAM H.	Torrance, Calif.	1st Lt.	USAF 8 AF	5.00
ALLEY, STUART C., JR.	North Muskegon, Mich.	2nd Lt.	USMC	5.00
AMBORT, ERNEST J.	Little Rock, Ark.	Capt.	USAF 5 AF	5.00
AMMON, ROBERT H.	Sinking Springs, Pa.	Maj.	USAF 8 AF	5.00
AMOSS, DUDLEY M.	Greenwich, Conn.	2nd Lt.	USAF 8 AF	5.50
AMSDEN, BENJAMIN C.	Buffalo, N.Y.	Lt.	USN	5.00
ANDERSON, A. L.		Lt.	USN	6.00
ANDERSON, CHARLES F., JR.	Gary, Ind.	1st Lt.	USAF 8 AF	10.50
ANDERSON, CLARENCE E.	Newcastle, Calif.	Lt. Col.	USAF 8 AF	16.25
ANDERSON, LESLIE E.	Cheverly, Md.	2nd Lt.	USAF 12 AF	5.00
ANDERSON, RICHARD H.	King of Prussia, Pa.	Lt.	USAF 7 AF	5.00
ANDERSON, ROBERT H.	Eau Claire, Wis.	Lt.	USN	10.00
ANDERSON, STANLEY M.	Indianapolis, Ind.	Flt. Off.	RAF 71 Sq	5.00
ANDERSON, WILLIAM Y.	Chicago, Ill.	1st Lt.	USAF 9 AF	7.00
ANDERSON, WYMAN D.	Cashton, Wis.	Capt.	USAF 9 AF	6.00
ANDREW, STEPHEN W.	Dallas, Tex.	Maj.	USAF 8 AF	9.00
ANDREWS, STANLEY O.	St. Petersburg, Fla.	Lt. Col.	USAF 5 AF	6.00

Name	Home Town	Rank	Service	Victories
ARASMITH, LESTER L.	St. Joseph, Mo.	Maj.	USAF 14 AF	5.00
ARON, WILLIAM E.	Oaklyn, N. J.	1st Lt.	USAF 15 AF	5.00
ASCHENBRENER, ROBERT W.	Lac-du-Flambeau, Wis.	Maj.	USAF 5 AF	10.00
AUST, ABNER M., JR.	Macon, Miss.	Capt.	USAF 20 AF	5.00
AXTELL, GEORGE C.	Cherry Point, N.C.	Maj.	USMC	6.00
BACCUS, DONALD A.	Los Angeles, Calif.	Col.	USAF 8 AF	5.00
BADE, JACK A.	Elk, Minn.	Capt.	USAF 13 AF	5.00
BAILEY, OSCAR C.	Corpus Christi, Tex.	Lt. Cdr.	USN	5.00
BAIRD, ROBERT	South Gate, Cailf.	Maj.	USMC	6.00
BAKER, DOUGLAS	Lindsay, Okla.	Cdr.	USN	16.00
BAKER, ELLIS C., JR.	Stillwater, Okla.	Capt.	USAF 5 AF	6.00
BAKER, ROBERT M.	St. Louis, Mo.	Maj.	USMC	7.00
BAKUTIS, FRED E.	Brockton, Mass.	Capt.	USN	11.00
BALCH, DONALD LUTHER	San Francisco, Calif.	Maj.	USMC	5.00
BALDWIN, FRANK B.	Philadelphia, Pa.	Maj.	USMC	5.00
BANK, RAYMOND M.	Chicago, Ill.	1st Lt.	USAF 8 AF	5.00
BANKEY, ERNEST E., JR.	Toledo, Ohio	Maj.	USAF 8 AF	9.50
BANKS, JOHN L.	Webster Groves, Mo.	Lt.	USN	9.50
BANKS, WILLIAM M.	Raleigh, W. Va.	Col.	USAF 5 AF	9.00
BARACKMAN, BRUCE MacD.	Meadville, Pa.	Cdr.	USN	5.00
BARDSHAR, FREDERIC A.	Seattle, Wash.	Cdr.	USN	8.00
BARE, JAMES D.	Wetumka, Okla.	Lt.	USN	6.00
BARKEY, ROBERT M.	South Field, Mich.	1st Lt.	USAF 15 AF	5.00
BARNARD, LLOYD GLYNN	Jacksonville, Fla.	Cdr.	USN	8.00
BARNES, JAMES M.	Binghamton, N.Y.	Lt. jg	USN	6.00
BARNES, TRUMAN S.	San Francisco, Calif.	Capt.	USAF 13 AF	5.00
BARRICK, JOHN F.	Tex.	Sgt.	RCAF 17 Sq	5.00
BARTELT, P. R.		Capt.	AVG	7.00
BARTLING, W. E.	Middleton, Ind.	Capt.	AVG	7.25
BASELER, ROBERT L.	Ardmore, Pa.	Col.	USAF 12 AF	6.00

Name	Home Town	Rank	Service	Victories
BASSETT, EDGAR R.	Scarsdale, N.Y.	Ens.	USN	9.00
BATTEN, HUGH N.	Huntington, W. Va.	Lt.	USN	7.00
BAUER, HAROLD W.	North Platte, Neb.	Lt. Col.	USMC	11.00
BAUMLER, ALBERT J.	Trenton, N.J.	Maj.	USAF 10 AF	13.00
BEAUDRY, PAUL H. N.	Springfield, Mass.	Ens.	USN	6.00
BEARDEN, AARON L.	Houston, Tex.	1st Lt.	USAF 10 AF	5.00
BEATLEY, RODMAN C.	Washington, D.C.	Lt. Cdr.	USN	6.00
BEAVERS, EDWARD H., JR.	Scranton, Pa.	Capt.	USAF 8 AF	5.00
BECKER, ROBERT H.	Shattuck, Okla.	Maj.	USAF 8 AF	7.00
BECKHAM, WALTER C.	Defuniak Springs, Fla.	Col.	USAF 8 AF	18.00
BEEBE, MARSHALL U.	Washington, D.C.	Cdr.	USN	10.50
BEERBOWER, DONALD M.	Hill City, Minn.	Capt.	USAF 9 AF	15.50
BEESON, DUANE W.	Boise, Idaho	Maj.	USAF 8 AF	19.33
BENNE, LOUIS	Johnstown, Pa.	Lt. Col.	USAF 15 AF	5.00
BENNETT, JOSEPH H.	Morton, Tex.	Capt.	USAF 8 AF	6.50
BENZ, WALTER G., JR.	Miami, Fla.	Col.	USAF 5 AF	8.00
BERKHEIMER, JACK S.	Temperance, Mich.	Ens.	USN	5.00
BERREE, NORMAN R.	Upper Darby, Pa.	Lt.	USN	9.00
BERTELSON, RICHARD L.	Minneapolis, Minn.	Lt.	USN	5.00
BEYER, WILLIAM R.	Danville, Pa.	Capt.	USAF 8 AF	9.00
BICKEL, CARL G.	El Monte, Calif.	Capt.	USAF 9 AF	5.50
BIEL, HIPOLITUS T.	St. Paul, Minn.	1st. Lt.	USAF 8 AF	5.33
BILLE, HENRY S.	Paradise, Calif.	Maj.	USAF 8 AF	6.00
BILLO, JAMES D.	Portland, Ore.	Lt. Cdr.	USN	5.00
BISHOP, LEWIS S.	Pensacola, Fla.	Capt.	AVG	5.20
BISHOP, WALTER D.	Kansas City, Kans.	Lt. jg	USN	5.00
BLACKBURN, JOHN T.	La Jolla, Calif.	Capt.	USN	13.00
BLAIR, FOSTER J.	Stroudsburg, Pa.	Lt. Cdr.	USN	5.00
BLAIR, SAMUEL V.	Minneapolis, Minn.	Lt. Col.	USAF 5 AF	7.00
BLAIR, WILLIAM K.	Coronado, Calif.	Lt. Cdr.	USN	5.00

Name	Home Town	Rank	Service	Victories
BLAKESLEE, DONALD J. M.	Fairport Harbor, Ohio	Col.	USAF 8 AF	12.50
BLAYDES, RICHARD B.	Houston, Tex.	Lt. jg	USN	5.00
BLICKENSTAFF, WAYNE K.	Chino, Calif.	Capt.	USAF 8 AF	10.00
BLUMER, LAURENCE E.	Walcott, N.D.	Capt.	USAF 9 AF	6.00
BLYTH, ROBERT L.	Charleston, S. C.	Lt.	USN	6.00
BOCHKAY, DONALD H.	No. Hollywood, Calif.	Lt. Col.	USAF 8 AF	14.83
BOCQUIN, VICTOR E.	Reading, Kans.	Maj.	USAF 8 AF	5.00
BOGGS, HAMPTON E.	Oklahoma City, Okla.	Capt.	USAF 10 AF	6.00
BOLT, JOHN F.	Sanford, Fla.	Maj.	USMC	6.00
BOLYARD, JOHN W.	Kingwood, W. Va.	Maj.	USAF 14 AF	5.00
BOND, CHARLES R.	Dallas, Tex.	Capt.	AVG	8.75
BONEBRAKE, ROBERT R.	Taylor, Tex.	Maj.	USAF 8 AF	5.00
BONG, RICHARD T.	Poplar, Wis.	Maj.	USAF 5 AF	40.00
BONNEAU, WILLIAM J.	Oakland, Calif.	Lt.Cdr.	USN	8.00
BONNER, STEPHEN J., JR.	Urbana, Ill.	Capt.	USAF 14 AF	5.00
BOOTH, ROBERT J.	Waukesha, Wis.	1st Lt.	USAF 8 AF	8.00
BORLEY, CLARENCE A.	Yakima, Wash.	Lt.	USN	5.00
BOSTROM, ERNEST O.	East Orange, N.J.	1st. Lt.	USAF 8 AF	5.00
BOSTWICK, GEORGE E.	Chippewa Falls, Wis.	Col.	USAF 8 AF	9.00
BOYINGTON, GREGORY	Burbank, Calif.	Lt. Col.	USMC	28.00
BRADLEY, JACK T.	Brownwood, Tex.	Col.	USAF 9 AF	15.00
BRADLEY, JOHN L.	Shreveport, La.	Lt. Col.	USAF 12 AF	5.00
BRASSFIELD, ARTHUR J.	Browning, Mo.	Cdr.	USN	7.00
BRAUN, RICHARD LANE	Cherry Point, N. C.	Lt. Col.	USMC	5.00
BREWER, CHARLES W.	Tulsa, Okla.	Cdr.	USN	6.50
BREZAS, MICHAEL	Bloomfield, N. J.	Capt.	USAF 15 AF	12.00
BRIDGES, JOHNNIE J.	Shelby, N.C.	Lt.	USN	6.25
BRIGHT, JOHN G.	Reading, Pa.	Maj.	AVG	7.00

Name	Home Town	Rank	Service	Victories
BRIGHT, MARK KENNETH	Anderson, Ind.	Lt.	USN	9.00
BROADHEAD, JOSEPH E.	Rupert, Idaho	Maj.	USAF 8 AF	10.00
BROCATO, SAMUEL J. JR.	Baltimore, Md.	Lt.	USN	6.00
BROOKS, JAMES L.	Roanoke, Va.	2nd Lt.	USAF 15 AF	13.00
BROWN, CARL A. JR.	Texarkana, Tex.	Cdr.	USN	10.00
BROWN, GERALD A.	Phoenix, Ariz.	Lt. Col.	USAF 8 AF	5.00
BROWN, HARLEY L.	Wichita, Kans.	1st Lt.	USAF 8 AF	6.00
BROWN, HARRY WINSTON	Amarillo, Tex.	Capt.	USAF 5 AF	5.00
BROWN, HENRY WILLIAM	Dallas, Tex.	Maj.	USAF 8 AF	17.20
BROWN, J. DANFORTH	Tampa, Fla.	Sq. Ldr.	RCAF	5.00
BROWN, JASPER R.	Old Glory, Tex.	Capt.	USAF 14 AF	5.00
BROWN, MEADE M.	Louisville, Ky.	1st Lt.	USAF 5 AF	6.00
BROWN, QUINCE L.	Bristow, Okla.	Maj.	USAF 8 AF	12.33
BROWN, ROBERT HAROLD	Medfield, Mass.	2nd Lt.	USAF 15 AF	7.00
BROWN, SAMUEL J.	Tulsa, Okla.	Capt.	USAF 15 AF	15.00
BROWN, WILLIAM, PERRY, JR.	Santa Ana, Calif.	Capt.	USMC	7.00
BROWNING, JAMES W.	Syracuse, Kans.	Capt.	USAF 8 AF	7.00
BRUELAND, LOWELL K.	Callender, Ia.	Maj.	USAF 5 AF	12.50
BRUNEAU, PAUL J.	San Diego, Calif.	Cdr.	USN	5.00
BRUNMIER, CARLAND E.	Bloomington, Calif.	Lt.Cdr.	USN	6.00
BRYAN, DONALD S.	Paicines, Calif.	Lt. Col.	USAF 8 AF	13.33
BRYAN, WILLIAM E.	Flint, Mich.	Lt. Col.	USAF 8 AF	8.50
BRYCE, JAMES A.	Altus, Okla.	Lt.	USN	5.25
BUCHANAN, ROBERT L.	North Baltimore, Ohio	Lt.	USN	5.00
BUCK, GEORGE T., JR.	Tchula, Miss.	Col.	USAF 15 AF	6.00
BUIE, PAUL D.	Nashville, Ga.	Capt.	USN	9.00
BURCKHALTER, WILLIAM E.	Great Neck, L.I., N.Y.	Lt. jg	USN	6.00
BURDICK, CLINTON D.	Brooklyn, N.Y.	1st Lt.	USAF 8 AF	5.50
BURGARD, GEORGE T.	Sunbury, Pa.	Capt.	AVG	10.75

Name	Home Town	Rank	Service	Victories
BURLEY, FRANKLIN N.	Monterey, La.	Lt. jg	USN	7.00
BURNETT, ROY O., JR.	Oswego, Ore.	Lt.Cdr.	USN	8.00
BURRISS, HOWARD M.	Granville, Ohio	Lt. jg	USN	7.50
BUSHNER, FRANCIS X.	Miami, Fla.	Cdr.	USN	6.00
BUTTKE, ROBERT L.	Sacramento, Calif.	Capt.	USAF 8 AF	5.50
BYRNE, ROBERT L.	St. Louis, Mo.	1st Lt.	USAF 9 AF	5.00
BYRNES, MATTHEW, S., JR.	Hamilton, Ont., Can.	Lt.	USN	6.00
BYRNES, ROBERT C.	Winfield, La.	1st Lt.	USAF 13 AF	5.00
CAIN, JAMES B.	Cramerton, N.C.	Capt.	USN	8.50
CALLAWAY, RAYMOND L.	Grove City, Minn.	Maj.	USAF 14 AF	6.00
CAMPBELL, RICHARD A.	Ferriday, La.	Capt.	USAF 12 AF	6.00
CANDELARIA, RICHARD G.	Los Angeles, Calif.	1st Lt.	USAF 8 AF	6.00
CARDER, JOHN B.	Red Oak, Ia.	Capt.	USAF 8 AF	5.00
CARE, RAYMOND C.	Angola, Ind.	Lt. Col.	USAF 8 AF	6.00
CARL, MARION EUGENE	Hubbard, Ore.	Lt. Col.	USMC	18.50
CARLSON, KENDALL E.	Red Bluff, Calif.	Capt.	USAF 8 AF	6.00
CARLTON, WILLIAM A.	Allen Park, Mich.	Maj.	USMC	5.00
CARMICHAEL, DANIEL A., JR.	Bexley, Ohio	Lt. Cdr.	USN	13.00
CARPENTER, GEORGE	Oil City, Pa.	Maj.	USAF 8 AF	13.33
CARR, BRUCE W.	Union Springs, N.Y.	Maj.	USAF 9 AF	14.00
CARR, GEORGE R.	Bogalusa, La.	Lt.	USN	11.50
CARROLL, CHARLES H.	Philadelphia, Pa.	Lt. Cdr.	USN	6.00
CARROLL, WALTER J., JR.	New York, N.Y.	1st Lt.	USAF 15 AF	8.00
CARSON, LEONARD K.	Clear Lake, Ia.	Maj.	USAF 8 AF	18.50
CARTER, JAMES R.	Spokane, Wash.	Lt. Col.	USAF 8 AF	6.00
CASE, WILLIAM NORTHROP	Vancouver, Wash.	Maj.	USMC	8.00
CASTLE, NIAL K.	Milwaukee, Wis.	1st Lt.	USAF 5 AF	5.00
CASWELL, DEAN	Edinburg, Tex.	Capt.	USMC	7.00
CESKY, CHARLES J.	Baltimore, Md.	Capt.	USAF 8 AF	8.50

Name	Home Town	Rank	Service	Victories
CEULEERS, GEORGE F.	Los Angeles, Calif.	Col.	USAF 8 AF	10.50
CHAMPION, HENRY K.	Greenville, Miss.	Lt.	USN	5.00
CHAMPLIN, FREDERIC F.	Eggertsville, N.Y.	Maj.	USAF 5 AF	9.00
CHANDLER, CREIGHTON	New Orleans, La.	Capt.	USMC	6.00
CHANDLER, GEORGE T.	Wichita, Kans.	Capt.	USAF 13 AF	5.00
CHANDLER, VAN E.	Waxhachie, Tex.	Maj.	USAF 5 AF	5.00
CHAPMAN, PHILIP G.	Fort Smith, Ark.	Maj.	USAF 14 AF	7.00
CHASE, LEVI R.	Cortland, N.Y.	Capt.	USAF 12 AF	10.00
CHEN, ARTHUR	Portland, Ore.	1st Lt.	AVG	5.00
CHENNAULT, CLAIRE	Waterhole, La.	Gen.	AVG/USAF	
CHENOWETH, OSCAR I.	Miami, Fla.	Cdr.	USN	8.50
CHICK, LEWIS W. JR.	Dallas, Tex.	Capt.	USAF 15 AF	6.00
CHRISTENSEN, FRED J.	Watertown, Mass.	Capt.	USAF 8 AF	21.50
CLARK, JAMES AVERELL, JR.	Westbury, L.I., N.Y.	Capt.	USAF 8 AF	11.50
CLARK, LAWRENCE A.	Huntington Park, Calif.	Lt.	USN	7.00
CLARK, ROBERT A.	Hartford, Conn.	Lt.	USN	7.00
CLEMENTS, ROBERT E.	Buena Vista, Ga.	Cdr.	USN	5.00
CLEVELAND, ARTHUR B.	Springfield, Ohio	1st Lt.	USAF 9 AF	5.00
CLINGER, DALLAS A.	Laramie, Wyo.	2d Lt.	USAF 14 AF	5.00
CLOUD, VIVIAN A.	Baltimore, Md.	1st Lt.	USAF 5 AF	5.00
COATS, ROBERT C.	Delhi, La.	Cdr.	USN	9.33
COCHRAN, PAUL R.	Hutchinson, Kans.	1st Lt.	USAF 12 AF	5.00
COEN, OSCAR H.	Wallum, No. Dakota	Flt. Lt.	RAF 71 Sq	5.50
COFFEY, ROBERT L. JR.	Johnstown, Pa.	Lt. Col.	USAF 9 AF	6.00
COLEMAN, THADDEUS T.	Eastman, Ga.	Lt. Cdr.	USN	10.00
COLEMAN, WILSON M.	Eutaw, Ala.	Capt.	USN	6.00
COLLINS, FRANK J.	Breckenridge, Tex.	Col.	USAF 12 AF	9.00
COLLINS, JOHN J.	New York City, N.Y.	Lt. Cdr.	USN	5.00
COLLINS, WILLIAM F.	Janesville, Wis.	Maj.	USAF 8 AF	5.00
COLLINS, WILLIAM M., JR.	Chevy Chase, Md.	Capt.	USN	9.00

			Vic-
Name	*Home Town*	*Rank* *Service*	*tories*
COLLINSWORTH, J. D.	Berger, Tex.	Lt. Col. USAF 12 AF	6.00
COLMAN, PHILIP E.	Roanoke, Va.	1st Lt. USAF 5 AF	5.00
COMPTON, GORDON B.	Dallas, Tex.	Lt. Col. USAF 8 AF	6.50
COMSTOCK, HAROLD E.	Fresno, Calif.	Maj. USAF 8 AF	5.00
CONANT, ARTHUR ROGER	Malibu, Calif.	Capt. USMC	6.00
CONANTS, EDWIN STANLEY	Lakeside, Calif.	Lt. Cdr. USN	6.00
CONDON, HENRY L.	Opelika, Ala.	1st Lt. USAF 5 AF	5.00
CONGER, JACK E.	Des Moines, Ia.	Lt. Col. USMC	10.50
CONGER, PAUL A.	Piedmont, Calif.	Maj. USAF 8 AF	11.50
CONROY, THOMAS J.	Kingsville, Tex.	Lt. USN	7.00
COOK, WALTER V.	Cincinnati, Ohio	Lt. Col. USAF 8 AF	6.00
COOLEY, WARREN C.	Cashion, Okla.	1st Lt. USAF 8 AF	6.00
COONS, MERLE M.	Gresham, Ore.	Capt. USAF 8 AF	5.00
COPELAND, WILLIAM E.	Carbondale, Ill.	Lt. Cdr. USN	6.00
CORDRAY, PAUL	Dallas, Tex.	Lt. Cdr. USN	7.00
CORIMER, RICHARD L. ("ZEKE")	Miramar, Calif.	Cdr. USN	10.00
CORNELL, LELAND B.	Newport, R. I.	Lt. Cdr. USN	5.00
COWGER, RICHARD D.	Ventura, Calif.	Lt. USN	6.00
COX, RALPH L.	Pasadena, Calif.	Capt. USAF 8 AF	5.00
COZZENS, MELVIN	Powell, Wyo.	Lt. jg USN	6.50
CRAGG, EDWARD	Cos Cob, Conn.	Maj. USAF 5 AF	15.00
CRAIG, CLEMENT M.	Washington, D.C.	Cdr. USN	12.00
CRAMER, DARRELL S.	Ogden, Utah	Lt. Col. USAF 8 AF	7.50
CRANFILL, NIVEN K.	Temple, Tex.	Col. USAF 8 AF	5.00
CRAWFORD, RAY	Alhambra, Calif.	1st Lt. USAF 12 AF	6.00
CRENSHAW, CLAUDE, J.	Monroe, Ia.	Maj. USAF 8 AF	7.00
CRIM, HARRY C., JR.	Xenia, Ohio	Lt. Col. USAF 7 AF	6.00
CROMBIE, WILLIAM F.	El Paso, Tex.	Maj. USAF 8 AF	5.00
CRONIN, DONALD F.	Baltimore, Md.	Lt. USN	6.00
CROSBY, JOHN T.	Jacksonville, Fla.	Lt. Cdr. USN	6.00
CROWE, WILLIAM E.	Norfolk, Va.	Lt. Col. USMC	7.00
CRUIKSHANK, ARTHUR, W.	Eglin AFB, Fla.	Col. USAF 10 AF	8.00

Name	Home Town	Rank	Service	Victories
Cullerton, William J.	Chicago, Ill.	1st Lt.	USAF 8 AF	6.00
Cummings, Donald M.	Clayton, N.Y.	Lt. Col.	USAF 12 AF	6.50
Cundy, Arthur C.	Tallahassee, Fla.	1st Lt.	USAF 8 AF	5.00
Cunningham, Daniel G.	Chicago, Ill.	Lt.	USN	7.00
Cupp, James N.	Red Oak, Ia.	Lt. Col.	USMC	13.00
Curdes, Louis E.	Fort Wayne, Ind.	Capt.	USAF 12 AF	9.00
Curtis, Robert C.	Washington, D.C.	Maj.	USAF 12 AF	14.00
Curton, Warren D.	Spring City Tenn.	Maj.	USAF 5 AF	5.00
Cutler, Frank A.	Cleveland, Ohio	Capt.	USAF 8 AF	8.50
Czarnecki, Edward J.	Wilmington, Del.	1st Lt.	USAF 5 AF	6.00
Dade, Lucian A., Jr.	Hopkinsville, Ky.	Lt. Col.	USAF 8 AF	5.00
Dahl, Perry J.	Mercer Island, Wash.	Capt.	USAF 5 AF	9.00
Dahlberg, Kenneth H.	Wilson, Wis.	1st Lt.	USAF 9 AF	14.00
Dahms, Kenneth J.	Winnebago, Minn.	Lt.	USN	7.50
Dalglish, James B.	Rome, N.Y.	Capt.	USAF 9 AF	9.00
Damstrom, Fernley H.	Oliva, Tex.	Capt.	USAF 5 AF	8.00
Daniel, William A.	Birmingham, Ala.	Col.	USAF 15 AF	5.00
Daniell, Jack S.	Birmingham, Ala.	1st Lt.	USAF 8 AF	5.00
Davenport, Merl W.	Detroit, Mich.	Lt.	USN	6.00
Davidson, George H.	Lake Como, Fla.	Lt. Cdr.	USN	7.00
Davies, James William Ellis	Bernardsville, N.J.	Flt. Lt.	RAF 79 Sq	7.00
Davis, Barrie S.	Zebulon, N.C.	1st Lt.	USAF 15 AF	6.00
Davis, Clayton E.	Brookfield, Vt.	Maj.	USAF 8 AF	5.00
Davis, George A., Jr.	Lubbock, Tex.	Lt. Col.	USAF 5 AF	7.00
Davis, Glendon V.	Parma, Idaho	Col.	USAF 8 AF	7.50
Davis, Leonard K.	Chicago, Ill.	Col.	USMC	5.00
Davis, Ralph H.	Lexington, Mass.	Lt. Cdr.	USN	7.50
Davis, Robert H.	San Diego, Calif.	Lt. Cdr.	USN	6.50
Dawkins, George E., Jr.	Rancho Santa Fe, Calif.	Capt.	USMC	5.00
Day, William C., Jr.	Red Lion, Pa.	Capt.	USAF 5 AF	5.00

Name	Home Town	Rank	Service	Victories
DAYMOND, GREGORY A. ("GUS")	Burbank, Calif.	Sq. Ldr.	RAF/USAF 71 Sq	9.00
DEAKINS, RICHARD S.	Jonesboro, Tenn.	Lt.	USAF 15 AF	5.00
DEAN, CECIL O.	Salina, Kans.	Capt.	USAF 12 AF	6.00
DEAN, WILLIAM A., JR.	Jourdanton, Tex.	Capt.	USN	11.00
DEAN, ZACH W.	Altoona, Kans.	1st Lt.	USAF 5 AF	7.00
DEAR, JOHN W., JR.	Meridian, Miss.	Lt.	USN	7.00
DE BLANC, JEFFERSON, J.	St. Martinville, La.	Capt.	USMC	9.00
DECEW, LESLIE	Bakersfield, Calif.	Lt. Cdr.	USN	6.00
DEGRAFFENREID, EDWIN L.	Shreveport, La.	Capt.	USAF 5 AF	6.00
DEHAVEN, ROBERT M.	Studio City, Calif.	Maj.	USAF 5 AF	14.00
DELLA, GEORGE	Strathmore, Calif.	Capt.	USAF 5 AF	5.00
DELONG, PHILIP CUNLIFFE	Jackson, Miss.	Maj.	USMC	11.17
DENMAN, ANTHONY J.	Greenwich, Conn.	Cdr.	USN	6.00
DENOFF, REUBEN H.	Chicago, Ill.	Cdr.	USN	5.00
DENT, ELLIOTT E., JR.	Birmingham, Ala.	1st Lt.	USAF 5 AF	6.00
DEWING, LAWRENCE A.	Walnut Grove, Calif.	Lt.	USN	5.50
DIBB, ROBERT A. M.	Los Angeles, Calif.	Lt.	USN	8.50
DICK, FREDERICK E.	Auburn, Me.	Capt.	USAF 5 AF	5.00
DIKOVITSKY, MICHAEL	Cleveland, Ohio	Capt.	USAF 5 AF	5.00
DILLARD, JOSEPH V.	Downey, Calif.	Capt.	USMC	6.33
DILLARD, WILLIAM J.	Longview, Tex.	Capt.	USAF 15 AF	6.00
DILLOW, EUGENE	Cobden, Ill.	Capt.	USMC	6.00
DOBBIN, JOHN FRANCIS	Brighton, Mass.	Col.	USMC	8.00
DOERSCH, GEORGE A.	Seymour, Wis.	Lt. Col.	USAF 8 AF	10.50
DONAHUE, ARCHIE GLENN	Texas City, Tex.	Lt. Col.	USMC	14.00
DONAHUE, ARTHUR GERALD	St. Charles, Minn.	Flt. Lt.	RAF	5.00
DONALDSON, I. B. JACK	Tulsa, Okla.	Capt.	USAF 5 AF	5.00

Name	Home Town	Rank	Service	Victories
DONER, LANDIS E.	Plymouth, Wis.	Cdr.	USN	8.00
DORRIS, HARRY W.	Harrisburg, Ill.	Maj.	USAF 15 AF	5.25
DORROH, JEFFERSON D.	Ontario, Ore.	Lt. Col.	USMC	6.00
DORSCH, FREDERICK J., JR.	Pittsburgh, Pa.	Capt.	USAF 15 AF	8.00
DOUGLAS, PAUL P., JR.	Paragould, Ark.	Col.	USAF 9 AF	7.00
DOYLE, CECIL J.	Marshall, Minn.	2d Lt.	USMC	5.00
DRAKE, CHARLES W.	Martinsville, N.J.	2d Lt.	USMC	5.00
DREGNE, IRWIN H.	Viroqua, Wis.	Col.	USAF 8 AF	7.00
DREW, URBAN L.	Detroit, Mich.	1st Lt.	USAF 8 AF	6.00
DRIER, WILLIAM C.	St. Louis, Mo.	Maj.	USAF 5 AF	6.00
DRISCOLL, DANIEL B.	Westport, Conn.	Lt. jg	USN	5.00
DRURY, FRANK C.	Danby, Mo.	Lt. Col.	USMC	6.00
DRURY, PAUL E.	Wynnewood, Pa.	Lt. jg	USN	6.00
DUBISHER, FRANCIS E.	Williamsburg, Ia.	Maj.	USAF 5 AF	5.00
DUBOIS, CHARLES H.	Richmond Heights, Mo.	Col.	USAF 10 AF	5.00
DUFFY, JAMES E.	Gardena, Calif.	Lt.	USN	5.00
DUFFY, JAMES E., JR.	Montclair, N.J.	Capt.	USAF 8 AF	5.20
DUFFY, RICHARD E.	Walled Lake, Mich.	2d Lt.	USAF 9 AF	5.00
DUKE, WALTER F.	Leonardtown, Md.	Capt.	USAF 10 AF	8.00
DUNAWAY, JOHN S.	Hilt, Calif.	1st Lt.	USAF 5 AF	7.00
DUNCAN, GEORGE C.	Arlington, Va.	Cdr.	USN	13.50
DUNCAN, GLENN E.	Houston, Tex.	Col.	USAF 8 AF	19.00
DUNCAN, ROBERT W.	Marion, Ill.	Lt. Cdr.	USN	7.00
DUNGAN, FRED L.	Yonkers, N.Y.	Lt. Cdr.	USN	7.00
DUNHAM, WILLIAM D.	Nezperce, Idaho	Col.	USAF 5 AF	16.00
DUNKIN, RICHARD W.	Huntington, Ind.	1st Lt.	USAF 12 AF	9.00
DUNN, BERNARD	Smackover, Ark.	Lt. jg	USN	5.33
DUPOUY, PARKER	Seekonk, Mass.	Capt.	AVG	6.50
DURNFORD, DEWEY F.	Columbus, Ohio	Maj.	USMC	6.33
EAGLESTON, GLENN T.	Farmington, Utah	Col.	USAF 9 AF	18.50
EASON, HOYT A.	Eclectic, Ala.	1st Lt.	USAF 5 AF	6.00
EAST, CLYDE, B.	Chatham, Va.	Maj.	USAF 9 AF	12.00

Name	Home Town	Rank	Service	Victories
EASTHAM, DAVID B.	Seattle, Wash.	Capt.	USAF 5 AF	12.00
EASTMOND, RICHARD T.	American Fork, Utah	Lt. Cdr.	USN	9.00
EBERTS, BYRON A.	Liberty, Mo.	Lt.	USN	6.00
ECCLES, WILLIAM G.	Los Angeles, Calif.	Lt. jg	USN	6.00
ECKARD, BERT	Huntington Park, Calif.	Lt.	USN	7.00
EDENS, BILLY G.	Tyronza, Ark.	Maj.	USAF 8 AF	8.00
EDER, WILLARD E.	Buffalo, Wyo.	Cdr.	USN	6.00
EDWARDS, EDWARD B., JR.	Lansdale, Pa.	Capt.	USAF 9 AF	5.50
EDWARDS, WILLIAM C. JR.	Newton, Mass.	Lt.	USN	6.00
EGAN, JOSEPH L., JR.	New York, N.Y.	Capt.	USAF 8 AF	5.00
ELDER, JOHN L.	Ebensburg, Pa.	Lt. Col.	USAF 8 AF	8.00
ELDER, ROBERT A.	Memphis, Tenn.	Maj.	USAF 8 AF	9.00
ELLIOTT, RALPH E.	Hoopestown, Ill.	Cdr.	USN	10.50
ELLIOTT, VINCENT T.	Pasadena, Calif.	Capt.	USAF 5 AF	7.00
ELLIS DAVIS, JAMES W.	Unknown	Flt. Lt.	RAF 79 Sq	8.00
ELWOOD, HUGH Mc J.	Oakmont, Pa.	Col.	USMC	5.00
EMERSON, DONALD R.	Pembina, N. D.	Capt.	USAF 9AF	5.00
EMMER, WALLACE N.	St. Louis, Mo.	Capt.	USAF 9 AF	14.00
EMMERT, BENJAMIN H., JR.	Erwin, Tenn.	Lt. Col.	USAF 5 AF	6.00
EMMONS, EUGENE H.	Lawrenceville, Ill.	1st Lt.	USAF 15 AF	9.00
EMPEY, JAMES W.	Bath, N.Y.	Capt.	USAF 15 AF	5.00
ENGLAND, JAMES J.	Jackson, Tenn.	Lt. Col.	USAF 10 AF	10.00
ENGLAND, JOHN B.	Caruthersville, Mo.	Lt. Col.	USAF 8 AF	17.50
ERICKSON, LYLE A.	Salt Lake City, Utah	Ens.	USN	5.00
EVANS, ANDREW J.	Montgomery, Ala.	Col.	USAF 8 AF	6.00
EVANS, ROY W.	San Bernardino, Calif.	Maj.	USAF 8 AF	6.00

Name	Home Town	Rank	Service	Victories
EVENSON, ERIC A.	Dodge City, Kans.	Lt.	USN	8.00
EVERHART, LEE R.	Petersburg, Ill.	Capt.	USAF 5 AF	6.00
EVERTON, LORAN D.	Crofton, Neb.	Lt. Col.	USMC	12.00
FAIRBANKS, DAVID C.	New York, N.Y.	Sqd. Ldr.	RCAF 247 Sq	15.00
FAIR, JOHN W.	Battle Creek, Mich.	Capt.	USN	6.00
FANNING, GROVER E.	Kansas City, Mo.	Maj.	USAF 5 AF	9.00
FARNSWORTH, ROBERT A., JR.	Jackson, Miss.	Lt. jg	USN	5.00
FARRELL, WILLIAM	Gardena, Calif.	Maj.	USMC	5.00
FASH, ROBERT P.	East St. Louis, Ill.	Lt.	USN	6.50
FAXON, RICHARD D.	Great Barrington, Mass.	Cdr.	USAF 12 AF	5.00
FECKE, ALFRED J.	Duxbury, Mass.	Cdr.	USN	7.00
FEIGHTNER, EDWARD L.	Newport, R. I.	Cdr.	USN	9.00
FELD, SYLVAN	Lynn, Mass.	Capt.	USAF 12 AF	9.00
FELTS, MARION C.	Roberta, Ga.	Maj.	USAF 5 AF	5.00
FENEX, JAMES E., JR.	West Lake, Pa.	Capt.	USAF 12 AF	5.00
FIEBELKORN, ERNEST C.	Los Angeles, Calif.	Capt.	USAF 8 AF	9.50
FIEDLER, ARTHUR C., JR.	Oak Park, Ill.	Maj.	USAF 15 AF	8.00
FIEDLER, WILLIAM F.	Akron, Ohio	Capt.	USAF 13 AF	5.00
FIELDS, VIRGIL C., JR.	Jay, Okla.	Maj.	USAF 12 AF	5.00
FINN, HOWARD J.	Belmond, Ia.	Maj.	USMC	5.00
FISCHETTE, CHARLES R.	Clyde, N.Y.	Maj.	USAF 12 AF	5.00
FISHER, DON HOMS	Miami, Fla.	Maj.	USMC	6.00
FISHER, EDWIN O.	Portland, Ore.	Capt.	USAF 9 AF	7.00
FISHER, RODNEY W.	San Francisco, Calif.	Capt.	USAF 9 AF	5.00
FISK, HARRY E.	Tacoma, Wash.	Capt.	USAF 9 AF	5.00
FISK, JACK A.	Peoria, Ill.	Capt.	USAF 5 AF	7.00
FLACK, NELSON D., JR.	Hatboro, Pa.	Maj.	USAF 5 AF	5.00

Name	Home Town	Rank	Service	Victories
FLATLEY, JAMES H., JR.	Green Bay, Wis.	Capt.	USN	6.50
FLEISCHER, RICHARD H.	Quincy, Mass.	Capt.	USAF 5 AF	6.00
FLEMING, FRANCIS M.	Portland, Ore.	Lt. Cdr. USN		7.50
FLEMING, PATRICK D.	Jamestown, R.I.	Cdr.	USN	19.00
FLINN, KENNETH A.	Walnut Creek, Calif.	Lt. jg	USN	5.00
FOLTZ, FRANK E.	Detroit, Mich.	Lt. Cdr. USN		7.00
FOLTZ, RALPH E.	Azusa, Calif.	Lt. Cdr. USN		5.00
FONTANA, PAUL JOHN	Sparks, Nev.	Col.	USMC	5.00
FORD, CLAUDE E.	Oildale, Calif.	Lt. Col.	USAF 12 AF	5.00
FORD, KENNETH M.	Whittier, Calif.	Lt. Col.	USMC	5.00
FORRER, SAMUEL W.	Fitzpatrick, Ala.	Cdr.	USN	5.50
FORSTER, JOSEPH M.	Gainesville, Fla.	Maj.	USAF 5 AF	9.00
FORTIER, NORMAN J.	Nashua, N.H.	Lt. Col.	USAF 8 AF	5.83
FOSS, JOSEPH JACOB	Pierre, S.D.	Maj.	USMC	26.00
FOSTER, CARL C.	Utica, Mich.	Lt.	USN	8.50
FOULIS, WILLIAM B., JR.	Houston, Tex.	1st Lt.	USAF 5 AF	6.00
FOWLE, JAMES M.	Miami, Fla.	Lt. Col.	USAF 8 AF	8.00
FOWLER, RICHARD E., JR.	Sweeney, Tex.	Lt.	USN	6.50
FOY, ROBERT W.	Oswego, N.Y.	Maj	USAF 8 AF	17.00
FRANGER, MARVIN J.	San Diego, Calif.	Lt. Cdr. USN		9.00
FRANKLIN, DWAINE R.	Deming, N.M.	Maj.	USAF 15 AF	7.00
FRANKS, JOHN M.	Easton, Pa.	Lt. jg	USN	7.00
FRANTZ, CARL M.	Brownsville, Pa.	1st Lt.	USAF 9 AF	11.00
FRASER, ROBERT B.	Genesee, N.Y.	Maj.	USMC	6.00
FRAZIER, KENNETH D.	Burlington, N.J.	Lt. Col.	USMC	12.50
FREEMAN, WILLIAM B.	Unknown	Capt.	USMC	6.00
FRENCH, JAMES B.	Oakland, Calif.	Lt.	USN	11.00
FRENDBERG, ALFRED L.	Hillsboro, N.D.	Lt.	USN	6.00
FRONING, ALFRED C.	LaParte City, Ia.	1st Lt.	USAF 9 AF	6.00
FRYER, EARL R.	Boyertown, Pa.	Capt.	USAF 8 AF	7.00
FUNK, HAROLD N.	LaHabra, Calif.	Cdr.	USN	7.00
GABRESKI, FRANCIS S.	Oil City, Pa.	Col.	USAF 5 AF	31.00

Name	*Home Town*	*Rank*	*Service*	*Vic-tories*
GABRIEL, FRANKLIN T.	Evanston, Ill.	Lt.	USN	8.25
GAILER, FRANK L., JR.	Great Neck, L.I., N.Y.	Lt. Col.	USAF 8 AF	5.50
GALER, ROBERT E.	Dallas, Tex.	Col.	USMC	13.00
GALLUP, CHARLES S.	Chicago, Ill.	1st Lt.	USAF 5 AF	6.00
GALLUP, KENNETH W.	Clint, Tex.	Col.	USAF 8 AF	9.00
GALT, DWIGHT B.	Silver Spring, Md.	Lt. Cdr.	USN	5.00
GALVIN, JOHN R.	Yardley, Pa.	Lt.	USN	7.00
GARDNER, WARNER F.	Cazenovia, N.Y.	Lt. Col.	USAF 15 AF	5.00
GARDNER, WILLIAM A.	Concord, N.H.	Capt.	USAF 5 AF	8.00
GARRISON, VERMONT	Mt. Victory, Ky.	Col.	USAF 5 AF	7.33
GAUNT, FRANK L.	North Platte, Nebr.	Capt.	USAF 13 AF	8.00
GAYLER, NOEL A. M.	Philadelphia, Pa.	Capt.	USN	5.00
GENTILE, DONALD S.	Piqua, Ohio	Capt.	USAF 8 AF	19.84
GERARD, FRANCIS R.	Lyndhurst, N.J.	Maj.	USAF 8 AF	8.00
GERICK, STEVEN	Pittsburgh, Pa.	Capt.	USAF 8 AF	5.00
GHOLSON, GROVER D.	Oxford, N.C.	Capt.	USAF 5 AF	5.00
GIBB, ROBERT D.	Lansing Mich.	1st Lt.	USAF 5 AF	5.00
GILE, CLEMENT D.	Pittsburgh, Pa.	Lt.	USN	8.00
GILLESPIE, ROY F.	Eugene, Ore.	Lt. Cdr.	USN	6.00
GIROUX, WILLIAM K.	Momence, Ill.	Maj.	USAF 5 AF	10.00
GLADEN, CYRUS R.	Salem, Ore.	Capt.	USAF 13 AF	5.00
GLEASON, GEORGE W.	Montrose, Colo.	Maj.	USAF 8 AF	12.00
GLENN, MAXWELL H.	Winnfield, La	Maj.	USAF 10 AF	8.00
GLOVER, FRED W.	Asheville, N.C.	Maj.	USAF 8 AF	10.33
GODFREY, JOHN T.	Woonsocket, R.I.	Capt.	USAF 8 AF	16.33
GODSON, LINDLEY W.	Colonia, N.J.	Lt.	USN	5.00
GOEBEL, ROBERT J.	Racine, Wis.	Lt. Col.	USAF 15 AF	11.00
GOEHAUSEN, WALTER J., JR.	Webster Grove, Mo.	2nd Lt.	USAF 15 AF	10.00
GOODNIGHT, ROBERT E.	Portland, Ore.	1st Lt.	USAF 9 AF	7.25
GOODSON, JAMES A.	New York, N.Y.	Lt. Col.	USAF 8 AF	15.00
GORDON, DONALD	Fort Scott, Kans.	Cdr.	USN	7.00
GOSS, EDMUND R.	Tampa, Fla.	Maj.	USAF 10 AF	6.00

Name	*Home Town*	*Rank*	*Service*	*Victories*
GOULD, NORMAN D.	Erie, Pa.	1st Lt.	USAF 8 AF	5.00
GRAHAM, GORDON M.	Taft, Calif.	Col.	USAF 8 AF	7.00
GRAHAM, LINDEL F.	Ridgewood, N.J.	Capt.	USAF 8 AF	5.50
GRAHAM, VERNON E.	St. Augustine, Fla.	Lt.	USN	5.00
GRANT, MARVIN E.	Racine, Wis.	Maj.	USAF 5 AF	7.00
GRAY, JOHN FLOYD	Champaign, Ill.	Lt. Cdr.	USN	8.25
GRAY, ROCKFORD V.	Cincinnati, Ohio	Maj.	USAF 8 AF	6.50
GREEN, HERSCHEL H.	Mayfield, Ky.	Col.	USAF 15 AF	18.00
GRESHAM, BILLY M.	Lake Charles, La.	1st Lt.	USAF 5 AF	6.00
GRIFFIN, JOSEPH HENRY	Chicasha, Okla.	Lt. Col.	USAF 10 AF	7.00
GRIFFIN, RICHARD J.	Jacksonville, Fla.	Cdr.	USN	8.00
GRIFFITH, ROBERT C.	Austin, Tex.	2nd Lt.	USAF 15 AF	5.00
GROSS, CLAYTON K.	Spokane, Wash.	1st Lt.	USAF 9 AF	5.00
GROSSHUESCH, LeRoy V.	Ogden, Utah	Lt. Col.	USAF 5 AF	8.00
GUMM, CHARLES F.	Spokane, Wash.	1st Lt.	USAF 9 AF	6.00
GUPTON, CHEATHAM W.	Durham, N. C.	Capt.	USAF 5 AF	5.00
GUSTAFSON, HARLAN I.	Norristown, Pa.	Lt.	USN	6.00
GUTT, FRED E.	Madison, Wis.	Capt.	USMC	8.00
HAAS, WALTER A.	McLean, Va.	Cdr.	USN	6.00
HABERMAN, ROGER A.	Long Beach, Calif.	Lt. Col.	USMC	7.00
HACKING, ALBERT C., JR.	Boston, Mass.	Capt.	USMC	5.00
HADDEN, MAYO A., JR.	Holland, Mich.	Cdr.	USN	8.00
HAGERSTROM, JAMES P.	Waterloo, Ia.	Lt. Col.	USAF 5 AF	6.00
HALL, GEORGE F.	West Palm Beach, Fla.	Capt.	USAF 8 AF	6.00
HALL, SHELDON O.	Pandoro, Ohio	Capt.	USMC	6.00
HALTON, WILLIAM T.	Brooklyn, N.Y.	Lt. Col.	USAF 8 AF	11.50
HAMBLIN, LOUIS R.	Ft. Bridger, Wyo.	Lt. jg	USN	6.00
HAMILTON, HENRY B.	Larue, Tex.	WO	USMC	7.00
HAMILTON, ROBERT M.	Baldwin, L.I. N. Y.	Lt.	USN	6.00
HAMMER, SAMUEL E.	Neal, Kans.	Maj.	USAF 10 AF	5.00
HAMPSHIRE, JOHN F.	Grants Pass, Ore.	Capt.	USAF 10 AF	13.00
HANES, WILLIAM F., JR.	Birmingham, Ala.	Capt.	USAF 15 AF	6.00

Name	Home Town	Rank	Service	Victories
HANKS, EUGENE R.	Philadelphia, Pa.	Lt. Cdr.	USN	6.00
HANNA, HARRY T.	Westfield, Ind.	1st Lt.	USAF 12 AF	5.00
HANSEMAN, CHRIS J.	Mendovi, Wis.	1st Lt.	USAF 8 AF	5.00
HANSEN, HERMAN, JR.	Kansas City, Mo.	Lt. Col.	USMC	5.50
HANSON, ROBERT MURRAY	Newtonville, Mass.	1st Lt.	USMC	25.00
HARDY, WILLIS E.	Corning, Calif.	Lt. Cdr.	USN	7.00
HARGREAVES, EVERETT C.	Milwaukee, Wis.	Lt. Cdr.	USN	8.50
HARMAN, WALTER	Santa Ana, Calif.	Lt. Cdr.	USN	5.00
HARMEYER, RAYMOND F.	New Orleans, La.	1st Lt.	USAF 12 AF	6.00
HARRIS, BILL (NMI)	Springville, Calif.	Lt. Col.	USAF 13 AF	16.00
HARRIS, CECIL E.	Cresbard, S.D.	Lt.	USN	24.00
HARRIS, ERNEST A.	Morristown, Tenn.	Capt.	USAF 5 AF	10.00
HARRIS, FREDERICK A.	Glendale, Ariz.	Capt.	USAF 5 AF	8.00
HARRIS, LEROY E.	Brownwood, Tex.	Cdr.	USN	12.00
HARRIS, THOMAS L.	Santa Paula, Calif.	1st Lt.	USAF 8 AF	5.00
HARRIS, THOMAS S.	Tamaroa, Ill.	Lt. Cdr.	USN	9.00
HART, CAMERSON M.	Westfield, N.J.	Capt.	USAF 8 AF	6.00
HART, KENNETH F.	Martinez, Calif.	1st Lt.	USAF 5 AF	8.00
HARTLEY, RAYMOND E., JR.	Kansas City, Mo.	Capt.	USAF 15 AF	5.00
HATALA, PAUL R.	Cleveland, Ohio	Capt.	USAF 8 AF	5.50
HATCH, HERBERT B.	Birmingham, Mich.	1st Lt.	USAF 15 AF	5.00
HAUVER, CHARLES D.	Poughkeepsie, N.Y.	Capt.	USAF 8 AF	5.00
HAVERLAND, CHARLES H., JR.	Hibbing, Minn.	Lt.	USN	6.50
HAVILAND, FRED R., JR.	Chicago, Ill.	Capt.	USAF 8 AF	9.00
HAWKINS, ARTHUR R.	Lufkin, Tex.	Lt. Cdr.	USN	14.00
HAWORTH, RUSSELL C.	Cedar Hill, Tex.	1st Lt.	USAF 8 AF	5.00
HAYDE, FRANK R.	Kansas City, Mo.	Lt. jg	USN	5.00
HAYES, THOMAS L., JR.	Brooks, Ore.	Lt. Col.	USAF 8 AF	8.50

Name	Home Town	Rank	Service	*Victories*
HAYWOOD, THOMAS	St. Paul, Minn.	Capt.	AVG	5.25
HEAD, COTESWORTH B., JR.	San Francisco, Calif.	Maj.	USAF 13 AF	12.00
HEARRELL, FRANK C.	Chula Vista, Calif.	Cdr.	USN	5.00
HEDMAN, ROBERT ("DUKE")	Webster, S.D.	Capt.	AVG	5.00
HEDRICK, ROGER R.	Hollywood, Calif.	Cdr.	USN	12.00
HEINZEN, LLOYD P.	Colorado Springs, Colo.	Lt.	USN	6.00
HELLER, EDWIN L.	Philadelphia, Pa.	Lt. Col.	USAF 5 AF	5.50
HENDERSON, PAUL M., JR.	Lakeland, Fla.	Lt.	USN	5.00
HENDRICKS, RANDALL W.	Youngstown, Ohio	Maj.	USAF 9 AF	5.00
HENNON, WILLIAM J.	Mound, Minn.	1st Lt.	USAF 5 AF	7.00
HENRY, WILLIAM E.	Bakersfield, Calif.	Cdr.	USN	12.00
HERBST, JOHN C.	Pala, Calif.	Col.	USAF 14 AF	15.00
HERNAN, EDWIN JAMES, JR.	Dallas, Tex.	Capt.	USMC	8.00
HIBBARD, SAMUEL B.	Harvard, Mass.	Cdr.	USN	7.33
HILL, ALLEN E.	Sterling, Ill.	Maj.	USAF 5 AF	9.00
HILL, DAVID L.	Victoria, Tex.	Maj.	AVG/USAF 10 AF	17.25
HILL, FRANK A.	Hillsdale, N.J.	Col.	USAF 12 AF	7.00
HILL, HARRY E.	Bakersfield, Calif.	Cdr.	USN	7.00
HILL, JAMES E.	Stillwater, Okla.	Lt. Col.	USAF 9 AF	5.00
HIPPE, KENNETH G.	Huntington, L.I., N.Y.	Lt. Cdr.	USN	5.00
HIRO, EDWIN W.	Chisolm, Minn.	Maj.	USAF 8 AF	5.00
HIVELY, HOWARD D.	Athens, Ohio	Maj.	USAF 8 AF	12.00
HNATIO, MYRON M.	Dearborn, Mich.	1st Lt.	USAF 5 AF	5.00
HOCKERY, JOHN J.	Independence, Mo.	1st Lt.	USAF 5 AF	7.00
HODGES, WILLIAM R.	Winston-Salem, N.C.	Capt.	USAF 8 AF	5.00

Name	Home Town	Rank	Service	Victories
HOEFKER, JOHN H.	Ft. Mitchel, Ky.	Capt.	USAF 9 AF	8.50
HOEL, RONALD W.	Duluth, Minn.	Cdr.	USN	6.00
HOFER, RALPH K.	Salem, Mo.	1st Lt.	USAF 8 AF	16.50
HOFFMAN, CULLEN J.	Atlanta, Ga.	Capt.	USAF 15 AF	5.00
HOFFMAN, JAMES E., JR.	Cleveland, Ohio	1st Lt.	USAF 15 AF	6.50
HOGG, ROY B.	Atlanta, Ga.	Capt.	USAF 15 AF	6.00
HOLLOWAY, BRUCE K.	Knoxville, Tenn.	B/Gen.	USAF 10 AF	10.00
HOLLOWAY, JAMES D.	Columbus, N.C.	2nd Lt.	USAF 15 AF	6.00
HOLLOWELL, GEORGE L.	Kansas City, Kans.	Lt.Col.	USMC	8.00
HOLMES, BESBY F.	San Francisco, Calif.	Capt.	USAF 13 AF	5.00
HOMER, CYRIL F.	Sacramento, Calif.	Maj.	USAF 5 AF	15.00
HOOD, WILLIAM L.	Benton Harbor, Mich.	1st Lt.	USMC	5.50
HOPKINS, WALLACE E.	Washington, Ga.	Lt. Col.	USAF 8 AF	6.00
HORNE, FRANCIS W.	Aucilla, Fla.	1st Lt.	USAF 8 AF	5.50
HOUCK, HERBERT N.	Cromwell, Minn.	Cdr.	USN	5.00
HOVDE, WILLIAM J.	Crookston, Minn.	Col.	USAF 5 AF	10.50
HOWARD, JAMES H.	St. Louis, Mo.	Lt. Col.	AVG/USAF 9 AF	9.33
HOWARD, ROBERT L.	Oakland, Calif.	1st Lt.	USAF 5 AF	6.00
HOWE, DAVID W.	East Hickory, Pa.	1st Lt.	USAF 8 AF	6.00
HOWES, BERNARD H.	Staughton, Pa.	1st Lt.	USAF 8 AF	6.00
HOYT, EDWARD R.	Denver, Colo.	1st Lt.	USAF 5 AF	5.00
HUBBARD, MARK E.	Wausau, Wis.	Col.	USAF 12 AF	5.00
HUDSON, HOWARD R.		Lt.	USN	5.00
HUFF, LLOYD G.	Mound City, Kans.	Capt.	USAF 13 AF	6.00
HUFFMAN, CHARLES W.	Rockville, Mo.	Lt.	USN	6.00
HUMPHREY, ROBERT J.		Lt.	USN	5.33
HUNDLEY, JOHN C.	Fort Stockton, Tex.	Maj.	USMC	6.00
HUNT, EDWARD E.	Los Angeles, Calif.	2nd Lt.	USAF 9 AF	7.50
HUNTER, ALVARO J.	Plessis, N.Y.	Maj.	USAF 5 AF	5.00

Name	Home Town	Rank	Service	Victories
Hurd, Richard F.	Dobbs Ferry, N.Y.	1st Lt.	USAF 12 AF	6.00
Hurlbut, Frank D.	Salt Lake City, Utah	Capt.	USAF 12 AF	9.00
Hurst, Robert	Grand Junction, Colo.	Lt.	USN	6.00
Hwang, John Pung-Yung	San Francisco, Calif.	Maj.	USAF 5 AF	13.00
Icard, Joe W.	Granite Falls, N.C.	1st Lt.	USAF 8 AF	5.00
Ilfrey, Jack E. M.	Houston, Tex.	Capt.	USAF 12 AF	8.00
Ince, James C.	Boulder, Colo.	Maj.	USAF 5 AF	6.00
Ireland, Julius W.	Baltimore, Md.	Lt. Col.	USMC	5.00
Jackson, Michael J.	Plainfield, N.J.	Maj.	USAF 8 AF	8.00
Jackson, Willie O., Jr.	Converse, La.	Col.	USAF 8 AF	7.00
Jamison, Gilbert L.	Olympia, Wash.	Capt.	USAF 8 AF	7.00
Jeffrey, Arthur F.	Picher, Okla.	Col.	USAF 8 AF	14.00
Jenkins, Otto D.	Kermit, Tex.	2nd Lt.	USAF 8 AF	8.50
Jensen, Alvin J.	Memphis, Tenn.	1st Lt.	USMC	7.00
Jensen, Hayden M.	St. Paul Minn.	Lt. Cdr.	USN	5.00
Jernstedt, Kenneth A.	Yamhill, Ore.	Capt.	AVG	10.50
Jett, Verl E.	Lompoc, Calif.	Lt. Col.	USAF 5 AF	7.00
Johnson, Arthur, G., Jr.	Litchfield, Minn.	Capt.	USAF 12 AF	8.50
Johnson, Byron M.	Lincoln, Neb.	Lt.	USN	8.00
Johnson, Clarence O.	Ada, Minn.	Capt.	USAF 12 AF	7.00
Johnson, Evan M.	Carlisle, Pa.	Capt.	USAF 8 AF	5.00
Johnson, Gerald R.	Eugene, Ore.	Lt. Col.	USAF 5 AF	22.00
Johnson, Gerald W.	Owenton, Ky.	Col.	USAF 8 AF	17.00
Johnson, Robert S.	Garden City, N.Y.	Lt. Col.	USAF 8 AF	28.00
Johnson, Wallace R.	Overland Park, Kans.	Lt.	USN	5.00
Johnston, John M.	Portland, Ore.	Lt.	USN	8.00
Jones, Charles David	Mineola, N.Y.	Maj.	USMC	6.00
Jones, Curran L.	Columbia, S.C.	Lt. Col.	USAF 5 AF	5.00

Name	Home Town	Rank	Service	Victories
JONES, CYRIL W., JR.	Athens, Tenn.	1st Lt.	USAF 8 AF	6.00
JONES, FRANK C.	Montclair, N.J.	Capt.	USAF 8 AF	5.00
JONES, JAMES M.	Epps, La.	Lt.	USN	7.00
JONES, JOHN L.	Paterson, N.J.	1st Lt.	USAF 5 AF	8.00
JONES, LYNN F.	Mercedes, Tex.	Capt.	USAF 10 AF	5.00
JONES, WARREN L.	Live Oak, Calif	2nd Lt.	USAF 15 AF	5.00
JORDAN, WALLACE R.	Long, Beach, Calif.	Col.	USAF 5 AF	6.00
JUCHEIM, ALDWIN M.	Grenada, Miss.	Capt.	USAF 8 AF	10.00
JULIAN, WILLIAM H.	Dallas, Tex.	Maj.	USAF 8 AF	5.00
KARGER, DALE E.	McKees Rock, Pa.	1st Lt.	USAF 8 AF	7.50
KARR, ROBERT A.	Waterloo, Ia.	Capt.	USAF 15 AF	6.00
KEARBY, NEEL E.	San Antonio, Tex.	Col.	USAF 5 AF	22.00
KEEN, ROBERT J.	Jacksonville, Fla.	Capt.	USAF 8 AF	6.00
KEITH, LEROY W.	Rio Hondo, Tex.	Lt. Cdr.	USN	6.00
KEMP, WILLIAM T.	East Peoria, Ill.	2nd Lt.	USAF 8 AF	6.00
KENDRICK, CHARLES	San Francisco, Calif.	1st Lt.	USMC	5.00
KENNEDY, DANIEL	Joliet, Ill.	Capt.	USAF 12 AF	5.00
KEPFORD, IRA C.	Greenwich, Conn.	Lt.	USN	17.00
KERR, LESLIE H., JR.	Evanston, Ill.	Lt. Cdr.	USN	6.75
KIENHOLZ, DONALD DAVID	Spokane, Wash.	Capt.	USAF 12 AF	6.00
KINCAID, R. A.	Oakland, Calif.	Cdr.	USN	5.00
KING, BENJAMIN H.	Oklahoma City, Okla.	Maj.	USAF 13 AF	7.00
KING, CHARLES W.	Columbus, Ohio	Col.	USAF 5 AF	5.00
KING, DAVID L.	Johnsville, Calif.	Capt.	USAF 9 AF	5.00
KING, WILLIAM B.	Norfolk, Va.	Capt.	USAF 9 AF	5.50
KINGSTON, WILLIAM J., JR.	Jersey City, N.J.	Lt.	USN	6.00
KINNARD, CLAIBORNE H., JR.	Franklin, Tenn.	Col.	USAF 8 AF	8.00
KINSEY, CLAUDE R.	Aurora, Ill.	Capt.	USAF 12 AF	7.00
KIRBY, MARION F.	Lometa, Tex.	Maj.	USAF 5 AF	5.00

Name	Home Town	Rank	Service	Vic-tories
KIRK, GEORGE N.	Moline, Ill.	Lt. jg	USN	7.00
KIRKLAND, LENTON F., JR.	Cairo, Georgia	Capt.	USAF 9 AF	5.00
KIRKPATRICK, FLOYD C.	Unknown	Lt.	USMC	5.50
KIRKWOOD, PHILLIP L.	Washington, D.C.	Lt. jg	USN	11.00
KIRLA, JOHN A.	Port Chester, N.Y.	Maj.	USAF 8 AF	11.50
KISER, GEORGE E.	Somerset, Ky.	Col.	USAF 5 AF	9.00
KLIBBE, FRANK W.	Anderson, Ind.	Lt. Col.	USAF 8 AF	7.00
KNAPP, ROBERT H.	Des Moines, Ia.	Maj.	USAF 5 AF	5.00
KNIGHT, WILLIAM M.	Sioux City, Ia.	Lt.	USN	7.50
KNOTT, CARROLL S.	Bakersfield, Calif.	1st Lt.	USAF 12 AF	5.00
KOENIG, CHARLES W.	Oakland, Calif.	1st Lt.	USAF 9 AF	6.50
KORALESKI, WALTER J., JR.	Detroit, Mich.	Capt.	USAF 8 AF	5.54
KOSTICK, WILLIAM J.	Memphis, Tenn.	Lt.	USN	5.00
KRUZEL, JOSEPH J.	Myrtle Beach, S.C.	Maj.	USAF 5 AF	5.50
KUENTZEL, WARD A.	Delano, Calif.	Capt.	USAF 12 AF	7.00
KUNZ, CHARLES MURPHY	Springfield, Mo.	Lt. Col.	USMC	8.00
LADD, KENNETH G.	Salt Lake City, Utah	Capt.	USAF 5 AF	12.00
LAIRD, WAYNE W.	Merced, Calif.	1st Lt.	USMC	5.00
LAKE, KENNETH B.	Memphis, Tenn.	Lt.	USN	6.00
LAMB, GEORGE M.	Magna, Utah	Maj.	USAF 9 AF	7.50
LAMB, ROBERT A.	Waldwick, N.J.	Maj.	USAF 8 AF	7.00
LAMB, WILLIAM E.	Washington, D.C.	Cdr.	USN	6.00
LAMOREAUX, WILLIAM E.	Casper, Wyo.	Lt.	USN	5.00
LAMPE, RICHARD C.	Globe, Ariz.	1st Lt.	USAF 15 AF	5.00
LANDERS, JOHN D.	Joshua, Tex.	Lt. Col.	USAF 5 AF	14.50
LANE, JOHN H.	Bakersfield, Calif.	1st Lt.	USAF 5 AF	6.00
LANG, JOSEPH L.	Hyde Park, Mass.	Capt.	USAF 8 AF	7.84
LARSON, DONALD A.	Yakima, Wash.	Maj.	USAF 8 AF	6.00
LARSON, LELAND A.	Bay City, Mich.	1st Lt.	USAF 9 AF	6.00

Name	Home Town	Rank	Service	Victories
LASKO, CHARLES W.	Nemacolins, Pa.	Lt. Col.	USAF 9 AF	7.50
LATHROPE, FRANKLIN C.	Blue Island, Ill.	2nd Lt.	USAF 15 AF	5.00
LAUGHLIN, CHAUNCEY H.	Ashland, Mo.	Capt.	AVG	5.20
LAWLER, FRANK	Coronado, Calif.	Capt.	AVG	8.50
LAWLER, JOHN B.	Baltimore, Md.	1st Lt.	USAF 15 AF	11.00
LAZEAR, EARL R., JR.	Bluefield, W. Va.	1st Lt.	USAF 8 AF	5.00
LEE, RICHARD J.	Affton, Mo.	Capt.	USAF 12 AF	5.00
LEIKNESS, MARLOW J.	Danville, Ill.	1st Lt.	USAF 12 AF	5.00
LENFEST, CHARLES W.	Boise, Idaho	Col.	USAF 8 AF	5.00
LENOX, JACK, JR.	Enid, Okla.	Capt.	USAF 15 AF	5.00
LENT, FRANCIS J.	Minneapolis, Minn.	Capt.	USAF 5 AF	11.00
LEONARD, WILLIAM N.	Norfolk, Va.	Cdr.	USN	8.00
LEPPLA, JOHN A.	Lima, Ohio	Lt.	USN	5.00
LESICKA, JOSEPH J.	Westmoreland, Calif.	Capt.	USAF 13 AF	9.00
LEVERETTE, WILLIAM L.	Lykesland, S.C.	Col.	USAF 12 AF	11.00
LEWIS, WARREN R.	Superior, Ia.	Lt. Col.	USAF 5 AF	7.00
LEWIS, WILLIAM H.	Pasadena, Calif.	Lt. Col.	USAF 8 AF	8.00
LIEBERS, LAWRENCE P.	Glendale, Calif.	1st Lt.	USAF 12 AF	7.00
LILES, ROBERT L.	St. Louis, Mo.	Lt. Col.	USAF 10 AF	6.00
LILLIE, HUGH D.	Grand Rapids, Mich.	Lt.	USN	5.00
LINDSAY, ELVIN L.	Palouse, Wash.	Lt. Cdr.	USN	8.00
LINES, TED E.	Mesa, Ariz.	1st Lt.	USAF 8 AF	10.00
LITTGE, RAYMOND H.	Altenburg, Mo.	Capt.	USAF 8 AF	10.50
LITTLE, JAMES W.	Pinecastle, Ky.	Lt. Col.	USAF 10 AF	5.00
LITTLE, ROBERT L.	Spokane, Wash.	Capt.	AVG	10.50
LOESCH, GREGORY K.	Baltimore, Md.	Capt.	USMC	8.50
LOISEL, JOHN S.	West Point, Neb.	Col.	USAF 5 AF	11.00
LOMBARD, JOHN D.	Ionia, Mich.	1st Lt.	USAF 10 AF	6.00
LONDON, CHARLES P.	Long Beach, Calif.	Capt.	USAF 8 AF	5.00
LONG, HERBERT H.	Miami, Fla.	Lt. Col.	USMC	10.00
LONG, MAURICE G.	Emmetsburg, Ia.	Lt. Col.	USAF 9 AF	5.50
LOPEZ, DONALD S.	Tampa, Fla.	1st Lt.	USAF	5.00

Name	Home Town	Rank	Service	Victories
LOUIE, CLIFFORD	Seattle, Wash.	Capt.	AVG	5.00
LOVING, GEORGE G., JR.	Lynchburg, Va.	Maj.	USAF 15 AF	5.00
LOWELL, JOHN H.	Denver, Colo.	Col.	USAF 8 AF	7.50
LOWRY, WAYNE L.	Mason City, Neb.	1st Lt.	USAF 15 AF	11.00
LUCAS, PAUL W.	Boone, Ia.	Capt.	USAF 5 AF	6.00
LUKSIC, CARL J.	Joliet, Ill.	1st Lt.	USAF 8 AF	8.50
LUMA, JOHN F.	Helena, Mont.	Flt. Off.	RCAF	5.00
LUNDIN, WALTER A.	Yonkers, N.Y.	Lt. Cdr.	USN	6.50
LUNDIN, WILLIAM M.	Chicago, Ill.	Lt. Col.	USMC	5.50
LUSTIC, STANLEY J.	Elbert, W. Va.	Capt.	USAF 7 AF	6.00
LUTTON, LOWELL C.	Kankakee, Ill.	1st Lt.	USAF 5 AF	5.00
LYNCH, JOHN J.	Alhambra, Calif.	Sqd. Ldr.	RAF 71 Sq.	12.00
LYNCH, THOMAS J.	Catasaugua, Pa.	Lt. Col.	USAF 5 AF	20.00
MACDONALD, CHARLES H.	Dubois, Pa.	Col.	USAF 5 AF	27.00
MACKAY, JOHN A.	St. Albans, Vt.	Maj.	USAF 12 AF	5.00
MAGEE, CHRISTOPHER LYMAN	Chicago, Ill.	Capt.	USMC	9.00
MAGOFFIN, MORTON D.	Deerwood, Minn.	Col.	USAF 9 AF	5.00
MAGUIRE, WILLIAM J.	Boston, Mass.	Capt.	USAF 8 AF	7.00
MAHON, KEITH	Oklahoma City, Okla.	Maj.	USAF 14 AF	5.00
MAHONEY, GRANT M.	Unknown	Capt.	RAF 79 Sq	10.00
MAHURIN, WALKER M.	Fort Wayne, Ind.	Col.	USAF 8 AF	20.75
MALLORY, CHARLES M.	Dunbar, W. Va.	Lt. Cdr.	USN	11.00
MALONEY, THOMAS E.	Cushing, Okla.	1st Lt.	USAF 15 AF	8.00
MANKIN, JACK C.	Kansas City, Mo.	Capt.	USAF 5 AF	5.00
MANKIN, LEE P.	Springfield, Mo.	Lt. Cdr.	USN	5.00
MANN, THOMAS H., JR.	Graysville, Ind.	Maj.	USMC	9.00
MANSON, ARMAND G.	Buffalo, N.Y.	Lt. jg	USN	7.00
MARCH, HARRY A., JR.	Washington, D.C.	Lt. Cdr.	USN	5.00
MARONTATE, WILLIAM P.	Seattle, Wash.	1st Lt.	USMC	13.00

Name	Home Town	Rank	Service	Vic-tories
MARSH, LESTER C.	Los Angeles, Calif.	1st Lt.	USAF 8 AF	5.00
MARSHALL, BERT W.	Greenville, Tex.	Col.	USAF 8 AF	7.00
MARTIN, ALBERT E., JR.	Warwick, R. I.	Lt.	USN	5.00
MARTIN, KENNETH R.	Greenwood, Mo.	Capt.	USAF 9 AF	5.00
MASON, JOE L.	Columbus, Ohio	Col.	USAF 8 AF	5.00
MASONER, WILLIAM J., JR.	Chicago, Ill.	Lt.	USN	12.00
MATHIS, WILLIAM H.	Nashville, Ga.	Capt.	USAF 7 AF	5.00
MATHRE, MILDEN E.	Cedar Falls, Ia.	Capt.	USAF 5 AF	5.00
MATTE, JOSEPH Z.	Randolph AFB, Tex.	Capt.	USAF 9 AF	5.00
MAXWELL, CHESTER K.	Alva, Okla.	Maj.	USAF 8 AF	5.00
MAXWELL, W. R.	Columbia, S.C.	Lt. Cdr.	USN	7.00
MAY, EARL	Milwaukee, Wisc.	Lt. Cdr.	USN	8.00
MAY, RICHARD HOBBS	Portland, Ore.	Lt. Cdr.	USN	6.00
MAYO, BEN I., JR.	Little Rock, Ark.	Maj.	USAF 8 AF	5.00
MAZZOCCO, MICHELE A.	Peekskill, N.Y.	Lt.	USN	6.50
McARTHUR, PAUL G.	Reform, Ala.	1st Lt.	USAF 9 AF	5.00
McARTHUR, T. H.	Caradan, Tex.	1st Lt.	USAF 12 AF	5.00
McCAMPBELL, DAVID	Bessemer, Ala.	Capt.	USN	34.00
McCARTNEY, H. ALLEN, JR.	Watertown, N.Y.	Maj.	USMC	5.00
McCAULEY, FRANK E.	Hicksville, Ohio	Capt.	USAF 8 AF	5.50
McCLELLAND, THOMAS G.	Albuquerque, N.M.	Lt.	USN	7.00
McCLURG, ROBERT W.	New Castle, Pa.	Maj.	USMC	7.00
McCOLPIN, CARROLL W.	Buffalo, N.Y.	Lt./ Col.	RAF/USAF	10.00
McCOMAS, ED O.	Winfield, Kans.	Col.	USAF 14 AF	14.00
McCORKLE, CHARLES M.	Newton, N.C.	Brig. Gen.	USAF 12 AF	11.00
McCORMICK, WILLIAM A., JR.	West Lawn, Pa.	Lt.	USN	6.00
McCUDDIN, LEO B.	Chula Vista, Calif.	Cdr.	USN	5.00

Name	Home Town	Rank	Service	Vic- tories
McCuskey, Elbert S.	Montgomery, Ala.	Cdr.	USN	14.00
McDaniel, Gordon H.	Sweetwater, Tenn.	1st Lt.	USAF 15 AF	6.00
McDonald, Norman L.	Framingham, Mass.	Maj.	USAF 12 AF	11.00
McDonald, R. ("Red")	Unknown	Ens.	USN	5.00
McDonough, William F.	Temple City, Calif.	Maj.	USAF 5 AF	5.00
McDowell, Don	Los Angeles, Calif	1st Lt.	USAF 9 AF	8.50
McElroy, James N.	Orlando, Fla.	Capt.	USAF 8 AF	5.00
McGarry, William D.	Los Angeles, Calif.	Capt.	AVG	10.25
McGee, Donald C.	Staten Island, N.Y.	Lt. Col.	USAF 5 AF	6.00
McGinity, Selva E.	Stilwell, Okla.	1st Lt.	USMC	5.00
McGinn, John L.	Luverna, Minn.	Maj.	USAF 13 AF	5.00
McGowan, Edward C.	Columbus, Ohio	Lt. Cdr.	USN	6.50
McGrattan, Bernard L.	Utica, N.Y.	Capt.	USAF 8 AF	8.50
McGuire, Thomas B.	San Antonio, Tex.	Maj.	USAF 5 AF	38.00
McGuyrt, John W.	Canton, Ohio	1st Lt.	USAF 15 AF	5.00
McKennon, Pierce W.	Fort Smith, Ark.	Maj.	USAF 8 AF	12.00
McKeon, Joseph T.	Maspeth, L.I., N.Y.	Capt.	USAF 5 AF	6.00
McKinley, Donald J.	St. Ansgar, Ia.	Lt.	USN	5.00
McLachlin, William W.	Louisville, Ky.	Lt.	USN	5.50
McLaughlin, Murry D.	Basin, Wyo.	1st Lt.	USAF 15 AF	7.00
McManus, John	El Toro, Calif.	Maj.	USMC	6.00
McMillan, George B.	Winter Garden, Fla.	Lt. Col.	AVG/USAF	8.25
McMinn, Evan D.	Pittsburgh, Pa.	Flt. Off.	USAF 8 AF	5.00
McPharlin, Michael G. H.	Toronto, Can.	Sqd. Ldr.	RAF/USAF 71 Sq	5.50
McPherson, Donald M.	Adams, Neb.	Ens.	USN	5.00
McWhorter, Hamilton, III	Athens, Ga.	Cdr.	USN	12.00

Name	Home Town	Rank	Service	Victories
MEGURA, NICHOLAS	Ansonia, Conn.	Capt.	USAF 8 AF	11.84
MEHLE, ROGER W.	Cincinnati, Ohio	Cdr.	USN	13.33
MEIGS, HENRY, II	New York, N.Y.	Lt.	USAF 13 AF	6.00
MENARD, LOUIS A.	Amery, Wis.	Cdr.	USN	9.00
MENCIN, ADOLPH	Ogelsby, Ill.	Cdr.	USN	6.00
MERONEY, VIRGIL K.	Pine Bluff, Ark.	Lt. Col.	USAF 8 AF	9.00
MERRITT, GEORGE L., JR.	Cumming, Ga.	Maj.	USAF 8 AF	5.00
MEUTEN, DONALD	Oakland, Calif.	1st Lt.	USAF 5 AF	6.00
MEYER, JOHN C.	Forest Hills, N.Y.	Lt. Col.	USAF 8 AF	24.00
MIKLAJCYK, HENRY J.	Syracuse, N.Y.	Capt.	USAF 8 AF	7.50
MILLER, ARMOUR C.	Cleverlock, N.Y.	Capt.	USAF 15 AF	6.00
MILLER, EVERETT	Pomona, Calif.	Capt.	USAF 15 AF	5.00
MILLER, JOHNNIE G.	Arlington, Tex.	Lt.	USN	8.00
MILLER, JOSEPH E.	Los Angeles, Calif.	Capt.	USAF 12 AF	5.00
MILLER, THOMAS F.	Portland, Ore.	1st Lt.	USAF 9 AF	5.25
MILLIKAN, WILLARD W.	Malvern, Ia.	Capt.	USAF 8 AF	13.00
MILLIKEN, ROBERT C.	Hanna, Wyo.	2nd Lt.	USAF 9 AF	5.00
MILLS, HENRY L.	Leonia, N.Y.	Maj.	USAF 8 AF	6.00
MILTON, CHARLES B.	Jasper, Fla.	Lt.	USN	5.00
MIMS, ROBERT	Dallas, Tex.	Lt. Cdr.	USN	6.00
MINCHEW, LESLIE D.	Miami, Fla.	Capt.	USAF 8 AF	5.50
MITCHELL, HARRIS E.	Richmond, Tex.	Lt.	USN	10.00
MITCHELL, HENRY E.	Vancouver, Wash.	Lt. jg	USN	6.00
MITCHELL, JOHN W.	San Antonio, Tex.	Col.	USAF 7 AF	11.00
MOATS, SANFORD K.	Mission, Kans.	Maj.	USAF 8 AF	8.50
MOLLAND, LELAND P.	South Fargo, N.D.	1st Lt.	USAF 12 AF	11.00
MOLLENHAUER, ARTHUR P.	Redwood City, Calif.	Ens.	USN	5.00
MOMYER, WILLIAM W.	Seattle, Wash.	Brig. Gen.	USAF 12 AF	8.00
MONK, FRANKLIN H.	Peoria, Ill.	1st Lt.	USAF 5 AF	5.00
MONTAPERT, JOHN R.	Van Nuys, Calif.	Lt. jg	USN	6.00
MOORE, JOHN T.	Montgomery, Ala.	Capt.	USAF 5 AF	7.00
MOORE, ROBERT W.	St. Matthews, Ky.	Capt.	USAF 7 AF	12.00
MORAN, GLENNON T.	Granite City, Ill.	Lt. Col.	USAF 8 AF	13.00

Name	Home Town	Rank	Service	Victories
MORANVILLE, HORACE B.	Guide Rock, Neb.	Lt.	USN	6.00
MOREHEAD, JAMES B.	Norman, Okla.	Lt. Col.	USAF 5 AF	7.00
MORGAN, JOHN L., JR.	Arlington, Tex.	Capt.	USMC	8.50
MORRILL, STANLEY B.	Willimantic, Conn.	1st Lt.	USAF 8 AF	9.00
MORRIS, BERT D., JR. (WAYNE)	Fallbrook, Calif.	Lt. Cdr.	USN	7.00
MORRIS, JAMES M.	Detroit, Mich.	Lt. Col.	USAF 8 AF	7.33
MORRISS, PAUL V.	Norcross, Ga.	Capt.	USAF 5 AF	5.00
MOSELEY, MARK L.	Atlanta, Ga.	Maj.	USAF 8 AF	6.50
MOSELEY, WILLIAM C.	Unknown	Lt.	USN	6.00
MUGAVERO, JAMES D.	Port Huron, Mich.	Capt.	USAF 5 AF	6.00
MULCAHY, DOUGLAS W.	Yonkers, N.Y.	Lt.	USN	8.00
MULHOLLEM, ROBERT F.	Chicago, Ill.	Capt.	USAF 10 AF	6.00
MULLEN, PAUL A.	Pittsburgh, Pa.	Capt.	USMC	6.50
MUNSON, ARTHUR H.	Utica, N.Y.	Lt.	USN	5.00
MURPHY, ALVA C.	Knoxville, Tenn.	Capt.	USAF 8 AF	8.00
MURPHY, JOHN B.	Darlington, S.C.	Col.	USAF 11 AF	6.75
MURPHY, PAUL C.	Meridian, Tex.	Lt. Col.	USAF 5 AF	6.00
MURRAY, ROBERT E.	Muncie, Ind.	Lt. Cdr.	USN	10.33
MYERS, JENNINGS L.	Ahoskie, N.C.	1st. Lt.	USAF 5 AF	5.00
MYERS, RAYMOND B.	Dundee, Miss.	Maj.	USAF 8 AF	5.50
NARR, JOSEPH L.	Unknown	2nd Lt.	USMC	8.00
NEALE, ROBERT H.	Seattle, Wash.	Capt.	AVG	15.50
NELSON, ROBERT J.	Sioux City, Ia.	Lt. Cdr.	USN	5.00
NEWKIRK, JOHN V.	Scarsdale, N.Y.	Capt.	AVG	10.50
NICHOLS, FRANKLIN A.	Wewoka, Okla.	Col.	USAF 5 AF	5.00
NOBLE, MYRVIN E.	Smithfield, Utah	Lt.	USN	7.50
NOOY, CORNELIUS N.	Smithtown, L.I., N.Y.	Lt. Cdr.	USN	19.00
NORLEY, LOUIS H.	Conrad, Mont.	Maj.	USAF 8 AF	11.33
NOVAK, MARVIN R.	Manitowac, Wis.	Lt. Cdr.	USN	5.00
NOVOTNY, GEORGE P.	Toledo, Ohio	1st Lt.	USAF 12 AF	8.00
OBERHANSLEY, JACK J.	Spanish Fork, Utah	Lt. Col.	USAF 8 AF	5.00
O'BRIEN, GILBERT M.	Charleston, S.C.	Maj.	USAF 8 AF	7.00

Name	Home Town	Rank	Service	Victories
O'BRIEN, WILLIAM R.	McPherson, Kans.	Capt.	USAF 8 AF	5.50
O'CONNOR, FRANK Q.	San Francisco, Calif.	Col.	USAF 9 AF	10.75
O'HARE, EDWARD H.	Chicago, Ill.	Lt. Cdr.	USN	12.00
OHR, FRED F.	Caldwell, Idaho	1st Lt.	USAF 12 AF	6.00
O'KEEFE, JEREMIAH J.	Biloxi, Miss.	1st Lt.	USMC	7.00
OLANDER, EDWIN L.	Northampton, Mass.	Maj	USMC	5.00
OLDER, CHARLES H.	Los Angeles, Calif.	Lt. Col.	USAF/AVG	18.25
OLDS, ROBIN	Washington, D.C.	Maj.	USAF 8 AF	12.00
OLSEN, AUSTIN LEROY	Seattle, Wash.	Ens.	USN	5.00
OLSON, NORMAN K.	Fargo, N.D.	Capt.	USAF 8 AF	6.00
O'MARA, PAUL, JR.	San Leandro, Calif.	Lt.	USN	7.50
O'NEILL, HUGH D.	Unknown	Lt.	USN	7.00
O'NEILL, JOHN G.	Gasport, N.Y.	Capt.	USAF 5 AF	8.00
O'NEILL, LAWRENCE F.	St. Louis, Mo.	1st Lt.	USAF 5 AF	5.00
ORTH, JOHN	Romeo, Mich.	Lt. jg	USN	6.00
OSHER, ERNEST K.	Graettinger, Iowa	Lt. Col.	USAF 12 AF	5.00
OSTROM, CHARLES H.	Miami, Fla.	Cdr.	USN	7.00
OUTLAW, EDWARD C.	Goldsboro, N.C.	Cdr.	USN	6.00
OVERCASH, ROBERT J.	Mooresville, N.C.	Lt. Col.	USAF 9 AF	5.00
OVEREND, EDMUND F.	Coronado, Calif.	Maj.	USMC/AVG	9.00
OVERFIELD, LOYD J.	Leavenworth, Kans.	1st Lt.	USAF 9 AF	9.00
OVERTON, EDWARD W., JR.	Arlington, Va.	Lt. Cdr.	USN	5.00
OWEN, EDWARD M.	Pacific Palisades, Calif.	Lt. Cdr.	USN	8.00
OWEN, JOEL A.	Skiatook, Okla.	Capt.	USAF 12 AF	5.00
OWENS, ROBERT G., JR.	Greenville, S.C.	Lt. Col.	USMC	7.00
PAISLEY, MELVYN R.	Portland, Ore.	Capt.	USAF 9 AF	5.00
PALMER, CYRIL DAMPIER	Cleveland, Ohio	Flt. Off.	RAF	5.00
PARHAM, FORREST F.	Kensington, Minn.	Maj.	USAF 14 AF	5.00

Name	*Home Town*	*Rank*	*Service*	*Vic- tories*
PARIS, JOEL B., III	Atlanta, Ga.	Maj.	USAF 5 AF	9.00
PARKER, HARRY A.	Milford, N.H.	Capt.	USAF 15 AF	13.00
PARRISH, ELBERT W.	Orlando, Fla.	Ens.	USN	7.00
PASCOE, JAMES J.	Poughkeepsie, N.Y.	1st Lt.	USAF 8 AF	6.00
PASKOSKI, JOSEPH J.	Macon, Ga.	Lt.	USN	6.00
PAULK, EDSEL	Vernon, Tex.	Capt.	USAF 15 AF	5.00
PAYNE, CARL W.	Columbus, Ohio	Col.	USAF 8 AF	7.00
PAYNE, FREDERICK R.	Santa Ana, Calif.	Col.	USMC	5.50
PEARCE, JAMES L.	Palos Verdes Estates, Calif.	Lt.	USN	6.00
PECK, JAMES ELDRIDGE	Berkeley, Calif.	Flt. Lt.	RAF 126 Sq	5.00
PERCY, GILBERT	Chico, Calif.	Maj.	USMC	6.00
PERDOMO, OSCAR F.	San Gabriel, Calif.	1st Lt.	USAF 20 AF	5.00
PETACH, JOHN E.	Perth Amboy, N.J.	Capt.	AVG	5.25
PETERSON, CHESLEY G.	Santaquin, Utah	Sqd. Ldr.	RAF/USAF 8 AF	7.00
PETERSON, RICHARD A.	Alexandria, Minn.	Maj.	USAF 8 AF	15.50
PHILIPS, DAVID P.	Jackson, Mich.	Lt.	USN	5.00
PHILLIPS, EDWARD A.	Blacksville, W.Va.	Lt.	USN	5.00
PHILLIPS, HYDE	Shelbyville, Ill.	Maj.	USMC	5.00
PICKEN, HARVEY P.	Minot, N.D.	Lt.	USN	9.00
PIERCE, FRANCIS E., JR.	Coronado, Calif.	Col.	USMC	6.00
PIERCE, JOSEPH F.	Duncan, Okla.	1st Lt.	USAF 8 AF	7.00
PIERCE, SAMMY A.	Ayden, N.C.	Maj.	USAF 5 AF	7.00
PIETZ, JOHN, JR.	Valley Stream, N.Y.	Maj.	USAF 5 AF	6.00
PIGMAN, GEORGE, W., JR.	New Orleans, La.	Lt.	USN	8.50
PISANOS, STEVE N.	Plainfield, N.J.	Maj.	USAF 8 AF	10.00
PITTMAN, JACK JR.	Amarillo, Tex.	1st Lt.	USMC	7.00
PLANT, CLAUDE W.	Portland, Ore.	Lt. jg	USN	8.50
POINDEXTER, JAMES N.	Milville, N.J.	Capt.	USAF 8 AF	7.00
POMPETTI, PETER E.	Philadelphia, Pa.	Maj.	USAF 8 AF	5.50

Name	Home Town	Rank	Service	Victories
POND, ZENNETH A.	Jackson, Mich.	2nd Lt.	USMC	6.00
POOL, KENNETH R.	Igloo, S.D.	1st Lt.	USAF 5 AF	5.00
POOL, TILMAN E.	Tulsa, Okla.	Lt.	USN	6.00
POPE, ALBERT J.	Atlanta, Ga.	Lt. Cdr.	USN	7.25
POPEK, EDWARD S.	Hackensack, N.J.	Lt. Col.	USAF 5 AF	5.00
PORTER, ROBERT BRUCE	Salena, Utah	1st Lt.	USMC	5.00
POSKE, GEORGE H.	Los Angeles, Calif.	Maj.	USMC	5.00
POST, NATHAN T.	San Francisco, Calif.	Col.	USMC	8.00
POUND, RALSTON M., JR.	Charlotte, N.C.	Lt. Cdr.	USN	6.00
POWELL, ERNEST A.	New Rochelle, N.Y.	Capt.	USMC	5.00
POWERS, JOE H., JR.	Tulsa, Okla.	Capt.	USAF 8 AF	14.50
POWERS, MACARTHUR	Inwood, L.I., N.Y.	Maj.	USAF 9 AF	7.50
PRATER, LUTHER D., JR.	Lexington, Ky.	Lt. Cdr.	USN	8.00
PREDDY, GEORGE E., JR.	Greensboro, N.C.	Maj.	USAF 8 AF	25.83
PRESCOTT, ROBERT W.	Forth Worth, Tex.	Capt.	AVG	5.25
PRESLEY, FRANK H.	Norfolk, Va.	Maj.	USMC	6.00
PRICE, JACK C.	Grand Junction, Colo.	Lt. Col.	USAF 8 AF	5.00
PRICHARD, MELVIN M.	Atlanta, Mich.	Lt. Cdr.	USN	7.25
PRIEST, ROYCE W.	San Antonio, Tex.	Maj.	USAF 8 AF	5.00
PRYOR, ROGER C.	Starkville, Miss.	Col.	USAF 14 AF	5.00
PUGH, JOHN FORREST	Brogan, Ore.	Capt.	USAF 8 AF	6.00
PURDY, JOHN E.	Dayton, Ohio	Capt.	USAF 5 AF	7.00
QUIGLEY, DONALD L.	Marion, Ohio	Lt. Col.	USAF 14 AF	5.00
QUIRK, MICHAEL J.	Port Henry, N.Y.	Lt. Col.	USAF 8 AF	12.00
RAINES, ROBERT J. ("CATFISH")	Burbank, Calif.	Cdr.	USN	6.00
RAMLO, ORVIN H.	Decorah, Ia.	Lt. Col.	USMC	5.00
RANKIN, ROBERT J.	Washington, D.C.	Lt. Col.	USAF 8 AF	10.00
RAY, C. B.	Tilden, Tex.	Capt.	USAF 5 AF	5.00
REBER, JAMES V., JR.	Reading, Pa.	Lt. jg	USN	11.00

Name	Home Town	Rank	Service	Victories
RECTOR, EDWARD F.	Marshall, N.C.	Capt.	AVG	10.50
REDMOND, EUGENE D.	Los Angeles, Calif.	Lt.	USN	9.00
REED, WILLIAM N.	Marion, Ia.	Maj.	AVG/USAF 14 AF	17.50
REESE, WILLIAM C.	Bear River, Utah	1st Lt.	USAF 8 AF	5.00
REEVES, LEONARD R.	Lancaster, Tex.	Maj.	USAF 10 AF	6.00
REGISTER, FRANCIS R.	Bismarck, N.D.	Lt. jg	USN	7.00
REHM, DAN R., JR.	New Orleans, La.	Lt. Cdr.	USN	9.00
REIDY, T. H.	Northfield, Ill.	Lt. Cdr.	USN	10.00
REINBURG, J. HUNTER	Fort Worth, Tex.	Lt. Col.	USMC	7.00
REISERER, RUSSELL L.	Los Altos, Calif.	Cdr.	USN	10.50
RENNEMO, THOMAS J.	Oreland, Pa.	Lt. Cdr.	USN	7.00
REULET, JOSEPH E.	Vacherie, La.	Lt. Cdr.	USN	5.00
REVEL, GLENN M.	Chase, Kans.	Lt. Cdr.	USN	5.50
REYNOLDS, ANDREW J.	Seminole, Okla.	Col.	USAF 5 AF	10.00
REYNOLDS, ROBERT	Orlando, Fla.	Capt.	USAF 9 AF	7.00
RHODES, THOMAS W.	Washington, D.C.	Lt. Cdr.	USN	5.00
RICHARDSON, ELMER W.	San Antonio, Tex.	Col.	USAF 14 AF	8.00
RIDDLE, ROBERT E.	Chicago, Ill.	2nd Lt.	USAF 15 AF	11.00
RIEGER, VINCENT A.	Denver, Col.	Lt.	USN	5.00
RIGG, JAMES F.	Saginaw, Mich.	Cdr.	USN	11.00
RIGHETTI, ELWYN G.	San Antonio, Tex.	Lt. Col.	USAF 8 AF	7.50
RILEY, PAUL S.	York, Pa.	1st Lt.	USAF 8 AF	6.50
RIMERMAN, BENN	Omaha, Neb.	Lt. Col.	USAF 8 AF	7.00
RITCHEY, ANDREW J.	Flint, Mich.	Capt.	USAF 9 AF	5.00
ROBBINS, JAY T.	Coolidge, Tex.	Col.	USAF 5 AF	22.00
ROBERSON, ARVAL J.	Los Angeles, Calif.	Maj.	USAF 8 AF	6.00
ROBERTS, DANIEL T., JR.	Los Angeles, Calif.	Maj.	USAF 5 AF	14.00
ROBERTS, EUGENE PAUL	Spokane, Wash.	Col.	USAF 8 AF	9.00
ROBERTS, NEWELL O.	Anderson, Ind.	Capt.	USAF 12 AF	5.00
ROBINSON, LEROY W.	Hopeville, Ga.	Lt.	USN	5.00
ROBINSON, ROSS F.	St. Paul, Minn.	Lt. jg	USN	5.00
RODDY, EDWARD F.	Cleveland, Ohio	Col.	USAF 5 AF	8.00
ROGERS, FELIX MIKE	Washington, D.C.	1st Lt.	USAF 9 AF	7.00

Name	Home Town	Rank	Service	Victories
ROSE, FRANKLIN, JR.	Piedmont, Calif.	Capt.	USAF 9 AF	5.00
ROSEN, RALPH J	Grayslake, Ill.	Lt. Cdr.	USN	6.00
ROSS, HERBERT E.	Fresno, Calif.	Maj.	USAF 12 AF	7.00
ROSS, ROBERT P.	Lillington, N.C.	Lt.	USN	5.50
ROSSI, HERMAN J., JR.	Wallace, Idaho	Lt. Cdr.	USN	6.00
ROSSI, JOHN R.	San Francisco, Calif.	Capt.	AVG	6.25
ROUNDS, GERALD L.	Fenton, Mich.	Maj.	USAF 12 AF	5.00
ROWLAND, ROBERT R.	Lodi, Ohio	Col.	USAF 5 AF	8.00
RUDER, LEROY A.	Mekossa, Wis.	1st Lt.	USAF 8 AF	5.50
RUDOLPH, HENRY S.	Howe, Ind.	Capt.	USAF 9 AF	5.00
RUHSAM, JOHN W.	Ventura, Calif.	Maj.	USMC	7.00
RUNYON, DONALD E.	Quonset Pt., R.I.	Lt. Cdr.	USN	11.00
RUSHING, ROY W.	McGehee, Ark.	Lt.	USN	13.00
RYNNE, WILLIAM A.	New Rochelle, N.Y.	1st Lt.	USAF 15 AF	5.00
SANDELL, ROBERT J.	San Antonio, Tex.	Capt.	AVG	5.25
SANGERMANO, PHILIP	Petersborough, N.H.	Flt. Off.	USAF 15 AF	8.00
SAPP, DONALD H.	Miami, Fla.	Lt. Col.	USMC	11.00
SAVAGE, JIMMIE E.	Dorchester, Tex.	Cdr.	USN	7.00
SAWYER, CHARLES W.	Emmett, Idaho	Maj.	AVG/USAF 14 AF	8.00
SCALES, HARRELL H.	Glendora, Calif.	Lt. Cdr.	USN	6.00
SCARBOROUGH, HARTWELL V., JR.		Maj.	USMC	5.00
SCHANK, THOMAS D.	Greeley, Colo.	1st Lt.	USAF 8 AF	5.00
SCHELL, J. L.	Weston, Conn.	Lt.	USN	5.00
SCHEIBLE, WILBUR R.	Akron, Ohio	Lt. Col.	USAF 8 AF	6.00
SCHERER, RAYMOND F.	Santa Ana, Calif.	Lt. Col.	USMC	5.00
SCHIEL, FRANK	Prescott, Ariz.	Capt.	AVG	7.00
SCHILDT, WILLIAM J.	Hamlin, N.Y.	Maj.	USAF 12 AF	6.00
SCHILLING, DAVID C.	Kansas City, Mo.	Col.	USAF 8 AF	22.50
SCHILTZ, GLENN D. JR.	North Canton, Ohio	Capt.	USAF 8 AF	8.00

Name	Home Town	Rank	Service	Victories
SCHIMANSKI, R. G.	Spokane, Wash.	Maj.	USAF 8 AF	6.00
SCHLEGEL, ALBERT L.	Cleveland, Ohio	Capt.	USAF 8 AF	8.50
SCHREIBER, LEROY A.	Plymouth, Mass.	Maj.	USAF 8 AF	12.00
SCHUH, DUERR H.	Douglas, Wyo.	1st Lt.	USAF 8 AF	5.00
SCHULTZ (SHOALS) ROBERT B.	Sandusky, Ohio	Capt.	USAF 14 AF	5.00
SCOTT, ROBERT L.	Macon, Ga.	Col.	USAF 10 AF	10.00
SEARS, ALEXANDER F.	Abilene, Tex.	1st Lt.	USAF 8 AF	5.00
SEARS, MELDRUM L.	Paris, Ill.	1st Lt.	USAF 12 AF	7.00
SECKEL, ALBERT JR.	Oak Park, Ill.	Cdr.	USN	6.00
SEE, ROBERT BYRON	San Francisco, Calif.	Capt.	USMC	5.00
SEGAL, HAROLD E.	Woodmere, L.I., N.Y.	Maj.	USMC	12.00
SEIDMAN, ROBERT K.	Pittsburgh, Pa.	1st Lt.	USAF 15 AF	5.00
SELF, LARRY R.	Dallas, Tex.	Lt. jg	USN	8.50
SHACKFORD, ROBERT W.	Medford, Mass.	Lt. Cdr.	USN	6.00
SHAFER, DALE E.	Waynesville, Ohio	Lt. Col	USAF 12 AF	8.00
SHANDS, COURTNEY	Washington, D.C.	Capt.	USN	6.00
SHAW, EDWARD O.	Spokane, Wash.	Capt.	USMC	13.00
SHAW, ROBERT M.	Pittsburgh, Pa.	1st Lt.	USAF 8 AF	8.00
SHIELDS, CHARLES A.	New Orleans, La.	Lt.	USN	5.00
SHIPMAN, ERNEST	Jackson Heights, L.I., N.Y.	2nd Lt.	USAF 15 AF	7.00
SHIRLEY, JAMES A.	Seneca, S.C.	Cdr.	USN	12.00
SHOMO, WILLIAM A.	Jeannette, Pa.	Lt. Col.	USAF 5 AF	8.00
SHOUP, ROBERT L.	Port Arthur, Tex.	1st Lt.	USAF 9 AF	5.50
SHUBIN, MURRAY JR.	Dormont, Pa.	Lt. Col	USAF 13 AF	11.00
SHULER, LUCIEN B.	Griffin, Georgia	1st Lt.	USAF 12 AF	7.00
SHUMAN, PERRY L.		Lt. Col.	USMC	6.00
SIGLER, WALLACE E.	Orange, Conn.	Maj.	USMC	5.33
SILBER, SAM L.	Baltimore, Md.	Cdr.	USN	7.00
SIMMONS, JOHN M.	Gadsden, Ala.	Maj.	USAF 15 AF	7.00
SIMMONS, WILLIAM J.	Los Angeles, Calif.	Col.	USAF 9 AF	6.00

Name	Home Town	Rank	Service	Victories
Singer, Arthur Jr.	Milwaukee, Wis.	Lt.	USN	10.00
Sipes, Lester H.	Omaha, Neb.	Cdr.	USN	5.00
Sistrunk, Frank	Phoenix, Ariz.	Lt.	USN	5.00
Skogstad, Norman C.	Barron, Wis.	Capt.	USAF 15 AF	12.00
Skon, Warren A.	St. Paul, Minn.	Lt. Cdr.	USN	7.00
Slack, Albert C.	Lufkin, Tex.	Lt. jg	USN	6.50
Sloan, William J.	Richmond, Va.	Maj.	USAF 12 AF	12.00
Smith, Armistead B., Jr.	Gastonia, N.C.	Cdr.	USN	10.50
Smith, Carl Eugene	Lufkin, Tex.	Lt. Cdr	USN	7.00
Smith, Clinton L.	Jackson, Miss.	Lt.	USN	6.00
Smith, Cornelius M., Jr.	Brooklyn, N.Y.	Lt. Col.	USAF 5 AF	11.00
Smith, Donovan F.	Niles, Mich.	Maj.	USAF 8 AF	5.50
Smith, Jack R.	San Simon, Ariz.	1st Lt.	USAF 15 AF	5.00
Smith, John C.	Portsmouth, Ohio	Maj.	USAF 5 AF	6.00
Smith, John L.	Lexington, Okla.	Col.	USMC	19.00
Smith, John Malcom	Owatonna, Minn.	Lt. Cdr.	USN	5.00
Smith, Kenneth B.	Watsontown, Pa.	Capt.	USAF 8 AF	5.00
Smith, Kenneth D.	Port Arthur, Tex.	Cdr.	USN	5.00
Smith, Leslie C.	Caruthers, Calif.	Col.	USAF 8 AF	7.00
Smith, Meryl M.	North East, Pa.	Capt.	USAF 5 AF	9.00
Smith, Nicholas J., III	Lynchburg, Va.	Lt. Cdr.	USN	6.00
Smith, Richard E.	Evansville, Ind.	Lt. Col.	USAF 5 AF	7.00
Smith, Robert H. ("Snuffy")	Eagle River, Wis.	Capt.	AVG 13 AF	8.00
Smith, Robert T.	Lincoln, Neb.	Capt.	AVG	8.67
Smith, Virgil H.	McAllen, Tex.	1st Lt.	USAF 12 AF	5.00
Snider, William N.	Vicksburg, Miss.	Maj.	USMC	8.50
Sonner, Irl V., Jr.	El Monte, Calif.	Lt. jg	USN	5.00
Southerland, James J.	Jacksonville, Fla.	Cdr.	USN	5.00
Sparks, Kenneth C.	Blackwell, Okla.	1st Lt.	USAF 5 AF	11.00
Spears, Harold L.	Newark, Ohio	Capt.	USMC	15.00
Spencer, Dale F.	Clymer, N.Y.	Capt.	USAF 8 AF	9.50
Spitler, Clyde P.	Oak Park, Mich.	Lt.	USN	5.00

Name	*Home Town*	*Rank*	*Service*	*Victories*
STAMBOOK, RICHARD E.	Torrance, Calif.	Lt. Cdr.	USN	11.00
STANCH, PAUL M.	Audubon, N.J.	Maj.	USAF 5 AF	10.00
STANGEL, WILLIAM J.	Waubun, Minn.	Capt.	USAF 8 AF	5.00
STANLEY, GORDON A.	Coronado, Calif.	Lt. Cdr.	USN	8.00
STANLEY, MORRIS A.	Alvin, Tex.	Maj.	USAF 8 AF	5.00
STANTON, ARLAND	New Milford, Conn.	Lt. Col	USAF 5 AF	8.00
STARCK, WALTER E.	Milwaukee, Wis.	Lt. Col	USAF 8 AF	6.00
STARKES, CARLTON B.	Moffett Field, Calif.	Cdr.	USN	6.00
STARNES, JAMES R.	Wilmington, N.C.	Maj.	USAF 8 AF	6.00
STEBBINS, EDGAR E.	Austin, Texas	Cdr.	USN	5.00
STEPHENS, ROBERT W.	St. Louis, Mo.	Col.	USAF 9 AF	13.00
STEWART, EVERETT W.	Abilene, Kans.	Col.	USAF 8 AF	7.83
STEWART, JAMES C.	Corona, Calif.	Col.	USAF 8 AF	12.50
STEWART, JAMES S.	Beverly Hills, Calif.	Lt.	USN	9.00
STEWART, JOHN S.	Worland, Wyo.	Lt. Col.	USAF 14 AF	8.00
STIMPSON, CHARLES R.	Salt Lake City, Utah	Lt. Cdr.	USN	17.00
STOKES, JOHN D.	Maplewood, La.	Lt. jg	USN	6.50
STONE, CARL VAN	Raleigh, N.C.	Lt.	USN	5.00
STORCH, JOHN A.	Long Beach, Calif.	Lt. Col.	USAF 8 AF	10.50
STOUT, ROBERT F.	Laramie, Wyo.	Maj.	USMC	6.00
STRAIT, DONALD J.	Verona, N.J.	Col.	USAF 8 AF	13.50
STRAND, WILLIAM H.	Pasadena, Calif.	Maj.	USAF 5 AF	7.00
STRANE, JOHN R.	Duluth, Minn.	Cdr.	USN	13.00
STRANGE, JOHNNIE C	Meridian, Miss.	Cdr.	USN	5.00
STREIG, FREDERICK J.	Pensacola, Fla.	Lt. Cdr.	USN	5.50
STURDEVANT, HARVEY W.	Pasco, Wash.	Lt. Cdr.	USN	6.00
SUBLETT, JOHN L.	Odessa, Tex.	Maj.	USAF 8 AF	8.00
SUEHR, RICHARD C.	Crafton, Pa.	Maj.	USAF 5 AF	5.00
SULLIVAN, CHARLES P.	Roanoke, Ill.	Col.	USAF 5 AF	5.00
SUMMER, ELLIOTT	Providence, R.I.	Capt.	USAF 5 AF	10.00
SUTCLIFFE. ROBERT C.	Trenton, N.J.	1st Lt.	USAF 5 AF	5.00

Name	Home Town	Rank	Service	Victories
SUTHERLAND, JOHN F.	Normandy, Mo.	Lt. Cdr.	USN	5.00
SWETT, JAMES E.	San Mateo, Calif.	Lt. Col.	USMC	15.50
SWOPE, JAMES S.	Killeen, Tex.	Cdr.	USN	10.00
SYKES, WILLIAM J.	Atlantic City, N.J.	Capt.	USAF 8 AF	5.00
SYMMES, JOHN C. C.	Lyons, N.Y.	Lt. Cdr.	USN	10.50
SYNAR, STANLEY T.	Muskogee, Okla.	Maj.	USMC	5.00
TALBOT, GILBERT F.	Olakmas, Ore.	Capt.	USAF 9 AF	5.00
TANNER, WILLIAM F.	Canastota, N.Y.	Maj.	USAF 8 AF	5.50
TAPP, JAMES B.	Eveleph, Minn.	Capt.	USAF 7 AF	8.00
TAYLOR, OLIVER B.	Palo Alto, Calif.	Col.	USAF 15 AF	5.00
TAYLOR, RALPH G., JR.	Durham, N.C.	1st Lt.	USAF 12 AF	6.00
TAYLOR, RAY A., JR.	Quanah, Tex.	Lt. Cdr.	USN	6.50
TAYLOR, WILL W.	Marion, Fla.	Lt. Cdr.	USN	5.00
TERRILL, FRANCIS A.	Tacoma, Wash.	1st Lt.	USMC	6.00
THACH, JOHN S.	Pine Bluff, Ark.	Capt.	USN	7.00
THELEN, ROBERT H.	Omaha, Neb.	Lt. Cdr.	USN	6.50
THOMAS, FRANKLIN C., JR.	Martinsburg, W. Va.	Maj.	USMC	9.00
THOMAS, ROBERT F.	Staten Island, N.Y.	Lt.	USN	5.00
THOMAS, WILBUR J.	Los Angeles, Calif.	Capt.	USMC	18.50
THOMPSON, ROBERT D.	Hubbard, Tex.	Capt.	USAF 15 AF	5.00
THORNELL, JOHN F., JR.	E. Walpole, Mass.	Maj.	USAF 8 AF	17.25
THWAITES, DAVID F.	Conshohocken, Pa.	Maj.	USAF 8 AF	6.00
THYNG, HARRISON R.	Barnstead, N.H.	Col.	USAF 12 AF	5.00
TILLEY, JOHN A.	Mill Valley, Calif.	Maj.	USAF 5 AF	5.00
TILLEY, READE FRANKLIN	Clearwater, Fla.	Pilot Off.	RAF 126 Sq	7.00
TINKER, FRANK G.	Little Rock, Ark.	Lt.	Spanish Civil War	8.00
TOASPERN, EDWARD W.	Barryville, N.Y.	Lt. jg	USN	5.00
TOPLIFF, JOHN W.	Tarpon Springs, Fla.	Lt. Cdr.	USN	5.00
TORDOFF, HARRISON B.	Mechanicsville, N.Y.	Capt.	USAF 8 AF	5.00
TORKELSON, ROSS E.	Everest, Kans.	Lt. Cdr.	USN	5.00

Name	Home Town	Rank	Service	Victories
TOVREA, PHILIP E., JR.	Phoenix, Ariz.	Capt.	USAF 15 AF	8.00
TOWNSEND, EUGENE P.	South Gate, Calif.	Lt.	USN	5.00
TRACY, F. W.	Kinston, N.C.	Lt. Cdr.	USN	6.00
TRAFTON, FREDERIC, O., JR.	Farmington, N.H.	1st Lt.	USAF 12 AF	5.50
TROUP, FRANKLIN W.	Decatur, Ala.	Lt. jg	USN	7.00
TROWBRIDGE, EUGENE A.	St. Paul, Minn.	Maj.	USMC	12.00
TROXELL, CLIFTON H.	Ravenna, Ohio	Maj.	USAF 5 AF	5.00
TRAUX, MYRON M.	Sullivan City, Tex.	Lt. jg	USN	7.00
TRULUCK, JOHN H.	Lynchburg, S.C.	Capt.	USAF 8 AF	7.00
TURLEY, GRANT M.	Aripine, Ariz.	2nd Lt.	USAF 8 AF	6.00
TURNER, CHARLES H.	Jacksonville, Fla.	Lt.	USN	6.50
TURNER, EDWARD B.	Spartanburg, S.C.	Lt. Cdr.	USN	7.00
TURNER, RICHARD E.	Estes Park, Colo.	Lt. Col.	USAF 9 AF	11.00
TURNER, WILLIAM L.	Idalou, Tex.	Col.	USAF 5 AF	10.50
TWELVES, WENDELL V.	Spanish Fork, Utah	Lt.	USN	13.00
TYLER, GERALD E.	Kalamazoo, Mich.	Maj.	USAF 8 AF	7.00
TYLER, JAMES O.	Ashland, Va.	Capt.	USAF 12 AF	8.00
UMPHFRES, DONALD E.	Philips, Tex.	Lt.	USN	6.00
VALENCIA, EUGENE A.	San Francisco, Calif.	Cdr.	USN	23.00
VALENTINE, HERBERT J.	Seattle, Wash.	1st Lt.	USMC	6.00
VANDEN HEUVAL, GEORGE R.	Staten Island, N.Y.	Maj.	USAF 8 AF	5.50
VAN DER LINDEN, PETER J.	Oaklawn, Ill.	Lt.	USN	5.00
VAN DYKE, RUDOLPH DANIEL	Dayton, Ohio	Lt. Cdr.	USN	5.00
VAN HAREN, ARTHUR, JR.	Phoenix, Ariz.	Lt.	USN	9.00
VARNELL, JAMES S., JR.	Charleston Tenn.	Capt.	USAF 15 AF	17.00
VAUGHN, HARLEY C.	Sapulpa, Okla.	Col.	USAF 12 AF	7.00
VAUGHT, ROBERT, H., JR.	Los Angeles, Calif.	Lt. Col.	USAF 5 AF	5.00

Name	Home Town	Rank	Service	Victories
VEDDER, MILTON N.	Los Angeles, Calif.	1st Lt.	USMC	6.00
VEJTASA, STANLEY W.	Circle, Mont.	Cdr.	USN	11.00
VINCENT, CLINTON D.	Natchez, Miss.	Brig. Gen.	USAF 10 AF	6.00
VINEYARD, MERRIWELL W.	Whitewright, Tex.	Lt. Cdr.	USN	6.00
VINSON, ARNOLD E.	Monticello, Mass.	Capt.	USAF 12 AF	7.00
VISSCHER, HERMAN W.	Portage, Mich.	Maj.	USAF 12 AF	5.00
VOGT, JOHN E.	Oklahoma City, Okla.	Capt.	USAF 7 AF	5.00
VOGT, JOHN W., JR.	Elizabeth, N.J.	Lt. Col.	USAF 8 AF	8.00
VOLL, JOHN J.	Goshen, Ohio	Maj.	USAF 15 AF	21.00
VORIS, ROY M.	Santa Cruz, Calif.	Cdr.	USN	7.00
VORSE, ALBERT O.	Woodside, Calif.	Cdr.	USN	7.50
VRACIU, ALEXANDER	East Chicago, Ind.	Lt. Cdr.	USN	19.00
WADE, LANCE C.	San Augustine, Tex.	Wg. Cdr.	RAF 145 Sq	25.00
WADE, ROBERT	Elkins Park, Pa.	Capt.	USMC	7.00
WAGGONER, HORACE Q.	Waggoner, Ill.	Maj.	USAF 8 AF	5.00
WAGNER, BOYD D.	Johnstown, Pa.	Col.	USAF 5 AF	8.00
WALKER, THOMAS H.	Mound, Minn.	Capt.	USAF 13 AF	6.00
WALKER, WALTER B., JR.	Stamford, Conn.	Lt. Col.	USAF 12 AF	5.00
WALSH, KENNETH A.	Washington, D.C.	Maj.	USMC	21.00
WANDREY, RALPH H.	Mason City, Iowa	Maj.	USAF 5 AF	6.00
WARD, LYTTLETON T.		Lt.	USN	5.00
WARFORD, VICTOR E.	Chickasha, Okla.	Col.	USAF 15 AF	8.00
WARNER, ARTHUR T.	Maplewood, N.J.	Lt. Col.	USMC	8.00
WARREN, JACK R.	San Jacinto, Calif.	Capt.	USAF 8 AF	5.00
WATERS, EDWARD T.	Highland Park, Mich.	1st Lt.	USAF 12 AF	7.00
WATKINS, JAMES A.	Crystal Springs, Miss.	Lt. Col.	USAF 5 AF	12.00
WATSON, RALPH J.	Centerburg, Ohio	Maj.	USAF 12 AF	5.00
WATTS, CHARLES E.	Van, Tex.	Lt. Cdr.	USN	8.75
WATTS, ORAN S.	Tulare, Calif.	1st Lt.	USAF 14 AF	5.00

Name	Home Town	Rank	Service	Victories
WEATHERFORD, SIDNEY W.	San Marcos, Tex.	1st Lt.	USAF 12 AF	5.00
WEAVER, CHARLES E.	Detroit, Mich.	Capt.	USAF 8 AF	8.00
WEAVER, CLAUDE, III	Oklahoma City, Okla.	Pilot Off.	RCAF	12.00
WEBB, WILBUR B.	Ardmore, Okla.	Lt. jg	USN	7.00
WEBB, WILLARD J.	Alton, Ill.	Maj.	USAF 10 AF	5.00
WEIGEL, GEORGE	San Francisco, Calif.	Capt.	AVG	5.00
WEISSENBERGER, GREGORY, J	Galveston, Tex.	Col.	USMC	5.00
WELCH, DARRELL G.	Goldthwaite, Tex.	Capt.	USAF 12 AF	5.00
WELCH, GEORGE S.	Wilmington, Del.	Maj.	USAF 5 AF	16.00
WELCH, ROBERT E.	Brown City, Mich.	Capt.	USAF 8 AF	6.00
WELDEN, ROBERT D.	Chicago, Ill.	1st Lt.	USAF 9 AF	6.25
WELLS, ALBERT P.	Long Beach, Calif.	1st Lt.	USMC	5.00
WENIGE, ARTHUR E.	Ashville, N.C.	Capt.	USAF 5 AF	6.00
WESOLOWSKI, JOHN M.	Detroit, Mich.	Cdr.	USN	7.00
WESSON, WARREN M.	Brooklyn, N.Y.	Capt.	USAF 8 AF	6.00
WEST, RICHARD L.	Chillicothe, Mo.	Capt.	USAF 5 AF	12.00
WEST, ROBERT G.	Parkersburg, Ia.	Lt. Cdr.	USN	5.00
WESTBROOK, ROBERT B.	Hollywood, Calif.	Lt. Col.	USAF 13 AF	20.00
WETMORE, RAY S.	Kerman, Calif.	Capt.	USAF 8 AF	22.59
WHALEN, WILLIAM E.	Hamilton, N.Y.	1st Lt.	USAF 8 AF	6.00
WHEADON, ELMER M.	Los Angeles, Calif.	Capt.	USAF 13 AF	7.00
WHISNER, WILLIAM T.	Shreveport, La.	Maj.	USAF 8 AF	15.50
WHITAKER, ROY E.	Knoxville, Tenn.	Maj.	USAF 9 AF	7.00
WHITE, HENRY S.	Los Angeles, Calif.	Lt. jg	USN	5.00
WHITE, JOHN H.	Kensett, Ark.	1st Lt.	USAF 12 AF	5.00
WHITE, ROBERT H.	Kansas City, Mo.	Capt.	USAF 5 AF	9.00
WHITE, THOMAS A.	Kelso, Wash.	Maj.	USAF 12 AF	6.00
WICKER, SAMUEL J.	Sanford, N.C.	Lt. Col.	USAF 8 AF	7.00
WILHELM, DAVID C.	Chicago, Ill.	1st Lt.	USAF 15 AF	5.00
WILKINS, PAUL H.	Billings, Mont.	2d Lt.	USAF 12 AF	5.00

Name	Home Town	Rank	Service	Victories
WILKINSON, JAMES W.	Swarthmore, Tex.	Capt.	USAF 8 AF	7.00
WILLIAMS, BRUCE W.	Salem, Oreg.	Lt.	USN	7.00
WILLIAMS, GERARD M. H.	Berkeley Heights, N.J.	Capt.	USMC	7.00
WILLIAMS, RUSSELL D.	Hamden, Conn.	1st Lt.	USAF 14 AF	5.00
WILLIAMSON, FELIX D.	Cordela, Ga.	Capt.	USAF 8 AF	13.00
WILSON, ROBERT C.	Jackson, Wyo.	Lt. Cdr.	USN	6.00
WILSON, WILLIAM F.	Strong City, Kan.	Capt.	USAF 8 AF	5.00
WINFIELD, MURRAY	Dearborn, Mich.	Lt.	USN	5.50
WINKS, ROBERT P.	Sumner, Ia.	1st Lt.	USAF 8 AF	5.50
WINSTON, ROBERT A.	Washington, Ind.	Cdr.	USN	5.00
WINTERS, THEODORE HUGH, JR.	St. Davids, Pa.	Cdr.	USN	8.00
WIRE, CALVIN C.	Wilmar, Calif.	Capt.	USAF 5 AF	7.00
WIRE, RALPH L.	Ada, Okla.	1st Lt.	USAF 5 AF	5.00
WIRTH, JOHN L.	Gary, Ind.	Lt.	USN	14.00
WISEMAN, LEE V.	Forbes, Kan.	Maj.	USAF 12 AF	5.00
WITT, LYNN E. JR.	Bowden, Ga.	Col.	USAF 5 AF	6.00
WOLF, JOHN T.	Garden Grove, Calif.	Lt.	USN	7.00
WOLFE, JUDGE E.	Flint, Mich.	Capt.	USAF 7 AF	9.00
WOLFORD, JOHN L.	Cumberland, Md.	Capt.	USAF 12 AF	5.00
WONG, JOHN (JOHN PUNG-YUNG HWANG)	San Francisco, Calif.	1st Lt.	USAF 14 AF	13.00
WOODHOUSE, HENRY DeC.A.	New York, N.Y.	Wg. Cdr.	RAF	5.00
WOODS, SIDNEY S.	Somerton, Ariz.	Lt. Col.	USAF 5 AF	10.00
WOODY, ROBERT E.	Roanoke, Va.	Lt. Col.	USAF 8 AF	7.00
WOOLEY, MILLARD JR.	Patterson, Calif.	Lt. Cdr.	USN	5.25
WORDELL, MALCOLM T.	New Bedford, Mass.	Cdr.	USN	7.50
WRENN, GEORGE L.	Charlotte, N.C.	Cdr.	USN	5.00
WRIGHT, ELLIS WILLIAM, JR.	Miami, Ariz.	Lt. Col.	USAF 5 AF	6.00
WRIGHT, MAX J.	Chappell, Neb.	Capt.	USAF 15 AF	5.00

Name	Home Town	Rank	Service	Victories
WYNN, VASSEURE F.	Dalton, Ga.	1st Lt.	USAF/RAF	6.00
YAEGER, ROBERT R., JR.	Hebbronville, Tex.	Capt.	USAF 5 AF	5.00
YEAGER, CHARLES E.	Hamlin, W. Va.	Maj.	USAF 8 AF	11.50
YEREMAIN, HAROLD	Fallon, Nev.	Lt.	USN	6.00
YORK, ROBERT M.	Old Orchard Beach, Me.	Capt.	USAF 8 AF	5.00
YOST, DONALD K.	Princeton, N.J.	Col.	USMC	8.00
YOUNG, OWEN DEWITT	Tenefly, N.J.	Lt.	USN	5.00
YUNCK, MICHAEL R.	Washington, D.C.	Lt. Col.	USMC	5.00
ZAESKE, EARLING W.	Highland Park, Ill.	Lt. jg	USN	5.50
ZEMKE, HUBERT	Missoula, Mont.	Col.	USAF 8 AF	17.75
ZINK, JOHN A.	Saint Mary, Ohio	Lt. jg	USN	5.00
ZOERB, DANIEL J.	Kingsport, Tenn.	1st Lt.	USAF 15 AF	7.00
ZUBARIK, CHARLES J.	W. Allis, Wis.	Maj.	USAF 8 AF	6.00

Twenty or More Victories

Name	Rank	Service	Score
BONG, RICHARD L.	Maj.	USAF	40.00
McGUIRE, THOMAS B.	Maj.	USAF	38.00
McCAMPBELL, DAVID	Capt.	USN	34.00
GABRESKI, FRANCIS N.	Col.	USAF	31.00*
JOHNSON, ROBERT S.	Lt. Col.	USAF	28.00
BOYINGTON, GREGORY	Lt. Col.	USMC	28.00
MacDONALD, CHARLES H.	Col.	USAF	27.00
FOSS, JOSEPH JACOB	Maj.	USMC	26.00
PREDDY, GEORGE E.	Maj.	USAF	25.83
HANSON, ROBERT M.	1st Lt.	USMC	25.00
WADE, LANCE C.	Wg. Cdr.	RAF	25.00
HARRIS, CECIL E.	Lt.	USN	24.00
MEYER, JOHN C.	Col.	USAF	24.00*
VALENCIA, EUGENE A.	Cdr.	USN	23.00

* Aces marked with an asterisk added to these scores by scoring victories in the Korean War. See Korean War lists.

Name	Rank	Service	Score
WETMORE, RAY S.	Capt.	USAF	22.59
SCHILLING, DAVID C.	Col.	USAF	22.50
JOHNSON, GERALD R.	Lt. Col.	USAF	22.00
KEARBY, NEAL E.	Maj.	USAF	22.00
ROBBINS, JAY T.	Lt. Col.	USAF	22.00
MAHURIN, WALKER M.	Lt. Col.	USAF	20.75*
CHRISTENSEN, FRED J.	Capt.	USAF	21.50
VOLL, JOHN J.	Maj.	USAF	21.00
WALSH, KENNETH A.	Maj.	USMC	21.00
ALDRICH, DONALD M.	Capt.	USMC	20.00
LYNCH, THOMAS J.	Lt. Col.	USAF	20.00
WESTBROOK, ROBERT B.	Lt. Col.	USAF	20.00

American Aces of the Korean War

Name	Home Town	Rank	Wing	Score
ADAMS, DONALD E.	Mt. Clemens, Mich.	Maj.	51	6.5
BAKER, ROYAL N.	McKinney, Tex.	Col.	4	13.0
BALDWIN, ROBERT P.	Los Angeles, Calif.	Col.	51	5.0
BECKER, RICHARD S.	Fleetwood, Pa.	Capt.	4	5.0
BETTINGER, STEPHEN L.	W. Caldwell, N.J.	Maj.	4	5.0
BLESSE, FREDERICK C.	Phoenix, Ariz.	Maj.	4	10.0
BOLT, JOHN F.	Sanford, Fla.	USMC Maj.	51	6.0
BORDELON, GUY P.	Franklin, La.	USN Cdr.	VC-3	5.0
BUTTLEMANN, HENRY	Bayside, N.Y.	1st Lt.	51	7.0
CREIGHTON, RICHARD D.	Baton Rouge, La.	Maj.	4	5.0
CURTIN, CLYDE A.	Portland, Ore.	Capt.	4	5.0
DAVIS, GEORGE A., JR.	Lubbock, Tex.	Maj.	4	14.0
FERNANDEZ, MANUEL J.	Miami, Fla.	Capt.	4	14.5
FISCHER, HAROLD E.	Swea City, Ia.	1st Lt.	51	10.0
FOSTER, CECIL G.	San Antonio, Tex.	1st Lt.	51	9.0
GABRESKI, FRANCIS S.	Oil City, Pa.	Col.	51	6.5
GARRISON, VERMONT	Mt. Victory, Ky.	Lt. Col.	4	10.0

Name	Home Town	Rank	Wing	Score
GIBSON, RALPH D.	Mt. Carmel, Ill.	Capt.	4	5.0
HAGERSTROM, JAMES P.	Waterloo, Ia.	Maj.	18	8.5
JABARA, JAMES	Wichita, Kan.	Maj.	4	15.0
JOHNSON, JAMES K.	Phoenix, Ariz.	Col.	4	10.0
JOLLEY, CLIFFORD D.	Salt Lake City, Utah	Capt.	4	7.0
JONES, GEORGE L.	Vero Beach, Fla.	Lt. Col.	4	6.5
KASLER, JAMES H.	Indianapolis, Ind.	1st Lt.	4	6.0
KINCHELOE, IVEN C., JR.	Cassapolis, Mich.	Capt.	51	5.0
LATSHAW, ROBERT T., JR.	Amarillo, Tex.	Capt.	4	5.0
LILLEY, LEONARD W.	Manchester, N.H.	Capt.	4	7.0
LOVE, ROBERT J.	San Bernardino, Calif.	Capt.	4	6.0
LOW, JAMES F.	Sausalito, Calif.	2nd Lt.	4	9.0
MARSHALL, WINTON W.	Beverly Hills, Calif.	Maj.	4	6.5
McCONNELL, JOSEPH, JR.	Apple Valley, Calif.	Capt.	51	16.0
MOORE, LONNIE R.	Ft. Walton, Fla.	Capt.	4	10.0
MOORE, ROBERT H.	Houston, Tex.	Capt.	51	5.0
OVERTON, DOLPHIN D., III	Andrews, S. C.	Capt.	51	5.0
PARR, RALPH S., JR.	Apple Valley, Calif.	Capt.	4	10.0
RISNER, ROBINSON	Oklahoma City, Okla.	Capt.	4	8.0
RUDDELL, GEORGE I.	Riverside, Calif.	Lt. Col.	51	8.0
THYNG, HARRISON R.	Barnstead, N.H.	Col.	4	5.0
WESCOTT, WILLIAM H.	New Lisbon, Wis.	Maj.	51	5.0
WHISNER, WILLIAM T.	Shreveport, La.	Maj.	51	5.5

Ten or more Victories

Name	Score
McCONNELL, JOSEPH, JR.	16.0
JABARA, JAMES	15.0

Name	Score
FERNANDEZ, MANUEL J.	14.5
DAVIS, GEORGE A., JR.	14.0
BAKER, ROYAL N.	13.0
BLESSE, FREDERICK C.	10.0
FISCHER, HAROLD E.	10.0
GARRISON, VERMONT	10.0
JOHNSON, JAMES K.	10.0
MOORE, LONNIE R.	10.0
PARR, RALPH S., JR.	10.0

American Aces of Both World War II and Korea

All officers are assigned to U.S. Air Force except as indicated.

Name	World War II	Korea	Total
BOLT, JOHN F. (USMC)	6.00	6.00	12.00
DAVIS, GEORGE A., JR.	7.00	14.00	21.00
GABRESKI, FRANCIS S.	31.00	6.50	37.50
GARRISON, VERMONT	7.33	10.00	17.33
HAGERSTROM, JAMES P.	6.00	8.50	14.50
THYNG, HARRISON R.	5.00	5.00	10.00
WHISNER, WILLIAM T.	15.50	5.50	21.00

Other Aces with Victories in World War II and Korea

All officers are assigned to U.S. Air Force except as indicated.

Name	World War II	Korea	Total
ADAMS, DONALD E.	4.00	6.50	10.50
ANDRE, JOHN W. (USMC)	4.00	1.00 night	5.00
BAKER, ROYAL N.	3.50	13.00	16.50

Name	World War II	Korea	Total
BETTINGER, STEPHEN L.	1.00	5.00	6.00
BRUELAND, LOWELL K.	12.50	2.00	14.50
CHANDLER, VAN E.	5.00	3.00	8.00
COLMAN, PHILIP E.	5.00	4.00	9.00
CREIGHTON, RICHARD D.	2.00	5.00	7.00
DELONG, PHILIP C. (USMC)	11.17	2.00	13.17
DURNFORD, DEWEY F. (USMC)	6.33	0.50	6.83
EAGLESTON, GLENN T. (USMC)	18.50	2.00	20.50
EMMERT, BENJAMIN H., JR.	6.00	1.00	7.00
HELLER, EDWIN L.	5.50	3.50	9.00
HOCKERY, JOHN J.	7.00	1.00	8.00
HOVDE, WILLIAM J.	10.50	1.00	11.50
JABARA, JAMES	1.50	15.00	16.50
JOHNSON, JAMES K.	1.00	10.00	11.00
LAMB, WILLIAM E. (USN)	6.00	1.00	7.00
LILES, BROOKS J.	1.00	4.00	5.00
LITTLE, JAMES W.	5.00	1.00	6.00
MAHURIN, WALKER M.	20.75	3.50	24.25
MATTSON, CONRAD E.	1.00	4.00	5.00
MEYER, JOHN C.	24.00	2.00	26.00
MITCHELL, JOHN W.	11.00	4.00	15.00
PRICE, HOWARD J.	4.00	2.00	6.00
RUDDELL, GEORGE I.	2.50	8.00	10.50
VISSCHER, HERMAN W.	5.00	1.00	6.00
WADE, ROBERT (USMC)	7.00	1.00	8.00

Top Fighter Aces of Other Nations in World War II

German Air Force

Maj. Erich Hartmann	352
Maj. Gerhard Barkhorn	301
Maj. Gunther Rall	275

United Kingdom (RAF)

Gp. Capt. James E. Johnson	38
Sq. Ldr. Marmaduke T. St. J. Pattle	34
Wg. Cdr. Brendan E. Finucane	32

New Zealand Air Force

Wg. Cdr. Colin F. Gray	27.5
Flt. Off. Edgar J. Kain	25
Wg. Cdr. E. D. Mackie	25

Royal Canadian Air Force (RCAF)

Flt. Lt. G. F. Beurling	31
Sq. Ldr. V. C. Woodard	20

South African Air Force

Maj. M. S. Osler	12
Maj. Cornelius A. Van Vliet	11
Capt. K. W. Driver	10

Russian Air Force

Maj. Gen. I. N. Kozhedub	62
Gds. Col. A. L. Pokryshkin	59
Gds. Capt. G. A. Rechkalov	56
Gds. Capt. K. A. Yevstigneev	56

Hungarian Air Force

Lt. Dezso Szentgyorgyi	30
Capt. Gyorgy Debrody	26
Lt. Laszlo Molnar	25

Belgian Air Force

Lt. Count Rodolphe C. deHemricourt deGrunne	13.0
S/Lt. V. Ortmans	11.0
Count I. DuMonceau deBergandal	7.5

Norwegian Air Force

Lt. Col. Sven Heglund	15.33
Capt. Helmar Gundt-Spang	10.33
Col. Kaj Birksted (Danish)	10.00

Italian Air Force

Maj. Adriano Visconti	26
Lt. Franco Bordoni-Bisleri	24
Lt. Leonardo Ferrulli	20

Czech Air Force

P/O. Josef Frantisek	28
W/Cdr. Karel M. Kuttelwascher	25
Capt. Alois Vasatko	13

French Air Force

Lt. Pierre Clostermann	33
Capt. Marcel Albert	23
Cdt. Jean E. F. DeMozay (War name: Marlaix)	23

Finland Air Force

Kapt. Hans H. Wind	75
Lt. Eino I. Juutilainen	74
Maj. Eino A. Luukkanen	54

Japanese Air Force

C.W.O. Hiroyashi Nishizawa	104
C.W.O. Shaichi Sugita	80
Lt. Saburo Sakai	64

Polish Air Force

Maj. S. Skalski	22.25
Lt. Col. W. Urbanowicz	17
	(plus 5 in CBI Theater)
Capt. E. Horbaczewski	16.5

Croatians (Fought against Russia under German flag)

Lt. Cvitan Galic	36
Lt. Jan Gerthofer	33
Oblt. Mato Dukovac	32

Rumanian Air Force

Prince Constantino Cantacuzino	60
Capt. Alexandru Serbanescu	55
Florian Budu	40+

Bulgarian Air Force

Lt. Stojanoff	14
Maj. Toplodolski	8

Glossary

Abort: A term used to describe a mission or flight turned back before its completion for reasons other than enemy action. Hence, "air abort" and "ground abort."

Air Force: The numbered Air Force (e.g., 8th Air Force) is a flexible organization of varying size. It usually has a single mission, such as defense, strategic or tactical. Its wings and squadrons are generally organized to report to an Air Division, which reports to the numbered Air Force.

Anchor: Applying the brakes or, in the air, reducing speed as rapidly as possible.

Anoxia: Hypoxia; the absence of oxygen in the blood, cells or tissues, generally experienced by pilots flying at high altitudes (above 14,000 feet) with a leaking oxygen mask.

Bail: Usually an abbreviation of bail-out. To escape from an aircraft by parachuting.

Balls Out: Full throttle, top speed. Taken from the steam controller on old steam engines, which whirled and were thrown to maximum point by centrifugal force.

Bandit: An enemy aircraft.

Barrel Roll: An aerial maneuver wherein an aircraft makes a complete roll; sometimes called a slow roll, but actually not quite the same maneuver.

Beat-up: Strafing objectives on the ground. Shooting up parked airplanes, an airfield, trains, etc., is a "beat-up."

Belly Land: To land an airplane with the landing gear shot away or retracted.

Big Friend: A friendly bomber.

Bird: An airplane is a bird to a pilot.

Bird Dog: A radio direction-finder. Also applied to a flyer who pursues girls persistently.

347

Black Cat: Navy nickname for a Catalina flying boat, often used to rescue pilots downed in the ocean.

Black Widow: Air Force nickname for the P-61 nightfighter.

Blocks: Airplane chocks, placed in front of the wheels while the aircraft is on the ground.

Bogey: Any flying aircraft or target that can be seen but is too far away to be identified as friend or foe.

Booger: Slang to booger off, to bug out to goof off. The British have another definition for the word.

Bounce: To attack an enemy aircraft from the air. Also used to describe a particularly rough landing.

Break!: To discontinue aerial combat suddenly; to peel off from a formation; to "break right" (or left) means a snap turn to avoid an enemy's attack.

Bust: To reduce a person in rank for disciplinary reasons.

Buzz-bomb: The pulse-jet powered V-1 used by the Germans in World War II

CAP: Combat Air Patrol; a term used extensively by Navy and Marine pilots.

CBI: China-Burma-India Theater of Operations.

CHICOM: Chinese Communists.

Chop Up: Same as beat-up, except that it is more generally applied to shooting up an enemy machine in aerial combat. Ripping an enemy plane to pieces with your own gunfire.

Clank: To become nervous or to freeze mentally.

Contour Chase: A World War I expression for hedgehopping, or flying at extremely low altitude.

Cold Turkey: A sure aerial kill. An easy mark or "sitting duck."

Creek: The Yalu River—a pilot's term in the Korean War for the boundary of their operations against the enemy.

Deck: The ground; the cloud level; the actual deck of an aircraft carrier. Usually used "down to the deck," meaning a pilot dove within a few feet of the ground.

Division: An Air Force organization normally consisting of two or more Wings of aircraft. Navy use (World War II) described a flight of four aircraft.

Ditch: To force-land an aircraft in the ocean, lake or other waters with the intention of abandonment.

Dogfight: An aerial battle. German term: "rhubarb."

Drink: The ocean, or sometimes a lake. Any body of water.

Driver: A pilot. As in, "This MIG driver was good."

Dry Run: A practice exercise or rehearsal. An intentional pass at a target completed without firing the guns or armament at it.

Egg Beater: Helicopter. Also called a chopper.

Ejected: Use of an ejection seat to bail out. A catapult seat in modern fighter aircraft forcibly ejects pilots from the aircraft when in distress.

ETO: European Theater of Operations.

Fat Dog: German expression for a large formation of bomb-laden bombers en route to their target.

Fighter Plane: Term applied to the whole range of fighting planes from World War I to the present day. Chasse (World War I), pursuit, scout, interceptor planes are variants of the fighter plane, as are long-range fighters, fighter bombers and tactical fighters.

Flaking: Term denoting the loss of aircraft aborting from a formation as it proceeds toward the target area.

Forced Landing: A landing forced upon an aircraft due to mechanical failure or any other reason.

Fruit Salad: An array of ribbons worn on a uniform. Sometimes refers also to ornamentation of peaked caps of higher-ranking officers.

Full bore: Top speed; full throttle; balls out.

G-suit: A specially designed suit intended to increase the number of G's a fighter pilot could take in high-speed maneuvers without blacking out. The G suit in essence prevented the pilot's blood from violently flooding into or draining from the extremities of his body.

Gaggle: A number of aircraft flying in loose formation.

Garbled: A transmission by radio-voice so confused by the elements, static or other interference that it is unreadable.

Glycol: A thick alcohol [$C_2H_4(OH)_2$] used as a coolant in liquid-cooled engines. If a bullet or cannon shell penetrated the cooling system, glycol would usually trail behind the stricken aircraft in a long white plume.

Go In: Crack up or crash. Also used in the past tense, as in "he went in near Abbeville."

Go-Juice: Gasoline or jet fuel.

Green 16: A term used to denote a new pilot in the formation. The color denotes his flight, the number his position.

Hack: Usually in the context of "hack down," meaning to shoot down. Often applied to bringing down a large aircraft.

Hammerhead: A stall. The aircraft climbs vertically almost to the stalling point, at which time full rudder is applied, causing the aircraft to reverse direction.

Hedgehop: To fly close to the ground, rising up over hedges, trees, houses, hills, etc. Sometimes called grass-cutting.

Honcho: The boss. An enemy pilot of standout ability.

Horizontal Trail: Usually the stabilator and elevators on the empennage of an airplane.

Hose Down: Strafing an area with machine-gun or cannon-fire from the air.

Hot: Coming in hot; landing faster than normal.

Hot Rock: A hot pilot, a skillful, clever pilot. To "get hot" means to begin running up a string of aerial victories.

Hun: World War I term used by the Allies for the Germans. Also "Jerry," "Heinie" and "Kraut."

Jink: Jerking an aircraft about in an evasive maneuver.

Jockey: Slang name for a pilot. Often "throttle jockey."

Joy Stick: Slang for the control stick of an airplane.

Jug: An engine cylinder. Also an affectionate name for the P-47 Thunderbolt in allusion to its shape.

Jump Sack: Parachute.

Kate: Allied name for Japanese Nakajima B5N2, a low-wing, single-engine torpedo bomber. Other Nakajima products were known as the Oscar, Myrt, Tojo, Frank, Helen, Irving, Jull and Nate.

Kill: To destroy an enemy aircraft. As a noun, a victory in aerial combat. Does not refer in its slang sense to the death of the enemy pilot. A "kill" may not involve the enemy pilot's death.

Korean War: A limited war in Korea between the United Nations and the forces of North Korea and Communist China—June 25, 1950, to July 27, 1953.

Lame Duck: A disabled or obviously malfunctioning aircraft.

Lead: (Rhymes with heed.) The action of aiming ahead of a moving target with a gun. The lead angle is the angle between the line of sight to a moving target and the line of sight to a point ahead of the target where the bullet will collide with the target. To "put in lead" or "pull lead" means to so head your aircraft that when you fire your guns you seemingly shoot far ahead of your target. In a dogfight, it is not always easy to turn inside the other aircraft sufficiently to "pull lead."

Loiter: To fly aimlessly about in the air, waiting.

Lone Wolf: A pilot who prefers to fly alone without a wingman, or who works alone instead of as a team. This mode of air fighting proved feasible only in the early days of World War I. Developing formation tactics made such fighting impossible.

Lufbery Circle: After Raoul G. Lufbery of World War I fame. A formation in which two or more aircraft would form a single defensive circle. Aircraft follow one another in this circle so that the guns of each aircraft protect the tail of the aircraft ahead of it. In Russia in World War II, as many as fifty Soviet aircraft were often observed in gigantic Lufbery Circles.

Macchi: An Italian aircraft manufacturing company which built numerous Italian warplanes, including the C-200, C-202 and C-205.

Mag: Abbreviation for magneto. A check of the flow of electricity from the magneto to the engine during engine runup before takeoff.

MAW: Marine Air Wing.

May Day: International distress signal by radiotelephone. Derived from French M'aider (Help me).

Old Head: A person who has been around a long time.

Old Man: The commanding officer: The Old Man can be any age.

O'clock: Usually preceded by a number from one to twelve and used to pinpoint the position of enemy aircraft relative to the friendly formation. "Bandit at three o'clock high" over the radio meant that an enemy aircraft had been spotted at the three o'clock position, i.e., to the right and high overhead.

Overshoot: To land long, overshooting the runway. Also applies to overleading when firing at an enemy plane in the air. In combat tactics: to bounce an enemy plane, usually fire and then "overshoot" the target, passing beyond the target.

P-400: The "C" model of the P-39 aircraft made by Bell Aircraft. It was exported to France and Britain and used by AAF pilots at Guadalcanal.

Panic Button: Literally, a control button or switch for use in some emergency. Figuratively, usually used to describe the action taken by a pilot who suddenly finds himself in a dangerous or untenable position.

Perch: Position of tactical advantage prior to initiating an attack on an enemy aircraft.

Pit: Short for cockpit—the pilot's office in an aircraft.

Port: Navy term meaning "left." "Starboard" denotes right.

Prang: A collision or crash of an airplane.

PTO: Pacific Theater of Operations.

Rack: To put an airplane into a sudden tortuous turn or maneuver.

Radial Engines: Aircraft engines with one or more stationary rows of cylinders arranged radially around a common crankshaft.

Raft: A life raft.

Rake: To sweep or strafe a target with machine-gun or cannon fire.

Recip: A reciprocating engine. An engine which develops its power in the back and forth movement of the pistons.

Reef: Change direction of an aircraft violently.

Rev: Revolution. To rev-up or increase the rpm of an engine.

rpm: Revolutions per minute.

Rhubarb: German term for aerial dogfight. RAF code word for aerial combat.

Robot: A device that operates mechanically. German aerial combat cameras were 35mm robot types, which took a picture every second. These robot pictures were of excellent quality and were used to confirm victories and illustrate proper techniques to student fighter pilots.

ROK: Republic of Korea.

Rotte: (German) A two-plane formation.

Sally: Allied name for the Mitsubishi Ki-213, a twin-engined heavy bomber of World War II.

SBD: Navy designation for the A-24 (USAAF) and SBD-3 of the U.S. Navy. A Douglas-built dive-bomber of World War II.

Schwarm: German designation for operational flight of four or five aircraft. A *Schwarm* consisted of two *Rotten*; three *Schwarms* made up a *Staffel*, four *Staffeln* a *Gruppe*.

Scissoring: A technique of flight by escort fighters in which the escorting aircraft from each side of the formation continually crisscross each other either from above or below the escorted formation. The Navy employed a system of scissoring called the "Thach Weave" after John Thach, one of their aces.

Scramble: The whole action involved in getting fighter interceptors into the air in the shortest possible time.

Scrub: To cancel a mission or sortie.

Sked: A schedule.

Slip: A slip occurs when an airplane yaws and slides ahead in forward flight or slides downward when the wings are banked.

Slot Man: The number four man in a formation if he takes position directly behind and slightly below the leader or number one man.

Slow Roll: The slow rotation of an airplane about its longitudinal axis, executed by (generally) coordinated manipulation of the controls.

Snaking: The tendency of an airplane to yaw from side to side at a certain frequency at high speeds.

Snap Roll: An aerial maneuver in which an airplane is made to effect a quick complete roll about its longitudinal axis. Generally quite uncoordinated manipulation of the controls.

Soggy: A pilots term often used to describe an unresponsive condition of an airplane, usually due to battle damage, e.g., "the controls were soggy."

Sortie: A flight or sally of a single airplane which penetrates into airspace where enemy contact may be expected.

Soup: Sometimes also called "pea soup." Fog or dense cloud.

Speed Brake: A flap designed for slowing down an airplane in flight.

Spit: Short for "Spitfire," fabled British World War II fighter.

Spike: To spike it. To force an airplane to land even though its speed is still well above landing speed.

Splash: Slang for crash or kill. The U.S. Navy used the word to indicate an enemy aircraft had been shot down in the ocean.

Split-ess: Sometimes known as Split-s or "split-arse" to the British. A maneuver in which the airplane makes a half-roll onto its back, and then dives in a curve, usually leveling off on a reversed heading at much lower altitude.

Squirt: A burst of machine-gun or cannon fire, usually directed at an enemy airplane.

Squirt job: A jet aircraft.

Stack: Abbreviation of "exhaust stack." Also, the holding of aircraft by altitude separations while waiting their turns to land. Sometimes used to denote a crash.

Steer: An instruction to steer or fly an aircraft on a given course or heading, as given to a pilot by a ground radio station.

Strafe: To rake objectives on the ground, such as troops, vehicles or emplacements with machine-gun or cannon fire or rockets from an airplane.

Straggler: An aircraft that cannot or does not keep up with the other aircraft in the formation.

Strip: A landing field.

Survival kit: A kit containing all the special items considered necessary or useful for a pilot to survive in the event of a forced landing, crash or bail-out over land or sea.

Tail Pipe: The pipe-like structure aft of a jet engine.

Tallyho: A code word called over the radio by a fighter pilot when he sights an enemy.

T-bolt: Slang for "Thunderbolt" (P-47).

TDY: Temporary duty. A period of duty away from one's home station.

Throttle-jockey: A pilot, usually a jet pilot.

Tin Fish: Torpedo.

Undershoot: To land short of the runway; to shoot under or behind a target.

Val: Allied name for Japanese Aichi D3A2 aircraft.

Wilco: Radio acknowledgment of instructions, meaning "will comply."

Windscreen: Windshield.

Window: Metal foil ribbon which causes extreme reflection on radar scopes, corrupting radar information. Also called "chaff."

Wingco: Short for "Wing Commander."

Zeke: An Allied code name for the Japanese Zero.

Zero: Mitsubishi Type O fighter plane. The Allies generally referred to all Japanese fighters as Zeroes, while actually there were numerous types, such as Hamp, Zeke, Tony, Tojo, etc.

ZI: Zone of Interior. The U.S.A.